Federalism and Intergovernmental Relations

Federalism and Intergovernmental Relations

Edited by
Deil S. Wright,
University of North Carolina at Chapel Hill in collaboration with
Harvey L. White,
North Carolina Central University

Published by the American Society for Public Administration

PUBLIC ADMINISTRATION LIBRARY

Published by the American Society for Public Administration

PAR Classics Series

I. **Professional Public Executives**
Edited by Chester A. Newland

II. **Perspectives on Budgeting**
Edited by Allen Schick

III. **Approaches to Organizing**
Edited by Robert T. Golembiewski

IV. **American Public Administration: Patterns of the Past**
Edited by James Fesler

V. **Federalism and Intergovernmental Relations**
Edited by Deil S. Wright and Harvey L. White

Monograph Series

1. **Applying Professional Standards and Ethics in the '80s: A Workbook & Study Guide for Public Administrators**
Edited by Herman Mertins, Jr. and Patrick J. Hennigan

2. **"The Study of Administration" Revisited**
James D. Carroll and Alfred M. Zuck

The American Society for Public Administration
1120 G Street, N.W., Suite 500
Washington, D.C. 20005

International Standard Book Number: 0-936678-06-2. Price: $12.95.

Contents

Preface

The invitation to edit this volume of *PAR* Classics was flattering to receive, challenging to execute, and satisfying to complete. Each aspect deserves brief comment.

The invitation and approval to engage in this enterprise could not have developed in a more complimentary and supportive manner. From Louis Gawthrop and Keith Mulrooney came words of enthusiasm and encouragement. From the ASPA Publications Committee and Council came expressions of need and formal endorsement. To be approached and enlisted in such an endeavor is personally and professionally gratifying, to say the least.

The task of identifying and selecting *PAR* items appropriate for this volume was more difficult than first expected. Two detailed and independent examinations of *PAR* volumes 1-43 (by White and by Wright) resulted in more than 200 items falling within a broad definition of federalism and intergovernmental relations. The reconciliation of these two separate lists produced a combined universe of nearly 300 items from which the final selections were drawn.

The total universe is provided as an appended bibliography. The citations there (and the final selections) reveal that we did not limit the universe or the final choices to regular articles or to articles and book reviews. Instead, our wide definitional net and format included items from reports of convention sessions, "Currents and Soundings," "Developments in Public Administration," and others. In short, we did not ignore a section, a category, or a page of *PAR* where the content might address issues of federalism and intergovernmental relations. For assistance with the bibliography and with many other parts of this project we express our thanks to John Paden, MPA graduate student at the University of North Carolina.

The scope and final size of our universe compounded the dual and interactive tasks of organizing the items and moving toward final choices. Our prior exposure to and experience in the field was helpful. A logical first category called for selections providing a review (or reviews) of developments in the field covering the half-century from the 1930s into the 1980s. Writers (in *PAR* and elsewhere) paid particular attention to the evolution of federalism and to the origin and development of intergovernmental relations starting in the late 1930s. It was therefore important, in our judgment, to provide readers an initial exposure to events, actions, and developments across these decades. Selections designed to implement this aim are found in Part II. Part I contains an introductory essay on four decades of changing relationships reviewed chiefly through the lenses provided by *PAR* articles.

In Part III we consciously narrowed or restricted our focus, relatively speaking. It could be contended that the issue area of urban and metropolitan development is hardly "narrow" by most standards. We acknowledge its perceived breadth. The scores of articles, symposia, book reviews, and other *PAR* items focusing on cities, metropolitan reform, housing, and urban problems reflect a wide array of issues. Our category (Part III) on metropolitan and urban development, however, is aimed at a cluster of geographic, organizational, functional, and process issues.

Intergovernmental financial patterns and relationships, policies and problems constituted a cluster of issues sufficiently large to form the basis for an entirely separate volume of *PAR* classics. The luxury of such space or discretion was not open to us. Our treatment of intergovernmental finances (Part IV) was therefore limited to only six selections from a universe of three-score items appearing in volumes 1-43 of *PAR*. We sought, with some difficulty, for a representative combination of articles on the full range of fiscal issues, e.g., intergovernmental aid, grantsmanship, imposition of tax limitations. We settled more for coherence than for full-fledged representativeness. In addition to a broad-gauged introductory selection, we included single articles on each of the three major types of federal aid—categorical, block, and general revenue funding. We end the section with a recent article intended to reflect the era of retrenchment and coping with cuts—how to say no, politely, to "losers" in the great grant game.

Intergovernmental management (IGM) is, at a minimum, a new phase of IGR and is perhaps an entirely new conceptual framework for analyzing activities within U.S. political/administrative systems. The problem solving and implementation dimensions of IGM tend to set it apart from the two older and contrasting concepts of federalism and of intergovernmental relations. This degree of distinctiveness was evident to us as we reviewed the contents of *PAR,* particularly in the past 10-15 years. We responded to this conceptual nuance and to *PAR* contents by creating a section (Part V) that we call The Management of Intergovernmental Implementation. As might be expected, it contains more articles by practitioners and all articles, regardless of author, have a more applied, problem-solving, action bias.

The preceding represents thumbnail sketches of our intellectual and operational processes pursued in executing this enterprise. Completing it resulted in feelings of satisfaction and accomplishment. We hope that readers—citizen, teacher, student, practitioner—emerge from encounters with the material in this volume with a similar sense of satisfaction, but not from our modest efforts. Rather, the satisfaction, and perhaps even enjoyment, should come from the quality and character of *PAR* itself, and from the authors and editors of *PAR* have made fine contributions to the study of federalism, intergovernmental relations, and intergovernmental management.

Deil S. Wright
Harvey L. White
Chapel Hill and Durham, N.C.
November, 1983

PART I

Introduction

Federalism and Intergovernmental Relationships: Evolving Patterns and Changing Perspectives

Contemporary federalism and intergovernmental relationships in the U.S. are rooted in two centuries of political and administrative experience. The four decades covered by *PAR,* of course, are a minor yet a very significant component of the longer span. The appearance of *PAR* in 1940 came in the immediate aftermath of two noteworthy developments in the 1930s. One was the "First New Federalism." The second involved the emergence of the concept of intergovernmental relations.

The First New Federalism

The New Deal response to the Great Depression was a set of policies that Jane Perry Clark called *The Rise of a New Federalism* (1938). The first selection in Part II by Frank Bane (2:95-103) devotes primary attention to the impressive collaborative national-state-local efforts achieved during World War II in implementing rationing programs. But Bane, who subsequently served as executive director of the Council of State Governments and as first chairman of the Advisory Commission on Intergovernmental Relations (1959-1969), briefly reviews notable cooperative experiences in the 1920s as well as the emergencies of the 1930s. He emphasizes these early efforts as precedents for the wholesale and herculean collaboration during the wartime emergency.

Bane is clear in noting that the wartime experiences, by building on prior foundations, "have made nearly every program of government a concern of federal, state, and local authorities alike" (2:101). These changing patterns and perspectives emerging from experience in the 1920s, the 1930s, and the wartime 1940s produced, in Bane's words, "the relatively new system of cooperative government." This new system was promptly labeled "cooperative federalism" and shortly after World War II "marble cake" was applied to this blending of national-state-local activities, first by Joseph McLean and later by Morton Grodzins (McLean, 1952; Grodzins, 1960).

Whatever the terminology, it is clear that *PAR* was born in a time of sea-change in national-state-local relations. Samuel Beer has written that "Roosevelt's nationalism was a doctrine of federal centralization and under his administration . . . the balance of the American federal system swung sharply toward Washington; this was a sharp break from normal expectations of the past, especially for the Democratic party, but also for the whole country" (Beer, 1978:7). Beer himself was a participant in that change process, working in Washington directly with New Deal brain-trusters Tugwell and Corcoran. He writes: "I vividly recall our preoccupation with persuading people to look to Washington for the solution to problems and our sense of what a great change in public attitudes this involved" (1978:8).

Initial efforts to describe this "great change" were taken by Clark, Bane, McLean, and others. Calling this new system a "New Federalism" seemed sensible and appropriate to these observers and participants. But for other analysts and activists, an entirely new concept seemed necessary to describe accurately and adequately these altered political and administrative conditions. The result was the origin and use of the term intergovernmental relations.

Intergovernmental Relations (IGR)

There is no need to devote time and space to the origin, development, and features of IGR. The topic has been amply discussed (Anderson, 1960; Graves, 1964; Wright, 1975). More pertinent is the close link between the development of the concept and its usage in virtually every volume of *PAR*.

Why should *PAR* have been the receptor and the outlet for articles dealing with this new phenomenon? There are several reasons but the most prominent was the centrality and significance of *administration* to the implementation of enlarged public programs precipitated by the Great Depression and World War II. From a wartime standpoint one perceptive observer (Bromage, 1943:35) noted that:

> cooperative government by federal-state-local authorities has become a byword in the prodigious effort to administer civilian defense, rationing, and

> other war-time programs. . . . Intergovernmental administration, while it is a part of all levels of government, is turning into something quite distinct from them all.

For Bromage, as well as for Bane, wartime experiences sharpened and crystallized their views and their concepts. But intergovernmental relations had been explicitly addressed by other authors prior to the outbreak of hostilities.

Two articles in the first volume of *PAR,* for example, were "Working Relationships in Governmental Agricultural Programs" (Vieg 1:141-148) and "Intergovernmental Contracts in California" (Stewart and Ketcham 1:242-248). The former essay discussed the melding of national-state-local linkages in the day-to-day activities of agricultural researchers, extension agents, soil conservationists, etc. Their regular contacts across governmental boundaries involved agricultural-related activities of promotion, inspection, and regulation.

The Stewart/Ketcham article identified over 200 interlocal contracts then (1940) in effect in the Los Angeles area covering nearly every major local function of local government. They generalized beyond the Los Angeles data and observed that ". . . throughout the country, in all kinds of functions and at all levels of government, administrative officials are proceeding by informal agreements or by formal contracts to put into effect programs that cut across the boundaries of independent areas" (1:248). A close reading of these and other articles in the 1940s reveals a full range of the features of IGR, e.g., informal exchanges, administrative linkages, day-to-day working relationships, and policy issues (especially finances).

More articles demonstrating the scope and depth to which IGR had pervaded *PAR* appeared around 1950. E. A. Lutz (1949) wrote a review, titled "Intergovernmental Relations at the Grass Roots" (9:119-125), of seven reports produced by several local Councils on Intergovernmental Relations. These councils were established in 1941 in four states (California, Georgia, Indiana, Minnesota) under a grant from the Spelman Fund. Citizen-based local councils were established in one or more counties within each state. A national coordinating committee had illustrious members, e.g., William Anderson, Frank Bane, Luther Gulick, Paul McNutt, and Harold D. Smith.

To show where the "field" stood in the late 1940s it is useful to cite statements underlying the creation of the councils, the problems they considered, and the judgments they made (Lutz, 9:119-120).

(1) That control over local affairs and local government has gradually been more and more centralized into the state and federal governments.
(2) That unless checked, this gradual drift will continue.

(3) That the rapid expansion of government has confused the minds of people at the "grass roots" and there is no clear cut understanding as to what phases of government should properly and profitably be federal, state, or local.
(4) That unless clarified and the trend reversed it may eventually undermine democratic government.
(5) That this gradual centralization of authority and control has been due in part to the feeling by those at the top and in control, that the people at the local level are not capable of handling the problems which arise.
(6) That the Council does not believe this to be true. It believes that the feeling has arisen, not as a result of the incapacity of the people, but rather as it is due to the absence of interagency coordination at the local level and a positive citizen interest and participation in the direction of "our government."
(7) That greater responsibility for operating and improving government services should rest in the hands of persons at the local level.

Citizen involvement and inter-level coordination were issues four decades ago, as well as today. So also was the problem of state budgeting for federal aid. A 1950 article by Emile Ader (10:87-92) considered "State Budgetary Controls of Federal Grants-in-Aid." The author found such controls "woefully lacking" and noted that "perhaps of even greater importance is the fact that requests for grant funds by the state operating departments are not channeled through the state budget offices" (Ader, 10:89).

A prime example of inter-level exchange was described in a 1951 article (11:103-108) by Stanley K. Crook, "The Pacific Coast Board of Intergovernmental Relations." This unique entity was organized on a voluntary, cooperative basis in 1945 under the joint sponsorship of key officials from all levels of government in the West Coast states. It had a membership of 71 officials and held quarterly meetings that rotated among the three regional cities of Seattle, Portland, and San Francisco. Cook, who worked as the administrator of the board, offered the following conclusions about the five-year efforts of the entity (11:108).

> In five years of successful operation the Pacific Coast Board of Intergovernmental Relations has demonstrated the feasibility and value of cooperation among all levels of government in the West Coast area. It has fostered a regard for the regional point of view in officials presumed to be confined jurisdictionally to the consideration of problems assumed also to be so confined. In so doing it has been able to bring about a regional point of view concerning basic regional requirements, and thereby to increase the chances for perception of the specialized character of those requirements in Washington, D.C. Finally, it has been successful in promoting good day-to-day working relationships

> between officials who must consult across governmental lines on official business. Perhaps the organization and work of the board offers a pattern for intergovernmental cooperation in other regions.

Despite the apparent "success" of the Board, it was disbanded in 1953 because of national-level domestic budget cuts and officials' declining interest. Its disappearance is probably representative of the fragile and fleeting nature of numerous cooperative endeavors.

The Academic Decade

The 1950s might appropriately be called the "academic" decade of federalism and intergovernmental relations. A national Commission on Intergovernmental Relations, launched in 1953, produced numerous studies, reports, and recommendations in 1955 (Commission, 1955). This official set of documents, however, was only the tip of an iceberg whose submerged segment constituted dozens of articles and books that focused on the field.

A selection in Part II by John M. Gaus (16:102-109) reviews the national Commission's *Report* and three scholarly books. Gaus' summary, scope, and synthesis stand on their own significant merit. His concluding comment that "we are an unfinished country" contained more foresight, however, than he could have anticipated about the on-coming 1960s.

The late 1950s was a time of continued studies, reviews, and proposals. From an action standpoint it was a period of comparative intergovernmental quiescence, punctuated mainly by a short-lived and unsuccessful effort to return some functions (and taxes) to the states (Grodzins, 1960). Simultaneous with that effort the House Intergovernmental Relations Subcommittee held extensive hearings on a wide range of intergovernmental administrative and policy issues. These hearings, in conjunction with other events and influences, resulted in the creation of the Advisory Commission on Intergovernmental Relations (ACIR) in 1959.

The ACIR, of course, became an official and, in some respects, a definitive as well as a detailed researcher/observer on IGR (Wright, 25: 193-202). Prior to the ACIR's creation, however, the presence of organized, focused, and sustained research on IGR was the exception rather than the rule. The topic of metropolitan problems, policies, and reforms was one subject that was exceptional and distinctive for the amount of sustained attention it received, in *PAR* and elsewhere.

In 1953 Victor Jones reviewed *eight* "Metropolitan Studies" (13:57-63) dealing with the problems in, and reform proposals for Atlanta, Birmingham, Chicago, San Francisco, Toronto and Washington (D.C.). Jones, a well-established metropolitan scholar, regretted the fact that there were no more metropolitan governments than in 1942, when his own book on the subject was published; nor was there progress since 1930 when the first wave of metropolitan interest and reform began. This hard fact remained despite Jones' noting the existence of "many more published and unpublished studies of government in metropolitan areas—official survey reports, doctoral dissertations, prize-winning essays and monographs" (13:58). The failure of reform proposals was likely to continue, Jones concluded, until research was done to "supplement the administrative and structural studies of metropolitan communities with studies of the metropolitan organization and relationships of attitude and opinion-forming agencies" (13:63).

Jones' synthesis of metropolitan organization and reform issues focused largely on interlocal and indigenous approaches to solving the problems of these burgeoning areas. A broader approach or strategy was emerging, however. This involved national-level actions and policies. It was exemplified in 1954 by Daniel R. Grant's article, "Federal-Municipal Relations and Metropolitan Integration" (14:259-267). Grant noted that "Virtually all of the metropolitan area studies devote considerable attention to every conceivable alternative solution or device for metropolitan integration, yet omit any consideration of federal intervention in a day when it is customary for frustrated cities to go to the federal government for help in any and all problems" (14:259). Grant's preferences for national involvement to promote metropolitan change emerged near the end of his essay. "The continued failure to evolve even a reasonable facsimile of integrated metropolitan government for any of the 170 standard metropolitan areas in the United States makes it clear that new avenues to integration need to be explored" (14:267).

Grant's call for active and even aggressive national involvement on metropolitan issues fell on barren soil in the "academic" 1950s. A steady stream of research and recommendations continued for the remainder of the 1950s and into the early 1960s. During the 1954-1964 decade no less than 15 *PAR* articles or book-review essays treated metropolitan problems directly or indirectly. But deliberate and purposeful national action on urban/metropolitan issues awaited the arrival of the 1960s activism and the broad political base that supported enactment of the Great Society programs. This was the period of the Second New Federalism.

The Second New Federalism

The transition from the "academic" 1950s to the "activist" 1960s was partly foreshadowed by the New Frontier policies of the Kennedy Administration. But it remained for Lyndon Johnson to consummate the powerful policy breakthroughs that flooded over and through the political dikes from 1964 to 1969.

The dramatic impacts of the Great Society programs on intergovernmental relations need not be recounted. Treatments of intergovernmental developments in the 1960s are numerous at both the summary and the detailed levels of analysis. A general and penetrating review by Beer, for example, lays bare the sharp differences between the politics of the second new federalism in the 1960s from that of the 1930s (Beer, 1978). Among the differences between the two periods Beer lists the following: technocratic takeover, the romantic revolt, participatory democracy, and cultural equality. Beer summarizes the contrasts between the 1930s and the 1960s as follows (1978:20).

> By comparison with the New Deal model of politics, the influence of parties and pressure groups had declined, while that of the expert and professional had risen. Likewise, in policy there were major departures. In their usual design, the new social programs had certain distinctive traits: they depended on government spending, to provide specific services, delivered by professionally trained persons, to certain categories of consumers, for the sake of designated outcomes. And, not least important, they were to be carried out not directly by the federal government but by agencies of state and local governments.

States and local governments were co-opted as third parties in major *national* efforts to govern by what Hugh Heclo has described as "government by remote control" (Heclo, 1978:92).

The speech in which Lyndon Johnson launched the Great Society (in 1964) also referred to a "creative federalism." The phrase was not developed or elaborated as an operative principle, but the scores of grant programs created under the Great Society rubric made the precise meaning of creative federalism an incidental point. By 1969, James Sundquist could confidently and accurately assert that "in the nineteen-sixties the American federal system entered a new phase" (Sundquist, 1969:1).

Sundquist further observed that "through a series of dramatic enactments, the Congress asserted the national interest and authority in a wide range of governmental functions that until then had been the province, exclusively or predominantly, of state and local governments," and added that "the massive federal intervention in community affairs came in some of the most sacrosanct of all the traditional preserves of state and local authority," education and local law enforcement (1969:1). But it was not merely the number or scope of functions aided by federal dollars that made the 1960s a "new phase." Sundquist, in a thoughtful analysis, highlighted the significance of "national objectives," "close federal control," and "centralization of objective-setting."

The sheer number of grant programs set this new federalism apart from all others that preceded or followed. In 1961, there were approximately 40 major grant programs, but by 1969 there were an estimated 150 major programs, 400 specific legislative authorizations, and 1300 different federal assistance activities for which monetary amounts, application deadlines, and use restrictions could be identified. Of the 400 authorizations, 70 involved direct national-local disbursements, thus bypassing the states. In dollar terms, federal aid more than tripled from $7 billion in 1960 to $24 billion in 1970. While the intergovernmental aspects of the New Frontier/ Great Society decade were often referred to as creative federalism, an equally apt description is "The Second New Federalism."

To what ends were these new and multiple federal initiatives directed? What were the chief issues addressed by this whirlwind of policy activism? At the risk of great oversimplification two major policy themes were prominent: first, an urban/metropolitan focus; second, attention to the disadvantaged through antipoverty programs and aid-to-education funds. The second policy theme needs little documentation. With respect to the first it can be noted that between 1961 and 1969 the percentage of all federal aid that went to urban areas (SMSAs) increased from 55 to 70 percent (from $3.9 billion to $14.0 billion).

Mere dollar amounts, however, are insufficient to convey the changed nature of national policies toward metropolitan and urban areas. In addition, the increasingly significant role of state policies emerged despite the conscious effort of many new federalism policies to bypass the states. Robert Wood, writing in *PAR* in 1970 on "Needs and Prospects" for intergovernmental research (30: 265-268), discussed an operational simulation exercise done for the Model Cities program. Despite the avowed intent of Model Cities to be a direct national-local program, bypassing the states, the simulation, according to Wood, "identified the [state] governor as a key figure in the delivery program" (30:267).

Norman Beckman addressed both national and state roles in his 1966 article (in Part III) on "How Metropolitan Are Federal and State Policies?" (26:96-106). Beckman described the increasingly active and "essential role" of the national government in metropolitan areas. He identified various avenues for "improved Federal and State practice" in addressing urban and metropolitan problems, and offered several criteria for guiding national and state policies: geographic adequacy, economies of scale, adequate and equitable resources, and responsibility for a wide range of functions. Beckman was optimistic about the directions and impacts of national as well as state actions. "The prospects look better than ever for treating Federal and State activities as part of a unity in achieving commonly accepted objectives for government in metropolitan areas" (26:105).

It should come as no surprise that the optimism expressed for "unity" and for "commonly accepted objectives" went unrealized. The difficulties of a concentrated and coordinated national assault on urban/metropolitan problems proved far more intractable than they appeared to analysts and activists in the 1960s. In addition, fundamental challenges were raised about the assumptions of metropolitan "reform" (see Warren, 24:180-187).

Our purpose here is not to recount those assumptions or review the arguments. Instead, we call attention to and include in Part III a 1974 article by Joan Aron that captures the rise and decline of metropolitan reform in the New York City metropolitan area. Although focusing primarily on New York, Aron references the experiments and experiences elsewhere. She concludes that "the metropolitan nostrums which have been proposed with such startling regularity in the past may not, in fact, be the most desirable way of coping with New York's problems" (34:264).

The "reform-to-revisionist" movement on metropolitan problems provides a useful motif for pursuing a closely related policy theme—the role of the national government in dealing effectively with urban, and especially central- or large-city problems. Three selections in Part III, drawn from a five-year span in *PAR* (1968-1973), confront issues associated with the dual problems of inner city decay and unprecedented suburban growth.

Robert Wood discusses the "Federal Role in the Urban Environment" (28:341-347) with a major emphasis on the creation and activities of the new Department of Housing and Urban Development. Wood was a top-level executive in HUD at the time (1968) he wrote. From that vantage point he saw HUD's departmental status as a means "to strengthen our legislative tools that we might begin fashioning, for the first time, a national urban strategy" (28:345).

Wood's optimism about and commitment to a national urban strategy would later be formalized into a legislative mandate for a biennial national urban policy report. But neither departmental status nor a formal legal mandate, alone or in combination, could bring about a nationally-directed solution to urban ills. The U.S. urban governance system was exceedingly complex and this complexity had been gradually recognized by urban policy strategists. One approach to overcoming weak national tools for affecting urban policy making was a requirement for citizen participation.

In "Federally Financed Citizen Participation" (32:421-427), another selection in Part III, Howard Hallman reviews the experience with national requirements for citizen/client participation in four federal aid programs: urban renewal, juvenile delinquency, community action, and model cities. Hallman addresses basic policy questions, e.g., should federal funds be used to support citizen participation? But he also provides a notable descriptive base about citizen participation, especially its broader origins than merely the "maximum feasible participation" requirements under community action programs. Finally, Hallman is explicit in raising the issue of tradeoffs between program/policy coordination and citizen participation. He notes that, "it appears that the two elements do not go together very well" (32:425).

For Norton Long, many aspects of the urban political and intergovernmental scene "do not go together very well." The Long selection in Part III discusses in a critical and incisive manner the question: "Have Cities a Future?" (33:543-552). Long's views are, characteristically, skeptical and revisionist with regard to existing national, state, and local policies. But Long's probing mind plumbs the depths, plateaus, and peaks of the urban policy terrain. On that rough landscape Long locates untapped resources and resilience: "Once we have freed ourselves from the dogma of their [cities'] powerlessness we may find that they, even in a nation-state, can be made as the best of the Greeks held—the instruments of a good and noble life" (33:552).

A sense of the activism, intensity, urgency, and contentiousness of this second new federalism period surfaced in a small fragment from *PAR* in 1969. Albert Abrams, President of the Capital District ASPA Chapter in Albany, New York, took both public administration and intergovernmental relations to task.

> The people don't give a damn about intergovernmental relations. It smacks of an excuse for inaction. The people want bread, not excuses.

Abrams' comments were part of the conflict, candor, and confrontation of the 1960s. Similarly, Sundquist, with the collaboration of David W. Davis, was extracting insights from in-depth probes of what had happened to federalism in the 1960s. A summary of their book, *Making Federalism Work,* appeared in a 1970 issue of *PAR* (30:625-630).

Sundquist and Davis looked at local-level organization structures for the coordinated delivery of Great Society programs in urban and in nonmetropolitan areas of the country. Their excavations into the buried strata of local government complexity and citizen activism unearthed many problems but few uniform solutions. At the national level, however, there was a centerpoint for intergovernmental strategy and action. They noted (30:630):

> If the American federal system is to be truly a *system* of relationships, rather than a jumble, it must be guided by a consistent set of principles. That guidance can come from a single source of authority—the President. He must define the principles and apply them in the legislation he proposes and in the way he directs the execution of the laws.

The Third New Federalism

Sundquist and Davis wrote descriptively and prescriptively in a time of the imperial presidency. They also looked retrospectively at the Johnson Administration's intergovernmental programs. Richard Nixon approached the presidency from an imperial perspective and looked prospectively at strategies to change intergovernmental programs and policies. Less than a year after his election he announced, with considerable fanfare, a set of "new federalism" proposals and principles aimed at shifting power and authority away from the national government and to states and local governments.

This third new federalism in one respect took a leaf directly from the pages of Sundquist and Davis. Nixon attempted to guide the federal system with "a consistent set of principles." These broad federalism "principles," to be discussed in a moment, should not obscure, however, the strong *managerial* tendencies that pervaded many dimensions of the Nixon presidency. It was Nixon who reorganized and renamed the national budget agency, Office of *Management* and Budget (OMB). In addition, Richard Nathan recounts President Nixon's misdirected managerial efforts to control the federal bureaucracy in the book, *The Plot That Failed: Nixon and the Administrative Presidency* (Nathan, 1975).

Intergovernmental Management. It should come as no surprise, therefore, that attention to the management of intergovernmental relations attained considerable prominence during the early 1970s at the same time as broader efforts were underway to produce major policy shifts (Wright, 1983). Ann Macaluso's article (in Part II) describes the background and work from 1973 to 1975 of the Study Committee on Policy Management Assistance (35:695-700). This collaborative effort between OMB and the National Science Foundation produced an extensive body of materials and a set of recommendations appearing in Part V as the "Executive Summary" of the Committee's report. The recommendations called for a major reorientation of federal assistance programs. Changes were proposed to reduce nationally-caused impediments to the effective *management* of state and local government activities.

The topsy-turvey growth of grant and other assistance programs had, by the 1970s, generated substantial apprehensions among officials at all levels about management capacity generally and about state-local policy management capacity in particular. Those concerns had been expressed in the latter days of the Johnson Administration. William Carey, whose short 1968 article opens Part V, thoughtfully and pointedly addressed the "gap between policy design, program definition, and effective delivery" (28:23). Additionally, Lawrence Howard (in a Part V selection) discussed a broad range of executive manpower issues in his 1973 article, "Executive Development: An Intergovernmental Perspective" (33:101-110). Howard's concern for the short supply of skilled administrators to manage the complex intergovernmental arrangements echoed and expanded a *PAR* editorial a few years earlier by Senator Edmund Muskie, "Manpower: The Achilles Heel of Creative Federalism" (27:193-194).

Issues involving the management of intergovernmental programs did not, of course, originate in, nor were they confined to the 1970s or to the third new federalism. As early as 1940 in *PAR* Lawrence Durisch examined intergovernmental aspects of implementing TVA policies—"Local Government and the TVA Program" (1:326-334). Program magnitudes, complexity, and ambitious aims, however, prompted a peaking of interest in implementation management since the 1970s. Our selections in Part V reflect this increased recent attention.

Three articles (Lovell, Mikulecky, Kettl) examine implementation chiefly from the local perspective. In one sense, these three "bottom-up" perspectives balance the first three selections (Carey, Howard, Study Committee) which adopt a national or "top-down" set of perspectives on implementing intergovernmental programs.

Professor Catherine Lovell finds that local jurisdictions adopt one or a combination of three basic coordination strategies in implementing grant programs. She concludes from eight case studies covering varied types of aid funding "that local and community institutions have the capacity to link the programs together in highly effective ways" (39:438).

City Manager Thomas Mikulecky offers a concise set of observations on strategies that local executives can and should use in dealing with the full array of intergovernmental interactions and influences. He cites "intergovernmental diplomacy" and playing the "regulation game" as two of several strategies open to an effective local administrator.

Professor Donald Kettl describes in somewhat different terms another strategy that local officials (in Richmond, Va., and elsewhere) have employed to implement federally-aided programs. That strategy, commonly called "contracting-out," involves the use of various local non-city groups and associations to deliver the federally-funded services and programs. The use of entities like neighborhood associations and non-profit organizations as intermediaries is Kettl's "fourth face" of the federal system.

Kettl's article can be beneficially read in conjunction with the Hallman article on citizen participation and the Long essay on the future of cities (Part III). One legacy of the participatory initiatives in the 1950s and mandates in the 1960s has been the presence and prominence of numerous activist groups and associations on the local scene. The "fourth face" strategy contains, however, a basic challenge to the governing integrity and sense of community and commitment that leaps to the reader's attention from the Long essay. If a city is little more than a conduit for receiving, transferring, and tracking funds, somewhat like an accountant, then is it still a city?

The concluding selection in Part V by Kearney and Garey is distinctive in at least two respects. First, the article on federalism and the management of radioactive wastes revolves chiefly around national-state relations. Second, as the title implies, it deals not with the intergovernmental exchange of "goods" but with national-state relations involving a "bad," namely, radioactive waste materials. Locating a place for radioactive residues is like finding a site for a LULU—a *l*ocally *u*nwanted *l*and *u*se. Incinerators, sewage plants, airports, and a variety of other "public" facilities are necessary; but intense protests arise from citizens against facilities to be located near their residences, schools, etc. Hence, the LULU acronym. Similarly, national government actions by the AEC, NRC, or the Department of Energy to locate sites for depositing radioactive wastes have generated storms of protests from state (and local) officials. The conflict, complexity, and other features of this national-state controversy lead Kearney and Garey to conclude that a new era of "contentious federalism" may be replacing the older conventional model in which cooperation was predominant.

Principles of the Third New Federalism. The emerging intergovernmental management issues did not, however, supplant high-voltage issues on the intergovernmental policy agenda placed there by Richard Nixon and the third new federalism. From an intergovernmental standpoint the accession of Nixon to the presidency produced a shift but not a major reversal of the momentum and trends built into intergovernmental policies during the preceding four decades. The president's conscious coinage of the "new federalism" term was part of a deliberate effort to deflect and redirect forces that were pushing the nation from *the* United States toward *a* "United State" (Lowi, 1978).

Nixon's new federalism was a set of policies developed with explicit rationale and noteworthy internal debate. The debate was conducted through a series of four internal advocacy papers written under the pseudonyms, Publius, Cato, Althusius, and Polybius (*Publius,* 1972). The clearest exposition and synthesis of New Federalism No. 3, however, appeared in a 1975 article by Richard Nathan, a chief architect of the term (Nathan, 1975).

Nathan highlighted the decentralist philosophy undergirding this new federalism by drawing distinctions between three aspects of domestic programs: (a) financing, (b) policy making, and (c) administration. He then noted that: "New Federalism, in effect, said that financial assistance from the federal government to the states should continue in the functional areas selected for decentralization, but that the policy making and administrative influence of the federal government should be reduced through revenue-sharing (both general and special) and related changes in the structure of other grants to states and localities" (Nathan, 1975:122). There was also a complementary component—functions for which a stronger national role and controls would be pursued. These included transfer payments and income security programs, functions involving high spillover effects (air pollution), and research/demonstration programs.

On the programmatic side, then, the "key idea," according to Nathan, was "a sorting out and a rearranging of governmental functions" (1975:121). This sorting process was to be accompanied by two prominent structural themes: (1) generalists (i.e., elected or appointed chief executives) and general purpose governments were favored over program/professional specialists, special districts, and quasi-governmental entities; and (2) among general purpose governments the new federalism policies were intended to be neutral, i.e., not favoring one type or level of government in distribution formulas or policy discretion. Both Macaluso's article in Part II and the Study Committee's Executive Summary in Part V explicitly reflect this "generalist" policy management orientation.

Despite structural and program policy shifts, three longer-term patterns persisted under the third new federalism. First, the absolute number of grant programs continued to rise. Second, the dollar amounts of federal aid continued to increase at the rate of 15-20 percent per year. Third, federal aid tended to become more concentrated in a few large, formula-grant programs.

For example, by 1976 more than 80 percent of all federal aid was disbursed through 25 major formula-based programs. This movement toward a small number of formula-type grant programs precipitated a shift toward what many participants called, "the formula game" or computer-based federal aid politics (Stanfield, 1978; Walker, 1979; Wright, 1980). These terms described strategies, ranging from the simple to the complex, designed to rig the various grant allocation formulas with factors favoring particular types of cities, counties, states, or regions. Among the most prominent of the large, formula-based aid programs was General Revenue Sharing.

General revenue sharing (GRS), as Nathan notes, was "the most important legislative enactment of New Federalism" (Nathan, 1975:128). Yet GRS produced mixed policy results when evaluated against the decentralist aims of the third new federalism. First, it was only incrementally expansive in terms of total federal aid to state and local governments. By 1976, GRS amounted to about 10 percent of $59.1 billion in total federal aid. (Note that between 1970 and 1976 federal aid in a six-year span had more than doubled from $24 billion to nearly $60 billion.) Second, GRS put an estimated 25-30,000 local jurisdictions in direct touch with the U.S. treasury *for the first time,* i.e., receiving quarterly GRS checks. For thousands of units (and local officials) with no prior direct involvement in the federal aid process, GRS dramatically increased their attention to events, interests, and opportunities on the Washington policy merry-go-round. In short, federal aid became as common as the morning cup of coffee to tens of thousands of officials in small cities and counties.

The longer-term legacy of these results is still unclear. In the short run, the third new federalism increased immensely the number and variety of local actors who viewed GRS and block grant programs (both old and new) as "entitlements." A possessiveness and a "right" to federal aid was clearly engendered by the separate and joint effects of the second and third new federalisms. One need only look at the explosion in federal grant case law to appreciate the significance of changed attitudes (ACIR, 1980a; Brown, 1980, 1981).

Intergovernmental Finances

Financial aspects of the U.S. federal system span the nation's complete constitutional history—from the Northwest Ordinance in 1787 to the most recent federal aid program enacted, expanded, reduced, or eliminated. Fiscal issues, in other words, transcend the bounds of the three new federalism periods previously reviewed and of the fourth one to be addressed shortly. It is important to note, however, the fiscal expansion was a salient feature of the first three new federalisms. Relevant figures support this general assertion.

Federal aid expenditures are shown below for fiscal years that cover 4-5 year periods for the Roosevelt, Johnson, and Nixon Administrations.

	Year	Outlays (in billions)
Roosevelt	1932:	.232
	1936:	.908
Johnson	1963:	8.507
	1968:	18.053
Nixon	1969:	19.421
	1974:	42.854

Extensive discussion of these respective increases is unnecessary. During each president's term the increase in federal aid to state/local governments rose sharply.

What may seem noteworthy is the continued rapid rise of federal aid during the third new federalism. The increases, however, cannot all be tallied and charged to President Nixon's account. On the contrary, at one point, 1973-1974, he battled the Congress, the courts, and state-local governments in his efforts to impound various grant-in-aid funds. What should be clarified is that the GRS and block grant fiscal strategies of the third new federalism resulted in major expansions in federal aid between 1969 and 1974.

More extensive and detailed figures on federal aid are informative. Annual data for nearly three decades are provided in Table 1. The absolute

Federal Grants-in-Aid in Relation to State-Local Receipts from Own Sources, Total Federal Outlays and Gross National Product, 1955-1983 (Dollar Amounts in Billions)

	Federal Grants-in-Aid (Current Dollars)					Exhibits:				
			As a Percentage of–			Federal Grants in Constant Dollars (1972 Dollars, GNP Deflator)			Grants for Payments to Individuals	
Fiscal Year	Amount	Percent Increase or Decrease (–)	State-Local Receipts From Own Source	Total Federal Outlays	Gross National Product	Amount	Percent Increase or Decrease (–)	Estimated Number of Federal Grant Programs	Amount	Percent of Total Grants
1955	$ 3.2	4.9	11.8	4.7	0.8	$ 5.3	n.a.	n.a.	$ 1.6	50.0
1956	3.7	15.6	12.3	5.3	0.9	5.9	11.3	n.a.	1.7	45.9
1957	4.0	8.1	12.1	5.3	0.9	6.2	5.1	n.a.	1.8	45.0
1958	4.9	22.5	14.0	6.0	1.1	7.4	19.4	n.a.	2.1	42.9
1959	6.5	32.7	17.2	7.0	1.4	9.6	29.7	n.a.	2.4	36.9
1960	7.0	7.7	16.8	7.6	1.4	10.2	6.3	132	2.5	35.7
1961	7.1	1.4	15.8	7.3	1.4	10.2	0	n.a.	2.9	40.8
1962	7.9	11.3	16.2	7.4	1.4	11.2	9.8	n.a.	3.2	40.5
1963	8.6	8.9	16.5	7.8	1.5	12.0	7.1	n.a.	3.5	40.7
1964	10.1	17.4	17.9	8.6	1.6	13.9	15.8	n.a.	3.8	37.6
1965	10.9	7.9	17.7	9.2	1.7	14.7	5.8	n.a.	3.9	35.8
1966	13.0	19.3	19.3	9.6	1.8	16.9	15.0	n.a.	4.5	34.6
1967	15.2	16.9	20.6	9.6	2.0	19.2	13.6	379	5.0	32.9
1968	18.6	22.4	22.4	10.4	2.2	22.5	17.2	n.a.	6.3	33.9
1969	20.3	9.1	21.6	11.0	2.2	23.4	4.0	n.a.	7.5	36.9
1970	24.0	18.2	22.9	12.2	2.5	26.2	12.0	n.a.	9.0	37.5
1971	28.1	17.1	24.1	13.3	2.7	29.3	11.8	n.a.	11.0	39.1
1972	34.4	22.4	26.1	14.8	3.1	34.4	17.4	n.a.	14.4	41.9
1973	41.8	21.5	28.5	16.9	3.3	39.5	14.8	n.a.	14.3	34.2
1974	43.4	3.8	27.3	16.1	3.1	37.7	–4.6	n.a.	15.3	35.3

Fiscal Year	Federal Grants-in-Aid (Current Dollars)		As a Percentage of–			Exhibits: Federal Grants in Constant Dollars (1972 Dollars, GNP Deflator)		Exhibits: Estimated Number of Federal Grant Programs	Exhibits: Grants for Payments to Individuals	
	Amount	Percent Increase or Decrease (–)	State-Local Receipts From Own Source	Total Federal Outlays	Gross National Product	Amount	Percent Increase or Decrease (–)		Amount	Percent of Total Grants
1975	$49.8	14.7	29.1	15.3	3.4	$39.6	5.0	448	$17.4	34.9
1976	59.1	18.7	31.1	16.1	3.6	44.7	12.9	n.a.	21.0	35.5
1977	68.4	15.7	31.0	17.0	3.7	48.8	9.2	n.a.	23.9	34.9
1978	77.9	13.9	31.7	17.3	3.7	51.8	6.1	498	26.0	33.4
1979	82.9	6.4	31.3	16.8	3.5	50.7	–2.1	n.a.	28.8	34.7
1980	91.5	10.4	31.7	15.8	3.6	51.2	1.0	n.a.	34.2	37.4
1981	94.8	3.6	29.4	14.4	3.2	48.5	–5.3	539	40.1	42.3
1982	88.8	–7.0	25.4	12.1	2.9	42.6	–12.2	441	37.8	45.5
1983 est.	93.5	6.3	n.a.	11.6	2.9	42.9	0.7	409	n.a.	n.a.
1984 est.	95.9	2.6	n.a.	11.3	2.7	41.8	–2.6	n.a.	n.a.	n.a.

Source: Advisory Commission on Intergovernmental Relations, *Significant Features of Fiscal Federalism, 1981-82 Edition,* Washington, D.C.: GPO, 1983, p. 66

amounts in the first column show long-term consistent and often major jumps in federal aid. The percentage figures in the second column show annual rates of increase in federal aid (for all but 1981-82).

The numerous double-digit rates show the sharp rises in intergovernmental aid. Curiously, the two highest rates of increase were in 1957-58 and 1958-59, the "academic" period of comparative quiescence. The rates are high, in part, because the base was low. But more directly pertinent is that the cause can be traced to a single large program—highway aid. This single aid program accounted for less than $1 billion in 1957, but was nearly $3 billion in 1959.

This sudden massive leap did not go unrecognized in *PAR.* Professor James Martin, who had also served as Kentucky State Highway Commissioner, critically examined the "Administrative Dangers in the Enlarged Highway Program" (19:164-172). Focusing primarily on the states, Martin concluded that "serious management breakdown has occurred only in states traditionally practicing a high degree of political patronage" (19:172).

Except for special circumstances in the 1950s, the highest rates of change appear in the mid-1960s and the early 1970s, coincident with the second and third new federalisms. The rates also remained at double-digit levels during the years 1975 through 1978. To explore and understand these varied federal aid changes we can usefully draw on a universe of more than 60 articles on intergovernmental finances that have appeared in *PAR.*

Not all these articles, of course, focused on federal aid. Some dealt with revenues and taxation. A few focused on state-local fiscal matters. Still others analyzed expenditure patterns and trends for national, state, and local jurisdictions. The most consistent, enduring, and frequent intergovernmental fiscal topic in *PAR,* however, has been the varied forms and different issues involving federal aid. Our selection of six articles in Part IV reflects this emphasis.

Our major focus on federal aid is not without hesitation or reservation, for two reasons. First, unsuspecting readers and new initiates to the study and practice of intergovernmental relations should be forewarned of the complexity and subtlety of intergovernmental finances. The fiscal facets of the federal system are like a thousand facets on rough-cut diamonds. Sharp edges, unexpected hues, and kaleidoscopic images are forthcoming from the "stones" extracted from the fiscal "mines" throughout the federal system.

A second reason advises caution on federal aid specifically, and on intergovernmental finances generally. This arises from what has been variously called, "fiscal fixation" or "monetary myopia." These catchy phrases have been coined to describe the inordinate and undue emphasis given to financial matters in the study and practice of intergovernmental relations. There is a seductive simpicity that often arises when "hard" and precise dollar figures are mobilized and manipulated to show changing power, influence, dependency, control, etc.

Fortunately, the very first selection in Part IV provides explicit help in countering these simplifying tendencies. Professor Daniel J. Elazar appropriately titled his article, "Fiscal Questions and Political Answers in Intergovernmental Finance" (32:471-478). Elazar, one of the most noted federalism scholars in the country, takes direct aim at:

> . . . the oft-encountered tendency to assess the respective policy roles of the various American governments by ascertaining what share of the total expenditure they contribute to the funding of specific programs. This short-hand but often misleading view is frequently encountered in the mass media where local programs are presented as federal ones on the assumption that the source of funds also indicates the locus of political control, a view that has been refuted time and again by studies of a whole host of intergovernmental programs.

Elazar's essay is not mainly cautionary, however. It is both analytical and assertive. Besides his strong emphasis on the political foundations undergirding fiscal relationships, Elazar elaborates three theories underlying federal aid, highlights some contradictory trends in national-local relations, and mentions state-local relations as a "hidden dimension" of the intergovernmental fiscal/political scene.

Elazar's article furnishes a valuable base from which to explore the three major types of federal aid—categorical grants, block grants, and general revenue sharing (GRS). One article appears on each of these components of the contemporary "tripartite system" of federal aid (ACIR, 1980b). Actually, this tripartite system is so recent in its arrival or birth that it walks unsteadily and would fall (fail) without active parental support. Thus far, from about 1970 to the present, major parental support and sustenance has come from the presidency, much as Sundquist and Davis predicted and prescribed in 1969.

Until enactment of the first major block grant (for law enforcement) in 1968, nearly all federal aid consisted of specific or specialized categorical grant programs. Within the categorical classification there was a further subdivision into project and formula grants. When President Nixon proposed his new federalism policies in 1969, it was estimated that 96 percent of all federal aid was dispensed through categorical grants. By 1972, as shown below, the complexion of federal aid components had changed even prior to the enactment of GRS.

	1972	1976	1980	1984
	(percentage of total federal aid)			
Categorical	90	78	79	81
Block	8	10	11	12
Shared revenue	2	12	10	7
Dollar amounts (in billions)	34.4	59.1	91.5	95.9

In recent years categorical grants have constituted about four-fifths of all federal aid. Despite this somewhat reduced proportion of all aid, categorical grants continue to be associated with grantsmanship and gamesmanship images.

The prominence as well as the politics involved in categorical grant awards make this form of aid the focus of considerable research and analysis. Gilbert and Specht examined the selection process that HUD followed in "Picking Winners" during the first-round funding for Model Cities in 1967-1968. They describe the manifest and latent functions of an elaborate grant evaluation and award process (PGRP). They reveal descriptively the extensive and involved nature of applying for federal categorical aid. But their analysis (in Part IV) also uncovers the way in which a "national" evaluation process is influenced by political forces, by HUD staff aspirations (and perhaps aggrandizement), and by the need for interagency participation and coordination.

Block grants have generally resulted from the consolidation of several categorical grants, e.g., Community Development Block Grant (CDBG). This was not the case for one of the earliest large block grant programs—the Safe Streets Act of 1968 (P.L. 90-351) which created the Law Enforcement Assistance Administration (LEAA). The creation and early experience of LEAA is the subject of Douglas Harmon's article in Part IV. Harmon provides an excellent analysis of the conflicts and competition engendered by the block grant idea as exemplified in LEAA. The block grant has been proposed as a major federal aid reform measure aimed at simplifying intergovernmental relations. Harmon found that this was not the case and concluded that the conflict and complexity associated with mechanism suggested that it "can be successfully introduced into only a limited number of policy fields" (30:152). His observation was accurate for the 1970s and for the 1980s as well.

Like the block grant idea, the concept of revenue sharing was a policy reform measure that traced its origins to the 1950s and even the 1940s (Hansen and Perloff, 1944). The intergovernmental policy ferment during the third new federalism resulted in the 1972 enactment of GRS (Beer, 1976; Dommel, 1974). A cottage industry soon emerged to monitor, describe, and evaluate the results of this novel and large intergovernmental innovation—

$30 billion for 38,000 state and local governments to spend over four years. The National Science Foundation, for example, sponsored over 20 research projects at a cost of $3 million to assess the impacts of state-local allocation decisions. One of the most significant aspects of the collective GRS research efforts was to focus not only on fund usage but also on the decision processes and the perspectives of decision makers.

The *PAR* article by David A. Caputo and Richard L. Cole in Part IV reflects these multiple interests. They relied on a survey of city officials to secure estimates of GRS outlays. They appropriately note, from their survey results, that "probably the most important impact of general revenue sharing funds may well be the general satisfaction of city officials with the program and the apparent increase in that satisfaction as the program continues" (35:142). That satisfaction resulted in powerful local lobbying efforts to continue GRS when renewal dates occurred in 1976, 1980, and 1983. The *local* efforts have been successful each time, but the states were eliminated as recipients in 1980.

All three types of federal aid are forms of federal assistance. But the meaning of "federal assistance" encompasses more than revenue sharing and block and categorical grants. A contract between the U.S. Bureau of Prisons and a state or local government for housing some federal prisoners would be a non-grant form of federal assistance. Cooperative agreements on joint research projects would also be a form of federal assistance, but may not be classified as a "grant." The Federal Grant and Cooperative Agreement Act of 1977 (P.L. 95-224) was enacted to reduce the considerable confusion that had pervaded federal/non-federal relationships.

Robert D. Newton was a member of the Grants and Contracts Division of the National Science Foundation when he addressed federal assistance issues and reforms in his 1978 article, "Administrative Federalism" (Part IV). Newton's article and the legislation sought to standardize terminology by distinguishing between (1) procurement, (2) cooperative agreements, and (3) grants. The crux of the difference between (2) and (3) is the expectation that grant transactions would have "minimum federal involvement" while cooperative agreements would be accompanied by "substantial federal involvement."

Perhaps the most noteworthy feature of the 1977 Act and of Newton's article is the mandate that national programs and national officials explicitly state their intended degree of involvement. A clear, explicit, and open statement of national purpose and control could be viewed skeptically for two reasons. First, the problem of securing such an above-board assertion is a difficulty that borders on the impossible. Second, attempting such a reasonable and rational aim attempts to eliminate the critical roles of ambiguity, flexibility, and compromise that are an important part of the intergovernmental bargaining and adjustment process.

The aftermath of P.L. 95-224 (and Newton's article) need to be noted. OMB launched a major study, mandated by 95-224, in 1978-1979. The study papers and documents exceeded in scope and size the materials produced by the Study Committee on Policy Management Assistance in 1975. A March 1980 report recommended a series of revisions and reforms in federal assistance management efforts (OMB, 1980). These proposals, however, were lost in the welter of policy shifts that occurred after the 1980 election. Indeed, the Intergovernmental Affairs unit in OMB was downgraded and decimated in the first few months of the Reagan Administration. This might seem to be an inconsistent course of action for President Reagan. The explanation is to be found in the brand of new federalism proposed and pursued by President Reagan from 1981 through 1983.

The Fourth New Federalism

The current form and manifestation of new federalism departs in several significant ways from the three previous forms (Wright, 1982). Speaking to state legislators at their national meeting in 1981, President Reagan employed terms that strongly supported "restoration" as an overall emphasis in the fourth new federalism, whose major features he prominently displayed in his 1982 State of the Union message. The President challenged the state legislators: "Together then let us restore constitutional government, let us renew and enrich the power and purpose of states and local communities, and let us return to the people those rights and duties that are justly theirs" (*Federalism,* 1981:36). The President's words and actions have made it clear that the Reagan Administration aimed at returning national-state-local relationships to a point probably between the first and second new federalisms.

The purpose here is neither to debate the wisdom of the fourth new federalism nor to estimate its restoration probabilities. Instead, we briefly describe the essential intergovernmental policy strategies that undergird the current new federalism and in that process attempt to clarify the extent to which this approach is, in fact, "new."

Four features or policy strategies are posited as representing the multiple and varied aspects of the fourth new federalism. These are: decongestion, devolution, decrementalism, and deregulation. Brief comments on each strategy are appropriate.

Decongestion. In conventional terms, this term describes the sorting out of government functions among levels of government. The Reagan Administration has accepted this policy strategy implicitly and explicitly. The Assistant to the President for Intergovernmental Affairs, Richard S. Williamson, has said that the President's federalism proposal "will cut administrative overhead and define precise product lines by sorting out responsibilities among the various levels of government" (ACIR, *Intergovernmental Perspective,* 1982).

The Administration's view of decongestion does not acknowledge that the full range of income maintenance programs is a national responsibility. Witness the original and ill-fated proposed "swap" with the states of Medicaid for Food Stamps and Aid to Families with Dependent Children (AFDC) programs. Many intergovernmental analysts, both objective observers and partisan advocates, have supported decongestion moves based on national assumption of income security programs (ACIR, 1980b, 1981).

The Administration's defense of its swap and turnback proposals rested on various rationales. Regardless of reason and conviction, however, it proved to be impossible to negotiate a consensus among state and local interest groups on the shifting of functions (Williamson, 1983; Farber, 1983). This component or feature of the fourth new federalism is moot.

Devolution. The term devolution seldom appears in discussions of U.S. intergovernmental relationships. This contrasts with its more extensive use in the United Kingdom and other unitary systems. This differential usage may be explained in part by the word's formal dictionary meaning: "a delegating of authority or duties to a subordinate or substitute." The term, however, is relevant to contemporary U.S. federalism and intergovernmental relations.

The concept of devolution applies to the Reagan Administration's proposals to turn over *resources* as well as programs to the states. This, of course, refers to the 1982 "turnback" proposals in which a trust fund would be created to finance the states' takeover of about 40 grant programs in the areas of transportation, community development, health, and social services. This element of the fourth new federalism is also moot.

But there is another part of the terrain on the current intergovernmental landscape that accords well with the devolution concept. This is the reinvigoration of the block grant idea. For the Reagan Administration, block grants are useful not only intrinsically, but also as stepping stones to turning back both programs and resources. As the 1981 Reconciliation Act (creating nine block grants) neared passage, the President emphasized the transnational nature of block grants to state legislators. "The ultimate objective . . . is to use block grants as a bridge leading to the day when you will have not only the responsibility for programs that properly belong at the state level but you will also have the tax resources now usurped by Washington returned to you" (*Federalism,* 1981:34).

The nine block grants enacted in 1981 devolved varying degrees of discretion on the states. But the implementation of the block grants revealed the Administration's independent resolve to shift discretion to the states. In August, 1981 the Secretary of Health and Human Services (HHS), Richard

Schweiker, wrote the following policy statement to the Governor of North Carolina: "After careful review of the statutory language and legislative history for each of the seven block grant programs [in HHS], I have decided that where the law provides this Department policy discretion, I will pass that discretion through to the states" (Beyle and Dusenbury, 1982:2).

On balance, then, it appears that devolution is an appropriate and relevant term for describing another major policy strategy of the fourth new federalism.

*Decrementalism. In*crementalism has been a standard term in the lexicon of budgeting, finance, and intergovernmental relations for over a quarter-century (Lindblom, 1959; Wildavsky, 1964). The term had become synonymous with the steady expansion of governmental programs and activities at all levels in steady *increments.* It was not until the late 1970s, highlighted in part by California's Proposition 13 vote, that public officials and analysts became acutely conscious of a no-growth, steady-state public sector. In fact, the no-growth pattern proved illusory; a more accurate description of the choices facing public decision makers were variously described as cutback management, doing more with less, and decrementalism.

PAR was an early and featured locus for the discussion of decrementalism. In 1978 Professor Charles Levine edited a *PAR* symposium of six articles on "Organizational Decline and Cutback Management" (38: 315-357). The urban dimension of resource reductions surfaced in two 1981 articles in a special issue on resource scarcity in urban public finance. Professor Jerry McCaffery described and argued for an emphasis on the revenue side of the budgeting ledger in his article, "Revenue Budgeting: Dade County Tries a Decremental Approach" (41:179-189). Professor Andrew Glassberg analyzed New York City financial policies and stringencies over a ten-year span. He placed that city's fiscal crisis on the broader urban scene in his article, "The Urban Fiscal Crisis Becomes Routine" (41:165-172).

It remained, however, for Carl Stenberg from the ACIR to put decrementalism and cutbacks in a broad intergovernmental context. Stenberg, now Executive Director of the Council of State Governments, reviewed 20 years of intergovernmental growth, change, and crisis in his 1981 article, "Beyond the Days of Wine and Roses: Intergovernmental Management in a Cutback Environment" (41:10-20). Stenberg's article is included as the final "review" article in Part II. Coincidentally, it appeared in the January/February issue of *PAR* simultaneous with the inauguration of Ronald Reagan as president.

Decrementalism has been such a prominently-featured theme of the fourth new federalism that it barely requires mentioning, much less special emphasis. A few figures should be entered for the record, however. Federal aid in FY 1981 was $94.8 billion and for FY 1982 the amount was $88.8 billion (see Table 1). For the first time in more than three decades an absolute decline had been recorded. Furthermore, there was a major drop in the number of grant programs. Not only were about 60 categoricals consolidated into nine block grants, but over 60 other categoricals were "zeroed out" in the budget crunching moves under the Omnibus Budget Reconciliation Act of 1981. As Table 1 indicates, the estimated number of grants dropped from 539 in 1981 to 409 in 1983.

That enactment process led one Senator (Durenberger of Minnesota) to observe, "We are at the point where one more round of this New Federalism—conducted in the frenzy of the budget process—will discredit the concept entirely" (*National Journal,* 1982). Other observers underscored more concisely the retrenchment dimension of Administration strategy: austerity equals decentralization (Calkins and Shannon, 1982).

The austerity theme is directly linked to the final selection in Part IV by Eugene S. Sunshine, "Minimizing the Disappointment of Successful Applicants in Grant Programs" (42:479-483). Sunshine concisely captures his direct involvement in the administration of grant programs by the New York State Energy Office. The problem of "dispensing disappointment" among numerous applicants was especially acute in the wake of 1982 new federalism cutbacks. Sunshine outlines a set of six strategies that helped the agency say no, politely and constructively, to applicants who could not be funded. In addition to an optimistic approach on coping with cuts, Sunshine's article focuses on a state agency's involvement in the implementation of a federal aid program. The role of state government and state agencies as middlemen in handling the bulk of federal aid funds is sometimes ignored or overlooked.

Deregulation. Policies aimed at reducing federal rules and regulations encompass much more than the regulatory "strings" attached to federal aid. But deregulation contains a significant intergovernmental subcomponent. The Presidential Task Force on Regulatory Relief, created in February, 1981, invited written comments on problems and changes needed in federal regulations. Of the 3,000 suggested changes, over 500 involved regulations affecting state and local governments (*Federalism,* 1981).

By the end of 1981, the Task Force had proposed or made final nearly 60 regulatory changes directly affecting state and local governments. Among these were: withdrawal of bilingual education rules and of federal regulations on school dress codes, proposed changes in Davis-Bacon and transportation of the handicapped regulations, and a review of regulations involving Medicaid and education of handicapped children.

Studies dealing with the intergovernmental issues and consequences associated with increasing federal regulations, including mandates, are extensive. No more than a few can even be referenced here (Beam, 1981; Kettl, 1981; Kettl, 1983; Lovell, 1979; Lovell, 1981; Petkas, 1981). In addition to producing a bias toward centralization, one study of "regulating the cities" under GRS, Comprehensive Employment and Training Act

(CETA), and CDBG programs noted that the rise in regulations "produced a growing administrative burden," "made the effective implementation of domestic policy more difficult," and "confused the lines of accountability for intergovernmental policy" (Kettl, 1981:114). For example, in the CETA *block grant* program the Federal Paperwork Commission "found one set of instructions 106 pages long among more than 150 transmittals to local governments in one region over a 27-month period—three transmittals every two weeks" (Kettl, 1981:122).

The "regulatory dimension" of federalism and intergovernmental relations has not gone unrecognized in *PAR*. Professor Catherine Lovell, one of the leading scholars on the subject, dealt with the subject broadly from the standpoint of federal and state mandates that have an impact on local governments (Lovell and Tobin, 41:318-331). The authors conclude that, (1) "mandates have resulted in extensive broadening of the activities of local governments while at the same time severely curtailing their autonomy," and (2) "in conjunction with the proliferation of grants-in-aid, mandating has expanded the dependence of local governments on the states and federal government for policy choices as well as resources" (41:329).

A scan of *PAR* in 1981 and 1982 yields several topics falling within the regulatory rubric. These include: state involvement in enforcement of federal surface mining and control legislation (Menzel, 41:212-219), loss of legal immunity by state and local officials (Groszyk and Madden, 41: 268-278), effects on state utility regulation of national public utility policy legislation (Vaughn and Sharpe, 41:387-391), the complexities and uncertainties of federal energy policies on state energy policies (Barkenbus, 42: 410-418), and the problems of securing local enforcement and compliance with state-mandated energy-conserving building regulations (Wilms, 42: 553-561). These illustrations and the space devoted to discussing "deregulation" are deliberate in intent. They signify a growing, significant, and problematic aspect of intergovernmental relations. It is perhaps ironic, as well as regrettable, that years of "fiscal fixation" may have partially obscured our vision of the "reality of regulation" that has emerged on the intergovernmental scene.

One concluding point might be made about the intergovernmental aspect of regulation and deregulation. The complexities of the problems involved in managing federal assistance are enormous. The 1980 Office of Management and Budget (OMB) study amply demonstrated and highlighted those complexities in terms of forms of assistance, varied types of assistance recipients, varying recipient capacities, multiple and conflicting purposes, and escalating assistance-related disputes (OMB, 1980). These complexities both demand and yet compound solutions to the problems of regulating and deregulating federal assistance activities. Persistence, varied approaches, problem-specific strategies, and caution about panaceas are probably the minimal hallmarks for progress in this difficult and sometimes arcane intergovernmental arena.

Concluding Comment. The current (fourth) variety of new federalism is, from a purely descriptive standpoint, especially deserving of the appellation "new." Each of the four dimensions represents a distinctive departure from past intergovernmental patterns. Decongestion, devolution, decrementalism, and deregulation constitute new intergovernmental strategies both in degree and in kind. Whatever the outcomes of these strategies, they signify that the nature of our federal system is an open and an evolving one. It is also a system of systems that will undoubtedly be analyzed and assessed in each subsequent volume of *PAR*.

References

Advisory Commission on Intergovernmental Relations (1980a). *Awakening the Slumbering Giant: Intergovernmental Relations and Federal Grant Law.* Washington, D.C.: GPO.

Advisory Commission on Intergovernmental Relations (1980b). *In Brief—The Federal Role in the Federal System: The Dynamics of Growth.* Washington, D.C.: GPO.

Advisory Commission on Intergovernmental Relations (1981). *An Agenda for American Federalism: Restoring Confidence and Competence.* Washington, D.C.: GPO.

Advisory Commission on Intergovernmental Relations (1982). *Intergovernmental Perspective,* 8 (Spring): 19.

Anderson, William (1960). *Intergovernmental Relations in Review.* Minneapolis, Minn.: University of Minnesota Press.

Beam, David R. (1981). "Washington's Regulation of States and Localities: Origins and Issues." *Intergovernmental Perspective,* 7 (Summer): 8-18.

Beer, Samuel H. (1976). "The Adoption of General Revenue Sharing: A Case Study in Public Sector Politics." *Public Policy,* 24 (Spring): 127-195.

Beer, Samuel H. (1978). "In Search of a New Public Philosophy," in Anthony King (ed.), *The New American Political System.* Washington, D.C.: American Enterprise Institute.

Beyle, Thad L. and Patricia J. Dusenbury (1982). "Health and Human Services Block Grants: The State and Local Dimension." *State Government,* 55 (Spring): 2-13.

Bromage, Arthur W. (1943). "Federal-State-Local Relations." *American Political Science Review,* 37 (February): 35.

Brown, George D. (1980). "Federal Funds and Federal Courts—Community Development Litigation as a Testing Ground for the New Law of Standing." *Boston College Law Review,* 21 (March): 525-556.

Brown, George D. (1981). "The Courts and Grant Reform: A Time for Action." *Intergovernmental Perspective,* 7 (Fall): 6-14.

Calkins, Susannah and John Shannon (1982). "The New Formula for Fiscal

Federalism: Austerity Equals Decentralization." *Intergovernmental Perspective,* 7 (Winter): 23-29.

Clark, Jane Perry (1938). *The Rise of a New Federalism: Federal-State Cooperation in the United States.* New York: Columbia University Press.

Commission on Intergovernmental Relations (1955). *A Report to the President for Transmittal to the Congress.* Washington, D.C.: GPO.

Dommel, Paul R. (1974). *The Politics of Revenue Sharing.* Bloomington, Ind.: University of Indiana Press.

Farber, Stephen B. (1983). "The 1982 New Federalism Negotiations: A View from the States." *Publius: The Journal of Federalism,* 13 (Spring): 33-38.

Federalism: The First Ten Months, A Report from the President (1981). Washington, D.C.: The White House.

Graves, W. Brooke (1964). *American Intergovernmental Relations: Their Origins, Historical Development, and Current Status.* New York: Scribner's.

Grodzins, Morton (1960). "The Federal System," in *Goals for Americans: The Report of the President's Commission on National Goals.* Englewood Cliffs, N.J.: Prentice-Hall. Published for the American Assembly of Columbia University.

Hansen, Alvin H. and Harvey S. Perloff (1944). *State and Local Finance in the National Economy.* New York: W. W. Norton.

Heclo, Hugh (1978). "Issue Networks and the Executive Establishment," in Anthony King (ed.), *The New American Political System.* Washington, D.C.: American Enterprise Institute.

Kettl, Donald F. (1980). "Regulating the Cities." *Publius: The Journal of Federalism, 1981.* Philadelphia, Pa.: Center for the Study of Federalism, Temple University.

Lindblom, Charles E. (1959). "The Science of Muddling Through." *Public Administration Review,* 19 (Spring): 79-88.

Lowi, Theodore J. (1978). "The Europeanization of America? From United States to United State," in Theodore J. Lowi and Alan Stone (eds.), *Nationalizing Government: Public Policies in America.* Beverly Hills, Calif.: Sage Publications.

Lovell, Catherine H. *et al.* (1979). *Federal and State Mandating on Local Governments: An Exploration of Issues and Impacts.* Final Report to the National Science Foundation. Riverside, Calif.: Graduate School of Administration, University of California.

Lovell, Catherine H. (1981). "Mandating: Operationalizing Domination." *Publius: The Journal of Federalism,* 11 (Spring): 59-78.

McLean, Joseph E. (1952). *Politics is What You Make It.* New York: Public Affairs Committee, Public Affairs Pamphlet.

Nathan, Richard P. (1975). "Federalism and the Shifting Nature of Fiscal Relations." *The Annals,* 419 (May): 120-129.

Nathan, Richard P. (1975). *The Plot That Failed: Nixon and the Administrative Presidency.* New York: John Wiley.

National Journal (1982), January 9.

Office of Management and Budget (1980). *Managing Federal Assistance in the 1980s.* Washington, D.C.: GPO.

Petkas, Peter J. (1981). "The U.S. Regulatory System: Partnership or Maze."

National Civic Review, 70 (June): 297-301.

Publius: The Journal of Federalism (1972). 2 (Spring): 95-146.

Stanfield, Rochelle L. (1978). "Playing Computer Politics with Local Aid Formulas." *National Journal,* (December 9): 1977-1981.

Sundquist, James with David W. Davis (1969). *Making Federalism Work: A Study of Program Coordination at the Community Level.* Washington, D.C.: Brookings Institution.

Walker, David B. (1979). "Is There Federalism in Our Future?" *Public Management,* 61 (January): 11-12.

Wildavsky, Aaron (1964). *The Politics of the Budgetary Process.* Boston, Mass.: Little, Brown.

Williamson, Richard S. (1983). "The 1982 New Federalism Negotiations." *Publius: The Journal of Federalism,* 13 (Spring): 11-32.

Wright, Deil S. (1975). "Intergovernmental Relations and Policy Choice." *Publius: The Journal of Federalism,* 5 (Fall): 1-21.

Wright, Deil S. (1980). "Intergovernmental Games: An Approach to Understanding Intergovernmental Relations." *Southern Review of Public Administration,* 3 (March): 383-403.

Wright, Deil S. (1982). "New Federalism: Recent Varieties of an Older Species." *American Review of Public Administration,* 16 (Spring): 56-73.

Wright, Deil S. (1983). "Managing the Intergovernmental Scene: The Changing Dramas of Federalism, Intergovernmental Relations, and Intergovernmental Management," in William B. Eddy (ed.), *Handbook of Organization Management.* New York: Marcel Dekker.

PART II

Themes Through Time: Evolving Patterns and Changing Perspectives

More than four decades of evolution and change in intergovernmental relations are recorded in *PAR*. Wartime emergency, peacetime quiescence, urban malaise, citizen activism, and fiscal retrenchment are only a few of the themes and problems caught in the crucible of national experience from the 1930s to the 1980s. The essay which constitutes Part I attempted to sketch some of the developments in federalism and intergovernmental relationships on a broad canvas. Here, in Part II, smaller, more focused cameos are provided by six articles that "sample" in selective depth the layers of political-administrative strata across nearly five decades.

Frank Bane was, in many respects, "Mr. Intergovernmental Relations." He held posts in national, state, and local governments, but he was probably most remembered for his roles as Executive Director of the Council of State Governments and as the first Chairman of the Advisory Commission on Intergovernmental Relations. Bane was in the Office of Price Administration in 1942 when he wrote about "an approach to the problem of public management that has been developing for at least three decades.' He called that approach "cooperative government," and he amply illustrated it with the administration of rationing programs during World War II.

Professor John Gaus of Harvard University dealt reflectively in 1956 with the intergovernmental changes and the ferment which had culminated in political issues during the 1952 presidential campaign. The occasion for Gaus' reflections was a flurry of books and reports that attempted to capture as well as to direct the shape of federalism and intergovernmental relations in the 1950s and beyond. Gaus acknowledged the changing configurations of social and political processes. He anticipated that more changes would occur.

Gaus' expectations of change were more than modestly realized. Two selections convey the mood and the modalities of intergovernmental developments in the 1960s. Albert Abrams provided a concise but intense sense of how intergovernmental relations was viewed in some quarters during that period. Abrams was a member of the staff of the New York legislature and president of the Capital District (Albany) ASPA chapter when he ventured (and vented) his views in 1969.

One effort to systematize some policy and many management aspects of intergovernmental operations was the joint OMB-NSF Study Committee on Policy Management Assistance. This group produced an extensive body of materials and a summary report in 1975. Ann Macaluso, an OMB staff member of the Committee, wrote a review of developments and issues that formed the basis for the group's deliberations and recommendations. Macaluso's article can also be read in conjunction with the "Executive Summary" of the Study Committee's report reprinted in Part V.

The concluding selection in this section was authored by Carl Stenberg. At the time Stenberg wrote the article he was with the ACIR but he currently serves as Executive Director of the Council of State Governments. The subtitle of his 1981 article covers two major intergovernmental themes of the 1970s and 1980s. The first is "intergovernmental management," a concept whose prominence has been mentioned and whose significance prompted us to cluster a set of articles in Part V on the subject.

The second term of major import in Stenberg's title is "cutback environment." If there is one policy theme that appears to have dominated recent and current intergovernmental issues, it is the controversy and conflict generated by cutbacks. Retrenchment and reduction, revolt and recession, decline and decrementalism are all terms that have been used to describe the fiscal shocks delivered to intergovernmental relations since the mid-1970s. Stenberg, of course, could not anticipate the impact of the fourth new federalism since his article appeared simultaneous with Reagan's inauguration. But the article is especially instructive not only because of its insightful review of previous "days of wine and roses" but also because of its prescience concerning intergovernmental issues for the 1980s and beyond.

FRANK BANE

Cooperative Government in Wartime

The rationing of sugar was the first program by which the government of the United States undertook to administer day by day an aspect of the life of every American. It followed soon after the rationing of tires and automobiles and made use of the same administrative machinery, which will doubtless be developed to serve as the basis for the whole system of rationing and price control. Barring the catastrophe of sudden defeat or the miracle of sudden victory, this machinery will have to be used for an ever increasing range of functions within the next few years, for it is essential to the mobilization of our material resources.

This administrative machinery was set up and put in operation within three weeks. On December 7 the Japanese bombed Pearl Harbor; on December 11 the Office of Production Management froze the supplies of rubber in the United States and began to look about for a method of rationing them; on December 14 the Office of Price Administration undertook the job; and by January 5 the system was in full operation, with the forms and procedures in the hands of regularly constituted authorities in virtually every county in the United States.

The program was unprecedented in American history. It was absolutely necessary, and, moreover, its necessity was generally recognized. Therefore the country welcomed and demanded measures that in ordinary times never would have been considered. Rationing had to be done; it was not a political issue. For that reason, it was not only a great administrative problem, but it was virtually unmixed with any but administrative considerations. As a result, the rationing program exemplified an approach to the problem of public management that has been developing for at least three decades and that, in less conspicuous ways, has brought about administrative unity in many other programs in which two or more of the so-called "levels of government" have participated.

Growth of Cooperative Government

This approach, for want of a better name, we may call "cooperative government." Within the multifarious pattern of state constitutions and local institutions and charters, it has enabled the American people to accomplish national objectives without doing violence to local, state, and regional habits. Almost unnoticed even by students of government, it has enlisted state and local agencies in active cooperation toward common purposes and has made local self-government an essential part of national teamwork.

From one point of view, the rationing machinery was hurriedly improvised. In a more realistic sense, it was built on the foundation of established habits of cooperation and long-standing traditions of administration.

The first decade of this century was a period of muckraking and enthusiastic municipal reform, especially in the industrial metropolitan communities of the Northeast and Middlewest. Nobody paid much attention at that time to the efforts of the pioneer public health administrators who were inaugurating the fight against hookworm in the southern states. Those pioneers could not rely on the expansion of municipal health departments for hookworm was a rural problem; and the diffuse structure of county government made full reliance on counties alone impossible. They accordingly furthered the establishment of county health officers who worked at first with private assistance and then under joint county and state supervisors.

At about the same time agricultural administrators, convinced that agricultural research and experimentation needed to be supplemented by active demonstration work in every locality, were developing the county agent. First employed with private funds and the encouragement of the Department of Agriculture to fight the boll weevil in the Deep South, the county agents came to be supported by local, state, and federal funds and to be supervised by county boards or local farm bureaus, state agricultural colleges, and the U.S. Department of Agriculture. Only after nearly a thousand county agents were actively at work did the federal government, through the Smith-Lever Act of 1914, put its relationship with them on a systematic basis.

During the 1920s thc county agent was an ever present example of the possibility of collaboration among all levels of government and an ever present refutation of the myth that the levels of government had to move majestically in separate spheres. The example was a fruitful one. The '20s are popularly considered the zenith of laissez faire, but in many states they saw the development of county welfare and health systems under state direction and supervision.

In Virginia, for example, the former Board of Charities and Corrections, which had given only very general supervision to county institutions, was abolished in 1922 and replaced by a state Board of Welfare. It took over much of the direction not only of state institutions but also of county institutions for the care of indigents, delinquents, and defectives. Furthermore it supervised county programs of outdoor relief and parole while all these county programs remained under the management of responsible local officials. In Virginia the problem was not complicated by any overlapping of counties and major cities, since in that state alone the two types of local authorities have mutually exclusive areas.

In the early '30s came the emergency relief programs. The Federal Emergency Relief Administration subsidized state relief programs, and the states generally worked through county governments in order to have a simple system for covering their entire areas, even if the municipalities had superior administrative machinery. The principal cities themselves and the leaders in municipal administration joined in the demand that the counties become the basis for welfare administration.

With all their faults the counties had two advantages: they were generally about the right size for local administration, and they covered, with no overlapping, the entire area of the United States. These considerations prevailed even in some states where counties had hardly administered any functions at all. In New Hampshire, for example, Governor John G. Winant called on the Brookings Institution to survey the administration of relief within the state and recommended its reorganization. New Hampshire's local government, like that of other New England states, has traditionally been the township. But New Hampshire, with fewer than a half million inhabitants, had two hundred odd townships and only ten counties. For economy and effectiveness of operation, the county was virtually made over into an administrative unit and given the functions of relief and welfare—under state supervision and with federal assistance.

The social security program greatly extended the system of federal-state cooperation since, except for the phase of old-age and survivors' insurance, it was administered entirely through the states and their subdivisions.

Most recently, the Selective Service System established at the national level only a headquarters office to coordinate the state and territorial offices and to serve as a liaison between the War and Navy departments and the general public. It delegated to each governor the enforcement of the selective service program in his state and the selection of a state director of selective service. The local boards, in turn, were given virtually autonomous power and maintained direct contact with the prospective trainees and their families and employers.

Most of these programs were based on grants-in-aid, but the fiscal relationship was no more important than the administrative relationship with which it was intertwined. The habit of cooperation, even though made possible by federal funds, amounted to a great deal more than the federal government's purchase of compliance; it depended on the general recognition of the necessity of a program and a unified administrative approach toward its management.

Most of these programs, too, were in the broad field of social welfare. As the nation more generally recognized the fact that it had national economic and social problems arising from the national development of industry and technology and world-wide trade, it undertook to solve them by national programs, which could be administered best by administrative systems cutting across the traditional levels of government.

But only with the Axis attack on the United States did we undertake in earnest to manage our entire economy. Social security and welfare programs help those persons who fare badly in our industrial system, but rationing and price control and war production management are complementary measures to administer the system itself.

War production management necessarily deals first and foremost with industrial organizations, but price control and rationing affect people directly. Therefore when rationing was first undertaken, and as it has been extended, it was built on the cooperative system of government that has become so firmly established in America rather than on either exclusively federal machinery or voluntary commercial cooperation.

Because of the necessity of immediate operation and of dealing with the personal problems of every inhabitant of the United States, decentralization was more than a luxury or a means of encouraging local responsibility—it was a stark necessity. When the Office of Production Management decided to turn over the administration of its rationing powers to the Office of Price Administration on the grounds that the OPA had a field organization, the OPA faced several crucial questions of management policy. On its answers to these questions it has established the national system of rationing, which is now intended to serve also as the basis for the administration of price control.

The first of these questions was whether to set up a purely federal field force like, for example, that of the Work Projects Administration or whether to turn the job over to state and local governments. The decision on this point was unequivocal. As far as law was concerned, rationing was a federal power and had to be enforced by federal agents. But as far as administration was concerned, it was decided to make an absolute division of authority or function and to turn over to the state and localities complete responsibility for their portions of the work.

Under this plan, the federal government was to develop the general policy and program in order to lay down the rules of the game. The state government was to organize, to supervise, and to direct its administration.

A local authority was to operate the program. The whole scheme was to depend on a complete and unqualified delegation of the necessary authority from the federal to the state level, and from the state to the local.

Organization in the States and Localities

Let us see how this system worked in the state governments and localities, first with respect to the tire and automobile rationing programs and then with respect to the sugar rationing program.

The whole approach depended on the existence in every state of a state defense council. These councils had been set up as auxiliaries to the governors in response to a request from the Division of State and Local Cooperation of the National Defense Advisory Commission in the summer of 1940, and in general they provided a system by which each governor could call on every department of the state government and on local authorities for participation in the war program.

On December 14, 1941, the OPA sent a telegram to every governor asking whether he and the state defense council would take full responsibility for organizing and directing the tire rationing program. Every state agreed to do so and to be ready to operate by January 5. Every state then appointed a rationing administrator who was accordingly designated by the OPA as a nonpaid federal agent.

The state furnished the necessary money, personnel, equipment, office space, and supplies. The state rationing administrator undertook to organize the local structure, designating municipal or county defense councils to be responsible for local operations. The quota for tires was assigned on a county basis, largely in proportion to the registration of commercial vehicles in each county, and therefore some local authority—either a defense council or a specially appointed county rationing administrator—had to be given authority to distribute the county quota among the local rationing boards.

The local boards of three members each were chosen by the local defense councils and their members, like the state and local rationing administrators, were appointed as unpaid federal agents on certification by the state rationing administrator. It then became the function of the local board to decide which persons should and should not receive tires in accordance with the national regulations.

The necessary field work for getting this structure set up uniformly was undertaken by some 20 volunteer and unpaid organizers on December 15. The organizers were brought together for a three-day conference (half of them in Washington, half in Chicago), and then each was assigned up to three states. In the meantime a regional organization under the OPA was being created, and the regional offices took over the supervision as soon as they were prepared.

In the first stage of operations the state and local offices went about their work with no financial assistance whatever from the OPA, except for the use of the penalty envelope and the necessary forms. Equipment and space were borrowed from existing agencies by the rationing administrators, and traveling was done in state cars. Personnel was borrowed from state and local agencies, volunteers were recruited from the volunteer participation bureaus of the Office of Civilian Defense and other sources, and a limited amount of clerical and stenographic assistance was secured from the WPA. The essential point, however, is that all these matters were the concern and responsibility of the state authorities; the OPA not only communicated with the state administrators alone, but it asked them to instruct the local authorities not to take any of their problems to Washington.

The state administrtor was not confined to any single pattern in setting up his local rationing organization. Both because the quotas were assigned on a county basis and to cover all the area of the state, the state administrator usually chose the county as the basis of operations.

But the state administrator set up more than one board to a county where local conditions made it advisable, as is shown by the fact that in the early months of the rationing program some 7,500 boards were established, while there are only 3,052 counties in the United States. In many local areas the state administrator divided up the county quotas and let city or town authorities choose their rationing boards.

The state rationing administrator, for example, decided whether a single board should be set up in a city or a board in each precinct, or he let the city defense council make the decision; what he did, or what he decided, was approved by the OPA. The state administrator could appoint a county administrator and delegate to him the job of determining quotas for the subdivisions of the county, or he could do the job himself. In either case, the choice and the responsibility were his, and the OPA did not interfere. Generally, the state administrator let the local council decide or followed its advice, on local organization problems.

The only exceptions to the rule of state responsibility were the cities of New York and Chicago, in which metropolitan defense councils had been created to deal directly with the federal government.

In the next stage, the OPA undertook to furnish state and local boards with paid employees to supplement the efforts of volunteers, especially in anticipation of the greater volume of work to be required by the sugar rationing program. It allocated the available funds for personnel among the states roughly according to three criteria: population, the registration of commercial vehicles, and the number of tire rationing boards. The state administrator then allocated the state's share among local boards and administrators. Likewise, he distributed where necessary a reserve quota of about 8 percent of the state quota to those counties containing unusual concentrations of eligible tire users as, for example, to the headquarters of a state highway department.

The object of the tire rationing program was to let tires go only to those who had to have them for purposes essential to public health and safety. The object of the sugar rationing program, on the other hand, was to allot sugar to everyone. The administrative structure and operations could follow the same principles but they had to be adjusted to take care of everyone at once. Furthermore, a system had to be devised without undue policing to permit everyone to get his share, and no one, whatever his wealth, to get more than his share.

The key to the new system for rationing sugar was the device of the ration stamp. Just as money makes possible the distribution of goods according to purchasing power with a minimum of inconvenience, so the ration stamp makes possible the allocation of their distribution according to need with a minimum of administrative supervision. The stamp simply flows along with money in the channels of commerce, passing from hand to hand with the exchange of goods. The dollar is the economic, the ration stamp the administrtive symbol.

To make the stamp system operate effectively, it was necessary first to register everyone and give him his stamp book; and second to provide a system of exchange to keep stamps of small denominations from accumulating in too great quantities and to see that the rationed goods are not sold without the collection of stamps.

The first task was the most difficult. The solution adopted was to enlist the help of the educational system of the country, since every political subdivision had a public school system. First the OPA enlisted the help of the U.S. Office of Education, which approved the plan; second, each state rationing administrator worked in cooperation with the state commissioner of education; third, the county rationing administrator made arrangements with the schools in the county for the work of registering both individual and commercial users of sugar and designated a custodian to take charge of the ration books and the necessary forms.

The OPA sent tire rationing forms only to the state administrators and let them distribute the forms within their respective states. But hundreds of millions of forms had to be printed for the sugar rationing program, and it was physically impossible to split the distribution of them into these two stages. The OPA therefore consigned the forms and ration books to the county clerk of each county in the country; the county clerk turned them over to the custodian appointed by the county rationing administrator; and the custodian was responsible for distributing them to the schools at the proper time.

As New Hampshire had to set up a system of county administration in order to handle her welfare problem, other New England states had to set up a county system for rationing. Massachusetts, for example, has no county clerks, and arrangements were made for the books to be delivered to the state commissioner of education and to be distributed by the state police force to the county custodians.

State rationing administrators and commissioners of education gathered in Chicago on March 21 and 22, 1942, to make final plans for the registration for sugar rationing and to iron out unusual problems. A two-day period, April 28 and 29, was set for the registration of commercial sugar users who buy from brokers or wholesalers in the 27,000 high school buildings in the country and a four-day period, May 4-7, for the registration of individual users in the 200,000 grade schools.

The Chicago meeting made possible a more uniform interpretation of rules and regulations, which OPA officials were present to explain, or to adjust. It also gave state administrators an opportunity to tell of unusual administrative difficulties—in one county in Utah a schoolhouse is 300 miles from the county seat, and the ration books had to be transported the last 40 miles on horseback—but these problems remained the responsibility of the state and local administrators. The typical reaction was, "This is a hell of a problem, but you tell us it's our job to get the books out and we'll do it."

The system of exchange of stamps was the next problem. The consumer was to turn over to the grocer his stamp along with his money to get his sugar supply. The grocer ws to pass on the stamps in exchange for the same quantities of sugar from the wholesaler, and so on to the refinery. And just as the customer's dimes may be exchanged for bills, so the stamps may be exchanged for large denomination certificates at the offices of the rationing administrator's 187 wholesale centers. The refinery must turn over to the OPA certificates accounting for the volume of sugar sold so that to a large degree the policing of the system is automatic.

As plans for the sugar rationing moved into their last stages, it became necessary to make available to the states limited funds for space, equipment, and communications, and to furnish paid stenographic and clerical personnel. The program was still to depend largely on volunteer or locally paid assistance, but funds were to be allocated to state administrators to use where absolutely necessary. Since the paid personnel, although under state or local supervision and control, was legally to be federal personnel, it was recruited through civil service channels.

In the management of any program it is necessary to choose between centralization and decentralization of operations. Each has its advantages and its evils. Decentralization leaves in the hands of local officials a great many decisions on which, in the eyes of a zealous central authority, they are bound to make frequent mistakes. The possibility of such mistakes is frightening to the central official, especially if he is by training and temperament more concerned with the subject matter of his program than with its management. He is accordingly tempted to institute a system of review of more and more decisions, and he hesitates to make a bold distinction between various types of problems in order to give to others the individual and particular cases, and control himself only the general aspects.

To yield to that temptation in the management of a national program is fatal. The old distinction between levels of government—reserving the programs most closely affecting the persons and property of citizens to the states and localities and entrusting the programs of national consequence to the central government—was a valid one in its time. The distinction cannot be made on the basis of *programs* today, for modern technology, modern economics, and modern communications have made nearly every program of government a concern of federal, state, and local authorities alike. But within each program a distinction can be made as to type of administrative activity or function: for example, the federal authority can determine those matters of most general concern, the broad policies and regulations; the state can take responsibility for organization and supervision and direction; and the locality can operate the program with respect to individual cases. Thus the relationship of the individual to national policy will be in the hands of those who best know local circumstances and are best able to judge individual cases, while at the other extreme the national authority will be free to devote its entire attention to broad issues of policy.

This relatively new distinction is fundamental to the relatively new system of cooperative government. It has never been applied more thoroughly than in the rationing system, and it is significant that the rationing system was set up hurriedly to deal with two things, rubber and sugar. In the past it was a man's own affair how often he wore out his tires and how much he sweetened his coffee, but nothing is more essential than rubber and sugar in modern mechanized and chemical warfare. The federal government had no choice but to interfere drastically with the individual's habits of transportation and diet, but it did well to restrict itself to general considerations and leave personal cases to the states and their subdivisions. Indeed, since it wanted to get the job done well, it had little choice.

Collaboration of Federal Agencies

Cooperative government usually involves not only collaboration among the so-called "levels of government" but among various departments and agencies of the federal government since in the modern world military, economic, and welfare programs are amazingly interdependent. The rationing program had unusually wide ramifications.

Rationing was undertaken under the authority granted to the President by the Vinson Priorities Act of 1941 and reaffirmed and expanded by the

Second War Powers Act, 1942. The President first delegated this power to the Office of Production Management, which in turn transferred authority to the OPA to administer the tire rationing program.

The basic quantities of rubber, automobiles, and sugar to be available for civilian use were determined by the Office of Production Management and its successor, the War Production Board, in consultation with the War and Navy departments. The WPB retains the responsibility for making this determination, and the OPA then takes over the responsibility for rationing the available supply. In the sugar program, the WPB allocates supplies to those consumers who buy directly from the refineries after they register through the employment offices under the Social Security Board.

The OPA called on the Office of Education for help in arranging for the registration of everyone in the United States and the distribution of ration books through the school system of the country. In providing clerical assistance to state and local rationing administrators it called first on the WPA and next on the Civil Service Commission. The Indian Service took over the job of registering all Indians for the rationing program, and the inspectors of the Wage and Hour Division of the Department of Labor helped the regional inspectors of the OPA check on the tire rationing system. The regions of OPA were based on those of the Office for Emergency Management in order to facilitate cooperation with other emergency programs.

Within the OPA, the rationing program involved certain staff determinations that were prerequisite to actual operations. The staff divisions working with WPB had to determine first the products to be rationed; then the amount available for civilian use; then the categories of individuals and services entitled to receive the products; and then the necessary rules and regulations.

To tighten up the relationships within OPA two important decisions were made in mid-April. First, on the theory that "field operations" could not be dissociated from other operations, it was decided to vest control in a director of operations, who would be in charge of the management and direction of the whole program, both in Washington and the field, but responsible to the Administrator. Second, it was decided to base the system of price control on the same type of cooperation with states and localities as the system of rationing.

As the administration of price control is added to the administration of rationing within the cooperative system, further federal financial aid will almost certainly be necessary. The state rationing administrators, originally chosen by the state defense councils and sworn in as federal officials without compensation, will become full-time, fully paid officials of the Office of Price Administration. At the same time, the volume of work will surely require the provision of more clerical personnel by the federal government.

The increase in federal contributions will, at a superficial glance, surely be taken to mean that the program has been "federalized" or fully nationalized in its controls. Of course it is impossible now to predict just what will be done with any program in the near future. But the benefits of decentralization and cooperative government can be retained as long as the local rationing boards or price administration boards are locally chosen, as long as the state administrators are designated by the states, and as long as the local and state administrators of the OPA are given substantial responsibility for the types of decisions and operations that so far have been entrusted to them. All of these conditions obtain under the present plans for the amalgamation of price control with rationing administration.

Perhaps this type of decentralization should be called "federalization" in a more accurate use of the term than that now current. The old theory of the federal system, based on a constitutional assignment of certain jobs to certain levels of government, has lost its reality under modern conditions. But a newer set of distinctions is possible. These distinctions must be administrative and must depend on an official and popular agreement to entrust considerable responsibility and authority in national programs to officials chosen by state and local governments. If maintained by common consent, they will constitute a new type of federalism that can be adapted readily to the changing demands of the modern world.

Those who interpret administrative developments in terms of a struggle for power among individuals or agencies or levels of government will find it difficult to understand the early history of America's first rationing program.

The agency that was made responsible for doing the job had no direct statutory authorization, but the necessary authority was delegated to it. The federal rationing agency got its program started without paid field employees and depended for its operations in the states and localities on volunteer personnel and contributions of office space and equipment. Its state administrators were chosen by another level of government, and its local officials were locally appointed. And the biggest single job that it undertook—the registration of the entire population—was done for it by the public schools, which many Americans usually consider not a part of "government" at all.

The organizing efforts of the OPA in the rationing program was devoted entirely to stimulating and freeing for action the energies of public officials over whom it had no power of compulsion. The program was undertaken not to restrict the distribution of commodities, for the necessities of war had done that, but to distribute most widely and equitably the supplies that were available for civilian use. The typical American did not want to compete with others for limited supplies of commodities; he wanted a system that would give him his share and no more. It was a mistake ever to refer officially to the "hoarding" of sugar, for many housewives who wanted to return surplus stocks to the grocers as soon as they were assured of an equitable rationing system would not do so after that derogatory term was popularized.

The rationing program had unusual advantages. It was an obviously necessary program, supported by the popularity of the war effort. It was a concrete and definite job, which could be judged by relatively simple standards. Hence it raised no political issues and depended less on litigation or prosecution than on voluntary compliance. In short, it came as close as any large-scale program could to an example of administration undisturbed by political and legal factors.

Thus isolated, perhaps administration can best be described as the accepting of responsibility. But whatever it is called, the administration of the rationing program showed that, given a common purpose, the American people can extend their system of cooperative government to accomplish swiftly, efficiently, and without coercion any objective that modern society or total warfare requires.

1942 (2:95-103)

JOHN M. GAUS

Federalism and Intergovernmental Relations

The Nation and the States, Rivals or Partners? by William Anderson. The University of Minnesota Press, 1955. Pp. 263. $3.75.

Federalism Mature and Emergent, edited by Arthur W. Macmahon. Doubleday and Company, 1955. Pp. 557. $7.50.

The Commission on Intergovernmental Relations, A Report to the President for Transmittal to the Congress. June, 1955. Pp. 311. $1.25.

The States and the Nation, by Leonard D. White. Louisiana State University Press, 1953. Pp. 103. $2.75.

When William Anderson published his *Federalism and Intergovernmental Relations; A Budget of Suggestions for Research* (from which the title of this review is gratefully borrowed) in 1946, the volume was reviewed in *The American Political Science Review* by Charles McKinley (Vol. 41, pp. 561-563). He closed his review with a reference to the 1940 Report of the Canadian Royal Commission on Dominion-Provincial Relations, and its research monographs, and the query, "Is there not a good case for a similar Domesday survey of the comparable aspects of federalism in the United States?" Leonard White, in his Edward Douglass White lectures at the Louisiana State University seven years later, published in the volume listed above, concludes with suggestions, one of which (at p. 97) calls for a "large-scale, top-level study of federal-state relations." Even as his lectures were issuing from the press, the new political leadership in Washington was authorizing the establishment of the Commission on Intergovernmental Relations, of which William Anderson was to be a member and for which he prepared *The Nation and the States.* Among the symposia arranged by Columbia University as a part of the exercises in celebration of its 1954 Bicentennial was that on federalism, organized by Arthur Macmahon, who in another of the volumes listed above has edited, introduced, and provided a setting of interpretation for the papers presented and discussed there.

Perhaps Professor McKinley is a bit overwhelmed at the deluge which has followed a little after his suggestion. Perhaps he remembers the preacher who in a drought prayed to the Lord for rain. At once the rains came—a deluge, a destructive flood; and on the followng Sunday, he was prompted to rebuke Him gently at such excess, pointing out that while rain had been asked for, "You shouldn't be ridiculous!" Certainly your reviewer feels overwhelmed—and at that the present list is only a part of the flood of writings on the topic that have recently appeared and that continue to appear. One thinks, for example, of the *Studies in Federalism,* edited by Robert R. Bowie and Carl J. Friedrich (Little, Brown and Co., 1954), or the just-issued report of the Eighth American Assembly at Arden House on *The Forty Eight States* (Graduate School of Business, Columbia University, 1955). And in the Autumn, 1955, issue of this *Review* Professor Hallie Farmer surveys some books on state governments in terms relevant to the present subject.

Yet however overwhelming the extent of the materials, a reviewer must attempt not only briefly to indicate the nature of the books assigned to him but to discuss their setting and their interconnections. The fact that the two authors and the editor-planner have had a major part in the development of the study of public administration invites some special—almost proprietary—attention in the *Public Administration Review.* What have "Our Boys" got to say on these matters which 50 years ago were left chiefly to the lawyers and historians?

I

Note first that Anderson's title of 1946, "Federalism and Intergovernmental Relations," is prophetic. The Commission was on "Intergovernmental Relations." Macmahon reserves one of his four parts for "Functional Channels of Relationship." White proposes not only the special commission noted above, but a "joint standing committee on federal-state relations." We have now, it seems, a wide agreement that a most fruitful line of inquiry into a federal system of government will not be confined to a striking of balance as to functions, powers, and conflicts of rival entities, but a continuing series of functional working "relations."

This is so obvious and accepted among us that to state it here may seem wasteful. But consider the domestic American setting in which these studies appeared. The Democratic party, which had been in power in the 20 years of depression, New Deal, war, and postwar activities was replaced by the Republican party. Those who had resented the programs of the New Deal, and all eager to cut down war and postwar activities and expenditures, could find some line of attack in denouncing the expansion as if it were at the expense of the states. (Note Anderson's discussion of such philosophies at pp. 236-238.) The special note of antiexecutive sentiment, reflected in the Twenty-second Amendment, is probably related also to general antigovernment views, perhaps also to war weariness; and a recourse to "states' rights" seems related to them all. Again, as the international situation has deteriorated and the dangers of atomic war have loomed, many have come to feel that so great are the tasks of foreign policy and defense inevitably falling upon the national government that positive efforts should be made to place as much of the domestic functions of government upon the states as possible. This view is strongly presented by White (p. 5).

But interest in the nature of a federal system of government has in the last ten years also been positive and creative because of the more widely shared heritage of the war. The search for some reconciliation of national states with larger inclusive systems whereby peace might be achieved and economic problems dealt with more effectively, and the development of resources expedited, has resulted in new federal systems or the refurbishing of old, both world wide and in Europe, Asia, and Africa. Some of the ablest public men and scholars of our time are at work on these matters.

One recalls what Wordsworth said of the institution-builders of his youth as laboring

> Not in Utopia—subterranean fields,—
> Of some secreted island, Heaven knows where!
> But in the very world, which is the world
> Of all of us, . . .

Part Four of the Columbia symposium contains the treatment of this important contemporary experience in federal government—the "emergent" phase, in Macmahon's characteristically felicitous phrase, on the international level.

Most striking of all, to this reviewer, is the direction of inquiry and recommendation in these books as to the American system. One cannot be certain how wide and deep the sharing of their thought may be—how far it is confined to political scientists, for example. Certainly it runs against the atmosphere of domestic opinion noted above. For their direction is toward a critical examination of the capacity of state governments to deal effectively with their present functions, or any kind which may be transferred to them from the national government. Behind such currents of thought are the researches and writings of two generations of scholars and investigators of government process and structure and of particular substantive fields. A characteristic example of this interpretation of institutional inadequacy from a careful analysis of substantive experience was the article by Vincent Ostrom entitled "State Administration of Natural Resources in the West" (47 *The American Political Science Review* 478-493, June, 1953). His conclusion is relevant to the tendency noted above:

> If the western states are to assume a greater role in the conservation and development of natural resources, they must first put their own houses in order. Resource programs need to be developed in terms of a comprehensive review and re-definition of agencies, values, assumptions and policies. There are a few signs on the horizon which indicate that possibly some states, California for example, may lead the way in an effort to redefine the role of the western states in natural resources administration. Otherwise, so far as resource development is concerned, the states are apt to become anachronisms like counties, to be tolerated as they muddle through.

Another contribution from the political scientists, particularly those most closely in touch with the conduct of state and local government, is a clearer grasp of the factors that have led to a wider use of national government, and of the extent to which policies of the national government have bolstered financially and extended the activities of both state and local governments. The recourse to verbal dogmas and phrases so long—and still—employed in discussion of our federal system, the search for sovereignty so beloved of orators, they largely reject for a more intensive and comprehensive recording of the influence of technology, prices and markets, and other economic matters, of war and defense, the shifts of population, and the more intensive drains upon natural resources.

II

There is not unanimity, however, with all this reflection of the cumulative studies of the operation of our system noted above. Some observations by White, for example, in the earliest published of the books under review, are challenged warmly by the later book, addressed to a different occasion, by Anderson. (Note Anderson's chapter on "The Self-Government of the States," which may be read as a reply to White.) White has used his three lectures as a means of expressing his views, as he approached the close of his long and crowded years of teaching, on this large and complex topic.

> . . . I do not assert that the states are in immediate danger, nor that much that has happened in transferring power and influence upward has been harmful. I do predict, however, that if present trends continue for another quarter century, the states may be left hollow shells, operating primarily as the field districts of federal departments and dependent upon the federal treasury for their support. This result would be bad for the federal government and would

> hold grave consequences for the kind of self-governing, local democracy that has been an essential part of our way of life.
>
> I shall consequently argue in these essays that the march of power to Washington should be reversed wherever it is possible, that the states should strengthen their capacity to take a greater share in the burden of government, and that they should preserve a wide range of freedom of action in programs jointly supported and administered. (p. 3)

This is his "own value choice at this period of American history." He follows at once, however, with a brief account of the evolution of our system, and a candid recording of the strength of the forces that have led to greater functions on the national level, but also notes expansion in state activities. He follows with a lecture on the continuing strength and importance of the states, improvements in their government, and the role of the Council of State Governments, "itself a constellation," and other associations at "1313"—"the national capital of state and local government in the United States"—whose life he has been able to observe from the first establishment of that center neighboring his university.

But he warns that the strength of the states must be used, and their improvement must continue; and ends with some suggestions for the use of their strength, and for the studies and committees referred to above. A special note is his tribute to emotional ties and loyalties centering in the states. He is more hopeful, too, than was Professor Hallie Farmer in her review, of a new turn in the cycle whereby states may again, as earlier in the century, experiment and pioneer. And he ends by a rejection of fatalistic acceptance of trends and an appeal that Americans "cease to complain about the march of power to Washington, and instead devote their talents for political invention to divert the flow of power to those areas where it can be wisely used and effectively controlled" (pp. 100-101).

This urbane, even-tempered, and reasonable presentation, characteristic of its author and appropriate to the lectureship, presents a look backward over one phase of White's life work, albeit not a central one, and offers a direction and tone of policy for a quarter century ahead.

III

Anderson's book has a different timing. It is a distilling under the conditions of heat necessary to that process, of the experience and thought of another teacher and scholar whose work from the beginning has been close to government locally and in the states, and who sees the role of the national government, given the forces depicted by White—and in more detail on a larger canvas by himself—as not only natural and rooted but complementary and for the most part desirable. His book carries the force of an argument addressed to a critical moment, with the tang of first-hand and detailed acquaintance from his studies of government—all government—in Minnesota. Probably the best review of his book and of the report of the Commission on Intergovernmental Relations was his own impressive and moving "A Political Scientist's Report to the Political Science Profession" at the Boulder meeting of the American Political Science Association last September. For the book includes a brief appraisal of the "climate of opinion" in which the commission met; an account of "the federal system in operation" which widens vistas from the focus on national-state relations to include the local governments, increasingly built into the federal system; a major Part II, prepared for the early use of the commission, on constitutional history, problems, and issues; a discussion, Part III, of "issues of policy and finance" illustrative of some typical institutional-functional developments, taxation, grants-in-aid; and analyses of the status, powers, and operation of the state governments and local governments. Running through these chapters is the theme of the interrelation of all three, the relating of function to the area of a problem, to constitutional and resources power, and to practical capacities and equipment.

At the beginning—"About This Book"—and at the end—"A Program of Constructive Action"—Anderson sets forth with eloquence clearly derived from deep feeling and from an effort to focus his long experience and study in these matters, his considered credo, to counterattack the views of those he believes mistaken in theory or ignorant of how our system really operates, or both, to remind us that our system has changed with conditions and should be expected to continue to change, and to list innumerable accomplishments we have achieved and innumerable lines of improvement needed in all levels and fields. "Work with and from what has already been devised to what is practically attainable. Do not reason out a theory unrelated to the facts and then prescribe it and force it upon those who must administer the program" (p. 252).

His credo at page xi in his introductory "About This Book," itself reflects his own militant assertion against elements in the "climate of opinion" he depicts in his first chapter:

> I believe that the system of government of the United States under the Constitution is probably the greatest achievement of the entire human race up to now in the construction of a political system that will provide strong and active government for every national and local need and emergency, and at the same time ensure a maximum of attainable personal liberty and popular control over what the government does. . . .
>
> I believe that the American people today, operating through their system of government, provide the most important, yes the one indispensable tower of strength among the free nations of the world as they face the forces of militant world communism.

Anderson's book was issued before the work of the commission was completed. His Boulder speech presents a retrospective view of its then completed history. We may urge upon him a new edition of his book, in which the speech would be published, along with a personal memoir of his experiences in the study, teaching, and consulting participancy in these matters. The very fact that his statement reflects an occasion, a moment of some tension and uncertainty of outcome, and displays deep feeling of one participating actively at the center of controversy, enhances its value to our profession.

In his presidential address at Boulder (46 *The American Political Science Reiew* 961-979), Charles McKinley remarked that he was "at best, agnostic about Professor Anderson's eloquent statement of conviction" quoted above. Yet he pointed out that "in the development of a science of politics" we are obligated to go beyond observation, description, and generalization "to search for clues from our own history and from comparative experience that may be helpful in the institutional adaptations most likely to resolve the problems of governance that lie ahead." Whatever differences in view as to our federal system may exist among White, Anderson, Macmahon, and McKinley, whose *Uncle Sam in the Pacific Northwest* (University of California Press, 1952) might well be grouped with the books under review, all unite in representing at its best among our political scientists that "search for clues . . . helpful in institutional adaptation."

IV

The *Report to the President* of the Commission on Intergovernmental Relations records (Appendix B, p. 285) the names of the many political scientists on its staff who contributed to its work. It will long be, like the *Report* of the President's Committee on Administrative Management in 1937, a part of our teaching materials. In spite of the controversial nature of the issues with which it deals and the nature of the controversies in the period of its preparation, and contrary to much expectation, it shifts the focus from immediate discontent and extreme dogmas to opportunities for long creative work on concrete questions. It frankly records that the outlook of its members "in concentrating on the intergovernmental aspects of a number of hotly debated policy issues . . . has frequently undergone substantial modification" (p. ix). As a result, it holds that:

> . . . The National Government and the States should be regarded not as competitors for authority but as two levels of government cooperating with or complementing each other in meeting the growing demands on both. Chiefly because of war and the recurring threat of war, the expenditures of the National Government have grown much larger than those of the States and localities. But State and local activities also continue to expand. Equally sig-

From this philosophy, the step to recommending attention to the improvement of all levels of government was natural. The genius and labors of Chairman Kestnbaum, the willingness of the members to hang together yet with outlet for recording at points personal and group reservation to particular passages, and what must have been outstanding staff work in preparation and drafting, combine to make this document valuable and significant. It is both, whether taken as a study in politics, as a shifting in emphasis and approach to our federal system, or as a recording of points of friction requiring continuing attention. Only one member registered general dissent, Senator Morse, because he felt that the report does not give "due emphasis to the rights and jurisdiction of federal sovereignty. . . . Nevertheless I recommend with enthusiasm the reading of the report by the American people" (p. 279).

The report is in two parts. The first is on more general topics—"The Evolution of the American Federal System," "The Role of the States," "National Responsibilities and Cooperative Relations," "Financial Aspects," and "Federal Grants-in-Aid." Part II consists of 12 chapters on "Intergovernmental Functional Responsibilities" from agriculture to welfare. Recommendations are not hurled *en masse* at the reader, but are interspersed at relevant points in the discussion. Comment of members in reservation or qualification as to the text are similarly scattered throughout. The effect is that one seems participating in discussion rather than witnessing the recording of dogmas or the striking of poses.

The general direction of the whole is that recorded here earlier—a shift from emphasis on conflict over constitutional doctrine (although this is at points present) to emphasis on the improvement of the operation of a system embracing three levels with variety and peculiarity in organization, process, and finance for each substantive field of relations. There is a shift from concern over "states' rights" to one for state responsibilities, capacity, and equipment. Thus state constitutional restrictions, legislative districting, and the recognition of new aspects of the problem of government in metropolitan regions give evidence of the use of data and observation hitherto neglected in much formal political debate on our federal system. Sixteen staff and study committee reports issued by the commission are listed (p. 295) covering a number of substantive fields and comparing grant-in-aid programs and their impact on state administration and finance.

The startling thing about the recommendations is that they are not startling, unless one recalls the atmosphere within which the commission was brought to birth. The call for continuing attention to intergovernmental relations in the Executive Office of the President (p. 87) has already been met by the appointment of Chairman Kestnbaum as special assistant to the President on the follow-up of the recommendations of the commission. (Note, for example, pp. 88-89, for more general suggestions.)

Recommendations for change within substantive fields reflect again less a tendency toward major shifts or transfers than a press for improvement in procedure and operation—warnings against the by-passing of "regularly constituted executive and budgetary channels at the state level," clarification of status of grant-aided state officials. White's suggestion that soil conservation functions be transferred to the states (all of them? the term is more ambiguous each year!) finds reflection in proposals at pp. 156-163. (Two senators, three representatives, even two Governors from the South, including Governor Shivers of Texas, dissent!) But pick your field, turn to the relevant chapter. A characteristic statement (p. 243):

> *The Commission recommends that the Congress and the executive branch of the National Government adopt the policy that capital costs of multi-purpose, basinwide water resource developments be equitably divided between the National Government and the States concerned, in the light of benefits received, ability to pay, and other attendant circumstances.*
>
> The right of the States and localities to share in the planning and execution of basinwide water development carries with it the corresponding responsibility of the inhabitants to pay a reasonable portion of the project costs.

Vocational education grants-in-aid may have done their job; but new categories may be needed. (The Constitution, like the tariff, may almost be said to be a local, or at least a functional, issue.) The statement (at pp. 145-149) of the problem of dealing with the wide array of substantive issues —which the commission did not dodge in taking what it calls "a more pragmatic approach"—is candid. The people's business must be carried on; no one group, or generation, can have wisdom and knowledge enough to strike off, at a given moment, what changes are desirable. But there is a big budget of useful work set forth here.

V

The heat of conflict present in some stages in the birth and life of the commission was not perceptible in the sessions at Arden House, during a week of January snows. The atmosphere was genial; and unity, or at least the greatest relationship possible among contributions to a symposium, was assured by the perfection-seeking industry and skill of Arthur Macmahon, planner and editor of *Federalism Mature and Emergent.* The essays are 22 in number, grouped in four parts, and interrelated and given setting by Macmahon's contribution of a general introduction entitled "The Problems of Federalism: A Survey" and introductory chapters to the three other parts. The first part is the most general—"Federalism: Its Nature and Role"; the discussants are Macmahon, Wheare, Neumann, Fischer, and Berle. Part II, "Basic Controls in a Maturing System" (Wechsler, Truman, Holcombe, Freund, Hart, Hays, and Dowling), considers "The Political Process," "The Courts and the Law," and "Legislative and Executive

Responsibilities in Managing a Federal System.'' In Part III, ''Functional Channels of Relationship'' (Gaus, McKinley, Handler, Weidner, and Blough), there are ''illustrative studies of functional fields'' (natural resources) and of ''overall aspects''—decision-making and fiscal. Part IV includes the papers on ''Supranational Union in Western Europe'' (Diebold, Svennilson, Clark, Bowie, and Friedrich). There is first presented ''The Economic Background and Functional Developments,'' and finally, ''The Project of a Political Community.''

Thus, while the other books under review here center upon American experience and within that on the administrative aspects of intergovernmental relations, the Columbia symposium has a wider range while retaining a reflection of the present moment when the federal principle is revealing new life and application. Such an effort at appraisal was natural and appropriate for Hamilton's Alma Mater, and the tone and character common to most of the essays is equally appropriate to one of the authors of *The Federalist Papers.* The recording of concrete experience is balanced by the search for meaningful definition and principle. There is reflection of current events and of present urgencies, but they are interpreted in the light of arrangements that seem peculiar and central to a unique form, process, and purpose as unfolded over the years.

The opportunity thus provided to take a wider view of federal government in varied settings of time, place, and purpose, with the running comment of an editor equipped to hold his contributors to a consideration of central issues and problems and determined to search out general principles from the varied contributions, has special value to us, engrossed in our present American problems. It was suggested above that the emphasis hinted in employment of the term ''intergovernmental relations,'' an emphasis on the operating of the federal system through policy and administration, is a shift away from an earlier emphasis on constitutional interpretation. But students of administration are students of political science as well. The daily news of conflict over segregation may remind us that there is more at stake than grants-in-aid or the responsibility for public employment exchanges, important as the contribution from each of these may be to the creation of conditions of life that ease the tensions and conflicts raising from other matters.

The Columbia symposium therefore has a double value. It records for the future student of federalism appraisals of its present manifestations after—should we say in the midst of?—a period of wars and rapid technical, economic, and social change. And it reminds the present student to stretch his outlook and deepen his search for more things than he is likely to dream of in his special field.

VI

Yet as one student turns from the symposium back to the other volumes reviewed here, he wonders whether all the questions McKinley may have had in mind in his review ten years ago have yet got stated afresh. The possible attachment of Americans to their states as entities of a more human scale is noted only by White, among the authors here. A prophecy by Frederick Jackson Turner in a paper 50 years ago (printed in *The Significance of Sections in American History,* Holt, 1932), leads one to a somewhat related consideration.

> . . . I make the suggestion that, as the nation reaches a more stable equilibrium, a more settled state of society, with denser populations pressing upon the means of existence, with this population no longer migratory, the influence of the diverse physiographic provinces which make up a nation will become more marked. They will exercise sectionalizing influences, tending to mould society to their separate conditions, in spite of all the countervailing tendencies toward national uniformity. National action will be forced to recognize and adjust itself to these regional interests. . . . Congressional legislation will be shaped by compromises and combinations, which will in effect be treaties between rival sections, and the real federal aspect of our government will lie, not in the relation of state and nation, but in the relation of section and section (pp. 313-314).

Well, we are probably less "settled," and perhaps more "migratory" than when Turner wrote. But there is a relevance of these remarks to the domestic news of the day about schools, roads, rivers, defense plant location and contracts, to our unfinished business of improved methods of relating limited resources to unlimited demands. The "treaties" are made through a Congress one House of which represents, as appropriate to a federal system, the corporate constituent units, of greatly varying population, resources, and needs. The better preparation of policy at each important strategic point of decision-making—electorate, party, legislature, and executive—engrosses our attention and effort. All of these studies add to our knowledge of how urgent is our need for such improvement because of the peculiarities of a federal system. Presumably it is guardian of unique qualities of place, people, and idea. Should we also enquire as to how far the conditions—technical and many others—that influence our life do make, as Turner suggested they would, for richness and variety? Perhaps we should note another passage of Turner's:

> . . . Men are not absolutely dictated to by climate, geography, soils, or economic interests. The influence of the stock from which they sprang, the inherited ideals, the spiritual factors, often triumph over the material interests. . . . Not seldom the ideals grow out of the interests. It is the statesman's duty

> and his great opportunity to lift his section to a higher and broader, a more far-seeing, conception of its interests as a part of the Union, to induce his section to accept the compromises and adjustments which he arranges with the leaders of other sections in the spirit of reconciliation of interests in the nation as a whole (*Ibid.,* pp. 337-338).

The political scientist is one among many who are needed in these continuing tasks of analysis of our changing society, even in studies of so apparently technical a subject as our federal system. Analyses of population, of the economy of areas (stimulated now as well by development aspirations of so many regions of the world), of custom, architecture, literature, and the arts have relevance to the student of the politics and administration of a federal system and intergovernmental relations. All over the world they say that American life is uniform and standardized. And when you drive along many of our main roads, for hundreds of miles you may experience this in the life and appearance of the highway. But turn off, and follow even for a short distance a secondary or local road, and you begin to discover difference, variety, the tang of character. How to use both, and improve both, is a joint enterprise. In these books the political scientists have contributed knowledge, experience, good temper, and a sense of strategy. But we are an unfinished country, and have yet to know our landscape.

1956 (16:102-109)

ALBERT J. ABRAMS

Making Public Administration Relevant

The cities are ablaze, angry fires burn in ghetto towns, looting and cop-jumping are "in," and frustrations burst like lava from a volcanic eruption, geysers of hate erupt striking blindly at the nearest symbol of those who have entrapped their hopes in slums and disease and poverty. Public administration dare not be irrelevant.

Our cities are choking with fumes from buses and cars and black-belching smokestacks. The cities are thirsting for pure water from rivers and lakes browned with sewage. Our cities are filled with ghost neighborhoods, shuttered stores, and the dried up dust of ambitions ground down into dirt. The unrepaired potholes are but one sign of the cities that have given up. Public administration dare not be alienated.

Progress is not a brew of puritan efficiency and morality, and structural and organization symmetry are pretty professional status symbols, but alas, the pretty blueprints are often mice mazes entrapping the constituency of public administration. Public administration dare not be white-collared any longer.

The people want jobs. They want decent schools. They want low-rent, high-quality housing. They want a block on which their kids can grow up decently apart from the pusher and pimp. They want public administration that is responsive and sensitive, that cares for people and not the artifices of management. They want a government that talks their language, that takes to the streets to meet the people where they are.

Public administration can no longer hide behind the dichotomy of policy and administration. We know administrators initiate, shape, limit, expand, inhibit, curve, accelerate policy. And the people are getting to know it. PA cannot run away and hide. It alone knows how to make governments govern. Let's get on with it. Let's become relevant.

The people don't give a damn about "intergovernmental relations." It smacks of the excuse for inaction. The people want bread, not excuses. The people want jobs, not intergovernmental explanations. The people want opportunity for their children, not intergovernmental expiations of guilt.

We in public administration, however, know that we've got to break through the mountain of law and lethargy embodied in intergovernmental relations if we are to make public administration relevant.

And so, while the American people think intergovernmental relations sound like a political science professor expounding, we've got to get over the obstacle course of IGR and get on with the domestic war against crime, against poverty, against a stench-ridden environment, against disease.

1969 (29:378)

ANN C. MACALUSO

Background and History of the Study Committee on Policy Management Assistance

The increasing interdependence of the levels of government—federal, state, and local—has been a feature of treatises on American government for many years. This interdependence is largely the result of federal intervention and initiation and the more passive acceptance by the state and local levels of these actions.

Federal involvement in state and local affairs has not, however, been brought about by logical, sequential steps. It has, rather, evolved without a common purpose or design. Beginning with the passage of the federal income tax, continuing with the social welfare measures in the 1930s, and culminating in the 1960s with multiple initiatives in programming, the federal role can best be described as a series of unintegrated, uncoordinated activities that have become a pervasive portion of state and local government affairs.

Most of these federal activities have consisted of administrative and fiscal actions. Often they have been taken without any assessment of their impact upon the functioning of state and local government. Such actions have not included concomitant development of organizational and institutional mechanisms through which administrative and fiscal impact might have been assessed, debated, and refined.

The following brief history is designed to show those few organizational actions which have taken place, together with key administrative and fiscal activities at the federal level. Taken together, these events provide the stage upon which the study of policy management assistance has been played. Some events have been narrow and specific. Others, particularly the federal fostering of citizen participation during the '60s, have brought into focus those emerging publics which have demanded their share of public resources. By making those demands, these groups have helped to shape the changing relationships among the several institutions of government in the United States.

Management in the Modern Era of Intergovernmental Relationships

Formal recognition of contemporary intergovernmental relations did not, in all probability, occur in the United States until 1953. Prior to that time, at least until the '30s, intergovernmental relations primarily concerned the judiciary branch of government. The demands of the Depression era created new social service programs and social legislation which sought to respond to needs of individuals on a national scale. The roles of state and local governments were incidental to national objectives, and no organizational or institutional relationships developed.

In 1953 the Kestnbaum Commission on Intergovernmental Relations was created by President Eisenhower. One of its major recommendations called for the establishment, in the Executive Branch, of "a permanent center for overall attention to the problems of interlevel relationships."[1]

Legislation creating the Advisory Commission on Intergovernmental Relations was passed in 1959. This response to the Kestnbaum Commission's recommendations followed a two-year study and recommendations by a joint committee of state and federal officials. This was the first time a group of the highest federal and state officials had met for such a purpose.

ACIR was created to monitor the operation of the American federal system. Consisting of 26 members who represent the various levels and branches of government, ACIR has conducted research studies and developed model legislation in areas identified by the Commission as being important. Its research studies contain action recommendations approved by the Commission. ACIR is currently the only federal organizational unit concerned solely with intergovernmental issues and relationships.

No additional direct responsibility for providing a liaison with state and local governments has yet been institutionalized. From time to time this function has been assigned to the Office of the Vice President or to the Domestic Council, at the choice of the President. Federal Regional Councils have also been given the responsibility to coordinate federal activities with state and local officials. This responsibility has been carried out on a "target of opportunity" basis.[2]

At the beginning of 1960, federal financial aid for specific public services was significant, but by no means a dominant aspect of government in the United States. Except for highways and welfare, federal aid did not constitute a sizeable proportion of state and local spending in any major functional area. The 44 programs which did exist were visible, comprehensible, and manageable. Most governors, mayors, or city managers could, if asked, enumerate all or most of the types of federal aid for which their jurisdictions were eligible.[3]

The new grant-in-aid programs passed in the '60s covered a wide range: open space, educational television, health services to migratory workers, manpower development and training, outdoor recreation, economic opportunity, elementary and secondary education, law enforcement assistance, solid waste disposal, highway beautification, and others.

The new grant programs fostered the growth of vertical administrative intergovernmental relationships, with power, money, and decisions flowing from program administrators to functional department heads in state and local governments—leaving cabinet officers, governors, county commissioners, and majors less and less informed as to what was actually taking place, and making effective horizontal policy control and coordination increasingly difficult at all levels of government. In addition, the active federal response to increased demands for citizen participation served further to fragment the policy and coordination function as policy makers were required to broaden their decision-making processes to reflect the viewpoints of a diverse and complex citizenry.[4]

The sheer volume of programs operating through a functional delivery system and the additional complexities generated by citizen participation raised a fundamental issue which is still not resolved in the intergovernmental system: "Where should coordination take place? At the point of origin of funds and programs, or at the point of delivery?"

The coordination issue began to be addressed in the mid-'60s through the development of interagency task forces and committees. Included among these were: the Joint Administrative Task Force, the Planning Assistance and Requirements Coordinating Committees, and the Federal Assistance Review. Certain presidential-level commissions, including the Council on Executive Reorganization, the Committee on Intergovernmental Personnel Systems, and the Advisory Committee on Management Improvement also dealt with the coordination issue. Executive orders which established authority for certain departments to convene meetings which staffs of other departments were expected to attend, as well as the conveyance of "lead agency" authority, were also used to bring about further coordination. Each of these committees and orders was dealing with the question of coordination at the point of origin, i.e., the point at which federal program funds, objectives, administrative regulations, and even designs originated.

Certain other program and administrative actions (the Model Cities program, A-95 review and comment procedures, Chief Executive Review and Comment requirements, block grants, etc.) were initiated by the federal government to bring about program and organizational coordination at the point of delivery—or at the point where federal control shifted to nonfederal control.

Each of these efforts attempted to bring the jurisdictional policy maker back into central focus as the accountable official. What is significant about these examples is that each was an ad hoc attempt to bring some order to the chaotic grant-in-aid system. No policy guidance or direction has existed under which these attempts reinforced each other and strengthened the intergovernmental system. Most of them have been transient in nature. They have also been isolated from each other and, frequently, from other programmatic actions taking place at the same time.

By the end of 1973, there was increasing recognition that ad hoc non-policy coordinated actions had not produced an integrated framework for the inter-federal system. In fact, there was increasing evidence to indicate that such actions had become dysfunctional.

Background of the Policy Management Study

A number of fairly specific actions were taken, beginning in 1973, designed to review and summarize, once again, the state of the health of intergovernmental organizational, administrative, and fiscal relationships. These actions resulted in the formation of the Study Committee on Policy Management Assistance in August 1974.

Formation of the Committee had particular antecedents in the following activities:

1. A study carried out by the Task Force on Technical Assistance in the fall of 1973.
2. A jointly-sponsored GAO/OMB Symposium on Technical Assistance to State and Local Governments held in April 1974 and a Workshop with Public Interest Groups in June 1974.
3. An OMB agency objective to strengthen the executive management capacity of state and local governments, set by former Director Ash in May 1974.
4. Issuance of OMB Bulletin 75-5, "Technical Assistance to State and Local Governments" in September 1974.

Each of the above activities is discussed in more detail below.

Task Force on Technical Assistance to State and Local Governments

In the fall of 1973, OMB conducted a five-part assessment and review of the New Federalism. A statement of ten principles, which was released in September, served as the basis of the study. Four of the study areas included natural resources programs, economics and general government programs, human resources, and community development programs. The fifth area covered intergovernmental cooperation and included cross-cutting intergovernmental issues, constitutional issues, and levels of functional responsibility; revenue-sharing; administration of federal assistance—decentralization, devolution, Federal Regional Council effectiveness, simplification of assistance—improving intergovernmental management—technical assistance, integration of planning programs, structure of governments—and implementation of New Federalism.[5]

The Task Force on Technical Assistance, composed of staff from Office of Management and Budget, and Departments of Housing and Urban Development, Labor, and Justice, reviewed the assistance programs of the Manpower Administration, Office of Education, Office of Community Planning and Development, Federal Highway Administration, Department of Agriculture Extension Service, and the Bureau of Intergovernmental Personnel Programs of the Civil Service Commission. For review purposes, the task force defined "assistance" very broadly to include the provision of funds, information, and staff services. It also categorized the *recipients* of assistance as follows: jurisdictional/policy level managers (elected officials, city managers, etc.), program administrators or managers, program operators, and individuals.

The task force also cursorily reviewed assistance provided by public interest groups, selected public service institutes, and certain non-profit organizations.

The task force findings were as follows:

- Most assistance follows traditional programmatic lines and supports program objectives.
- Assistance provided by non-governmental institutions is heavily supported by federal funds which are available from a limited number of sources.
- Very little assistance is provided to jurisdictional policy makers and managers.

The task force hypothesized that these findings, based on a selected sample of federal organizations, would extend generally to *all* federal domestic agencies and departments.[6]

OMB/GAO Symposium—Public Interest Group Workshop

In April 1974, the Office of Management and Budget and the General Accounting Office jointly sponsored a one-day symposium to review the technical assistance programs of the federal government. Participants included assistant secretary-level officials from most of the domestic departments and agencies plus participant-observer representatives from the public interest groups.[7]

The symposium was followed by a one-day workshop in June with representatives of six of the public interest groups (International City Management Association, National League of Cities/U.S. Conference of

Mayors, National Association of Counties, Council of State Governments, and the National Legislative Conference—now National Council of State Legislatures). Participant-observers from several federal agencies also attended.[8]

There was general agreement at both the symposium and the workshop that technical assistance, as well as other forms of federal assistance, needed more thorough review and assessment with particular attention to identifying those sources of assistance to jurisdictional policy makers. Participants also expressed general concern about the adverse impact which reinforced and improved functional delivery systems had on management of jurisdictional policy and priorities.

OMB Objective To Strengthen Executive Management Capacity of State and Local Governments

During the Spring Budget Review in May 1974, information gathered from the Technical Assistance Task Force and the symposium was presented to (then) Budget Director, Roy Ash, concerning the apparent lack of federal executive management assistance for jurisdictional policy makers and managers. Although the findings of the New Federalism study had not been released by the White House and OMB, there was increasing concern about the potential impact general revenue sharing and the new block grant programs would have on state and local governments. This concern was expressed via the media and from the Congress. Director Ash directed that a one-year study of existing federal assistance, executive management needs, and current status of executive management of state and local governments be undertaken. He further directed that a coordinated federal strategy for strengthening executive management be prepared for review and implementation in the spring and summer of 1975.[9]

OMB Bulletin 75-5

Bulletin 75-5 was the primary instrument used by OMB, and subsequently by the Study Committee on Policy Management Assistance, to identify and assess the current status of technical assistance provided by the federal government to state and local governments. Sent to 41 departments and agencies, Bulletin 75-5 specifically defined technical assistance as "assistance in the form of funds, manpower or contracts, training, seminars, workshops, conferences, technology transfer, research utilization, personnel exchange, on-site Federal manpower assistance, information services and dissemination, and other similar activities."

The Bulletin further defined the recipient target group as

> . . . elected officials and chief administrative officials of State and local governments. Among others, this includes: elected and appointed chief executive officers and their staffs, such as governors, mayors, city or county managers and chief administrative officers; State and local legislative bodies and their staffs, such as State legislatures and city or county councils; and the heads of major program areas or departments, such as a State Secretary of Health or a City Director of Public Safety.[10] [11]

As hypothesized by the task group on technical assistance, Bulletin 75-5 results indicated very little federal assistance available to jurisdictional managers.[12] The most significant sources appeared to be: the HUD 701 program and research program for capacity building;[13] the Intergovernmental Personnel Act program under the U.S. Civil Service Commission; project research and demonstration grants from the Office of the Secretary of HEW; and some National Science Foundation research and demonstration grants.[14] The Department of Labor Comprehensive Employment and Training Act funds, which also appeared to offer some capacity-building resources, went through mayors, who served[15] as prime sponsors.

Formation of the Study Committee on Policy Management Assistance

Concurrent with development of Bulletin 75-5, OMB formulated plans for an interagency committee. Its representation was to come from those departments and agencies which had been identified as providing assistance to jurisdictional policy makers and managers. The decision to utilize an interagency study team, rather than a committee of academic representatives or of outside consultants, was reached for two reasons:

- It was assumed that staff from federal level departments and agencies would have access to state and local government representatives through their own delivery systems; and
- It was recognized that these personnel would have already identified some of the problems faced by jurisdictional policy makers because of problems inherent in federally funded program delivery systems.[16]

The Study Committee heard presentations from university officials, state and local government representatives, federal program managers, and "provider" institutions for approximately the first three months of its existence. It began to collect reports on the status of policy management (meetings were held weekly), and NSF filled in gaps in Committee understanding by commissioning a series of papers from existing or potential "actors" in the policy management scenario (published as Volume III of the Committee Reports).

Enthusiasm on the part of the Committee, other interested participants, and those who made presentations began to build as the dimensions (and problems) of the current "government-by-program" picture emerged. While the implications of considering alternatives to government-by-program appeared to be beyond the Study Committee's purview, members felt it vital to follow through on the need to *manage* intergovernmental relations. This became a primary focus for the Study Committee.

The report of the Committee, therefore, considered two areas of emphasis:

1. Improved management of the intergovernmental system.
2. Policy management as a favored mechanism to redress the imbalances of "government-by-program."

The Committee's report was submitted to Executive Branch policy makers, congressional staffs and leaders, and the general public in three volumes:

1. An "Internal Report" submitted to Director Lynn, OMB, the secretaries of the major departments, the Comptroller General, and the Chairman of the Civil Service Commission (entitled *Framework of a Strategy for Policy Management Assistance To State and Local Governments,* Volume I, April 1975).
2. A "Public Report" which contained the "Internal Report" material, but which provided additional contextual and background material (entitled *Strengthening Public Management in the Intergovernmental System,* Volume II, undated).
3. A third volume which contained all of the papers commissioned by NSF, together with working papers developed by the staff as the study progressed (entitled *Report of the Study Committee on Policy Management Assistance: Background Papers and Resource Materials,* Volume III, undated).

A supporting videotape, containing perspectives and views of state and local officials on the intergovernmental system and management needs was also developed with the help of the Department of Labor and United States Information Agency.

The Study Committee recognizes that its findings and recommendations will be subject to general debate and dialogue, and that implementation may be slow and incremental. It believes, however, that changes of the nature it has proposed are vital to the health of the federal system and inevitable, if the autonomy, accountability, and responsibility of the partners in that system are to survive.

Notes

1. *Report of the Kestnbaum Commission on Intergovernmental Relations* (Washington, D.C.: U.S. Government Printing Office, 1953).
2. *Role and Missions of the Federal Regional Councils—FY 1975 Guidelines,* Memorandum for Federal Regional Council Chairmen, Office of Management and Budget (Washington, D.C., June 3, 1974).
3. For a more complete listing of such actions, see *Framework of a Strategy for Policy Management Assistance to State and Local Governments,* Volume I, Study Committee on Policy Management Assistance.
4. *Eleventh Annual Report of the Advisory Commission on Intergovernmental Relations* (Washington, D.C.: U.S. Government Printing Office, 1970).
5. Although the full report of the New Federalism study was never officially released, the statement of principles received wide distribution; Office of Management and Budget, *New Federalism Study, Principles and Questions* (Washington, D.C., September 26, 1973).
6. Office of Management and Budget, *The New Federalism—Report on Technical Assistance* (Internal document), an unreleased report (Washington, D.C., November 1973).
7. Office of Management and Budget, *Summary of GAO/OMB Symposium on Technical Assistance* (Washington, D.C., April 16, 1974).
8. Office of Management and Budget, Summary of Meeting of Public Interest Groups and Selected Agency Representatives on Technical Assistance to State and Local Governments (Washington, D.C., June 27, 1974).
9. Office of Management and Budget, *Management and Operations Spring Review—Director's Review Decisions* (Internal document) (Washington, D.C., May 16, 1974).
10. Office of Management and Budget, OMB Bulletin 75-5, *Special Analysis of Federal Technical Assistance Provided to State and Local Governments* (Washington, D.C., September 5, 1975).
11. Heads of major program areas of departments were included for two reasons: (1) It was feared that data recovered without such inclusion would be too insignificant to warrant collection. (2) Such assistance might be reprogrammed to provide support for elected and chief administrative officials.
12. Study Committee on Policy Management Assistance, *Framework of a Strategy for Policy Management Assistance to State and Local Governments,* Volume I, Appendix B; Higgs, Louis D., *Mapping the Federal Assistance Effort: The Pieces of a Puzzle, but Where's the Picture,* A preliminary analysis and interpretation of federal agency responses to OMB Bulletin 75-5 (Washington, D.C., 1975).
13. The HUD 701 program is the grandfather of all management assistance efforts to state and local governments. Its program emphasis has shifted over its life span from comprehensive plan support, to management support, and, most recently, to support for housing and land use planning. Similarly, its recipient

group has included varying mixes of state, local general purpose governments and inter-local planning bodies from time to time. Most projects which have management assistance components, however, can be traced in whole, or in part, to the 701 program.

14. The NSF R&D grants have been used primarily to build capacity in institutions, which are then expected to assist local governments, state executive officers, and even some state legislatures. Such assistance is weighted toward science and technology.
15. CETA grants were the first block grants to be directed to elected officials as "prime sponsors." Previous block grants (partnership in health, law enforcement assistance) had been funded through areawide mechanisms, whose governing bodies contained mixes of program deliverers, consumers (in some cases), and representatives of elected officials.
16. HEW, OEO, DOL, EDA, and other agencies have been exploring the "vertical relationships" problem since the mid-1960s.

1975 (35:695-700)

CARL W. STENBERG

Beyond the Days of Wine and Roses: Intergovernmental Management in a Cutback Environment

For more than 20 years, the theory of "cooperative federalism" has strongly influenced teaching, research, and practice in the intergovernmental relations field. According to this view, the operation of the federal system practically since its inception has been characterized by a sharing, rather than the separation of powers and responsibilities.[1] Activities associated with the performance of governmental functions—making policy, raising revenues, administering services—are said to have been cooperative and collaborative ventures in nearly every area. This role sharing requires accessibility, negotiations, and mutual accommodation on the part of the members of the "intergovernmental partnership."

The rising popularity of cooperative federalism has been accompanied by a growth in the size and scope of governmental activity, especially at the national level. Many of the constitutional, judicial, and political barriers to the expansion of the federal government's involvement in domestic affairs have fallen. The federal role has become "bigger, broader, and deeper," particularly in areas that were traditionally state and local responsibilities.[2] As a result of these changes, contemporary intergovernmental relations bear little resemblance to those of two decades ago.

Although pressures for greater involvement continue to be exerted, countervailing conditions also are present. Inflation, unemployment, energy shortages and costs, and tax payer unrest have affected nearly all governments. If these developments produce major and lasting shifts in national domestic priorities, spending commitments, and fiscal capacity, more fundamental adjustments in intergovernmental relations can be expected during the 1980s.

To some degree the expansion of federal resources, influence, and power is consistent with the sharing and partnership themes of cooperative federalism. However, the nature, pace, extent, and impact of this phenomenon raise issues that are not adequately addressed by proponents of this theory. Moreover, as governmental growth rates slow or decline and intergovernmental management moves from an expansionist to a cutback orientation, a reformulation of cooperative federalism appears warranted to take into account the forces of competition, conflict, and centralization and the stresses that these changes place on a dynamic, highly intergovernmentalized system and those who function within it.[3]

Intergovernmental "Growing Pains"

The effects of the federal government's assumption of more and more responsibility for dealing with domestic problems since the 1960s have been profound and pervasive. They also have occasionally been perplexing and paradoxical.

Grant-in-aid programs have been one of the chief vehicles for this growth. They provide a good illustration of how and why federal expansion occurred, and what the impact has been on the theory and practice of intergovernmental relations. At least six features of their recent evolution are worth noting.

1. *Growth:* The dollar amounts of federal aid to state and local governments have climbed from approximately $7 billion in FY 1960 to an estimated $88.9 billion in FY 1980. The annual rate of growth during the last two decades has been about 15 percent. Federal aid has risen from less than 2 to 3.4 percent of the Gross National Product and from 14.7 to 23.2 percent of total state-local expenditures over this period.[4] In *per capita* and constant dollar terms, the $159 figure for 1980 was over three and one-half times that of 20 years earlier. The number of programs mushroomed from approximately 130 in 1960 to more than 500 in 1980, although there has been no consensus on these figures despite several efforts to catalog federal grants and to computerize information about them.[5] Moreover, strong doubts persist about whether state and local officials are well aware of available assistance, and whether the flow of funds into their jurisdictions can be accurately tracked.

2. *Instruments:* The types of instruments for dispensing federal assistance have become more numerous and diverse. A variety of intergovernmental transactions occur under formula and project grants, block grants, general revenue sharing, procurement contracts, as well as grant and cooperative agreements. Yet, determining which instruments to use to accomplish national purposes most efficiently, effectively, and equitably has proven to be a stiff challenge for assistance program architects. Striking and maintaining a proper balance between recipient flexibility in resource allocation and implementation decisions, on the one hand, and grantor stewardship and accountability, on the other, have also been quite difficult. Because of confusion or disagreement over these matters, the label used to

describe aid programs—such as "block grant"—has often been an oversimplified or misleading reflection of the intergovernmental relationships that occur within it. Reauthorization proceedings have tended to blur, rather than clarify, these issues even further.

3. *Participants:* Over the past decade, virtually all states and general purpose local governments have become participants in federal programs. When school districts and special districts are taken into account, it has been estimated that nearly 80 percent of the approximately 80,000 units of state and local government in the United States receive federal aid.[6] Adding to the scope and complexity of the intergovernmental partnership are organizations like Federal Regional Councils, multistate and substate regional planning and development agencies, private non-profit organizations, and neighborhood bodies which have been established to plan for, administer, coordinate, and spend federal monies. While participation is voluntary, the bulk of assistance dollars is dispensed to "entitlement" jurisdictions often on very attractive matching terms. Economically and politically, then, it is difficult for them to turn down low-cost or costless funds that would otherwise go elsewhere, even if they have a distorting effect on priorities. Moreover, some aid recipients, such as large central cities in the northeast and midwest, have little or no choice because they have come to depend heavily on this source of revenues to sustain their service delivery systems. Others, like many regional planning bodies, owe their existence to federal funding.

4. *Uncertainty:* More federal funds are now available to more public and private sector organizations for more purposes than ever before. The capacity of recipients to utilize these monies effectively, however, has been impaired. In particular, there has been uncertainty over whether sufficient amounts required to launch or continue a program will be available when they are needed, and whether they may be used for recipient priority purposes. Advance planning, program development, and personnel decisions are made especially difficult by the annual grant cycle and by delays in processing applications.

5. *"Strings":* Federal program conditions have become extensive, expensive, intrusive, and increasingly unenforceable. Traditional "watchdog" requirements of a planning, application, maintenance of effort, reporting, and audit nature continue to be attached to grants-in-aid. In recent years the federal government has used assistance programs to help achieve national social policy goals, such as affirmative action, environmental quality, historic site preservation, and citizen participation. Some 59 of these "cross-cutting" requirements apply to federal aid programs regardless of purpose. More than half of them are less than 10 years old.[7] Old and new style conditions have generated comprehension, cost, and compliance concerns on the part of both grantor and grantee. These con-

cerns have been exacerbated in recent years by decisions of the U.S. Supreme Court which have greatly reduced the scope of sovereign immunity and increased the possibility of state and local officials being sued for their actions or inactions in administering federal programs.[8]

6. *Bypassing:* The jurisdictional "leapfrogging" tendencies of federal agencies and congressional committees have become more pronounced. They have created difficulties in subnational planning, coordination, and implementation activities. States in particular have been affected. They have been bypassed in the administration of approximately 25 percent of federal assistance, even though many have assumed key roles in the same programs areas—like community development and employment training—that are being handled on a federal-local basis.

Three Basic Questions

Unquestionably, most of the federal assistance programs spawned during the 1960s and 1970s had laudable objectives. Federal monies supported efforts to tackle tough social and physical problems; they stimulated new undertakings; they helped develop more systematic ways of identifying interfunctional linkages and coordinating efforts, and they encouraged improvement of recipient organizational arrangements, personnel systems, as well as planning and management capacities. This intervention on such a massive scale was accompanied, however, by mounting concerns on the part of public officials and their constituents. These concerns can be summarized in three basic questions:

- Who does what?
- Who pays the bill?
- Who is responsible?

The answers to these questions have significant implications for the course of intergovernmental management, as well as federalist theory, in the 1980s.

Who Does What?

The extensive intergovernmental sharing and occasional competition in planning, policy making, administration, financing, and regulation have blurred the constitutional division of authority and responsibility. It is especially difficult, if not impossible, to identify those services over which local officials now exercise complete control because nearly all have become intergovernmental enterprises.

As recently as the late 1950s, police and fire protection, land use, and education were considered to be of an exclusively or predominantly local nature. Of course, some sharing of responsibility did take place. As Morton Grodzins asserted at that time: "From abattoirs and accounting through zoning and zoo administration, any governmental activity is almost certain to involve the influence, if not the formal administration, of all three planes of the federal system."[9] Two decades later, the key difference was the degree of federal penetration into subnational affairs. In many respects, the federal government had become the senior member of the intergovernmental partnership, largely through the grant-in-aid device.

Federal programs have sprung up "like dandelions after a spring rain."[10] Sometimes this has occurred with an almost complete disregard by program proponents for what is already on the statute books as well as what is a proper area of national intervention. To illustrate the proliferation of contemporary grants-in-aid, consider that there are at least: 7 different highway safety grants, each focusing on a specific activity like bridge replacement or seatbelts; 6 forest programs; 23 grants for pollution control and abatement; 36 varieties of social services assistance; and 78 grants for elementary, secondary, and vocational education.[11]

Few matters have been immune from being defined as a national problem that warrants a new aid program and perhaps a new office or agency to administer it. A review conducted by the Advisory Commission on Intergovernmental Relations (ACIR) of federal aid bills introduced in Congress in recent years reveals a wide range of activities that are considered by some members to be national, not purely subnational, problems.[12] The list of *existing* federal aid programs includes:

- school security
- urban gardening
- pothole repair
- noise control
- training for use of the metric system
- arson
- home insulation
- urban park facilities
- meals-on-wheels
- jellyfish control
- snow removal
- police disability payments
- aquaculture
- displaced homemakers
- bridge replacement and rehabilitation
- rat control
- education of gifted children
- alcohol abuse
- homemaker and residential repair services for the elderly
- development of bikeways
- solid waste disposal
- aid to museums
- runaway youth
- art education
- rural fire protection

To underscore this point further, the following activities have been *considered* by Congress as potential areas of national involvement:

- cat and dog spaying and control
- group life insurance for policemen
- library operating expenses
- tree maintenance and planting

spouse abuse
population education
camp safety
zoos
conversion of school property to other uses
education for good citizenship and ethics
control of beverage containers
mosquito control
detection of glaucoma
retraining of surplus teachers
regulation of boxing
repair of public facilities
jail construction

The appropriateness of federal involvement in many of these areas, from the standpoints of both national interest and on-going state and local activity considerations, is highly questionable.

Several factors account for the expansion of the federal government's role in and impact on state and local operations, and the accompanying concerns about redundancy and inappropriateness. These include:

- Pressures from many quarters for tangible national level responses to perceived and articulated problems like urban decay, poverty, illiteracy, hunger, and crime;
- Presidential commitments to develop programs intended to help both people and places in need of assistance;
- Inadequacy of the property tax and other local revenue sources to meet steadily rising personnel, program, and infrastructure costs;
- Unwillingness of some states to provide their localities with increased financial assistance or the discretionary authority necessary for them to tackle their problems;
- Concerns that pressing problems like deteriorating environmental quality, poor health care, substandard housing, inadequate transportation, and unemployment could not be effectively addressed within local and sometimes even state boundary lines, and that national remedial actions or the formation of new multistate and substate organizations were necessary to handle these responsibilities;
- Federal desires to stimulate state and local expenditures in national priority areas;
- Federal agency claims for separate program status to reflect important differences in their missions, clienteles, and ways of doing business;
- Desires on the part of individual members of Congress to gain political credit or simply "do good" by serving as entrepreneurs in behalf of new or expanded federal domestic initiatives; and
- Vigorous and occasionally vicious lobbying by state and local elected officials as well as functional specialists for a bigger share of federal aid to support their operations.[13]

Who Pays the Bill?

Notwithstanding the various problems associated with participation in grant programs, states and localities have eagerly turned to the federal overnment for fiscal relief. They have formed associations to lobby for programs benefiting their units generally. They have set up Washington offices to represent their individual jurisdictional interests. They have hired grants-in-aid coordinators to track down and acquire available federal funds. These jurisdictional (as opposed to functional or issue) lobbyists, who Samuel Beer has labeled "topocrats," have become articulate in demonstrating that state or local problems are of national significance and skillful in working with executive branch agencies, congressional committees, and interest groups in shaping legislation.[14]

A human factor which should not be overlooked in attempting to understand the governmental growth phenomenon is what has been called the "law of appropriateness." Basically, this law holds that the level of government or agency most appropriate to deal with a problem or provide a service is one's present employer, while some other jurisdiction is most appropriate to deal with a problem or provide a service is one's present employer, while some other jurisdiction is most appropriate to finance the activity.[15] In other words, the expansion of the federal government's role is partly attributable to the natural inclination of state and local officials to seek financial support from higher levels while retaining program discretion and administrative control. From the federal point of view this division of labor makes sense since it is normally more desirable and feasible, economically as well as politically, to use local or state agencies as service deliverers than to attempt to carry out this task directly.

During the same period that the federal government's role in domestic affairs expanded, major changes took place at the state level. Constitution revision, legislative reapportionment, executive branch reorganization, and fiscal reform efforts produced more powerful governors, more representative legislative bodies, more streamlined administrative structures, and more balanced revenue systems. As a result, significant increases were made in state aid for education, social welfare, health and hospitals, and transportation purposes, as well as for general assistance to local governments. A number of states launched programs targeted on their more needy urban communities. These actions, coupled with the expansion of federal-local relationships, helped accelerate the "intergovernmentalization" process.

In sum, governments at all levels have been responsive—if not hyper-responsive—to rising public demands for more and better services over the past two decades. The federal government has increasingly assumed the role of "banker" and with it, "regulator" and "equalizer." States and localities, while playing these roles to a lesser degree, have been the prime "implementors" in the federal system.[16]

In the view of one observer, these actions have produced "hyperlexis," a "pathological condition caused by an overactive law-making gland."[17] The explosion of statutes, ordinances, and regulations has contributed to confusion and uncertainty over which level of government or public officials were ultimately responsible for the delivery of services. The growing separation between revenue raising and spending responsibilities also has generated concerns about accountability.

Who Is Responsible?

Given the number of programs and participants and the diversity of purposes, it is not surprising that accountability for the proper use of public monies has been difficult if not impossible to pinpoint and maintain. Nevertheless, a variety of approaches have been attempted to achieve this objective, including auditing and paperwork requirements, decentralized and generalist-oriented decision making, as well as cross-cutting and programmatic conditions.

Federal funds are extremely difficult to trace once they are deposited in state or local bank accounts. They simply become revenues whose origin and objectives may be easily blurred or distorted. Due to this "fungibility" factor, accounting often becomes more of a leap of faith than an exercise in precision. Perhaps reflecting the frustration and futility involved here, a recent General Accounting Office study of 73 grant recipients revealed that 80 percent of their federal funds were not even audited by grantor agencies.[18]

On the other hand, state and local auditors may be rather zealous in trying to track the flow of outside monies into their budgets and ensure that they have been properly used by recipient agencies. Occasionally, this quest for accountability may lead to unnecessary frequency and duplication of efforts in the audits of some programs, gaps and inconsistencies in the coverage of others, and little or no attention being given to still others. While some agencies set aside office space which is regularly used by federal, state, local, and independent auditors, others are visited only once a year by a representative of their audit agency.

Despite these facts of grant-in-aid life, the amount of paperwork required on the part of recipients to "document" their use of federal monies has reached staggering proportions. Plans, applications, financial reports, and technical materials travel from city hall or county courthouse through a chain of regional, state, and federal intermediaries before arriving in Washington. The sheer volume of required information, and the usually large number of participants across the country, make intensive scrutiny a luxury that program administrators and auditors of grantor agencies cannot normally afford. These constraints are especially severe in a period of staffing freezes and travel cutbacks, unless the federal agency has an effective field structure.

Despite much rhetoric about the evils of paperwork, these formal trappings of accountability persist. Many administrators readily agree that some paperwork is essential and reasonable in order to provide assurances to grantor agencies that federal monies are needed and are being spent as planned, as well as for grantee internal management purposes. Requirements for applicants to supply what they perceive to be unessential or trivial information, however, generate complaints that they must go through several costly and time-consuming "rituals" in order to obtain federal money. These criticisms are particularly strong when a state or local unit attaches requirements to federal funds as they pass-through its budget office or program agency, but contributes little or nothing financially to the undertaking.

The concerns about recipient accountability that pervade many congressional committees, federal agencies, and Washington-based interest groups are reflected in the structure of federal assistance as well as in the nature of cross-cutting requirements and the design of particular program procedures. Of course, federal monies have become somewhat more discretionary from the state and local perspective due to the enactment of the health, law enforcement, employment and training, community development, and social services block grants as well as general revenue sharing. Among other things, these programs sought to strengthen the position of state and local elected officials and administrative generalists in decision making as a means of enhancing accountability.

Despite our nation's "grassroots government" traditions, accountability is difficult to establish at the local level. The ballot box provides only a crude indicator of priorities and performance. Most elected chief executive and legislative officials are part-timers, and have difficulty keeping track of available outside funds and monitoring how they are spent. And well-insulated local bureaucracies may owe their allegiance and perhaps longevity to state and federal counterpart programs and, hence, take cues from their administrators.

At the state level, prospects for accountability have been enhanced by decreases in the number of state agencies and separately elected department heads, increases in the professional staffing of governors' offices, and improvements in planning and budgeting. Only recently, however, have legislatures demonstrated a serious interest in oversight through the enactment of sunset laws and procedures for reappropriating federal funds before they can be spent by state agencies.

Partly due to these limitations, as well as to interest group pressures, with each block grant reauthorization, Congress has added new categories of assistance, targets of program emphasis, and earmarked accounts.[19] The revenue sharing program likewise has been used as a vehicle for Congress to ensure, among other things, that local governments will encourage citizen participation in the budgetary process and that their books will be periodically subjected to an independent audit. These requirements, and many of the 59 cross-cutting conditions, are not merely procedural in nature and limited in impact. Nor are they intended only to reinforce accountability. Instead, they seek to impose national standards or influence recipient behavior across a range of intergovernmental policies and operations.

The advent of cross-cutting requirements and their popularity among interest groups suggests that the "creeping conditionalism" phenomenon will continue. This will occur regardless of whether the contents of the various compliance documents have any relationship to reality, whether they facilitate or impede program management, or whether their cumulative effects on individual recipients are recognized.[20] It also suggests that, while much lip service is given to the cooperative nature of the intergovernmental partnership, there is considerable distrust and skepticism on the part of the federal partner toward states and localities—and vice versa.

One effect of the fragmentation and redundancy of contemporary federal programs is that many buck-passing opportunities are provided. Federal officials, for example, have blamed state or local officials for programmatic shortcomings. Local officials have criticized the "feds" for unpopular actions or policy decisions such as fair housing programs or community-based corrections projects. At the same time, however, they may have welcomed such intervention implicitly as a way of triggering or hastening necessary but different actions. Both local and federal officials have pointed to the states' insensitivity, reluctance, or inability to provide needed assistance or authority to their local governments as justification for establishing direct relationships.

From the standpoint of accountability, then, there are too many fingers in the intergovernmental service delivery pie. In the final analysis, when everyone is responsible for some aspect of service delivery, no one can really be held responsible. While there is much accounting in the form of seeking compliance with paperwork requirements and other conditions and the development of audit trails, there is actually little genuine accountability.

Rethinking the Responses

Many observers believe that the "days of wine and roses" are over as far as expansion of the federal government's role in domestic affairs through grants-in-aid is concerned. Commitments to increase defense spending, desires to reduce deficit financing and to balance the budget, and concerns about the solvency of the social security system have placed further pressure on the so-called "controllable" portion of the federal budget. With respect to the public sector generally, and the federal assistance component particularly, the management environment is changing from conditions of resource growth and rising expectations to conditions of resource stability or decline and failing expectations.

Evidence that these shifts are underway is provided by developments on the federal assistance front. From FY 1978 to FY 1981, the rate of federal aid growth slowed to 7.8 percent, half the annual figure for the preceeding 20 years.[21] In real terms, this slowdown represented an annual decline in the buying power of federal dollars. Another indicator is the desire of federal executive branch and congressional officials, and the willingness of state and local interest groups, to consider reducing outlays in certain grant areas, prioritizing existing programs, and making jurisdictional, functional, and discretionary authority trade-offs.[22]

Applying the fiscal brakes at the national level will have wide-spread and unpleasant effects on state and local governments. Clearly, it will hit hardest those units which have become increasingly dependent on federal aid to finance their operations over the past two decades. It will mean that more battles will be fought in Congress over formulas for entitlement programs. More vigorous competition will take place between and among states, localities, and non-governmental aid recipients for available project grants or discretionary funds. Quite possibly the friction between the "sunbelt" and "frostbelt" states that has resulted from the movement of people and industry to the southeast and southwest and the impact of regionally differentiated federal economic development policies will be exacerbated, and spread to other areas like severance taxes on energy production. Local governments will have to rely on their own revenue sources or state aid for a larger share of their expenditures. They will have to become more concerned about the costs and benefits of participating in federal programs from the standpoints of administrative overhead as well as the price tag on assuming services started with federal seed money.

The initial responses to resource scarcity have been a mounting interest in cutback management strategies and greater emphasis on economy, efficiency, and productivity. While the longer-term implications of an "era of limits" on budgets, personnel, and services are more difficult to gauge, columnist David Broder has predicted that ". . . the next two decades will be as much a period of institutional rehabilitation and repair as the last two decades were a time of disparagement and destruction of the machinery of our government."[23]

Any effort to respond to the fiscal and managerial stresses that are currently being placed on the federal system must inevitably confront the three basic questions raised earlier. In so doing, it will be necessary to rethink some of the conventional wisdom of intergovernmental reform. It will also be necessary to reconsider the applicability of some of the tenets of cooperative federalism theory to this changed environment.

Coping with a low-growth, no-growth, or retrenchment oriented intergovernmental system will require policy makers and administrators to take a variety of remedial actions. Many past and present policies, practices, and proposals will need to be re-examined, and new ones developed. The general types of responses that will very likely emerge from this process are of a procedural, structural, and functional nature.

Procedural Responses

Since the mid-1960s, the administrative and fiscal problems associated with the growth of federal grants-in-aid have been dealt with by a wide range of procedural remedies. These include:

- Assigning certain agency heads authority to convene meetings to discuss matters that cross departmental boundaries;
- Creating interagency committees to study various issues, decide jurisdiction over applications, and launch or coordinate presidential domestic policy initiatives;
- Developing management circulars to, among other things, facilitate access of the public, state and local officials, and interest groups to agencies during the regulation drafting process, coordinate local developments with areawide and statewide plans, unify financial and administrative requirements, standardize cost principles, and streamline audits;
- Furnishing prospective applicants with better federal program information;
- Issuing presidential directives to agencies to reduce paperwork requirements, simplify administrative machinery, and accelerate application processing;
- Providing ways to lessen overhead expenses through merging planning and administrative requirements and expanding the time periods they cover, standardizing and simplifying cross-cutting conditions, allowing recipients to certify their compliance with applicable federal laws and regulations in lieu of submitting extensive documentation, and reducing the number of information requests made by grantor agencies and the collection of nonessential data; and
- Calling attention to the fiscal, regulatory, and other impacts of pending legislation on potential recipients by requiring the inclusion of a statement of the anticipated effects.

These and other procedural initiatives have generally increased interagency and intergovernmental communications and coordination or, in the case of recently adopted procedural reforms, can be expected to do so. Yet, their overall impact has been limited by a number of factors, including the absence of a solid legal foundation in some cases, agency rivalry in others, and personnel and time constraints in still others. In addition, improvements of this type are usually of a "nuts and bolts," process, and technical nature, and their results are not often immediate or timely. Not surprisingly, then, they fail to generate much visibility, commitment, and sustained interest among top careerists and political executives.

Despite their mixed record, procedural reforms will continue to be the most frequently used tool for intergovernmental management improvement. Their popularity stems from a number of sources. In particular, since they do not require the enactment of legislation, implementation can proceed in a relatively expeditious manner. If the changes prove successful, they can even help pave the way for legislation as happened, for instance, with the Integrated Grant Administration experiment during the early 1970s, which led to the passage of the Joint Funding Simplication Act of 1974. At the same time, if problems arise during implementation, "fine tuning" can be done.

On the other side of the coin, some of the advantages of procedural changes from the point of view of the implementing agencies may be considered disadvantages by those in the Executive Office of the President, as well as state and local governments. These improvements, after all, are normally carried out in an incremental manner and at a pace set largely by the responsible agencies. From their perspective, the adjustments in policy, procedure, or program operation are frequently permissive rather than mandatory. Even in the case of presidential directives, they can be gradually eased into the mainstream of intergovernmental administration, placed on the backburner, or avoided entirely.

This agency reluctance or resistance often causes recipients to be skeptical about the impact of well-publicized presidential partisanship—it is partially rooted in the long absence of an effective central management agency to facilitate and monitor agency follow-up efforts, and to secure compliance. Until a strong central management presence is felt in the Office of Management and Budget (OMB) or elsewhere in the federal executive branch, the effects of administrative improvements will be limited because they will be too heavily dependent on agency good will to carry them out.

In addition to better central management machinery, the prospects for procedural reforms achieving their goals would be bolstered by giving greater recognition in program design and implementation to the wide diversity that exists among recipients' commitments and capacities. Congress and some federal agencies tend to assume that all states are equally willing and able—or unwilling and unable—to administer and finance particular services. They also assume that all localities possess the same amount of discretionary authority. The inclusion of certain midwest townships and New England counties in general revenue sharing, despite their limited functional responsibilities, underscores this point.

As a result of this view, even when significant improvements have been made they may be ignored. This was the case in 1978, with respect to the states' role in the national urban policy, and in 1980, concerning their future participation in general revenue sharing. In both instances, the efforts of a growing number of states to establish programs to provide general financial assistance to local governments and bear a greater share of the costs of certain services, to target resources on distressed communities, and to plan and coordinate urban and regional policies comprehensively were overlooked or downplayed.[24]

Adapting differential treatment processes to intergovernmental management systems would reinforce the need for state and local governments to continue to put their own houses in order. After all, many of the mandates and conditions that accompany federal funds reflect congressional and agency views that recipients lack the necessary planning and management personnel and procedures to implement national programs effectively and to account for federal funds properly. Under this approach, however, the more progressive recipients would not be penalized, nor would the less progressive ones be rewarded.

Jurisdictional targeting, in an administrative sense, is much more difficult than fiscal targeting, where relevant data to measure need and capacity are normally available (even if not completely reliable), and the distributional effects of various formulas can be readily discerned via computer print-out. Indeed, not much progress has been made in developing methods to measure and incorporate in legislation the varying commitments and capabilities of aid recipients or to defer to their judgments in intergovernmental planning and management since a suggestion along these lines was offered in the late 1960s by James Sundquist.[25]

While many political, administrative, and legal obstacles exist, the shrinking size and buying power of aid dollars make the need for a more sophisticated and differentiated approach to intergovernmental management compelling. Some movement in this direction is already underway, and more can be expected. Experiments with certification procedures, requirement waivers, application packaging and expediting, and the like are important steps toward improved implementation. An example of how greater selectivity could be introduced into program design is the so-called "buy in" approach to direct federal-local relationships. In legislation authorizing programs of this type states could be given the option to participate, with the degree of their involvement in channeling funds, reviewing local plans and applications, and performing other administrative roles determined by the extent of their commitments. This could be measured by such factors as the establishment of an appropriate administrative agency, employment of sufficient professional personnel, development of a comprehensive plan, adoption of local consultation procedures, and provision of a substantial portion of the non-federal matching costs or other funds to support relevant local programs. If a state did not wish to be involved, direct federal-local relationships would prevail.[26] This approach has been considered in federal housing and community development, employment training, and law enforcement programs, and adopted in the latter, but has much wider applicability given the number of areas in which the states are being bypassed.

The pace of procedural reforms could be hastened, and the results enhanced, if officials of the different levels and units of government that share implementation responsibilities became less skeptical and cautious and more trusting in their dealings with one another. If this were the case, many of the intergovernmental rituals they follow would be unnecessary. Accordingly, many of the overhead costs, burdens, delays, headaches, and frictions associated with intergovernmental management would be reduced. And perhaps the spirit of cooperative federalism would be better reflected in actual practice.

Structural Reforms

A second, and more ambitious, reform involves restucturing assistance programs. Several concerns about the problems inherent in the highly fragmented contemporary federal assistance system have helped kindle interest in this approach. The duplication among functionally related programs and the agencies that administer them is inefficient and unnecessarily expensive from a federal administrative costs standpoint. The program mix is so confusing to some prospective applicants that it acts as a deterrent to their participation. Others, which can afford to hire grants coordinators or set up Washington offices, may actually benefit from program fragmentation by playing agencies off against one another in an effort to obtain the most funds on the easiest terms. Another concern here is the narrowness of the authorized uses of federal programs. This specificity often means that recipients cannot use available funds for their greatest needs, and that federal monies may have a distorting effect on their budget priorities.

Grant consolidation proposals have a long history, yet the enactment record is rather modest. The most significant period of consolidation activity was 1966-1974 when 32 categorical programs were merged into block grants in the health, employment and training, and community development areas. Besides consolidating a number of functionally related programs, these block grants accorded recipients significant amounts of flexibility in applying federal monies to their priority needs. In addition to these enactments, during this period Congress consolidated several maternal and child health and crippled childrens' services programs and libraries, learning resources, and innovative education programs into two larger categorical grants. After a three-year hiatus, in 1977 and 1978 Congress approved consolidations in the insular areas, forestry, and elderly programs. None have been enacted since that time.

While these actions are somewhat encouraging to grant reformers, two facts should not be overlooked. First, "recategorization" has affected each block grant, with the range of recipient discretion often being significantly narrowed with each reauthorization. Second, the so-called congressional-federal agency-interest group "iron triangle" has continued to spawn categorical programs—including some 50 new grants from 1975-1978—as well as to resist successfully the consolidation of major existing ones in areas such as food and nutrition, vocational education and rehabilitation, transportation, and water and sewer.[27]

Even though the pressures to preserve the categorical *status quo* remain strong, the redundancy and specificity of contemporary programs are luxuries the intergovernmental system can no longer afford. The overall slowdown of federal aid growth rates, the willingness on the part of some public officials to trade off certain categoricals for the continuation of more discretionary forms of assistance, and the potential spotlighting effect of "sunset" type evaluations on programs that are ineffective or have outlived their usefulness suggest that grant consolidation activity will increase in the years ahead. The ultimate outcome of the efforts, of course, rests heavily on the president taking the initiative and lending his support to consolidations, as well as on the Congress fairly and expeditiously considering those proposals that are offered. It also depends on the backing these efforts receive from state and local officials.

Functional Reforms

The pinpointing of functions being performed and/or financed by the federal government for devolution to subnational units has surfaced from time to time since the 1950s, but it has really not been taken seriously by intergovernmental policy makers. As the United States entered the decade of the 1980s there were some indications that this issue would be raised again, and perhaps more carefully considered, at the national level.

As demands on the federal budget grow in the years ahead, it is likely that national policy makers will look to the "controllable" sector—particularly assistance programs—for elimination or devolution targets. There are few precedents here, most of which can be traced to the work of the Joint Federal-State Action Committee between 1957 and 1959, whose recommendations that federal waste treatment and vocational education programs be shifted to the state level were ignored by Congress and not supported by state officials.[28] The "new federalism" domestic policy of President Richard Nixon emphasized the need to devolve or decentralize certain functions being performed at the national level or by the central offices of federal agencies, as well as to hold the line on expenditures for other activities. This philosophy was reflected in actions taken by the administration to spin off anti-poverty programs, cap social service outlays, curtail environmental protection projects, and cash-out housing and education programs and substitute vouchers.[29]

An "era of limits" could well provide an excellent climate for launching a rational sorting-out process. OMB's examination of appropriate forms of financial assistance pursuant to the Federal Grant and Cooperative Agreement Act of 1977 is a step in this direction, as is the study by the Advisory Commission on Intergovernmental Relations of "The Federal Role in the Federal System."

The proliferation of small project grants for a wide range of activities of questionable national significance but unquestionable interest group importance, the continuing pressure from some regions, states, and localities for massive infusions of federal funds, and the dismal experience with federal program terminations since the 1950s all suggest that any sorting out process may be an exercise in political futility. Yet, it is essential that this effort at least get underway, and that criteria be developed to help guide policy makers. Particularly significant here is the call for a national convocation on federalism that was made during the summer of 1980 by the National Governors' Association and ACIR. Others have since echoed this sentiment for a variety of philosophical and political reasons. Potentially a convocation of federal, state, local, private sector, and citizen representatives could focus attention on the real meaning of the 10th amendment and other parts of the Constitution, increase understanding of how and why governmental growth has occurred at all levels, determine the areas where involvement on the part of the federal government or of states and localities is inappropriate or undesirable and should end, and develop strategies for "decongesting" the federal system and shifting functional and financial responsibilities. The philosophical and practical considerations behind this sorting out effort have been pointed out by Governor Bruce Babbitt of Arizona:[30]

> To those of us who came of age in the 1960s, 'states rights' evoke memories of a racist governor standing in the schoolhouse door, and malapportioned legislatures. Two decades later, some of us are having second thoughts about what the government should and should not do. . . . Governors like myself, trying to innovate in resource management, medical care and environmental issues, find ourselves cornered by rigid federal regulations at every turn. If we are beginning to sound like George Wallace or John C. Calhoun, it is not because

> we share their objectives; it is because we believe that the government, acting in pursuit of many noble goals, has not produced what it promised and is rapidly destroying the power of state and local governments to do a better job.

As an example of the kind of functional and financial shifts that might be considered, a case could be made for immediate assumption by the federal government of existing programs aimed at meeting basic human needs, including full federal financial responsibility for Aid to Families with Dependent Children, Medicaid, and General Assistance, and gradual assumption of the costs of employment security, housing assistance, medical benefits, and nutrition. At the same time, many of the remaining federal aid programs should be scrutinized for termination, phase-out, and consolidation opportunities. The most likely candidates are: the approximately 420 categorical grants that together comprise only about one-tenth of total federal assistance to state and local governments; programs in functional fields like law enforcement where federal monies amount to less than 10 percent of total government outlays; grants that have high administrative costs relative to the federal financial share; and programs which could be wholly or predominantly funded by state or local government tax revenues or user fees, or could be shifted to the private sector.[31]

As these suggested trade-offs suggest, those engaged in any sorting out process must carefully weigh the proper role for the federal government to play against that of the state, local, and private sectors. In particular, desires for more economy and efficiency in the structure and operation of intergovernmental programs need to be balanced with the desires for greater equity. While the federal aid system has not significantly redistributed resources to most disadvantaged states and regions, nevertheless fiscal equity remains an important objective of many programs. Especially in periods of retrenchment, it is essential that the redistributive effects of federal programs on needy places as well as people receive considerable attention. In addition, opportunities must remain open for new needs to be expressed and acted on at appropriate governmental levels.

A strong impetus to these efforts could be provided if local and state lobbyists and the public become less eager to press for increasing the federal government's fiscal role in domestic affairs, better aware of the institutional consequences of this expansion, and more willing to suggest potential targets of opportunity. As the *Wall Street Journal* put it in an editorial comment on the National Conference of State Legislatures' meeting in July 1980: "States have improved markedly in their administrative ability in recent years . . . and they may find life easier if they just avoid taking federal money wherever possible. And the voters could turn things around altogether if they stopped thinking of their Congressmen as caseworkers and held them to account at the polls for the laws they pass."[32]

Implications for Theory and Practice

The 1980s could well be a crossroads period for the theory and practice of American federalism. Major changes have occurred in intergovernmental relations at a rapid rate, and they will undoubtedly continue. The ensuing stresses and strains that have been placed on governmental institutions and public officials have grown with the size and complexity of federal-state-local relationships. While change is inevitable, it needs to be channeled and controlled so as to minimize or avoid potentially dysfunctional or destructive consequences. The procedural, structural, and functional reforms outlined above can help adapt intergovernmental management to the political, economic, and social realities of the 1980s.

At the same time that these and other remedial actions are being examined, it is necessary to consider the theoretical underpinnings of the federal system in light of contemporary intergovernmental relationships. The events during the past two decades call for a re-examination and elaboration of certain components of cooperative federalism. While this is not the place to attempt to analyze this issue fully, it is appropriate to raise a number of questions that stem from the developments that have been discussed.

- What are the proper functional responsibilities of the three levels of government?
- What patterns of shared and separated governmental roles are appropriate?
- What is the effect of extensive sharing of certain responsibilities on accountability for results?
- Under what circumstances, and with what conditions, should the federal government assume direct responsibility for performing certain functions if state and local participation in aid programs declines?
- Is the widening gap between intergovernmental revenue raising and spending authority desirable?
- How can the expansion of direct federal-local relationships to include jurisdictions other than "mega-cities" be justified?
- What are the effects of direct federal private sector relations on state and local governments?
- Why are the states not more widely recognized as the so-called "keystones of the governmental arch" by the architects and implementors of federal programs?
- Have local and state governments become too dependent fiscally on the federal government and, in making cutbacks, should they be willing to sacrifice their priorities in order to retain federal funding?
- On what basis should the federal government give preferential treatment in allocating resources to particular localities, states, and regions of the country?

- Why have skepticism and distrust between the different levels of government apparently grown concurrent with significant increases in the amount of intergovernmental activity, and how can a trust factor be built into relationships between officials representing different levels, units, and agencies?
- Why do functional specialists continue to seek to end-run generalists in the intergovernmental policymaking and administration despite the major strides that have been made in modernizing the executive and legislative branches?
- What is the role and influence of "topocrats" in intergovernmental decision making, and how successful have they been in overcoming the functional forces that run vertically through the federal system?
- What is the impact of an increasingly activist judiciary on the allocation of functions between the levels of government, the raising and distribution of revenues, and the performance of services?
- Can the growing interest in applying "layer cake" federalism to certain governmental activities be reconciled with a "marble cake" approach to others?
- How has the growth of the federal government's revenue raising and resource allocation roles, the decline of the national political parties, and the willingness of some members of Congress to act as *de facto* state or local officials affected the decentralized operation of the federal system?

These questions, and many others, deserve more attention than they have received to date by those concerned about federalist theory. Coupled with the reforms in intergovernmental practice suggested above, much progress could be made toward restoring balance in the federal system and making cooperative federalism a reality rather than a slogan in the 1980s.

Notes

1. Morton Grodzins, *The American System: A New View of Government in the United States,* edited by Daniel J. Elazar (Chicago: Rand McNally & Company, 1966).
2. U.S. Advisory Commission on Intergovernmental Relations, *A Crisis of Confidence and Competence,* The Federal Role in the Federal System: The Dynamics of Growth (Washington, D.C.: U.S. Government Printing Office, July 1980).
3. Charles H. Levine and Paul L. Posner, "The Centralizing Effects of Austerity on the Intergovernmental System," paper prepared for delivery at the 1979 Annual Meeting of the American Political Science Association, Washington, D.C., August 31-September 3, 1979; and Deil S. Wright, *Understanding Intergovernmental Relations* (North Scituate, Mass.: Duxbury Press, 1978).
4. U.S. Office of Management and Budget, *Special Analyses Budget of the United*

States Government Fiscal Year 1981 (Washington, D.C.: U.S. Government Printing Office, 1980), p. 254.

5. U.S. Advisory Commission on Intergovernmental Relations Staff Compilation. See also: *A Catalog of Federal Grant-in-Aid Programs to State and Local Governments: Grants Funded FY 1978* (Washington, D.C.: U.S. Government Printing Office, February 1979).
6. Advisory Commission on Intergovernmental Relations, *A Crisis of Confidence and Competence,* p. 84.
7. U.S. Office of Management and Budget, *Managing Federal Assistance in the 1980s* (Washington, D.C.: U.S. Government Printing Office, March 1980), pp. 20-26.
8. *Maine v. Thiboutot,* 100 S. Ct. 2502 (1980).
9. Morton Grodzins, "The Federal System," in *Goals for Americans* (New York: The American Assembly, 1960), pp. 266-267.
10. Seth S. King, "Why Have One When Many Will Do?" *The New York Times Magazine,* September 16, 1979, p. 115.
11. U.S. Advisory Commission on Intergovernmental Relations, "Grant Consolidation: Time for Action," *Information Bulletin* No. 77-2, September 1977, p. 2.
12. Wayne F. Anderson, "Intergovernmental Aid: Relief or Intrusion? *National Civic Review* (March 1980), p. 130.
13. Cynthia Cates Colella, "The Creation, Care and Feeding of Leviathan: Who and What Makes Government Grow," and David R. Beam, "The Accidental Leviathan: Was the Growth of Government a Mistake?" *Intergovernmental Perspective* (Fall 1979), pp. 6-19.
14. Samuel H. Beer, "Federalism, Nationalism, and Democracy in America," *American Political Science Review* (March 1978), pp. 9-21.
15. David J. Kennedy, "The Law of Appropriateness: An Approach to a General Theory of Intergovernmental Relations," *Public Administration Review* (March/April 1972), pp. 135-143.
16. Edward K. Hamilton, "On Neoconstitutional Management of a Constitutional Problem," *Daedalus* (Spring 1977).
17. Bayless Manning, "Hyperlexis: Our National Disease," *Congressional Record,* March 16, 1978, p. S. 3948.
18. U.S. General Accounting Office, *Grant Auditing: A Maze of Inconsistency, Gaps, and Duplication That Needs Overhauling,* June 15, 1979, p. ii.
19. Advisory Commission on Intergovernmental Relations, *Block Grants: A Comparative Analysis* (Washington, D.C.: U.S. Government Printing Office, October 1977).
20. Catherine H. Lovell, et al., *Federal and State Mandating on Local Governments: An Exploration of Issues and Impacts* (Riverside: University of California, June 20, 1979); and U.S. Congressional Budget Office, *Federal Constraints on State and Local Government Actions* (Washington, D.C.: U.S. Government Printing Office, April 1979).
21. Office of Management and Budget, *Special Analyses Budget of the United States Government Fiscal Year 1981,* p. 239.
22. Congressional Budget Office, *Reducing the Federal Budget: Strategies and*

Examples (Washington, D.C.: U.S. Government Printing Office, February 1980).

23. *Washington Post,* September 18, 1980.
24. National Academy for Public Administration and U.S. Advisory Commission on Intergovernmental Relations, *The States and Distressed Communities: The 1980 Annual Report* (Washington, D.C.: U.S. Government Printing Office, 1981).
25. James L. Sundquist and David W. Davis, *Making Federalism Work: A Study of Program Coordination at the Community Level* (Washington, D.C.: The Brookings Institution, 1969), pp. 247-252.
26. Carl W. Stenberg, *State Involvement in Federal-Local Grant Programs: A Case Study of the "Buying In" Approach* (Washington, D.C.: U.S. Advisory Commission on Intergovernmental Relations, December 1970).
27. U.S. Advisory Commission on Intergovernmental Relations, *A Catalog of Federal Grant-in-Aid Programs to State and Local Governments: Grants Funded FY 1978,* p. 1.
28. Grodzins, "The Federal System," pp. 267-268.
29. Richard P. Nathan, *The Plot That Failed: Nixon and the Administrative Presidency* (New York: John Wiley & Sons, 1975).
30. Bruce Babbitt, "On States' Rights," *New York Times,* September 9, 1980.
31. U.S. Advisory Commission on Intergovernmental Relations, *An Agenda for American Federalism: Restoring Confidence and Competence* (Washington, D.C.: U.S. Government Printing Office, 1981).
32. *Wall Street Journal,* July 21, 1980.

1981 (41:10-20)

PART III

Metropolitan and Urban Problems, Policies, and Prospects

The 1960s represented a "new phase" of intergovernmental relations—a second new federalism. This phase was typified by an acceleration in the number and scope of functions aided with federal dollars and accompanied by increased federal aid that emphasized "national objectives," "close federal control," and "centralization of objective-setting."

The articles in this section (Part III) exemplify two prominent themes that characterized the second new federalism. One was an urban/metropolitan focus; the second centered attention on citizens and clients of federal aid programs, especially the disadvantaged. The five selections highlight a cluster of geographic, organizational, functional, and process issues that occupied center-stage during the second new federalism.

Norman Beckman, in 1966 on the staff of ACIR, discusses the role of the national and state governments in finding solutions to problems in metropolitan areas. He examines issues of geographic adequacy, economies of scale, and adequate and equitable resources. He outlines various strategies for reforming metropolitan governments, e.g., comprehensive and functional planning requirements, local government control over the use of special districts, strict statutory standards for new incorporation in metropolitan areas, and special priority for general purpose government when awarding federal and state grants.

The second selection also reflects a concern for the "state of affairs" in metropolitan America almost a decade later. Written in 1974 by Joan B. Aaron of New York University, this article reviews the rise and decline of metropolitan reform in the New York City metropolitan area. It also references reform experiences of other communities across the nation and questions whether some form of regional government is the answer to the problems of metropolitan areas.

The third article in this section examines the federal involvement in urban areas. Robert Wood, a top-level executive at HUD in 1968, notes the dual problem of reversing patterns of decay while meeting the challenges of new growth in urban areas. Answers to several basic policy questions are posited as prerequisites for a solution to urban problems. A structural strategy, the establishment of HUD as a cabinet-level department, is offered as evidence on movement toward a legislative mandate for answers to basic policy questions.

Howard Hallman reviews experience with national requirements for citizen participation in various federal aid programs from the 1950s to the early 1970s. He examines policy questions relative to the use of federal funds to support citizen participation, e.g., "Who should hire and supervise the [community] organizer?" "Where does the money come to pay their salaries?" He also provides information on variations in federally required citizen participation from urban renewal and juvenile delinquency to community action and model cities. Particular emphasis is placed on the dilemma between citizen participation and coordination: "Where resident participation has been strong, relatively little coordination has occurred. Where coordination has been emphasized, resident participation has been weak."

The concluding selection in this section was written by Norton E. Long of the University of Missouri-St. Louis. Long explores the political and economic prospects for the survival of American cities. He argues that although political science and economics "have done little to measure the cost effectiveness of public services . . . we are not helpless before the question of whether cities or even neighborhoods are consequential or trivial for their citizens and their inhabitants." He uses examples such as the low infant mortality rate in Hong Kong and the low crime in an Italian American neighborhoods as indicators of the type of contribution that citizens and cities can make to "the improvement of the human condition." Cities have "slack resources" which, if utilized, could contribute to "local community building and rebuilding." Long strongly criticizes the general acceptance of the powerlessness of cities and their citizens. He also questions policies that proceed from such assumptions of powerlessness, policies that produce cities which are little more than "empty husks."

NORMAN BECKMAN

How Metropolitan Are Federal and State Policies?

Like the weather, everybody talks about the need for restructuring local government in metropolitan areas but nobody does anything about it. In the words of Thomas Reed, "So far we have accomplished little more than the world's record for words in proportion to cures effected."[1] The problems are real enough: uneven allocation of fiscal resources among the many local governments in a metropolitan area, disparities in levels of service among central city and suburban jurisdictions, economically inefficient scale of operation, excessive spillover of costs and benefits, and unresolved areawide problems.

Heavy emphasis in the extensive literature to date has been on the use of intra-metropolitan machinery—annexation, extraterritorial powers, interlocal contracting, councils of governments, urban counties, control of special districts, and city-county consolidations, etc.[2] Less attention has been given to the vertical (federal-state-local, federal-local, state-local) dimension in which all governments in metropolitan areas must also operate; yet both the horizontal and the vertical systems of intergovernmental relationships should be understood before creation of alternative structure is recommended. Even the severest critics must admit that, like the bumblebee and the old "PBY," however imperfect or illogical, the present system does work. For this, state and federal governments must get a large share of the credit.

This article is designed, first, to describe how federal and state agencies play an increasing, essential role in encouraging action which meets the following criteria for sound local government in metropolitan areas—*geographic adequacy, economies of scale, adequate and equitable revenue sources, and responsibility to the public for a wide range of functions;* the second, to identify some areas for improved federal and state practice in achieving these objectives. The attempt is to document and explain changes in federal and state policies developed largely in the last five to ten years toward urban development and governments in metropolitan areas; policies which, like Mr. Disraeli's empire, are being acquired in a fit of absent-mindedness.

Geographic Adequacy

Governments performing urban services should have a geographic area of jurisdiction adequate for effective performance. For many governmental functions today, particularly those concerned with natural resources, the environment, and communication, area is crucial to effectiveness. Yet, since logical service areas for different functions and subfunctions vary, no "set" of boundaries for local governments is demonstrably more satisfactory than existing boundaries, just as, in all the discussions of the greater sense inherent in dividing the country into "natural" regions, rather than states, there has been no agreement on "natural" regional boundaries.

In recent years, federal agencies have shown considerable ingenuity in achieving necessary areawide administration, while preserving the role of the general governments affected. Planning and other performance requirements under federal grant and loan programs can go far toward achieving rational physical development projects, even in an area that is politically fragmented. Aids for functional and comprehensive planning have become legion in number if not in name.[3]

For certain functions nothing less than nation-wide planning will assure adequate performance. Thus, aid under the Federal Aid Airport Program is limited to projects which are part of the National Airport Plan. Similarly, each federally aided construction project under the Interstate Highway Program must constitute an improvement in the federally approved national highway system. For other functions, regions less than national but not necessarily confined to any existing political boundaries are preferable. All federal water resource projects must be part of a comprehensive river basin plan. Assistance under the Public Works and Economic Development Act of 1965 is made not to individual communities but to "economic development districts" and "areas" experiencing substantial and persistent unemployment. Under the same Act, joint federal-state regional action planning commissions similar to the Appalachian Regional Commission are authorized in multi-state regions meeting certain economic criteria.

It is at the metropolitan level that the major administrative innovations have been developed, mainly in the last five years, to assure geographically adequate planning and development. In 1960, the term "metropolitan" could scarcely be found in federal law or regulation. Today, most new grant-in-aid programs and more than one-third of the existing federal programs affecting urban development encourage broader jurisdictions for areawide coordination of projects, in law, in official policy statements, and in definitions of eligible projects.[4]

The principle of geographically adequate development as a condition of federal assistance is now the official policy of the Executive Branch, as indicated in the President's message on "Problems of the Central City and Its Suburbs."

A few of the more outstanding examples of this new element in federal performance requirements follow. The Federal Highway Act required that, beginning July, 1965, no funds can be approved for a project in any urban area of more than 50,000 population unless there is an established continuing comprehensive transportation planning process for the urban area as a whole. By December, 1965, it was reported that this transportation planning process was ". . . underway in all 224 urbanized areas of more than 50,000 population and in many smaller areas as well. In the majority the process is fully adequate to permit evaluation of any proposed transportation system and in most of the remainder it can provide reasonable bases of review of individual projects. The fears of some that the planning requirement of the 1965 Act would serve to delay the federal-aid highway program have proved unfounded."[5] Whether these planning operations will undermine or strengthen comprehensive metropolitan planning agencies remains to be seen; nevertheless, the 1965 requirement marked a milestone in intergovernmental affairs by linking local governments in the entire urbanized and urbanizing area with the state highway agency and by directly joining policymaking to implementation.

Under the open space land program of the Department of Housing and Urban Development, the Secretary is authorized to make grants only if he finds that there is a comprehensive planning program for the entire urban area, and that the land to be acquired for open space use is important to the execution of a comprehensive plan. The Urban Mass Transportation Act of 1964 carries language that is increasingly becoming boilerplate for legislative draftsmen. Grants can be made only to carry out a program "for a unified or officially coordinated urban transportation system as part of the comprehensively planned development of the urban area. . . ."

Although less use has been made of incentives to achieve effective areawide administration, two recent examples, however, can be cited. The 1965 amendments to the Federal Water Pollution Control Act authorize an additional 10 percent grant for those sewage treatment construction grant projects that are certified by an official state, regional, or metropolitan planning agency as being in conformity with a comprehensive plan of development. The Economic Development Act authorizes the Secretary of Commerce to increase the amount of grant assistance by 10 percent if the redevelopment area is situated within a designated economic development district, is actively participating in the economic development activities of the district, and if the specific project is consistent with an approved district economic development program.

The President, in his March "Cities" message, reaffirmed the new operating procedures in a proposal to establish a $100 million annual grant program for urban water and sewage facilities:

> The Federal Government cannot and should not require the communities which make up a metropolitan area to cooperate against their will in the solution of their problems. But we can offer incentives to metropolitan area planning and cooperation.

The incentive turns out to be a "condition of Federal assistance" that "these grants will be contingent upon comprehensive areawide planning" of the facilities to serve an entire region, taking into account foreseeable growth needs. Following enactment of this legislation in the first session of the 89th Congress (along with three other entirely new waste water control grant programs, bringing to six the number of water pollution control grant programs, each administered by a different federal agency) the Department of Housing and Urban Development issued regulations governing eligibility for project grants. Four planning elements are required:

1. the project is consistent with a short-range areawide water or sewer system program;
2. the areawide program is based on long-range, area water and sewer planning;
3. water and sewer planning is part of long-range, areawide comprehensive planning; and
4. comprehensive planning is conceived and carried out to attain urban area goals and objectives under the policy direction of local elected officials.[6]

The approval is not limited to physical development activities. Illustrating what Humpty Dumpty meant when he said to Alice, "When I use a word it means just what I choose it to mean—neither more nor less," the new *Community Action Program Guide* issued under the Economic Opportunity Act, containing instructions for applicants, defines "community" as:

> . . . any urban or rural, or urban and rural, geographical area, including but not limited to a State, metropolitan area, county, city, town, multi-city unit, or multi-county units. Generally, a community should be coterminous with a major political jurisdiction such as a city or county, or with a group of political jurisdictions exercising responsibility for related public programs. In metropolitan areas, whenever feasible, the community should include all of the urbanized or urbanizing portions of the area.
>
> A community shall cover a geographical area of sufficient size and population to allow for the effective utilization of human physical and financial resources in an attack on poverty. Communities containing very small populations are encouraged to combine their efforts with adjacent jurisdictions to ensure the creation of an adequate resource base. . . .

The states have made less use of planning requirements or incentives, but, rather, have tended to act as administering agents or have imposed standards and responsibilities on local governments in a manner politically and legally inappropriate for federal agencies. The states have an increasingly substantial record of direct action in regional planning, provision of water, recreational facilities and open space, air and water pollution control, and, in the East, subsidies to regional mass transportation. In regional development, Connecticut took the lead in 1955; today, 15 regions have been defined, and 7 regional planning agencies have been activated, covering 80 percent of the state's population. California regional planning legislation in 1963 automatically created regional planning districts when two-thirds of the local governments declare there is a need for such a district. New York State's Office of Regional Development has recommended the designation of development regions and the creation of regional councils to prepare comprehensive regional plans. Georgia has divided the state into 16 planning districts.

Some states have taken away or modified small local governments' zoning powers in the interests of more effective planning for a larger area, supporting a technical staff competent to provide continuing attention to development problems, and discouraging excessive fiscal zoning practices on the part of small municipalities. The State of Kentucky in 1964 removed the zoning power entirely from municipalities under 1,000 population. In Indiana a single Metropolitan Planning Commission and Board of Zoning Appeals has been established, and all local boards abolished in the Indianapolis-Marion County Metropolitan Area. The State of New York in 1960 provided for county review of local development actions of county-wide significance. Connecticut has provided for similar review of certain town zoning decisions by the regional planning agency.

These are promising beginnings, but hardly more, as indicated. Lest this review end on too "Pollyanna" a note, it may be appropriate to quote from a 1964 resolution of the National League of Cities:

> Certain Federal programs encourage undesirable sprawl by financing partial public facilities and urban housing which (1) do not take into account population trends; (2) are not required to meet adequate standards; (3) require or permit the creation of special districts that bypass general governments; or (4) are not part of a plan that will affect the overall growth of the area. Among Federal agencies involved in these practices in the fields of public facilities and urban housing are: Farmers Home Administration, Community Facilities Administration, Federal Housing Administration, Veterans Administration, Area Redevelopment Administration and its Accelerated Public Works Programs, the Rural Areas Development Program of the Department of Agriculture and the General Services Administration's surplus real property disposal program.[7] Passage of the Resolution was followed by creation of a Joint Task

Force on Substandard Urban Expansion supported by the League and the National Association of Counties.

As previously indicated, the majority of federal aid programs for urban development still do not encourage areawide jurisdiction over the planning and administration of urban development programs, but accept whatever areas of jurisdiction (usually strictly local) the states and localities make available. Population limitations in such grant programs as rural electrification, public facility loans, and sewage treatment plants similarly tend to discourage areawide programs for planning and administration. A financial bonus for smallness of area covered is actually given in the urban renewal program to communities under 50,000 population in the form of three-fourths rather than two-thirds federal matching grants.

Economies of Scale

References to economies of scale to be realized from performing urban services on a large scale are common in metropolitan reorganization literature, though significant research to date is limited.[8]

Federal Functional Planning, Joint Performance, and Special Districts

Most federal aids in urban areas are for special types of facilities which are most effective when planned as systems. Planning a functional and systematic network of each type of facility, e.g., water supply, sewage disposal, transit, and even hospitals, is necessary to achieve economies of scale and avoid haphazard location of facilities.

From 43 federal urban development programs examined,[9] these facts emerged: 15 federal aid programs require conformance with official plans for the function being assisted; 4 require review only, not necessarily conformance; and 11 stipulate that aid projects be "not inconsistent" with existing functional plans. Programs requiring conformance to local or metropolitan-wide functional plans, in addition to those cited above having areawide planning requirements, include such basic urban services as urban renewal, area redevelopment projects, advances for public works planning, and FHA mortgage insurance (only with regard to housing in urban renewal areas or for relocation of displaced families).

Federal programs in large metropolitan areas with inadequate functional planning requirements tend to be those of less significance for urban development and include public facility loans (limited to communities under 50,000), reclamation projects, and agriculture loans to associations for water supply projects.

Nearly one-half of federal urban development programs require some degree of state involvement. State supervision in many of these casses can be exercised to aid coordination across local political boundaries, if not between different types of aid. Thus, federally aided projects for hospital facilities, sewage treatment construction grants, and highways must conform to and be included in a state plan.

Another way of promoting economies of scale is to authorize or encourage two or more governmental units eligible for federal aid to participate jointly in a cooperative project. Specific legislative authority for this type of aid exists in about a quarter of the federal programs and at least another quarter which administratively authorize joint projects. Thus, the Public Housing Administration deals with joint city-county and, in a few cases, multi-county housing agencies. In cases where single jurisdictions are too small to finance local staffs individually, joint housing authorities are being administratively encouraged. Ceilings of $1.2 million on grants for waste treatment works for individual projects are raised to $4.8 million when more than one community participates under the 1965 Water Quality Act.

Federal agencies have generally taken a pragmatic approach in establishing organization requirements for grant eligibility. In a recent Senate survey of grant programs, only one in four federal aid officials felt that the involvement of special districts in the administration of their programs raised problems in coordinating their program with local governments and other federal activities at the local level.[10] The primary federal interest is to assure professional performance and achievement of specific program objectives, rather than strengthening the general purpose units of government, the cities and the counties. Most federal aid is available to both general purpose and special units of local government. The special purpose units, generally endorsed, and required by about one-quarter of all federal programs, ostensibly to achieve an appropriate work load and resultant economies of scale, include regional planning agencies, local area redevelopment organizations, industrial development authorities, rural area development committees, irrigation districts, and water user associations. The proposed Intergovernmental Cooperation Act contained in the President's Budget Message for 1966 includes a section granting general local governments priority over special districts in eligibility for federal aids. In addition, where special districts do receive federal grants, they would be required to provide full information concerning the request to the local governments in the area.

All of these approaches taken by the federal government, functional planning requirements and assistance, authorization and encouragement of joint performance by local governments, eligibility of special districts, increase the potentialities for achieving economies of scale in urban services.

The States Act in the Name of Efficiency

The marked decline in independent school districts was the brightest finding of the 1962 Census of Governments, because consolidation resulted in economies of scale. Here the states have been most successful in rationalizing the performance of a basic governmental service, largely through offering the incentive of extra aid if school districts consolidated, but also through direct mandate. Credit should also be given to the political efforts of the teaching profession, which saw in consolidation a means of raising educational standards and, at the same time, getting a living wage.

Currently, states are acting to preserve existing economies of scale through control of new municipal incorporations. At least seven states have, in the last two years, established regulatory machinery, either in the form of a state agency, or, as in California, by creating a local agency formation and annexation commission in every county. One of the key elements in this kind of legislation is the statutory standards that review commissions must take into account including "the present cost and adequacy of governmental services and controls . . . and the probable effect of the proposed action and of alternative courses of action on the cost and adequacy of local governmental services and regulation in the area and in adjacent areas."[11]

A 1963 Georgia enactment, authorizing state financial incentives and technical assistance where political subdivisions establish joint undertakings, may serve as an example for other states. A very significant piece of state legislation enacted in 1965 is the joint resolution in Utah, proposing a new article of the state constitution authorizing creation of "metropolitan region governments." If adopted by the voters, this amendment will permit countywide metropolitan government to assume the powers and functions of existing cities and special districts in an area and to provide for the necessary revenue.

The Great Equalizer

Government should be able to raise adequate revenue and do it equitably. "Some observers contend that public finance, not governmental structure, is the nub of the metropolitan problem. They argue that, given sufficient funds and equitable distribution, most of the difficulties, whether traffic, blight, or pollution, can be overcome without major changes in the existing governmental pattern."[12] The uneven allocation of fiscal resources at the differing levels of service among local governments in metropolitan areas is becoming exacerbated as central city and suburban populations, especially in our larger and older metropolitan areas, are becoming increasingly distributed along economic and racial lines. Here, in achieving financial equity, the federal and state governments have a crucial role to play.

As Alan Campbell has written, "National-State-local federal fiscal interdependence is one of the major aspects of the interdependence of the entire system."[13] Federal and state aid form "the bridge between expenditure assignment and tax assignment. This function of aid demonstrates the interrelatedness of the total system and shows the crucial role played by intergovernmental flows of funds."[14]

Intra-metropolitan redistribution of tax revenue has been limited to occasional use of sales and payroll taxes. The flow is essentially from the federal and state governments to the local governments. The direction of this flow recognizes the superior tax base and the mobility of people, industry, and, indeed, of problems throughout the nation.

Both federal and state grant programs, especially since the '30s, have given statutory recognition to underlying differences in relative local capacities to raise funds. The case for equalization provisions in grants-in-aid to governments in metropolitan areas is strong. Given the wide diversity in fiscal capacity among these local governments, more nearly uniform minimum program levels can best be obtained through equalizing grant provisions. Both the Hoover Commission and the Kestnbaum Commission studies concluded that equalization provisions should be incorporated in grant programs.

Professors Cohen and Grodzins, as part of a larger study documenting the essential consistency that marks the economic impacts of federal and state-local governments concluded that, while federal taxes were found to have a greater redistribution effect than state-local taxes, the state-local tax system, despite its dependence on the property tax, had an equalizing effect of its own. On the other hand, state-local expenditures had a greater redistribution effect than federal expenditures. "Considering taxes and benefits together, both levels of government redistribute income in the direction of greater equality, the federal government more so than the state-local governments. . . . Equalization of income is assumed to be a desirable fiscal policy. Sharing passes the [consistency] test because both governments together transfer income from higher to lower income groups."[15]

Federal and state equalization among the many local governments in any given metropolitan area takes three basic forms: (1) use of allocation and matching formulas in grants; (2) use of a progressive system of tax collection; and (3) the program purposes to which the tax funds are put.

Intergovernmental Fiscal Aid

Most federal grant programs and some state programs have two distinct but related provisions which determine how much each state or local government will get. First is the so-called allocation or apportionment formula which relates to the manner in which the federal appropriation is apportioned among the state and local recipient governments. The typical newer federal grant program takes into account program need as measured by the total population or by some other index, such as incidence of disease, plus an index of financial need, to assure that poorer jurisdictions will get more funds. State grants for education tend to be inversely related to property value and directly related to number of students or population of school age. Welfare aid is related to the number of welfare eligibles.

The other provision pertains to the matching funds required to be raised by state and local governments as their share of aided program costs. The federal government has generally adopted personal income in each state as an index of relative matching capacity. States have tended to rely on the equalized value of taxable property for their index of capacity.

There has been a discernible trend in recent years for the federal government to pay a larger part of total project costs, e.g., the 90-10 highway program (half the funds are spent in metropolitan areas) and urban renewal, or a larger share of the cost of minimum payments, as in public assistance. Project and demonstration grants also have a greater equalizing effect in that they tend to be directed to communities and individuals in the greatest need. These approaches minimize the importance of the matching provisions. Some states where general assistance is locally financed have emergency state aid programs for areas in greatest need. Certain new federal programs, such as the Economic Opportunity Act, and the Education, Appalachia, and Economic Development Programs go primarily to the poorest jurisdictions for support of a range of local programs.

Preliminary findings in a Brookings-supported study of intergovernmental systems and fiscal patterns in metropolitan areas being conducted by Alan Campbell and Seymour Sacks, add to our understanding of the complex world of state-local fiscal and functional relationships. State aid, and likewise federal aid, is found on the whole to be additive to local tax efforts. In metropolitan portions of states, however, state aid today is only two-thirds as high as it is in non-metropolitan communities. The nature of the state aid pattern, of course, varies considerably by state, depending on pattern of political power in state legislatures.

With more than half the states now having completed reapportionment on the basis of population, and the rest in process of following suit, additional aid can be anticipated, especially for the currently under-represented suburban areas. As suburban jurisdictions ringing central cities grow older, it will be hard, both politically and administratively, to separate suburban from city interests. The end result is likely to be a redirection of the present rural orientation of State aids into metropolitan areas.

Tax, Tax, Tax

Equalization in financing of local government services is also achieved through federal and state tax systems. The use of federal and state personal and corporate income taxes to finance grants-in-aid produces considerable equalization through application of uniform and progressive national and state tax rates. The federal and state governments collect the great bulk of all taxes in the United States today—83 percent (65 percent—federal, and 18 percent—state); 17 percent is collected by local governments. In 1963, federal and state tax revenues represented 23 percent of national income, while local tax revenues totaled only 4.6 percent.[16] This is all the more significant with respect to the ability of governments to raise revenues and raise them equitably, when it is realized that local governments rely almost exclusively on the property tax which is not so carefully geared either to ability to pay taxes or to benefits derived from governmental programs. The long-range trend in governmental finance has been toward a sustained growth in the size of state payments to local governments, with a consequent property tax relief and additions to state taxes.[17]

At the interstate metropolitan area level, Robert Dixon[18] has advocated creation of federal-interstate agencies to meet mass transit, air pollution, land use planning, and water resources needs. To break the pattern of limited use of the interstate compact as "low level devices for low level patterns," he advocates a levy of special taxes within the interstate metropolitan level for use solely within the region. Professor Dixon argues that the Constitution's uniformity clause applies only to general federal tax levies which must be used to support federal activities throughout the United States, and is no constitutional barrier to a federal area tax to support area projects.

The notable current issue in federal-state-local fiscal relations is the Heller plan to turn over almost unconditionally to the states about $2.5 billion in federal tax revenues each year. National expenditures have increased in the last decade by some 25 percent, while state and local expenditures expanded approximately five times as fast. At the same time, a growing economy is bringing in increased billions each year in federal revenues.

The nation's governors asked that the President give it fresh consideration. Many mayors, and organized labor in general, are against the plan because they fear little money channeled through states would get to the cities. A politically acceptable approach has not yet been worked out, but would likely involve an increase in the equalization effects, through apportionment formulas or "earmarked" grants to meet specific urban needs, or both.

Spend, Spend, Spend

The purposes to which grant funds are put probably have the greatest equalizing effect of all. Increasing federal and state aids for such programs as economic opportunity, depressed areas assistance, urban renewal, low and moderate income housing, medicare, mass transit, water supply, sewage disposal and sanitation, and education all indicate a shift of federal and state interest from rural to urban concerns, and to human as well as physical needs.

The latest *Catalog of Federal Aids to State and Local Governments*[19] identified 115 programs of national aid containing 216 separate authorizations. Some 17 major new grant programs were initiated in the 88th Congress. Both the number of grants and dollar amounts involved were exceeded in the first session of the 89th Congress by the enactment of 17 major new grant programs and the expansion of a number of others, led by one and a half billion dollar enactments for elementary and secondary schools which the President described as "the most significant step of this century to provide widespread help to all of America's school children." Other new grants dealing even more specifically with metropolitan-wide problems include the Public Works and Economic Development Act, grants for basic water and sewer facilities, grants for advance acquisition for land, river basin planning, land development insurance, the Water Quality Act, solid waste disposal, highway beautification, and even a grant (89-344) for "reimbursement to States and localities for sidewalk repair."

No one of the equalization arrangements in federal and state aid, allocation and matching formulas, use of progressive tax systems, program purposes achieves great equalization. The cumulative effect, however, is substantial.

Local Government Responsibility

The decentralized character of American political party organization and the district system of election for the U.S. House, and for many state legislatures assure both protection against federal and state domination and solicitous concern for the fate of local jurisdictions.

The main ingredient in the marble cake of American federalism is the grant-in-aid which acknowledges the superior ability of local governments to minister to the service needs of their residents. Federal and state aids and local "home rule" provisions in state constitutions and statutes rest upon an acceptance of city and county responsibility for the whole range of urban services. Although grants are available to special districts as well as to general purpose jurisdictions, the great bulk of local expenditures are made by the general governments. Of all direct local government expenditures in

1964, municipalities account for 33 percent, counties 20 percent, townships 4 percent, school districts 38 percent, and all special districts only 5 percent.[20]

Even for federal grants administered on a regional basis, federal agency guides and requirements have emphasized the importance of adequate representation of and consultation with local officials. Two recent examples, in addition to the Highway and Water and Sewer Facilities grant requirements referred to above should be cited. The Department of Housing and Urban Development, in awarding "701" metropolitan planning assistance grants, must be satisfied that all parts of the region are adequately represented on the planning body. The planning agency must establish a "check point" procedure for review of recommendations on preliminary drafts of planning proposals by the chief executive and legislative body of the localities in the planning area and by other affected local, state, and federal agencies. In addition, working with councils made up of elected officials in the metropolitan area is recommended as desirable practice. This has been facilitated by new authority under the Housing and Urban Development Act of 1965 (89-117) for the Secretary to make available two-thirds matching grants to support the activities of such councils, including studies of common legal, governmental, and administrative problems in the area. The Economic Development Act requires the Secretary of Commerce, before making grants to an economic development district, to give local general government officials "a reasonable opportunity to review and comment upon proposed projects." The Secretary is also directed to "encourage participation by appropriate local governmental authorities in" the designation of such districts.

Many federal programs, including urban renewal and public housing, require creation of citizens' advisory groups to insure participation by local residents. The new Economic Opportunity program has gone so far in requiring participation by the poor in the development and administration of programs that many mayors complain that their responsibility as elected officials is being undermined.

Toward a Strategy for Metropolitan Areas

The foregoing has been a review of federal and state efforts in recent years to adapt policies and programs into what Henry Hart has called: "a more discriminating form of cooperative federalism"[21] to meet the needs of government in metropolitan areas. What is in order now is to develop and pursue a more consistent federal and state strategy to achieve the objectives of geographic adequacy, economies of scale, adequate and equitable financing, and strengthened responsibility and accountability of local general governments in metropolitan areas.

National and state activities should occur in the form of a comprehensive reform effort, and as individual opportunities present themselves. A reform effort for metropolitan areas should include a number of basic policies:

> Comprehensive and functional planning requirements should be applied in all federal and state aid programs significantly affecting urban development, and incentives provided for joint participation by local governments in programs lending themselves to areawide administration.
>
> The states should give local governments in metropolitan areas tools to control the use of special districts, including: requiring approval by the local general government of land acquisition by special districts; making local approval a condition precedent to the creation of special districts; setting various standards for local governments; and providing for their dissolution if the governments in the area are willing to take over responsibility for the special district function.
>
> The states should establish strict statutory standards for new incorporations within metropolitan areas. States should also review financial aid arrangements, to eliminate provisions which encourage local government proliferation or subsidize otherwise unviable local governments.
>
> More determined use should be made of state regulatory powers and performance standards in such fields as urban water supply and sewage treatment to ensure orderly and economic urban fringe development consistent with comprehensive land use goals.
>
> Federal formula grant programs to state and local governments should take into account relative disparities in fiscal capacities and needs among local governments in metropolitan areas, and should aim at a reasonably uniform level of program performance throughout the country.
>
> States should revise their grant distribution formulas to equalize local property tax loads among local jurisdictions in metropolitan areas, and should finance at least half of the cost of programs which meet needs least likely to be directly related to the availability of public resources, such as general public welfare assistance and special programs of public education. States should also pay part of the non-federal share of such essentially federal-local programs as urban planning, urban renewal, low income housing, airport development, hospitals, sewage treatment and public water and sewer facilities, mass transit, and regional planning.
>
> Because of the crucial role in state-local fiscal relations played by education, each state should make a critical review of its present school grant formula to insure that it provides for a minimum educational level below which no community falls, and that it contains factors designed to measure as accurately as possible local tax effort and diverse community

educational requirements (e.g., taking into account higher per pupil costs in urban slum areas).

State enabling legislation for establishing metropolitan planning agencies should be reviewed to insure a dominant role for the elected officials of the area, including assurance of adequate representation of central cities in such bodies. State legislation should authorize creation of councils of elected officials with responsibility for administering the metropolitan planning program, including the federally required continuing comprehensive transportation process.

Finally, the general purpose governments of the nation—cities, counties, and, in New England, towns—should be granted priority in the receipt of federal and state grants for urban development or assistance, with special districts eligible only when local governments, singly or jointly, cannot or will not do the job.

It may be argued that the strategies proposed here will perpetuate, by patching up, the present system of overlapping and fragmentation. It can equally be argued that performance requirements in federal and state aids, incentives to joint action, greater equalization in financial arrangements, and strengthening of general government responsibilities, can (through precedent and penalties for autonomy) work toward reducing barriers to more general governmental reorganization.

The strategy outlined is only half the battle for furthering the objectives stated above. The other half includes the whole range of horizontal interlocal devices, from liberalized annexation to review of local zoning, to Dade County type federation and to Nashville-Davidson County consolidation. Many of the proposals made, however, would have relevance even if areawide governments were established throughout the United States.

The specifics of how to adapt existing programs along the lines recommended are well known. Precedents have been established in individual federal programs, by individual states, and by local governments in metropolitan areas. Extensive hearings have been held on major aspects of this subject; e.g., comprehensive local and metropolitan planning requirements; favoring the eligibility for federal aids of units of general local government —cities, towns, and counties—in contrast to special purpose districts and authorities; requiring advance notice on acquisition, change of use, and disposition of land. Model state bills are available.[22] New proposals are being made for the development of common areawide planning requirements to be used by all federal agencies in a metropolitan area and for greater consistency in regional office boundaries. At least seven states have now created State Offices of Local Affairs concerned with proposed and existing legislation affecting the structure and financing of local governments, coordinating state activities in urban areas, and encouraging joint action among local governments in solving common problems.

A crucial federal role is increasingly being played—and has promise of being played even more effectively—as programs are focused on problem parts of the metropolitan area and as fiscal policies recognize the changing demands on state and local tax systems. Spurred by increasing urbanization, rapid reapportionment, the competition and stimulus of federal activities, and better understanding of how to deal with urban problems, states are likely to play a more and more significant role of oversight and assistance to their urban areas. The most dynamic governors today are those—both Republicans and Democrats—who are leading the fight in their states for urban oriented programs to meet broad metropolitan area problems, serving not only Democratic central cities but Republican suburbs as well.

The prospects look better than ever for treating federal and state activities as part of a unity in achieving commonly accepted objectives for government in metropolitan areas. This will involve a major role in metropolitan areas for federal and state governments—a role that is likely to be good politics, and good administration, for a long time to come.

Notes

1. Thomas H. Reed, "Hope for Suburbanitis," *National Civic Review,* December 1950, p. 542.
2. See Roscoe C. Martin, *Metropolis in Transition: Local Government Adaptation to Changing Urban Needs* (Housing and Home Finance Agency, Washington, D.C., September 1963) for a series of contemporary case studies, and Advisory Commission on Intergovernmental Relations, *Alternative Approaches to Governmental Reorganization in Metropolitan Areas* (Washington, D.C.: Government Printing Office, June 1962) on the strengths and weaknesses of ten such reorganization approaches.
3. National Association of Counties, *Comprehensive Planning . . . Federal Assistance Programs* (Technical Advisory Report Number 2, Washington, D.C.). Lists some 20 different federal agencies' programs of assistance for comprehensive planning, basic data collection, and transportation and public facilities planning.
4. Advisory Commission on Intergovernmental Relations, *Impact of Federal Urban Development Programs on Local Government Organization and Planning* (Washington, D.C.: Government Printing Office, 1964), p. 16.
5. E. H. Holmes, "Progress and Events Since the First National Conference on Highways and Urban Development." Remarks at the Second National Conference on Highways and Urban Development, Williamsburg, Virginia, December 12-16, 1965, p. 5.
6. Department of Housing and Urban Development, *Water and Sewer Facilities Planning Requirements: A Program Guide* (Washington, D.C., November 29, 1965), p. i.
7. National League of Cities, *National Municipal Policy* (Washington, D.C., 1965), pp. 71-72.

8. See Harvey E. Brazer, *City Expenditures in the United States* (New York: National Bureau of Economic Research, Inc., 1959); Advisory Commission on Intergovernmental Relations, *Performance of Urban Functions: Local and Areawide* (Washington, D.C.: Government Printing Office, 1963); and Werner Hirsch in *Public Expenditure Decisions in the Urban Community* (Washington, D.C.: Resources for the Future, Inc., 1963).
9. Advisory Commission on Intergovernmental Relations, *Impact of Federal Urban Development Programs on Local Government Organization and Planning* (Washington, D.C.: Government Printing Office, 1964), p. 18.
10. U.S. Congress, Senate Committee on Government Operations, Subcommittee on Intergovernmental Relations, *The Federal System as Seen by Federal Aid Officials,* 89th Cong., 1st Sess., p. 84.
11. *California Government Code,* Section 54786.
12. John C. Bollens and Henry J. Schmandt, *The Metropolis: Its People, Politics, and Economic Life* (New York: Harper and Row, 1965), p. 340.
13. Alan K. Campbell, "National-State-Local Systems of Government and Intergovernmental Aid," *The Annals,* May 1965, p. 95.
14. *Ibid.,* p. 103.
15. Jacob Cohen and Morton Grodzins, "How Much Economic Sharing in American Federalism?" *The American Political Science Review,* March 1963, p. 19.
16. Campbell, *op. cit.,* p. 99.
17. Federation of Tax Administrators, *Tax Administrators News,* Vol. 29, No. 4, April 1965, p. 1.
18. Robert G. Dixon, Jr., "Constitutional Bases for Regionalism: Centralization; Interstate Compacts; Federal Regional Taxation," *The George Washington Law Review,* October 1964, pp. 47-88.
19. U.S. Senate, Subcommittee on Intergovernmental Relations of the Committee on Government Operations, *Catalog of Federal Aids to State and Local Governments* [Supplement, January 1965] (Washington, D.C.: Government Printing Office, 1965).
20. U.S. Bureau of the Census, *Governmental Finances in 1963-64* (Washington, D.C.: Government Printing Office, 1965).
21. Henry C. Hart, "The Dawn of a Community-Defining Federalism," *The Annals,* May 1965, p. 149.
22. See Hearings before the Subcommittee on Intergovernmental Relations, Committee on Government Operations, United States Senate, on S. 561, "The Proposed Intergovernmental Cooperation Act of 1965," 89th Congress, first session, and recent annual issues of *Suggested State Legislation,* Committee of State Officials on Suggested State Legislation, The Council of State Governments.

1966 (26:96-106)

JOAN B. ARON

Regional Governance for the New York Metropolitan Region: A Reappraisal

For the past decade or so, it has been customary for urban scholars and researchers in the New York metropolitan region (and elsewhere) to explore the performance of functions in the metropolitan area, find them lacking in almost all particulars, make a diagnosis of political fragmentation, and recommend some form of institutional change. Instances of fragmented decision making and proliferation of public and private bodies can be cited for every functional field.[1] The usual prescription is to call for some variant of regional mechanism—generally multipurpose in nature, areawide in jurisdiction, and representative in character. Such an entity, it is suggested, might then be given the power to initiate and implement policies to guide and manage regional development.

Within the past year, however, the usual emphases appear to have been overlooked or, at a minimum, temporarily shelved. With the issuance of reports on regionalism by the New York State-created Scott Commission, and its counterpart, the New York City-sponsored vanden Heuvel Commission, we have an opportunity to review the latest proposals for the provision of regional services in the New York metropolitan area.[2] On the one hand, the Scott Commission proposes the creation of "multiple functional regions"—based upon a service district for each urban function, a notion that is reminiscent in intent to the concern for "administrative efficiency" that dominated much of the thinking of the earlier theorists in public administration. On the other hand, the vanden Heuvel report demonstrates an unmistakable tendency to deemphasize proposals for institutional change in favor of policy changes which can be implemented at present by existing levels of government. While the two reports differ significantly in almost every possible respect, including length, depth of analysis, and policy prescriptions, they do possess this one curious element in common: Neither opts for the creation of a single regional government—in sharp contrast to the traditional remedies which have long governed our assumptions concerning regional needs.

If this reading of the recommendations of the reports is accurate, it would tend to indicate that at least two prestigious commissions in the New York area have come around full circle to a willingness (at least for the time being) to accept current institutional mechanisms as givens in the region's political environment. Questions can then be raised: Why, for example, is there this new shift in emphasis from radical institutional change? Why is a new interest in policy displacing the traditional preoccupation? And what is the significance of this change for solving metropolitan problems? To try to answer these questions, one must review some of the more significant proposals for institutional change in the New York region in recent years as well as the responses from local, state, and federal levels of government.

The publication of the ten-volume Harvard survey of physical, social, economic, and political developments in the tri-state region is one of the high water marks of scholarly investigation of the New York region. Among the volumes, Robert C. Wood's *1400 Governments,* published in 1961, still stands as an accurate description of the region's political economy and can serve as the starting point of our review of recent history. In this work, Wood is quite specific about his notion of desirable regional objectives, namely:

> . . . the establishment of a governmental structure which possessed the jurisdiction and the authority to make decisions about alternative forms of Regional development, more or less consciously and more or less comprehensively . . . there would be some type of regional organization empowered to set aside land for recreational purposes on the basis of a Regional plan. . . . There would be some type of regional organization empowered to subsidize commuter transportation, if this were in accord with a general plan. And . . . the organization should probably be responsible to a Regional electorate and draw revenue from a common revenue pool.[3]

In outlining the major features of a government sufficient to redirect the pattern of economic development in the region, Wood (like the Scott Commission ten years later) was undoubtedly influenced by the early works of James W. Fesler, Arthur Maass, and others concerning the determination of the proper governmental level for the performance of public functions. Wood, himself, was a contributor to the Maass work, joining in the effort to highlight the importance of political integration, or the "power to govern generally" in addition to the administrative and economic criteria that had been the controlling concepts up to that time.[4]

At or about the same time, a number of regional spokesmen were making similar suggestions concerning the establishment of new governmental mechanisms for the New York region. During the 1950s, for example, Luther Gulick, the Citizens Budget Commission, the Regional Plan Association (RPA), and Mayor Robert Wagner had all publicly proposed the creation of a coordinating regional mechanism to bring together all strands of governmental action.[5] And Wallace Sayre, who was then completing his own massive survey of the political system of New York City, headed a committee on metropolitan governmental affairs for RPA which found that "a leadership institution . . . [was] indispensable to the growth, prosperity and well being of the New York metropolitan region."[6]

During the 1960s and early 1970s, proposals for metropolitan reorganization that would be appropriate to the New York region continued to be made. These covered a broad range of recommendations from minor structural changes such as councils of governments to the use of regional planning commissions with strong coordinating powers (like Twin Cities), and the creation of multipurpose service districts and even "metropolitan states."[7] One of the better known, prepared by the Committee for Economic Development, *Reshaping Governments in Metropolitan Areas* (1970), called for a "two tier" governmental system for metropolitan areas, in which the responsibility for providing urban services was shared between a metropolitan level and a community level, based upon the federation model of the Municipality of Metropolitan Toronto. For large metropolitan areas (of which New York must be considered a prime example), it was suggested that city boundaries be extended to include the entire metropolitan area, and community districts created therein to safeguard local needs.

The "federation" concept was applied to the New York region in late 1971 when City Planning Commissioner Martin Gallent called for the creation of a "Regional Federation" to exercise governmental and fund-raising powers presently given to existing authorities. It received further attention when Alan K. Campbell, project director of the CED study, presented fiscal and non-fiscal data to reinforce his proposals for centralization and decentralization of New York City. At or about the same time, Mayor Lindsay proposed his notion of "National Cities" through which the cities might bypass the states and deal directly with the federal government on matters of "trade, finance and social welfare."[8]

"Regional Government" by Local, State, and Federal Action

In the light of these continuing proposals for mechanisms of New York regional governance, what has been the response of the many levels of government operative in the region?

During the 1950s the region's local governments were the major participants in the effort to create a tri-state regional governing mechanism. In 1956, under the aegis of Mayor Wagner of New York City, the chief elected officials of local communities in the region formed a voluntary association, the Metropolitan Regional Council (MRC), to develop solutions to common regional problems. (It was the MRC to which Wallace Sayre had referred when he spoke of the region's need for a "leadership institution.") By the late 1950s MRC decided it would be more effective as a regional policy-developing body if it could gain legal recognition of its efforts as an interlocal advisory board devoted to "association, consultation and study." MRC was successful in securing legal status from the three states; its fortunes took a sharp plunge downward when it was unable to secure ratification of the interlocal agreement from some of the more important suburban communities in the region. Despite a commitment to regional cooperation by many of the local chief executives, parochial legislative bodies and insular community groups were unwilling to join in a regional effort which might lead to diminution of local autonomy. By 1965, another regional agency, the Tri-State Transportation Commission, had already emerged as the official regional planning agency, and MRC could no longer attain an unrivalled position of regional leadership.

In the 1960s the initiatives for supporting regional approaches in the New York region shifted from the localities to the states and federal government. Because of federal requirements for comprehensive planning in different functional fields, particularly in federally aided highway programs, the three states in the region created the Tri-State Transportation Commission in 1965 by interstate compact to perform comprehensive planning in transportation and related land use problems. Since its inception, Tri-State has been an advisory body only—with no operational responsibilities. Although it now serves as the regional review body for local applications for federal aid in many functional fields, it lacks power to enforce its recommendations and its jurisdiction is limited to regional development projects which use federal funds. Tri-State's planning responsibilities were expanded in 1971 and its name was changed to the Tri-State Regional Planning Commission, but its coordinating powers remained unchanged.

In addition to Tri-State, the three states have, individually, created their own mechanisms for policy formation and regional development. New York has been particularly active in responding to specialized urban pressures, making use of public authorities to handle a variety of functional problems in the New York metropolitan region. The 12-county Metropolitan Transportation Authority and the statewide Urban Development Corporation are two instances of New York's public authorities which have been developing regional programs in the transportation and housing fields. Like the Port Authority of New York and New Jersey, each has developed into a strong, single-purpose government in its own right. The creation of the Hackensack Meadowlands Development Commission by New Jersey to oversee the development of the largest remaining tract of undeveloped land in the region is another example of state-initiated metropolitan action.

Despite these individual state efforts, not one of the three states has shown any inclination for establishing the single, general-purpose structure for the New York region advocated by the political reformers. In fact, New York's path to regional action has been characterized by John Bebout, a prominent urban scholar, as "a rudimentary, regrettably unintegrated, ad hoc system of regional governance, for limited purposes."[9]

A metropolitan form of government inspired by federal action seems equally remote at present. On the one hand, the federally supported regional bodies, MRC and Tri-State, lack power to guide regional development. In addition, the federal government fails to make use of its regional bodies in the New York area for programs other than "metropolitan" and transportation planning. Although a large number of federal programs require regional approaches, such as economic development, community action, comprehensive health planning, law enforcement planning, water pollution control, air quality control, and manpower area planning, federal agencies deal with a variety of non-regional bodies to channel their funds and implement their programs. Federal revenue sharing is the latest program to bypass the regional entities in favor of a direct allocation of funds to the states and localities.

1970s—Is Regional Government the Answer?

At present, then, the New York region has made little progress toward securing general-purpose regional machinery to formulate regional policy and manage regional development. The region's pronounced tendency toward maintenance of the institutional status quo, coupled with the extreme difficulty of securing political support for structural innovation, may furnish a partial explanation for the alternative proposals suggested by the city and state study commissions.

Another, more significant, explanation may lie in the uncertainty of meaningful improvements in the quality of urban life once reorganization is achieved. Recent research indicates that the outcome of metropolitan reorganizational efforts may not be commensurate with expectations of metropolitan reformers. The findings show that the alternative metropolitan systems have not yet achieved the economic improvements that were sought or yielded the material benefits that were desired.[10]

It has been found, for example, that metropolitan reorganization does not typically relieve tax pressures; nor does it create economies in the provision of public services. In those metropolitan areas where attempts were made to equalize services among disparate communities (as in Nashville-Davidson County, Tennessee, and Toronto, Canada), the service level generally rose to that of the community with the highest level of service in question—thus leading to a per capita increase in service costs. Frequently, as in Nashville Metro, metropolitan reorganization has generated a sense of rising expectations among the residents of the metropolitan community for additional services. Increased service demands have led to increased levels of public spending which have eliminated, in turn, the hoped-for economies.

Recent findings also indicate that metropolitan reform does not per se guarantee a reduction of service and fiscal disparities among the different communities in a metropolitan area. In some "reformed" metropolitan areas, because of the creation of different service zones, existing patterns of service inequality have remained unchanged.

Experience discloses, too, that metropolitan reorganization does not necessarily lead to a redistribution of existing financial resources among the component parts of a metropolitan community. Instead of providing for a more equitable sharing of resources that are raised locally, a redistribution from wealthy to needy communities appears more likely to occur when resources originate *outside* the metropolitan system—that is, when resources for redistributive programs are supplied by state or federal levels of government.[11]

Finally, metropolitan reform has not led to a change in the level of citizen interest or satisfaction with governmental institutions or political machinery. While data for the measurement of citizen interest in the quality of urban life prior to—and following—reform efforts are sparse, a Nashville survey indicates that citizen satisfaction with the performance of urban functions following reorganization did not change markedly. The evidence also shows that citizen participation in reformed governments is very limited. In both Miami and Toronto, voter participation in metropolitan politics declined, when compared with voter registration and turnout in pre-reform elections.

These somewhat unexpected findings suggest that the metropolitan nostrums which have been proposed with such startling regularity in the past may not, in fact, be the most desirable way of coping with New York's problems. Neither the region's central cities nor its most needy groups—the minorities and the poor—would be certain to benefit. The findings also suggest that the creation of metropolitan government need no longer be viewed as the first priority of regional business. As the vanden Heuvel report has pointed out, basic changes in substantive policy and intergovernmental fiscal relationships can be made right now if existing governments wish to move ahead. The experience of reformed governments elsewhere confirms this judgment; to wait for institutional change might cause unnecessary delays and, in the long run, might not even be worth the effort.[12]

Notes

1. A recent study of the management of water resources in the region, for example, finds that water is supplied by a patchwork of more than 400 independently

managed and partly connected water agencies. Because of the lack of an integrated system, some areas experience shortages at the same time that water is locked in elsewhere. See Michael R. Greenberg, et al., "A Geographical Systems Analysis of the Water Supply Networks of the NYMR," *Geographical Review* (July 1971), pp. 340-347. RPA, *Waste Management,* 1968, and Tri-State Regional Planning Commission, *Managing the Natural Environment,* 1970, offer further examples of fragmented regional services.

2. State Study Commission for New York City, Task Force on Jurisdiction and Structure, *Concept of Multiple Functional Regions in the Tri-State Metropolitan Region,* September 1972, and New York City Commission on State-City Relations, *The New York Metropolitan Region: Problems of Growth—Proposals for Change,* December 1972.
3. Robert C. Wood, *1400 Governments: The Political Economy of the New York Metropolitan Region* (Cambridge: Harvard University Press, 1961), p. 192.
4. James W. Fesler, *Area and Administration* (University, Ala.: University of Alabama Press, 1949), and Robert C. Wood, "A Division of Powers in Metropolitan Areas," in Arthur Maass (ed.), *Area and Power: A Theory of Local Government* (New York: Free Press, 1969).
5. Luther H. Gulick, "The Next Twenty-Five Years in Government in the New York Metropolitan Region," address to the 25th Anniversary meeting of RPA, October 6, 1954; Harold Riegelman, counsel to the Citizens Budget Commission, address proposing a metropolitan council of municipalities, January 12, 1955; RPA *News,* No. 48 (1955) and No. 49 (1956); and Robert H. Wagner, "Problems of the Metropolitan Area," address to the American Municipal Association, Miami, Florida, November 18, 1955.
6. *New York Times,* January 9, 1959, p. 16. See also Wallace S. Sayre and Herbert Kaufman, *Governing New York City: Politics in the Metropolis* (New York: Russell Sage Foundation, 1960), p. 596.
7. For an early discussion of different forms of metropolitan reorganization, see Roscoe C. Martin, *Metropolis in Transition: Local Government Adaptation to Changing Urban Needs* (Washington, D.C.: Housing and Home Finance Agency, 1963). For more recent examples, see Stanley Baldinger, *Planning and Governing the Metropolis: The Twin Cities Experience* (New York: Praeger, 1970); Joseph F. Zimmerman, "Direct State Action to Help Solve Metropolitan Problems," *State Government* (Winter 1971), pp. 37-41, and "Substate Regional Government: Designing a New Procedure," *National Civic Review,* Vol. 61 (June 1972), pp. 286-290; and Richard Burton, "On the Relevance of Governmental Reorganization to National Urban Growth Policy," The Urban Institute (Working Paper 750-90, July 1971).
8. Martin Gallent, "Regional Federation Essential for Area," *New York Times,* November 14, 1971, sec. 8, p. 1; Alan K. Campbell, Statement to the New York State Study Commission For New York City, February 2, 1972; and John V. Lindsay, "For New 'National Cities,' " *New York Times,* June 9, 1971, p. 43.
9. John E. Bebout, *Regional Planning Issues,* Part 1, Hearings before the Subcommittee on Urban Affairs of the Joint Economic Committee, 91st Congress, 2nd Session, 1970, p. 131.
10. See particularly Steven P. Erie, John J. Kirlin, and Francine F. Rabinowitz,

"Can Something Be Done? Propositions on the Performance of Metropolitan Institutions," in Lowdon Wingo (ed.), *Reform of Metropolitan Governments* (Washington, D.C.: Resources for the Future, 1972), pp. 7-43; and Melvin B. Mogulof, *Five Metropolitan Governments* (Washington, D.C.: The Urban Institute, 1972), *passim.*

11. Wingo, p. 33, and Mogulof, pp. 54-55, 106. Minnesota's fiscal disparities law, which provides for the sharing of 40 percent of the growth in commercial-industrial property tax base among the units of government in the Twin Cities metropolitan area, is clearly unusual in its redistributive aspects.
12. For further discussion of this point of view, see Vincent Ostrom, Charles Tiebout, and Robert Warren, "The Organization of Government in Metropolitan Areas: A Theoretical Inquiry," *American Political Science Review,* Vol. LV (December 1961), pp. 831-842, and Robert Warren, *Government in Metropolitan Regions: A Reappraisal of Fractionated Political Organizations* (Davis, Calif.: University of California, Davis, Institute of Governmental Affairs, 1966).

1974 (34:260-264)

ROBERT C. WOOD

Federal Role in the Urban Environment

Urban areas, particularly inner cities, have in the '60s been undergoing what many have termed a domestic revolution of rising expectations. Whether we meet these expectations is dependent on our capability to:

- reverse patterns of decay, reinforced by almost a century of neglect
- meet the demands of unprecedented growth.

I need not belabor statistical support for this thesis. Urban decay and growth are well documented—125 million urban Americans in 1967, 280 million by the year 2000; 20 million poor presently trapped in slum areas living in substandard, dilapidated housing.

To begin reversing patterns of decay while meeting new growth we must answer the basic policy questions:

How do we provide a decent living environment—housing, schools, public facilities, recreational areas—for these 20 million Americans presently living in slum areas? How do we overcome generations of inability to feel a sense of belonging to a community? How do we offer free accessibility to decent housing in all parts of the urban areas? How do we build housing in sufficient volume to meet our national goal of "a decent house for every American family"?

Simultaneously, we must face the question of how we deal with growth. How do we distribute over 100 million new urban Americans who will be deposited across the country by the year 2000? How much do we add on to the old metropolitan cities now growing at three times the average rate of the nation? How many will spill out into the larger suburbs to form the linear cities from the East and West Coasts, and from St. Louis up to Chicago? How many will find opportunity and hope in existing communities of 100,000 or 200,000 or 50,000? How many will really find new homes, new jobs, new activities in the heartland of America—the 16 states that grow at the rate of one-quarter as fast as the national average? How many can expect realistically to be in new communities?

The national government has begun to address itself to these questions, and our responses are now taking shape. I suggest that our ability to begin shaping responses has been greatly aided by a cabinet-level department concerned with Housing and Urban Development.

My propositions are threefold:

- Departmental status has under the pressure of events evolved rapidly into an instrument for focusing national attention on urban problems;
- Departmental status has provided a mechanism for bringing internal and external cohesiveness—private and public, federal, state, and local—to urban problems;
- Departmental status has allowed us to strengthen the legislative tools that we might begin fashioning a national urban strategy.

The Fight for Cabinet Status

Reflecting back to the late 1930s and through the 1950s, one can identify mounting pressures for federal urban representation.

First came the President's Committee on Administrative Management with studies and recommendations that led to the Federal Works Agency, the Federal Security Agency, and the Federal Loan Agency. Then the National Housing Agency was designed to meet the more urgent needs for war housing and community facilities—bringing together parts of programs formerly administered in Federal Works and Federal Loans, from Interior and elsewhere. Changes came again when the National Housing Agency was converted into the Housing and Home Finance Agency. As urban areas grew at unprecedented rates and problems multiplied, the logical step forward was cabinet status.

However, not until the late 1950s and early 1960s was a Department of Urban Affairs seriously debated. The debates took on new tones of seriousness with the:

- endorsement of a department in the 1960 Democratic platform;
- awakening of academic interest to the problems of our urban areas;
- growing commentary of public officials; and
- an administration proposal to create a department in 1961.

And with this increasing concern opponents and proponents stepped forward and began publicly stating their positions.

Opponents drove home the incompatibility of a department to that part of established administrative doctrine focusing on abstract organizational criteria when they wrote:

> To admit it would be to introduce a maverick into the administrative corral. The work of such a department, if all the programs carried on by the federal government affecting cities were placed under its jurisdiction, would necessarily cut across the functions of a great many agencies and departments.[1]

And more important, they questioned whether the chief executive was strengthened[2] by bringing together a number of agencies before a president could grasp any firm notion of what he wished the new assembly of programs to do. In such a situation, they argued that the President stood in danger of losing initiative in executive direction and that the burdens of the presidency would be increased, not reduced.

Thus, they offered a counter proposal to form a new staff agency concerned with gathering facts on which the president and his department and line department to administer urban programs. This agency would be concerned with gathering facts on which the president and his department and agency chiefs might form an appropriate policy.

Pro-department forces did not answer these allegations—their arguments were not directed at administrative tidiness of a department. On this level the opponents would have won hands down.[3] Nor did they argue for consolidation of every possible urban program into a single department.

Instead, they rallied around the simple concept of a spokesman for urbanites. Typical was Senator Joseph Clark's desire for a "voice at the summit" where national policy was made:

> We need a vital center of thought and action—an executive and a staff with a broad responsibility for studying the problems of metropolitan areas and for thinking creatively about the role of the Federal Government, in the solutions. . . . An agency which daily administers planning grants, urban renewal and slum clearance, public housing, and community facility loans can best nourish the creative thinking that is the missing ingredient.[4]

Thus, "representativeness" was the goal of proponents—"representativeness" in the sense of being able to disagree with the chief executive or to influence him in terms other than logical arguments, not in terms of a "consultive" or "advisory" capacity. And only a cabinet member possessed the necessary set of bargaining advantages peculiarly adapted to this task.

So, in the final analysis, neither administrative precision nor tidiness in organizational arrangements, but political power became the kernel of the proponents' position.

Placing in perspective the political predicament of urbanists in the 1960s, their desire for political leverage becomes obvious. In short, every citadel of political power and influence—the myths of our national political folklore, the attitudes of the voters, the self-interests of the politicians, the legalism of the courts, the parochialism of the legislatures—had proven antagonistic. Thus, the urbanists' appeal to Washington was a strategy of last resort.

Organizing for Urban Representation

Finally after five years of academic and political debate, of congressional trial, and of gradual public awakening to urban problems came the passage of the 1965 Act, which President Johnson termed "the single most important breakthrough in the past 40 years." This Act provided for the creation of a new cabinet-level Department of Housing and Urban Development.[5]

Technically, the Housing and Home Finance Agency was elevated to cabinet status. But more was required than a *pro forma* merger of related functions and programs under a newly created cabinet member. This Act:

- chartered a broad operating role for the Department and the Secretary in relation to other federal agencies and other levels of government.
- vested in the Secretary full powers to integrate and administer expanded programs and activities of the Department.
- allowed the Secretary a great deal of discretion in organizing the Department.[6]

First on the agenda was converting HHFA into a department. Already HHFA was faltering under increasing burdens of complex programs and activities with financial involvement reaching the $7.3 billion mark. Housing programs had multiplied and diversified—including a college housing loan program, supervision of the FNMA, loans for prefabricated housing, mortgage insurance programs for housing in urban renewal areas, housing for the elderly and the handicapped.

Also included in the HHFA urban portfolio in 1965 were several urban planning programs—grants for sewers, schools, and hospitals, loans and grants for community facilities, grants for open space land, loans and grants to assist mass transportation and urban beautification.

The task, however, was greater than a mere regrouping of existing programs. In President Johnson's words:

> In the next 35 years, we must literally build a second America—putting in place as many houses, schools, apartments, parks and offices as we have built through all the time since the Pilgrims arrived on these shores.[7]

He continued that although physical challenges were awesome, challenges to the spirit were even greater and more demanding:

> It is not enough for us to erect towers of stone and glass, or to lay out vast suburbs of order and conformity. We must seek, and we must find ways to preserve and to perpetuate in the city the individuality, the human dignity, the respect for individual rights, the devotion for individual responsibility that has been part of the American character and the strength of the American system.[8]

So the President's vision of the Department's mission was that our program be designed to rebuild our cities socially as well as physically. To accomplish this mission it was clear that we needed to begin administratively linking together the many urban aid programs and envisaging the city in terms of total urban development. First the activities and programs had to be oriented toward broad problem solving—regardless of historical distinctions or past organization separation. Second, traditional agencies and program tools had to be integrated to meet total objectives and to compel interrelated approaches.

Under the dictates of the departmental Act, the first grouping brought together those programs related to the private mortgage market.

A second grouping included those programs dealing essentially with central city problems—urban renewal, public housing, development of neighborhood centers, and provision of open space and beautification in dense central areas. Also included was relocating urban families.

The third program grouping was concerned with metropolitan areas and the urbanizing countryside. This included grants for preserving open space, for developing areawide water and sewer systems, for urban mass transportation, for advance land acquisition.

A fourth category brought together the Department's demonstration programs—model cities and the new developmental work in intergovernmental relations.

Departing from accepted standards in public administration, this organizational grouping did not allocate neat, self-contained program packages to top officials; or assign either a line role or a staff role to top officials.

But this organization was not based on an assumption that our programs should be neat, self-contained packages. It anticipated an inevitable overlap. This grouping was based simply on the theory that problems of the inner city were more closely related than those faced by the urbanizing fringe while taking into account the similarity of the problems faced by both areas.[9]

To effectively administer such separate yet related programs it was deemed desirable that assistant secretaries be concerned both with program execution and with Department-wide interrelationship.[10] Each was given a program area and at the same time made collectively responsible for serving as the general staff for the Secretary of the Department. They were expected to be not only advocates for their programs but to work jointly to achieve the Department's mission.

In addition to these program groupings, three steps were taken to assure a more effective Department:

- Consolidation of the Department's administrative functions under an assistant secretary for administration.
- Appointment of a deputy under secretary for policy analysis and program evaluation to compare programs, sharpen policy objectives, and review the extent to which the Department is carrying out its objectives.
- Designation of a Budget Review Committee to compare programs and make recommendation to the Secretary on the allocation of departmental resources.

HUD—Two Years Out

So, given a lengthy fight for Cabinet status and the considerable efforts devoted to organizing for an effective voice in national policy, it is fair to begin raising the question of accomplishments. What has the Department contributed to our capability to meet urban problems?

Three discernible trends merit comment. First, a cabinet department has provided an instrument through which we might begin developing an integrated and cohesive federal approach to urban programs. As mentioned, early proponents of a cabinet department never envisioned all federal programs touching on urban affairs being brought under the umbrella of HUD. Had that been the goal, we would have failed miserably in two years—water pollution is still under the auspices of Interior, air pollution under HEW, urban area airports divided between the new Department of Transportation and FAA, while the highway program is located in the Department of Transportation. Instead, our policy from the beginning was simply to follow the directions set forth in the 1965 legislation and the subsequent "Convenor Order."

The 1965 Act creating the Department stated that HUD shall "exercise leadership at the direction of the President in coordinating federal activities affecting housing and urban development. . . ."[11] Under the so-called "Convenor Order"[12] the Secretary is authorized to convene meetings of Departments and agencies having responsibilities related to urban problems. Neither the statute nor the Executive Order was intended to give HUD *carte blanche* to related government programs. They have been used to achieve coordination and greater cohesiveness among all federal agencies dealing with urban problems. The "Convenor Order" has allowed us to move from the constraints of standing "interdepartmental committees" into more flexible techniques of problem solving. Secretary Weaver can call together all departments concerned with a specific problem in informal working groups and task forces. After the job is completed, the committee disbands.

The second contribution of departmental status has been the opportunity to develop broader bases of support for urban programs. Traditional support groups, such as housing-related industries, have turned their concerns from relatively specific and technical interests to the entire range of urban development. Moreover, an entirely new company of actors have appeared on the urban scene: churchmen, educators, welfare groups, and labor and business organizations.

Voluntary and professional organizations are now actively involved as sponsors of our low-income housing projects. And, increasingly, private industries are committing their talents and resources to rebuilding our cities and producing a larger supply of low-income housing.[13] HUD has been working with numerous businessmen—from industry, finance, and manufacturing—in a mutual effort to provide new inputs into urban programs.

Finally, departmental status has allowed us to strengthen our legislative tools that we might begin fashioning, for the first time, a national urban strategy.

The basic philosophy of this strategy is quite simple. It says that the classic function of cities everywhere and for all times has been to give people options—to allow them to choose where they want to live, where they want to work and where they want to play.

This legislation proposes to move against the constraints, the inflexibilities, that in the last 20 years have hobbled these choices and robbed us of some of the opportunities.

The first link forged in this urban strategy is the 1966 model cities program, which proposes to make livable again entire neighborhoods in our older cities and to reclaim the opportunity for residential urban life.[14] Communities must be willing to meet performance standards and create a comprehensive plan—including programs for physical, economic, and social development.

The federal government responds by making available traditional types of aid to fit the components of the comprehensive plan. We also give the community a supplemental grant to use at its own discretion to fill in the chinks. This program provides incentives for a community to examine its needs deeply and to pull together a total, coordinated response.

Although still in its early stages, this program is moving ahead. Sixty-three model cities are now producing action plans for restoring entire residential neighborhoods and for bringing to bear physical and social human development plans in a staged sequence of five years, or about one-half the average time required in urban renewal. This initial effort alone will aid some one million families—or four million people. Recognizing the vast potential of this program, President Johnson requested that Congress provide $2.5 billion for model cities special grants over the next three years.[15]

The second link in our strategy is metropolitan incentive grants designed to improve planning on an areawide basis. President Johnson has proposed that Congress provide $55 million next year to assist planning for orderly growth of urban areas.[16] Also, he asked Congress to authorize $10 million for a program of areawide incentive grants to construct public facilities that are part of a comprehensive plan.

Both of these programs will attempt to make orderly and coherent the process of metropolitan growth. Given adequate funding, these grants will be provided to metropolitan areas that are willing and able to undertake development based on a comprehensive plan.

The third link in this urban strategy is the development of new communities. Initial efforts came in the 1966 Act[17] which provided insurance guarantees for the development of new communities.

Now this administration proposes a bold and creative program—the New Communities Act of 1968. Noting the options New Communities can offer, the President said:

> In America—where the question is not so much the standard of living, but the quality of life—these new communities are worth the help the government can give.[18]

Underlying this proposal is a recognition of the numerous problems associated with building new communities. The simple fact is that, in the past, developers of new communities have been hard pressed and others discouraged by the large capital outlays required to develop a new community. High initial funds are demanded—often ranging to $70 million for land and public facilities and roads and water and other utilities. Compounding a high initial outlay is the long development period and the corresponding slow return on investment. In view of these difficulties, private capital, unaided, cannot be expected to choose new communities investment over more attractive short-term, higher profit alternatives.

And it is basically to these financial difficulties that the federal government has responded with the new communities proposal. Major innovative financing techniques—federally guaranteed cash flow, debentures with interest and amortizations payments—are included in this proposal. These new aids will offer the needed flexibility to assist developments of new communities of wide-range of types and localities.

With federal assistance to encourage experimentation we can begin determining if new communities will:

- Unlock new techniques in construction to increase the quality and supply of housing;
- Permit economies of public facilities not possible in sprawling suburbs;
- Lower land costs;
- Provide a range of housing designs and costs to suit all tastes and income groups;
- Preserve a harmony with the beauty of our land;
- Provide a market for new technologies and innovations in facilities and services; and
- Create new job opportunities.

In two years the new Department of Housing and Urban Development has made a discernible contribution to developing an urban strategy designed to overcome present blight and meet future growth.

Our strategy is not to cry catastrophe or disaster. It is not one that sets this American urban experience as one which finds us spinning out of control. It has a sense of deep concern of how a country, rich and powerful, can tolerate such a voice of despair that comes out every summer in its midst. And it is basically a philosophy of building.

And this strategy does not accept an either/or proposition to the road of urban future. It does not abandon the great capital investments of great cities. It does not suppose that suburban areas created from the generation of 1946 to 1967 will disappear. It does not suppose that this nation is so robbed of imagination, of ingenuity, of creativity that we cannot build cities that will attract the flowing migration.

Instead, it is strategy—moving on several tacks at once—to meet new orders of magnitude, to accommodate the demands of 100 million new urban Americans, and to bring this country out of its urban generation of city-building whole.

Notes

1. Robert H. Connery and Richard H. Leach, "Do We Need a Department of Urban Affairs," *The Western Political Quarterly,* XIII:1 (1960), p. 109. For more extensive discussion see Connery and Leach, *The Federal Government and Metropolitan Areas* (1960).
2. This was the guiding principle of the President's Committee on Administrative Management and the two Hoover Commissions which have followed it. President's Committee on Administrative Management, *Report of the President's Committee 3.*
3. In terms of the Bureau of the Budget specifications for a reorganization plan,

neither common purpose, process, clientele, place, or time were readily discernible in federal programs concerned with urban problems. Housing mortgage insurance and guarantee programs had as their objective the provision of "decent environment" for individual households; the federal highway program was concerned with building a national road network adequate for defense purposes. The certification of veterans' eligibility and the inspection of property bore little if any resemblance to the skills and procedures involved in advising local officials how to plan for their community growth. The clientele of the renewal program, depending on one's perspective, was either the resentful former tenants one dispossesses or the wealthier new tenants who take title. Each of these activities had claimants scattered across the continent and worked with municipalities at every stage of urban development.

4. "Toward National Federalism," lecture series on *The Federal Government and the Cities,* George Washington University (1960).
5. 79 STAT 667, P.L. 89-174 (1965).
6. Only these two major organizational changes were spelled out in the Act:

   (A) The Act specified that there shall be within the Department a Federal Housing Administration headed by one of the assistant secretaries, who would also be the federal housing commissioner.

   (B) The Act transferred intact to the new Department the former Agency's mixed-ownership corporation, the Federal National Mortgage Association, with the Secretary as chairman of its board of directors.
7. Remarks of President Johnson at the signing ceremony creating a new cabinet Department of Housing and Urban Affairs, September 9, 1965.
8. *Ibid.*
9. For example, this organization recognized that most public housing is located in central cities, but all is not; that urban transportation systems while essentially providing a link throughout the entire metropolitan area have profound effects on the central city—housing, commerce, land values.
10. Congress had itself set this pattern when it stipulated that one assistant secretary should be at once the federal housing commissioner and the Secretary's principal adviser in connection with programs related to the private mortgage market—thus by law enjoining him to perform a mixed line and staff function.
11. 79 STAT 667, P.L. 89-174 (1965).
12. Executive Order No. 11297, 31 F.R. 10765 (1966).
13. For example, the nation's life insurance companies established a $1 billion pool for investment in improved housing and in job-creating efforts in slum areas.
14. 80 STAT 1255, P.L. 89-754, 89th Congress, 2nd Session, T.I (1966).
15. Message to Congress, The Crisis of the Cities, February 22, 1968. In addition, the President requested for fiscal year 1969 an additional $500 million in urban renewal funds to be used exclusively in model cities.
16. In 1966 Congress authorized, but did not fund, such a program of incentive grants. 80 STAT 1261, P.L. 89-754, 89th Congress, 2nd Session, T.II (1966).
17. 80 STAT 1271, P.L. 89-754, 89th Congress, 2nd Session, T.IV (1966).
18. *Op. cit.,* n. 15.

1968 (28:341-347)

HOWARD W. HALLMAN

Federally Financed Citizen Participation

During the last 20 years increasing amounts of federal funds have been directed toward citizen participation in public programs. Although in the total federal budget the dollars so invested are miniscule, the nature of the participatory process is controversial enough that two questions are repeatedly asked: Should federal funds be used to support citizen participation? If so, how should this be accomplished?

In this article, I explore answers to these queries by reviewing the experience under four programs: urban renewal, the juvenile delinquency/gray area projects, community action, and model cities. This review will show that there has been an evolving and steadily broadening concept of what is proper and of how federal and local agencies should proceed.

Urban Renewal in the '50s

When federal aid for urban redevelopment was first provided under the Housing Act of 1949, there was no requirement for citizen participation except through public hearings. However, by that time a number of cities had had some experience of neighborhood involvement in city planning, and a body of knowledge and opinion had developed.

In one of the first "textbooks" for redevelopment practitioners, Slayton and Dewey observed that community organization was useful to the urban redevelopment program for three reasons. First, it "helps in eliciting information on the attitudes and interests of those in redevelopment areas." Second, it provides "a vehicle for discussing a proposed plan with the residents before it is announced." Moreover, "opposition that has resulted from fear and lack of understanding may be at least lessened. If, in addition, the plan reflects some or many ideas of the residents, they may not be anxious to oppose what they may look upon as their own handiwork." Third, "it is a means of making the democratic process more effective," for "the redevelopment process offers the community an excellent opportunity to encourage participation in planning."[1]

The Housing Act of 1954 (which broadened the program and changed its name to "urban renewal") gave citizen participation a push by requiring it as part of the "workable program for community improvement," which was a precondition for receiving federal funds. Most cities responded by creating a citywide advisory committee composed of leading citizens with little or no representation from the neighborhoods affected by urban renewal. But a few places sought greater citizen participation at the neighborhood level, and, as they did, they confronted a dilemma that has arisen again and again in other programs. To achieve effective participation, community organizers are needed.[2] But who should hire and supervise the organizers? Where does the money come to pay their salaries?

In Philadelphia, a city which was a leader in the '50s, staff of public and citywide citizens agencies struggled with this problem and concluded the following:

> The staffing to develop the citizen participation process is critical. In the ideal situation, it would come from voluntary sources, indicating community readiness both in leadership and financing to carry the full share of responsibility. However, the magnitude of the problems and the large number of areas needing Urban Renewal treatment, would indicate that in most instances the expenditure of the government funds is both appropriate and essential for insuring citizen participation which is genuinely representative and effective.
>
> Although experimentation is needed, it would seem that the private agency which is skilled in this field of community organization would be best equipped to do this job. . . .[3]

Between the lines, what this said was that the Redevelopment Authority should give funds to the Health and Welfare Council or Citizens' Council on City Planning so that they could hire community organizers. But with one exception, this was not done, and instead the public agencies handled this function directly in an effort which was "partly community organization and partly community relations."[4] The one exception was a contract between the Redevelopment Authority and the Citizens' Council for City Planning under which the latter provided a community organization staff for the giant Eastwick Project. By and large, the "c.o." services were effective in eliciting citizen interest and support, but a by-product was the virtual silencing of the board of the Citizens' Council in any public debate over the Eastwick plan.[5]

In at least two other large cities during the '50s, public agencies attempted to perform community organizing directly, but in both the internal contradictions were eventually too great to bear. Community organization staff of the Detroit City Plan Commission organized residents in the

Mack Concord Project, but after the residents, with the assistance of the organizers, opposed a gasoline service station that the city planners wanted, publicly financed community organizing soon came to an end. The Baltimore Urban Renewal and Housing Agency established a community organization division, but eventually its first director left and its effectiveness declined due to unbearable tensions between the organizers on the one hand and the planners and administrators on the other.

Juvenile Delinquency and Gray Area Projects

The next round of experience worth noting is the projects supported by the President's Committee on Juvenile Delinquency and by the Ford Foundation's gray area program during the first half of the '60s. While most of them were run by private, nonprofit agencies, they were operating with federal funds and with Ford funds, which are of a quasi-public character.

In 1964 Peter Marris, an astute Englishman, spent the year observing the Ford-supported projects, and found that they were following three basic strategies of reform.[6] The first strategy was to recognize the power of established institutions and to seek to influence them through a coalition governing board and joint-staff activities of various agencies. The second strategy was to use research and analysis to find rational solutions to urban problems. The third strategy was "to arm the disadvantaged with more powerful weapons in their own defense." He noted:

> Each appeals to a different aspect of the democratic process: its search for consensus, its pragmatism, its respect for the aggressive assertion of sectional interest. Each becomes sterile divorced from the others: unless challenged by their users, institutions become preoccupied with their own survival; without a willingness to seek accommodation, protest becomes a self-regarding posture of defiance; without knowledge good intentions blunder in the dark, while the pursuit of knowledge dwindles into irrelevance without the pressure of political realities and immediate need.

He concluded that one organization cannot wholeheartedly follow each of these three strategies at once. Instead, he proposed a more diversified pattern of organization where each strategy has its own champion:

> Firstly, it suggests an organization close to, if not part of city hall, which also commands the respect of agencies outside the mayor's jurisdiction. . . . Secondly, it suggests organizations to study the consequences of social policy, and to make the analysis on which the policy should rest. . . . Thirdly, it suggests organizations, independently funded, that will help the least fortunate to exploit their rights.

Community Action Program

The Community Action Agencies that were being organized as Marris wrote proceeded to learn basically the same lesson for themselves. The charter for the Community Action Program—Title II of the Economic Opportunity Act of 1964—gave these new agencies three assignments: provision of services, mobilization of public and private resources, and achievement of maximum feasible resident participation.

The fledgling Office of Economic Opportunity emphasized all three. It mandated a broadly representative board of directors, and by the second year used one-third as a working guideline for the proportion of representatives of the poor (made official by Congress in 1966). It entered into negotiations with other federal agencies to work out ways to bolster the coordinating role of Community Action Agencies, and Congress wrote a role for them into the Elementary and Secondary Education Act of 1965 (only to water it down in a 1966 amendment). OEO also pushed for rapid impact of local programs and developed a series of nationally packaged and promoted programs—Head Start, Foster Grandparents, Project Enable, Legal Services, etc.

In the public press and the halls of Congress, resident participation got most of the attention during the first year as OEO pushed for board representation for the poor. In a handful of communities these representatives gained a majority of the board seats, and those CAAs tended to place more stress on social action than upon services or coordination. Here and there neighborhood organizers stimulated protest movements. While altogether the dollars spent for aggressive citizen participation were small, the controversy which this stirred up was grist for the journalists' mill.

But by 1967 the dominant emphasis of Community Action Agencies was the provision of services, mostly those funded by OEO. Coordination of a wider range of antipoverty programs was not happening in most communities. Resident participation was being achieved in a number of ways:

> membership on the governing board, employment of residents especially as subprofessionals, neighborhood boards and area councils, delegate agencies controlled by persons served, program advisory committees, parent groups for Head Start and school programs, independent citizen organizations, neighborhood meetings, newsletters, and, in rare instances, social protest.[7]

While these methods did not measure up to what the staunchest advocates of citizen participation wanted during the first years of the Community Action Program, they were far beyond the practices of urban renewal agencies in the '50s. And in spite of the controversy that raged around maximum feasible participation, Congress extended the program in 1965, 1966,

1967 and 1969—restricted in this way and that, but with the participation requirement retained.

In program terms, the price of continued emphasis upon citizen participation was restriction of the role of the CAAs. Other federal agencies were not willing to trust them to handle their local programs, and the advocates of coordination in the Bureau of the Budget, who once placed their hopes on the CAAs, turned their attention to other devices for achieving local coordination of federal programs. For reasons I will examine later, citizen participation drove out coordination.

Model Cities Program

What replaced community action in the favor of federal officials concerned with coordination was the Model Cities Program. Established by Demonstrations Cities and Metropolitan Development Act of 1966, this new program used different terms to describe many of the same functions undertaken previously by the juvenile delinquency/gray area projects and by the Community Action Agencies. The act provided federal funds for various projects and activities, and required a city to have "administrative machinery . . . for carrying out the program on a consolidated and coordinated basis" and "widespread citizen participation."[8] However, the local program must have the approval of the local governing body, which meant that Model Cities was under the ultimate control of city government in contrast to Community Action, in which city control was optional.

When the first planning grants were awarded in November 1967, HUD issued each city a "discussion paper," which usually led to local reorganization of the model city structure. A year later HUD described the kind of City Demonstration Agencies (CDA) that emerged:

> Most CDA structures include a coalition policy-making group, a central planning group, a central residents advisory or coordinating group, a technical group, CDA staff, and anywhere from 8 to 15 planning committees.
>
> In most cities, planning task forces (or planning committees) are deliberately heavily weighted with neighborhood people. . . . Most task forces are chaired by city officials, but some are chaired by elected or selected neighborhood residents and others and have a neighborhood resident as co-chairman of each task force.[9]

Based upon a sample of these first-round cities, Sundquist and Davis found five types of model cities agencies:[10] unicameral (city hall controlled); bicameral (a city CDA and a separate neighborhood resident's organization), which was subdivided into unified (equal partners), city hall oriented, and neighborhood oriented; and resident controlled.

As planning progressed, unicameral types tended to move toward one of the bicameral schemes as residents demanded and obtained a greater voice in decisions on use of funds. Although HUD has no systematic analysis of the current situation, it appears that in most places residents of the model neighborhoods have the de facto right to approve or disapprove the program before it goes to city council, but in probably less than one-fifth of the cities do residents have a formal (de jure) veto over programs.

In some communities mayors or city councils have vetoed program components favored by the residents, but rarely have they added programs on their own. The vast majority of plans have been adopted through a bargaining process in which the residents play an important role—a much stronger role than under Urban Renewal, but usually less than under Community Action.

Since Floyd Hyde became Assistant Secretary for Model Cities in 1968, greater stress has been placed upon the mayor's role. As a result, some mayors seem to have asserted themselves and have gained greater control, and this has usually meant weakening the role of the residents. However, the mayor still has to bargain with model neighborhood residents, and his control is considerably less than it is over traditional line departments of municipal government.

As to the program content, once again the dominant pattern is a comprehensive package of services, funded mostly by the primary federal agency (HUD's Model Cities Administration). Coordination of a bundle of programs financed by other sources has not emerged, and the HUD-prescribed planning methodology has proved to be far too complicated and quite unrelated to the local bargaining process through which the first-year supplemental funds were allocated. Between citizen participation and coordination, the latter looms larger in Model Cities because of the connection with the mayor, who has—potentially at least—more clout than any other of the previous coordinating bodies. But it has yet to be shown that other federal agencies are willing to utilize the local Model Cities Agencies as the vehicle to coordinate their local programs.

In Retrospect

In the '50s there were those of us who were skeptical of utilizing public funds to promote resident participation because we doubted that the community organizers would have enough freedom of action. The experience of those urban renewal agencies which tried to do community organizing directly bore this out. With private sources insufficient, the best answer seemed to be making public funds available to an established voluntary agency, but this rarely happened.

The juvenile delinquency/gray area projects went the nonprofit route, but with their coalition boards they were hard pressed to go all out for neighborhood action. Nonetheless, they advanced previous efforts, particularly in the use of residents in staff positions.

At first some persons tried to move the Community Action Program into social protest and nonpartisan political action, but that was farther than those who controlled OEO would allow. But after five years, even though it has sometimes been misdirected, mismanaged, and misinterpreted, CAP has a record of notable achievements in resident participation. Several thousand citizen organizations have been formed in urban and rural poverty areas. New leaders, numbering in the tens of thousands, have emerged from among the poor, near-poor, and minority groups, including many militants who now call the poverty program "mickey-mouse," but who got considerable experience on the CAP payroll. Within the last four years a new type of neighborhood institution—the community corporation—has come into being. Community action groups have kept the Model Cities Program "honest" in its effort to achieve "widespread citizen participation," far surpassing what HUD ever did before in any of its programs. And the tripartite board of the Community Action Agencies is one of the few places in today's polarized society that poor people, public officials, and civic leaders from the "establishment" unite in a common endeavor.

Model Cities has benefited from this experience, and while it has a different alignment of power, with city government being stronger, it has "legitimized" the use of board members selected by residents of a particular neighborhood in a process different from the traditional municipal election or mayoralty appointment. And in spite of the reluctance of some HUD officials, a number of model city agencies are using community corporations as a means of organizing and delivering services. In some places where the Community Action Agency has gone stale and its neighborhood advisory councils represent mainly "old guard" leaders, the Model Cities Agency has achieved much more vital and representative citizen participation. And Model Cities, through the bicameral scheme of organization, is also fostering communication between different elements of urban society.

Compared to 1960, a remarkable amount of citizen participation is now being financed by federal funds—both directly in the form of community organizers and resident-controlled organizations, and also indirectly in the form of participation on the governing boards of publicly financed agencies.

Citizen Participation versus Coordination

As noted earlier, all of these programs of the '60s have essentially been comprehensive service projects in the inner city with a mixture of resident participation and coordination added. Where resident participation has been strong, relatively little coordination has occurred. Where coordination has been emphasized, resident participation has been weak. Thus, although a pure separation may not be possible, it appears that the two elements do not go together very well, but instead require different kinds of structural arrangements, as Marris suggested five years ago.

On the one hand, coordination emphasizes the centripetal force of community power. This is because, by and large, voluntary coordination is not very effective since the tough issues are those on which no participating agency will yield easily. Therefore, there has to be some form of sanction to assure coordination, such as the authoritative relationship of the hierarchical organization or the control of monetary resources and physical facilities. The exercise of these controls comes most easily when they are in the hands of one person or relatively few. Since in public programs we are rightly concerned with accountability, we want such persons to be responsible to the people through the processes of representative democracy. This points toward the mayor and other elected officials as the ones who should have responsibility and authority for allocating funds and for assuring that they are used in a manner that achieves coordinated action.

On the other hand, citizen participation is a centrifugal force. As involvement increases, more actors enter the arena and more diverse views are presented. Competition for scarce resources comes into play, and various interest groups contend against one another. The *demos* are in the forefront, and it is up to their representatives to bargain in order to achieve a workable compromise, or to use an older expression, to seek the "general will."

An organization interested in increasing citizen participation of necessity has to be less concerned with tight operation, which is more the concern of coordination. Moreover, the mayor and others in control of resources are extremely reluctant to delegate part of the coordinating responsibility to the "noisy assembly," and while many mayors support the Community Action Program, they have no intention of it becoming a major coordinating vehicle. And in those cities where neighborhood residents have taken control of the model cities machinery, mayors have disowned the program as a municipal instrument for coordination of a wide variety of programs.

In some places, the Model City Agency for the present has been able to keep its governing board to a small enough size so that it can provide representation to the model neighborhood while still being able to serve as a coordinator. But when the Model City Program becomes citywide in scope, as Secretary Romney has said it should, other neighborhoods will desire representation and so will citywide interest groups which will want to get in on the decision-making process of allocating what will be much larger resources. This means that the model city board will either become as large as many community action boards are now, or will be reconstituted more along the lines of other municipal commissions with three, five, seven, or nine members, not trying to give every interest a seat, but relying on the broader political processes which select and regulate the mayor and city council. If the board becomes quite large, it will not be an effective vehicle for coordination, and it might just as well merge with the community action board; but then a new coordinating instrument will be needed. If the city-wide Model City Agency has a small board and concentrates on coordination, it will be less likely to promote and assist citizen participation, which will need to be expressed through another mechanism.

Two Organizations Needed

Seeing this dilemma at the time of the change of national administrations, several persons and study groups proposed that there be separate organizations for coordination and citizen participation.[11] I believe that this is still a valid though not an easy solution.

Perhaps the biggest obstacle is that there is too much history and too much inertia behind the present arrangement. Change is an uncertainty. Too many of the contending agencies have had to fight too hard for their place in the sun and would be reluctant to risk shifting to a different role. This would be particularly true of Community Action Agencies, which are in the most precarious position since they have scarcely any supporters left in the Executive Branch, not even at OEO.

Therefore, to the extent that realignment is promoted as federal policy, the Administration, as a precondition, needs to make a fresh commitment to the concept of citizen participation. This it could do within the framework of its own rhetoric, making the following case.

We have in the United States what our founding fathers called a "republican form of government,"[12] or what today we might describe as a "representative democracy" (thus giving us a choice of the nomenclature of the two major parties). The essence of this system is that the government derives its "just powers from the consent of the governed,"[13] with consent understood to be an active force, not merely passive acquiescence. Historically, we have developed ever new ways of gaining this consent: the electoral process, the political party, the convention, the direct primary, initiative, referendum, recall, boards and commissions, advisory councils, public opinion polls, and the simulated referendums that elected officials have going in their heads at all times. The new forms of citizen involvement that have emerged during the past decade should be seen as an extension of the trend toward ever broadening the workings of American democracy, of enriching and providing new variations in the republican form of government.

In this context it is quite appropriate for the federal government to give attention to citizen participation. This can be done in many ways, perhaps chiefly by setting forth the procedures through which federal programs operate, such as requiring accountability by duly elected officials, public hearings, and other methods to gauge public opinion, proper representation of all affected groups in the decision-making processes. In addition, the federal government can directly encourage and assist greater participation in the governmental processes by persons who tend to be left out.

It is quite proper, therefore, for the federal government to take positive action that enables citizens to become more fully involved in the governmental processes and to engage in self-help activities. In effect this adds a fourth level to the federal system, and in a country the size of the United States the national, state, and municipal tiers need to be supplemented by organizations at the neighborhood level. While there is no magic in decentralization (and indeed some programs need greater centralization, such as a national standard for family assistance), there is much to be said for seeking the level closest to the people for organizing program operations. This is now advocated by the far right and the new left, as well as many conservative, moderate, and liberal voices in between.

From this philosophy flows the notion that federal funds can appropriately go to a local organization that has as its purpose the development of citizen self-help capacity through resident-controlled neighborhood institutions. Since this function cannot be easily performed by the municipal instrument for program coordination, as we have seen, a separate organization is needed. Such an organization could be a part of city government, or it might be a quasi-public agency organized as a private, nonprofit corporation. It should be governed by a board which represents various elements of the community, including local government, leaders of the "establishment," and representatives of the persons served. Its chief purpose would not be to deliver services but rather to assist residents to organize and conduct their own activities. Thus, its functions would include technical assistance, training, and monitoring use of funds flowing through it to neighborhood organizations. This outline, of course, describes the Community Action Agency, shorn of the coordination task which it cannot perform anyway and revitalized to focus clearly on the mission of citizen development.

If national, state, and municipal leaders have the vision to recognize the need for greater citizen involvement and for local and neighborhood instruments through which this can be achieved, they would not only support this function but would also be more tolerant of the inevitable roughness of bringing previously left-out citizens into greater participation in public programs. "Where there is no vision, the people perish."[14]

Backed by leadership support, the renewed Community Action Agency has the potential for doing what seemed infeasible in the '50s: channel federal funds to support neighborhood organizations. Interestingly to me, the tripartite board of which I was personally skeptical for several years may be one of the greatest assets, for it gives legitimacy to this endeavor and provides communications between separated elements of society. Moreover, it is one step removed from elected officials who, if directly responsible, might be under severe pressure to block the promotion of citizen actions, but can instead be relieved of the blame for mistakes while benefiting from the accomplishments.

At the neighborhood level residents need the opportunity to decide what is the most appropriate way to organize. This may mean consolidation of several existing organizations that serve the same territory under different programs, or it may mean the continuation of more than one organization. What is essential is that the decision be based upon the residents' perspective, not upon the will of distant bureaucracies, each of which wants its own neighborhood organization, as is too often the case today. This suggests that the renewed Community Action Agency might serve as a catalyst in behalf of all federal agencies for helping a neighborhood to find its best method of organization (just as the Model Cities Agency, expanded to citywide operations, might be the local catalyst to produce coordination of federal programs). This, however, does not relieve other federal programs from the responsibility of setting ground rules which encourage widespread citizen participation. And one of the functions of the Community Action Program would be to promote participation in the involvement processes of these other programs and to assist neighborhood institutions in securing funds from these sources.

To be sure, perfect harmony will not be produced through these arrangements, but there will be provided more orderly ways for achieving fuller involvement of the people in the effort to "establish Justice, insure domestic tranquility, . . . promote the general welfare, and secure the Blessings of Liberty,"[15] which is why the United States was constituted in the first place.

Notes

1. William L. Slayton and Richard Dewey, "Urban Redevelopment and the Urbanite," in Coleman Woodbury (ed.), *The Future of Cities and Urban Redevelopment* (Chicago: The University of Chicago Press, 1953), pp. 427-429.
2. This was one of the major conclusions of a study entitled *Community Organization for Citizen Participation in Urban Renewal* by William C. Loring, Jr., Frank L. Sweetser, and Charles F. Ernst (Cambridge: The Cambridge Press, 1957).
3. *Citizen Participation in Urban Renewal,* a statement prepared by the Philadelphia Area Planning Conference, January 1957, p. 5.
4. Howard W. Hallman, *Education to Forward Urban Renewal in Philadelphia* (Philadelphia: Philadelphia Housing Association, 1958), p. 21.

5. A conclusion based upon the author's personal observations.
6. Peter Marris, *The Strategies of Reform,* a paper presented at a conference on community development held in San Juan, Puerto Rico, December 1964, mimeo. 11 pp.
7. *Economic Opportunity Amendments of 1967,* report of the Committee on Labor and Public Welfare, U.S. Senate, Senate Report No. 563, 90th Congress, 1st Session, p. 37 (the author was director of the Senate study).
8. Section 103 (a), Demonstration Cities and Metropolitan Development Act of 1966, P.L. 89-754. The Act has other requirements which differ from community action, such as a concern for civic design and historical preservation, but this article is concentrating on the similarities.
9. U.S. Department of Housing and Urban Development, *Citizen Participation in Model Cities,* Technical Assistance Bulletin No. 3, December 1968, p. 4.
10. James L. Sundquist and David W. Davis, *Making Federalism Work* (Washington, D.C.: The Brookings Institution, 1969), p. 96.
11. Sundquist and Davis, *op. cit.,* chapters 2 and 3; Howard W. Hallman, *The Future of the Poverty Program,* December 1968; Antipoverty Conference held at Airlie House under the auspices of the Urban Coalition, *Options for the Future,* January 1969; and unpublished report of a task force appointed by then President-elect Nixon and chaired by Richard Nathan, then at The Brookings Institution.
12. Note Article IV, Section 3 of the U.S. Constitution: "The United States shall guarantee to every State in this Union a Republican form of government. . . ."
13. *The Declaration of Independence.*
14. *Proverbs,* 29:18.
15. Preamble to the Constitution of the United States of America.

1972 (32:421-427)

NORTON E. LONG

Have Cities a Future?

Some eight years ago at Bloomington in the course of an incisive talk on "Problems in the Study of Urban Politics," James Wilson remarked, "Who governs? is an interesting and important question; an even more interesting and more important question, it seems to me, is what difference does it make who governs?"[1] In his later remarks I think he gives an answer I would interpret as saying that to most people it makes very little difference. He says, "The most obvious indicators of the quality of life in our cities—per capita income, median school years completed, home ownership, morbidity rates, participation in cultural activities—are not much affected by the form or functioning of city government . . . the life chances of an individual are much more the function of aggregate national and regional factors (economic growth, the structure of the labor market, national security) than of factors over which local officials and 'power structures' have much control."[2] I think this has been the dominant view in American political science. It seems to say that local government is in terms of important matters a pretty trivial affair. The acceptance of this view, however, has non-trivial consequences.

Professor Dahl's classic study of New Haven, *Who Governs?* yields much the same conclusion. In the axioms of the local system it appears "the existing socio-economic structure must be taken as given, except for minor details. . . . Until recently the political stratum has assumed that the physical and economic features of the city are determined by forces beyond their control."[3] Marx would have found little to disagree with in this. Indeed, he might well have found *Who Governs?* an admirable description of what he meant by "bourgeois democracy." The interesting question of how leaders and followers in New Haven have come to accept the social and economic structures as immutable or at least insignificantly mutable by local action is, one supposes, what Bachrach and Baratz have in mind in their concern with the politics of non-issues.

The definition of the city as largely powerless to significantly affect the lives of its inhabitants for good or ill gives the best of good reasons for the apathy that Professor Dahl and others have found so prevalent among the citizens. Politics becomes a form of entertainment, a distraction, a circus rather than a serious instrument for the improvement of the human condition, e.g., the spectator sport perspective that Scott Greer found in St. Louis. If the city is powerless to significantly alter in desired ways the important dimensions of the lives of its citizens, it can at best become a conduit for external sources of power to do the things it might wish but is fiscally and politically incapable of doing. This conception of the city explains the mayor's emerging role as beggar-in-chief for federal and state funds. The problems of the city are seen as basically lack of money and the solution to the problems are seen as basically purchasable, only given enough money. The economism of this view is clear and it fits nicely with the conception of the urban scene as a market of competing real estate amenities, a view given classic exposition by Thiebout, Ostrom, and Warren.

The solution of the city's problems by money alone becomes more and more dubious. (Few ever say money alone will do it, but what else is needed is rarely specified. When it is, as in Congressman Reuss' polemic for revenue sharing, organizational proposals remain unrelated to substantive desired outcomes.) The City of New York, as Lyle Fitch points out, has spent more, much more, than anyone else is likely to with no appreciable improvement. Fred Powledge quotes William F. Buckley, Jr., to the effect that "if New Haven's per capita success at getting money were shared by all other U.S. cities, the nation would have been spending $146 billion on urban programs." As Powledge states, "Federal urban renewal allocations to New Haven were equivalent to $790 for each man, woman, and child."[4] Summing up what money did in New Haven, he finds little beyond a few buildings whose architecture he doubts will stand the test of time.

If we do our arithmetic, New York and New Haven's experience should cast doubt on the ability of any amount of money to accomplish much through the current ways we spend it. We may, indeed we probably will, spend more on health, education, police, and other public goods, but whether these expenditures will be more productive than past ones is extremely dubious. Not only is this the case because public goods are mostly services and the service industry shows little capacity to increase in productivity—William Baumol's thesis—but even more because our politics gives little incentive for increases in productivity. Beyond this, many of the alleged public goods turn out in practice to be little better than public patent medicines—health cures that don't produce measurable improvements in specifiable people's health; education that is unaccompanied by measurable outcomes in literacy; policing that costs more and is accompanied by rising crime, some of it caused by the police. Our experience with foreign aid should have taught us the limits of an external infusion of money without an appropriate modification of infrastructure. The foreign aid outcome—elite enrichment, monuments, inflation, and increased military expenditures—has a painful resemblance to the outcomes of aid to the American city and even to the LEAA's penchant for spending on police hardware. Those who have called for a Marshall Plan for the cities have rarely pursued the analogy enough to ask what would it take to revive the economies of the cities. What they have usually had in mind was little more than the magnitude of the aid.

The City as an Economy

Rarely are cities thought of as economies, as enterprises that must pay for their imports with exports. The existence of the city as a sub-community within the larger community of the state and the nation obscures its status as an economy, one that must keep books, and make them balance. Bertal Ohlin in his *Interregional Trade* showed how readily the subordinate communities of a nation could be conceptualized in international trade terms. An economics that has concerned itself almost exclusively with macro-Keynesianism and whose conception of local economies derives from national income shares has no realistic conception of the interaction patterns that constitute the nation's local economies. Political scientists, in undue awe of economists, have assumed the local economies to be mere by-products of a national economy hung in the sky above them, independently controlling them without being controlled by them. From this view, a nation of sick cities, to use Mitchell Gordon's expression, could have a well national economy from whose health and wealth they could be restored. The plain fact is that an urban nation of sick cities would be a sick nation.

Failure to look at the city as an economy whose books must be balanced and whose expenditures must in good part be treated as investments has resulted in treating municipal expenditures largely as pure consumption. The consumption is a kind of merit goods consumption that is self-justifying, independent of the consequences in the lives of citizens. One does not look at the municipal budget and ask what one is getting in health, education, security, housing, and, given scarce resources and the priorities of human values, whether the mix is right. Patrick Crecine's recent volume on urban finance almost suggests that one can't know. Meltsner and Wildavsky seem to argue that one should leave municipal budgeting alone, even in a near bankrupt city such as Oakland. If a city were conceptualized as a humane local producer and consumer cooperative, it would make the best of good sense to ask how one was using scarce resources and whether the return on them was as good as it might be.

The poor have a special interest in how the city spends its money. As

Leon Keyserling points out, some 50 percent of the incomes of those earning $2,000 and under goes for taxes. They pay higher shares of their incomes than anybody else; although, since they pay scarcely any income tax, the affluent don't see them as taxpayers at all. When you have very little income to begin with and half of it is taken in taxes, you might like to have some assurance that that half is being well spent for your welfare. Indeed the poor can rejoice that the economists assure them that this is the case. It is consoling to know that one is a high-cost citizen and that schools, the hospitals, and the police are coming at a bargain rate. Many low-income ingrates fail to appreciate the service. Some even prefer to hang on to their income in serviceless suburbs or rural areas. Invincible ignorance or immaculate membership in the Chicago school of economics, take your choice. Many, and not only the poor, feel that the municipal service bureaucracies serve largely themselves and that their ministrations do little to educate the youth, make safe the streets or heal the sick. The labels are there, the performance yardsticks and their application—a task Herbert Simon abandoned without as a consequence abandoning theorizing—remain underdeveloped and unapplied. Perhaps this again but shows the triviality of local government, though a 50 percent bite from one's meager income is scarcely trivial.

Even though political science and economics have done little to measure the cost effectiveness of public services and their measurable contributions to the improvement of the human condition, we are not helpless before the question of whether cities or even neighborhoods are consequential or trivial for their citizens and their inhabitants. As long ago as 1965, Hong Kong had an infant mortality rate a third better than that of St. Louis in 1971. The technology for achieving the better performance is not a trade secret of Hong Kong. The interest in the relevant categories of babies may be. In St. Louis, "The Hill," an Italian neighborhood, has a crime rate lower than not only the rest of the city, but than most, if not all, of the suburbs as well. Acting through their own organizations, the residents of "The Hill" have assisted strong young Italian families to buy homes and settle there. As a result, while housing in much of the city is in decay, on "The Hill" it is well kept and demand outruns supply. "The Hill" cares for its houses, the appearance and the safety of its streets, its children, and the employment of newcomers from Italy to its midst. It amounts to a neighborhood cooperative for the protection, welfare, and advancement of its members. Along many non-trivial dimensions of the human condition—security, employment, education, self-respect to name but four—it is a powerful instrument to improve the lot of the members of the local territorial community.

Perhaps the functioning of an ethnic neighborhood will not be regarded as an instructive political model of what a city might be and what the political requisites for the city being non-trivial might be. Sayre and Kaufman conceptualize the politics of New York as a game for prizes. In most such games there are prizes for the few winners. The winnings come from the pot made by those drawing the blanks. One might be less concerned about the blanks if the conduct of the business of the city—the by-product of the contest for prizes—were as collectively beneficent as the market of the classical economist was theoretically supposed to be. Neither New York nor New Haven lends support to the view that the contest for prizes, even when the federal government donates them munificently, is likely to result in a sustained collectively beneficent outcome. The ethnic neighborhood of "The Hill" provides a more promising model though it has the vice of depending on intentional beneficence.

Use of Slack Resources

Professor Dahl offered a great deal of hope for the little man in *Who Governs?* He made a point that is frequently played down by those who see tyranny in all powerful oppressive systems. His point was that almost everyone had slack resources and that given competence and organization, that slack could be mobilized and made to count. The concept of slack resources need not be confined to political resources. It holds for economic resources as well. Most people, even the very poor, have inefficiently used resources and in addition suffer from individually and collectively destructive behavior. Malcom X in his *Autobiography* gives as graphic and convincing a picture of how competent use of slack resources can transform not only an individual but a large number of individuals. Malcom depicts the difference in the lives of people made by membership in a Black Muslim Church. Without infusion of outside funds, with income at official poverty levels, people by the transformation of their behavior from individually and collectively self-destructive patterns and by the efficient uses of their limited resources radically alter their lives for the better.

There is nothing unique about the capacity of the Black Muslim Church to effectively alter the lives of poor people. Amish, Mennonites, and others have taken unpromising land amidst conditions of poverty and organized their members into a society capable of efficiently using resources, with power to significantly shape their environment and with a most significant capacity to confer a sense of self-respect and purpose. This last seems odd speaking of a city. Given the history of the city such as Fustel de Coulanges recounts in his *Cité Antique,* how odd that it should seem odd. Yet we are so completely possessed by the conception of the politically and economically eviscerated city of liberalism, capitalism, and the nation-state that the older Greek, medieval, renaissance, and even early modern conception of the city as a self-determining cooperative for ordering and advancing the common life and well-being of its citizens seems strange and well nigh utopian. It is not so long ago that the conception had meaning. Examples of communal societies within the larger society of the state and nation capable of profoundly influencing the lives of their members still exist to remind us that in principle, even today, local territorial communities within the larger political orders need not be trivial. Hence, in principle at least, cities need not be trivial. Cities to become powerful, self-directing cooperatives need citizens as churches require communicants. Whether cities with deeply loyal citizens are compatible with the nation-state and the national market of capitalism is a serious question. Rousseau and other nationalists have feared they would break the general will and be, in Hobbes' pungent phrase, so many worms in the entrails of the national body politic.

It is not accidental that the city of national liberal capitalism has progressively weakened its hold on its citizens even when its budget and its bureaucracy have swollen beyond recognition. Nisbet, in his *Quest for Community,* has discussed how the local community has lost function, which at first seems strange given the enormous growth of local activity. Yet when one contrasts the Black Muslim or Amish churches with the contemporary American city, the loss of function becomes readily apparent. Roland Warren in his *Community in America* traces the logic by which vertical organizations—national corporations, unions, professions, bureaucracies, markets—have eroded the autonomy of local horizontal organizations—the cities, the towns, the neighborhoods, the churches, and even perhaps the families. The completion of the erosion, as he shows, involves the vertical organizations in a common fate. National corporations and national unions alike have vulnerable feet of local clay. Even the national government pays unwilling tribute to the enduring significance of the local order when not only congressmen's secretaries but congressmen and ambassadors as well suffer the consequences of a horizontal local society no longer able or willing to maintain a normative order. The rediscovery of the neighborhood and the local community as necessary vital constituents of the body politic proceeds apace. Given our overseas preoccupation, we have given far more thought to nation building than to local community building and rebuilding.

Samuel B. Warner in his *Street Car Suburbs* gives a history of the transformation of the older city to the anti-city of the metropolitan area. He shows how by 1900 "the growing parochialism and fragmentation resulted in a steady relative weakening of social agencies. Weakness, in turn, convinced more and more individuals that local community action was hopeless or irrelevant. From this conviction came the further weakening of the public agencies. The self-defeating cycle, begun by the street car metropolis, has continued with increasing severity to this day.

"The inattention of late nineteenth century Bostonians to the fragmentation of their community life was not an accidental oversight, it was a matter of principle, the principle of individualistic capitalism.''[5] Warner's account does not differ from the standard account of the growth of metropolitan areas except with respect to this last and essential point. The fragmentation is not accidental, an oversight, but a matter of principle, the principle of individualistic capitalism. This is important because it accounts for the grave and insuperable difficulties that have faced those who wished to put together what they saw as the fragments of what should have been pieces of the larger political whole. The enduring hold of ''the principle of individualistic capitalism'' accounts in no small degree for the almost unbelievable lack of serious concern with a politics of metropolitan city building. The Committee for Economic Development and its political science advisors treat ''Reshaping Government in Metropolitan Areas'' as if it were no more than a corporate reorganization. A political organization to produce what would—if it achieved its ostensible social objectives—amount to no minor revolution is not even discussed. The executive-centered coalition of notables and experts had a long run under favoring circumstances in New Haven. Its staying power and continuing achievement should have provoked thought.

These views are curiously lacking an appreciation of the value and vitality of going political concerns and the difficulty of conjuring them into life where they do not exist. They stem from the tendency of the liberal capitalist ideology to devalue politics and even to forget to what degree economics itself depends on a politics creating the conditions under which it can function. Lester C. Thurow of MIT, testifying before the Joint Economic Committee of Congress, recalls what is often forgotten by political scientists as well as economists. He says, ''People oftentimes forget what is the first statement of any Economics I textbook. . . . If a market economy starts off with what society regards as an optimal distribution of income it does nice things. We tend to remember the nice things and forget the fundamental if statement. If it is on the right track it does nice things.

''The real function of Government is to adjust the distribution of income to put it on the right track, whatever that is.''[6] As Professor Dahl's study of New Haven indicates, leaders and followers are likely to forget the politically problematic nature of the social and economic structure and that one of the major purposes of a government is precisely not only to sustain the social and economic structure but to alter it. The political process by which alteration is rendered unthinkable is worth more thought than we have given it.

Powerlessness

We have come largely to regard our cities and their citizens as powerless. This acceptance of the powerlessness of cities and individuals accounts, to a considerable extent, for the uncritical assumption that the socio-economic structure is not susceptible of meaningful alteration. Even if individuals could exert some power over the cities, it would do no good since the cities themselves are empty husks. Some such view would appear to be held by Frances Piven and Richard Cloward who see the attainment of power at city hall by blacks and the poor as largely bereft of meaning. The grounds for this dim view are largely economic and even somewhat less than that, fiscal. Many cities are impoverished; therefore, they can do little and are worth little. This is to see an alteration in the city's politics as of little account. It is in full accord with the economism of purchased solutions. Robert Wood found the expenditures of New York suburbs to vary with density and per capita income, not with Democratic or Republican politics or city manager plan. Harvey Brazer's findings seem to lend further support to this statistical explanation. But what should one conclude? That politics makes no difference or that Democratic or Republican, city manager plan or other plan makes little difference? Ergo, does it follow that no kind of local politics could make a substantial difference or that only these kinds of political differences matter little on the most critical dimensions for most people? What they do determine is who wins what prizes in essentially the same game whose larger results remain much the same.

Left, right, and center are hung up on money not only as the root of all evil, but seemingly the source of all power. The city suffers from two disabilities, its declining revenue base and the departure of much of its middle class and much of its business. Old jobs have left for the suburbs and new jobs are largely locating there. These are the basics of the case for the powerlessness of many of the cities. They are bolstered by much of the conventional wisdom of what to do about our ills. Thus the Advisory Commission on Intergovernmental Relations says,

> The economic welfare of an individual in midcentury America, with its emphasis on occupational specialization, depends primarily upon the amount of education he achieved. Education largely determines occupation, and occupation in turn largely determines income. . . . Where educational, occupational, and income levels are generally low, substantial public health and welfare services are likely to be needed, but the financial resources required to provide them may be inadequate.[7]

This seems to suggest that differences in education are the main key to income and welfare. This certainly seems to be something the city could do something about. The reason it can't, or that one infers it can't, is that it hasn't enough money. We are told that the quality of education is largely a function of money spent. If this is so, then there is no way for the impoverished city to give its youth an even half-way equal chance. But is it so? It has been nationally reported that Amish one-room schools with a

17-year-old teacher have students who do as well on standard tests as pupils from the most expensive suburban schools. Marilyn Gittel in her study of New York's experiments in local control reports, "Participation in the policy process had one overwhelming beneficial effect on the participants: It led to heightened feelings of efficacy and self-esteem."[8] While the experiments were too short to be evaluated and the new administrators highly conventional in their methods orientation, a political approach to the problems of the school showed promise. As she points out, "Educational programs—compensatory programs—had been declared failures by such impressive studies as the Coleman Report (Equality of Educational Opportunity) and the U.S. Civil Rights Commission Report (Racial Isolation in the Schools). Both these studies recommended primarily a political solution to the crisis in public schools."[9] William Ryan in his powerful book *Blaming the Victim* suggests the main explanatory variable accounting for massive pupil failure to be the expectations of the teachers. This is a factor subject to alteration by politics, although, as Albert Shanker would know, two can play at that game.

There seems a logic worth testing in the notion that self-esteem and a sense of causal efficacy of an ability to alter the environment by one's own efforts rather than merely to passively adapt to it, are powerfully related to success in the learning process. It also seems likely that children learn and take important cues from their parents. If parents show a sense of causal efficacy in utilizing instruments of community control, such as a neighborhood school board, a needed lesson might be provided for their children. The isolation of the schools from politics itself teaches lessons—lessons of powerlessness, incompetence, apathy, and passivity.

One can not, surely not an educator, downgrade education. Yet its magic efficacy may have been over sold in an effort to both explain and as well to justify and legitimate the gross disparities of income that affect our cities.

In his prepared testimony to the Joint Economic Committee, Lester Thurow states, "From 1949 to 1969 the share of total income going to the lowest quintile has dropped from 3.2 percent to 2.6 percent and the share going to the highest quintile rose from 44.8 percent to 46.3 percent. Education has been becoming more equally distributed yet income has been becoming more unequally distributed."[10] Thurow maintains that our hopes for education removing or at least reducing some of the more glaring inequalities of the society have depended on the validity of a wage competition model as an explanation of the labor market. He finds that a job competition model with far different consequences is a more adequate explanatory tool. Thurow points out "only 30 percent of the observed income differences between black and white males can be attributed to personal characteristics. The remaining 70 percent is explained in terms of demand side phenomena (wage and job discrimination, full employment, etc.)."[11] Given the validity of a job competition model, a strategy such as that employed in World War II to deliberately change the sociology of wage differentials is required.

Such a strategy becomes all the more important given the distribution of jobs between the inhabitants of cities and non-residents. Secretary Romney in a talk in St. Louis made the point clear. He said, "The city continues to provide more job opportunities for non-city residents than for residents of the city."[12] Lyle Fitch says over half the jobs in Newark are held by people who live outside the city and nearly one in three residents is on welfare.[13] For St. Louis, Newark, and other cities, it appears that despite the loss of jobs to the suburbs and the greater growth of new jobs in the suburbs, the people of the city would do pretty well jobwise and incomewise if they could have the jobs now filled by non-residents. These jobs filled by non-residents are not just those in the private sector, but also those held by police and school teachers. The city by its own practice legitimizes the claim that qualified personnel can neither be recruited from its midst nor retained if city residence is required.

Sharing the Poor

The official wisdom sees the problem of poverty and income change to be solved more by the redistribution of the poor throughout the metropolitan area than by the political efforts of the poor acting through their city. The policy might be characterized as one of sharing the wealth through sharing the poor. Thus the Advisory Commission on Intergovernmental Relations says, "To a large extent, the task of assuring equal economic and social opportunity to metropolitan residents becomes one of creating a free and adequate housing market."[14] The argument for attempting to open the suburbs to the city's poor and blacks to achieve a better balance between needs and resources is reinforced by the argument that the poor and the black need access to the suburbs to gain housing near enough to the growing edge of unskilled and low-skilled jobs. Sol Linowitz of the Urban Coalition and Paul Davidoff of the Suburban Action Institute both urge the opening of suburbs to the poor and the black for this purpose. Were there a "Real City" with a political process powerful enough to enforce the kind of labor and housing market the theories of the classical economists require, such a policy might be a promising way of achieving some of the redistributivist objectives that the proponents of metropolitan or "Real City" solutions claim to intend.

Metropolitan areas would be—as many reformers have claimed—communities without government but awaiting the touch of a creative and powerful politics to give them birth. Any candid review of the politics of metropolitan reform in the United States will reveal its anemic nature; it offers scant promise of producing the major social change the proponents of reform envisage. Metropolitan Toronto, the classic case on the continent and the exemplar of the CED, was put together and reassembled by the provincial legislature. The diminution of its constituent parts suggests it to be in process of becoming to all intents a single city. It resembles our own now rather old experiment, New York City, a case that reminds one that American legislatures have the power and on occasion have used it to reshape local governments in significant ways. The rarity of the action suggests the chances of reoccurrence.

The literature of metropolitan reform and the comparative studies of governmental performance are disappointing in their abstract, *a priori,* and dogmatic character, the absence of observation. Despite the existence of Metropolitan Toronto and Los Angeles' Lakewood Plan, we have little or no developed rationale for choosing between them on the basis of measured observables reflecting desirable significant changes in the human condition. Public choice theorists argue with impeccable logic but with almost a Downsian unconcern for the isomorphism or lack of isomorphism of their assumptions with observed reality. The protagonists of metropolitan reform show scarcely any great interest in empirical observation. Thus the Committee for Economic Development and its academic advisors can say, "America's metropolitan problems have produced two relatively separate streams of suggestions for reform. One is concerned with substantive problems—education, transportation, housing, welfare, pollution. The other analyzes the structure that governs metropolitan areas. Although the interrelationship between structure and substance is occasionally mentioned, it is seldom analyzed in depth. The result is that the connection between the substantive problems and governmental structure is only vaguely understood."[15] How odd that this confession of ignorance should not have at least inhibited the academic advisors from advocating major changes in government. Perhaps they didn't expect to be taken seriously or, as Charles Hyneman remarked in another connection about administrative reform, this is an adventure in theology, metaphysics, and esthetic.

According to Charles Haar and his associates,

> The current development of urban regions has proceeded in the absence of effective metropolitan planning. The results have been far from disastrous: Essential services have been provided. . . . The American governmental system has indeed responded to the most serious challenges of urban growth, and a major part of this response has been increasing Federal assistance in community development. As a result, the most pressing needs have been met, and few real crises have been allowed to develop.[16]

Despite these good marks, Haar and associates believe the metropolitan system, although fortunately non-disastrous to this point, should be given conscious direction. Their reasons are much the same as those Lloyd Rodwin gives for the choice of an urban growth strategy. After reviewing the woeful deficiency in analytic tools and even of solid information, Rodwin remarks, "Decisions are daily being made which fix tomorrow's patterns of development. Many governments might prefer to make these decisions consciously."[17] And this is the best of reasons for having a government to make decisions consciously—so that hopefully one can at least learn and in the process improve one's practice. The task of government is to take one out of the state of nature and change the unintended play of forces into an ordered set of intended and corrigible outcomes.

Yet this is easier said, by far, than done. Dean William Wheaton has this to say, "One could compare Houston, which has had no planning, with any of a score of cities of comparable size and recency of development, which have had the most advanced planning, and find no discernible important differences."[18] Depressing, but refreshingly candid coming from the dean of a school that turns out city planners. Another piece of candor from the Advisory Commission on Intergovernmental Relations,

> References to economies of scale to be realized from performing urban services on a large scale are common in public administration literature. However, with few exceptions these references are not substantiated with specific objective studies of what has happened when the administration of various urban services has been moved from a smaller to a larger unit of government.[19]

Would that the Commission take its own implicit warning and make the requisite objective studies before handing down prescriptions without evidence of their efficacity. Perhaps one should not regard the American public as invincibly ignorant, but as rather being possessed of a commendable sales resistance to sloppily researched proposals and arrogant pontification.

Sales resistance, however, is not cognitive competence. A profound and one might say warranted distrust of experts can result in a corrosive cynicism and alienation that perhaps contributes more to the sense and actuality of powerlessness than anything else. Political science has not helped much. It has largely confined itself to institutional description with little concern for relating outputs to inputs and even less to reasoned evaluation of outputs. Eugene Meehan has written persuasively of the faulty epistemology that has dogged the discipline, leading it up blind alleys and failing to yield explanations capable of providing useful intervention strategies. Meehan has found that this epistemological disaster has not been unrelated to the discipline's romance with logical positivism and the consequent disbelief in the possibility of a reasoned process of evaluation. The lack of utilitarian orientation has the aspects of a becoming modesty among those who scarcely expect their wares to be put to any use except as testimonial advertising or conspicuous intellectual consumption of a Veblenian honorificence. The editing device of such an enterprise in default of the test of practical use becomes that of the mutual admiration society.

Meehan is not alone in his concern that lack of practical orientation has led and must lead to sterility. Warren Ilchman in a footnote to a review of his recent book says, "What we try to do in *The Political Economy of Change* is to encourage social scientists to move away from the metaphysics of systems and functionalism . . . and to move towards the analysis of real-world political choices."[20] Donald Campbell, the Northwestern social psychologist, has called for the study of reforms as experiments in the hope not only to add to the sacred lore of science but also for the mundane purpose of finding out what really works.

It is strange that political science has rarely showed signs of regarding the levels of cognitive competence as being of serious political significance. In international relations where the editing device of war gives point to comparative weapons technology, we show at least a limited concern for the state of knowledge. Elsewhere perhaps because of the value relativism of our logical positivism we disregard the possibility of knowledge and treat variations as matters of taste. Of course to the extent that the knowledge of political science is metaphysical in character, its real-life consequences are akin to the consequences of metaphysics in other spheres. One can not review the literature of cities or other aspects of the discipline without the sense that testable and tested political knowledge could be immensely useful. Indeed such knowledge could make major contributions to the amelioration of the human condition. The attainment of testable knowledge is not easy. Donald Campbell, who combines the virtues of a practicing scientist with an interest in philosophy of science, makes painfully clear the rarity of the critical experiment and the unambiguous conclusive answer to the most well-conducted inquiry. This is under the best of circumstances—how much more difficult with the fragmentary and polluted data yielded by the uncontrolled laboratory of public affairs. Beyond this and compounding it further is the political consequentiality of knowledge; of course were it inconsequential we would not want it either. The current fate of PPBS is indicative of the concern of those selling patent medicines for a Pure Food and Drug Administration. Stanley Botner suggests, "that, however ineffective, PPBS was *too* effective for the groups presently dominating the budgetary bargaining process."[21] Difficult as the attainment of knowledge may be, if there was any one thing that got us down from the trees and out of the caves, it was the human capacity to think to some purpose and the fruitful use of that capacity. The political city as the Greeks knew was the sociological requisite for the fullest and best use of the talents of men. The city was where you could, if you would, put it all together.

Where the Buck Stops

The city and to some extent the neighborhood are where the buck stops. Here in the lives of observable people we can see the actual outcomes of government programs. As a representative sample of the range of the human condition, the city provides a living standard of evaluation. As a system of people and their roles it provides a meaningful whole that can be made operational; in terms of the functional autocracies of substantive bureaucracies, the city can police and intentionally and corrigibly direct their unintended collective impact. How important the visible needs and desires of the city's population are for the coordination of federal bureaucracies is readily inferrable from Martha Derthick's fine study, *New Towns In-Town.* Most federal attempts at coordination have found coordination for its own sake empty. Coordination has to be for the sake of quite specifiable people; and if it is really to be for their sake, they had better, as Lord Lindsay urged, have some say as to whether the shoe fits.

The Greek city was viewed by the classic Greek philosophers as a momentous discovery setting Greeks apart from barbarians. While the Greek conception of the city has been treated as irrelevant for the subordinate modern city, it may still have relevance for the ills that affect us. Paratroopers may descend on Little Rock and troop carriers roll in Newark and Detroit, but an effective order other than one of subjection requires the restoration of a local legitimacy. The ethical unravelling of the American local community is widely apparent. Its restoration is high on any responsible agenda. While Patrick Moynihan speaks somewhat scornfully of a "Maximum Feasible Misunderstanding," the demand for popular participation in the programs affecting people's lives is wholly in accord with the best civic traditions of the west. Potentially anarchical as Plato and other enemies have always seen the democratic thrust, its alternative can be little other than servile acquiescence. Thucydides captured the good and the bad of the tremendous unleashing of popular energies in democratic Athens. Centuries later we may be sadder but scarcely wiser as to whether the possibilities of achievement are worth the undoubted risks.

Professor Dahl in his presidential address concerned himself with the scale and functioning of the good city. His model must have been the city he describes in *Who Governs?*—not as described but as possible. Reading Fred Powledge's *Model City,* another and later account of New Haven's experiences, one is struck first with the seeming pomposity of the undertaking, with its shabby real estate promotions, federal deals, and public relations huckstering, and then with the tragedy that this most heralded of the nation's efforts with its share of generous if untutored idealism should have come to so little account. Powledge sees the failure in the executive-centered coalition's unwillingness to share power with the neighborhoods, the poor, and the black community. He finds a lack of will at the root of the failure. Perhaps, but a lack of knowledge might be a more accurate diagnosis. More knowledge would have avoided a Potempkin village erected on the basis of federal funds with no self-sustaining local structure capable of standing on its own when the federal largesse dried up. The departure of the New Haven new breed to greener pastures is the best of commentaries on the failure of the New Haven model to develop continuing citizenship and leadership. New Haven's response to the loss of federal funds teaches again the lesson of local powerlessness. Few things could be more unfortunate than the drawing of such a conclusion. Was it inevitable that local resources could not have been developed to produce a model city capable of standing on its own, capable of using but not hopelessly dependent on precarious federal funds? Black Muslim and Amish churches, "The Hill" in St. Louis, and ethnic communities elsewhere suggest that cities with resources, however meager by American standards—large by those of the world—should be able to maintain themselves. Surely they can be making their resources, however limited, truly serve them.

Max Weber said when the city lost its walls, the city ceased to be. Literally interpreted this means when the city ceased to be a fortress and the citizens ceased to be soldiers defending that fortress, the city as previously known came to an end. But is the literal meaning to be taken literally? Can the modern city be symbolically walled, civicly if not militarily defended, and imbued with a rich and purposeful common life capable of capturing the minds and hearts of men? If the city is not mere land whose buildings and location may obsolesce but a territory infused with value by valued, continuing institutions linking the generations, the city need not lose function as Sternlieb and Finger suggest it has. The city is a territorial embodiment of human capital, an institution that provides shared purposes, a theater, and an instrument of action for the realization of human values. A city may be this; but clearly, as Warner noted in his *Street Cur Suburbs,* the city of liberal individualistic capitalism has been ceasing to be such a city. Its civility, such as it is, derives from an older city. The price of the erosion of that older city is becoming painfully clear.

For no one must this be more poignant than for the new black mayors inheriting a city fiscally impoverished and spiritually eviscerated. Professor Wilson in his perceptive study of "Negro Politics" makes the point that Negro politicians look to the dominant white model of the period when they came politically of age. The model to which the black mayor is all too likely to look is New Haven. William Nelson, Jr., in his study of Gary makes the sad but not surprising finding, "we need only point out that much of

Mayor Hatcher's present popularity rests on the continuing viability of his federal programs. These programs represent the Achilles' heel of the Hatcher administration. A significant cutback in such programs by the federal government, the onset of a serious scandal involving a major federal program, or the failure of these programs to live up to their grandiose promises could produce a wave of resentment aimed directly at the mayor's office. Essentially, Hatcher has built his popularity in the black community on the back of forces beyond his control. Consequently, a drastic change in direction of these forces could have disastrous repercussions on the future of his administration.

"What is needed most in Gary at the present time is a community-based, community-oriented political organization that can begin the process of institutionalizing Black Power. Such an organization can provide some assurance that whatever the fate of the leader the progress of the movement will not be unalterably deterred."[22] Nelson speaks to the peculiar condition of blacks for whom the still existent city is a powerful device to establish an identity and living space within the dominant and dominating larger society.

But blacks are not the only ones who are trying to create a new society within the womb of the old—or at very least to revivify American purposes to the point where they can command the uncoerced allegiance of young and old. Robert Goodman in *After the Planners* speaks of a guerilla architecture pioneering the new in the midst of the old. We used to see the states as the laboratories of innovation in American democracy. The cities are far more likely to be. Once we have freed ourselves from the dogma of their powerlessness we may find that they, even in the nation-state, can be made as the best of the Greeks held the instruments of a good and noble life.

Notes

1. James Q. Wilson, "Problems in the Study of Urban Politics," a paper prepared for a conference in commemoration of the 50th anniversary of the Department of Government, Indiana University, Bloomington, November 5-7, 1964, p. 3.
2. *Ibid.,* p. 8.
3. Robert A. Dahl, *Who Governs?* (New Haven: Yale University Press, 1961), p. 94.
4. Fred Powledge, *Model City: One Town's Efforts to Rebuild Itself* (New York: Simon and Schuster, 1970), p. 19.
5. Samuel B. Warner, *Street Car Suburbs,* cited in Charles M. Haar, *The End of Innocence of a Suburban Reader* (Glenview, Ill.: Scott Foresman, 1972), p. 167.
6. Statement of Lester C. Thurow, "Hearings Before the Joint Economic Committee, Congress of the U.S.," 92nd Congress, 2nd Session, March 21, 22, 23 and 24, 1972 (Washington, D.C.: U.S. Government Printing Office), pp. 168-169.
7. The Advisory Commission on Intergovernmental Relations, *Metropolitan*

Social and Economic Disparities: Implications for Intergovernmental Relations in Central Cities and Suburbs (Washington, D.C.: The Commission, January 1965), p. 13.
8. Marilyn Gittel, *et al., Demonstration for Social Change, An Experiment in Local Control* (New York: Institute for Community Studies, Queens College, 1971), p. 39.
9. *Ibid.,* p. 87.
10. Thurow, *op. cit.,* p. 172.
11. *Ibid.,* p. 174.
12. Remarks Prepared for Delivery by George Romney, Secretary, U.S. Department of Housing and Urban Development, at the St. Louis Metropolitan Area Leadership Option Meeting at Ralston Purina Auditorium, St. Louis, Missouri, April 6, 1972, p. 7.
13. Letter from Lyle Fitch to the author, July 18, 1972.
14. Advisory Commission on Intergovernmental Relations, *op. cit.,* p. 91.
15. Committee for Economic Development, *Reshaping Government in Metropolitan Areas* (New York: The Committee, 1970), p. 23.
16. Charles H. Haar, *et al.,* "The Effectiveness of Metropolitan Planning for Committee on Government Operations" (Washington, D.C.: U.S. Government Printing Office, 1964).
17. Lloyd Rodwin, *Nations and Cities, A Comparison of Strategies for Urban Growth* (Boston: Houghton Mifflin, 1970), p. 14.
18. William Wheaton, "Metro-Allocation Planning," *Journal of the American Institute of Planners,* Vol. XXXIII (March 1967), quoted in Bollens and Schmandt, *The Metropolis: Its People, Politics and Economic Life,* 2nd edition (New York: Harper & Row, 1970).
19. Advisory Commission on Intergovernmental Relations, *Performance of Urban Functions: Local and Areawide* (Washington, D.C.: The Commission, September 1963), p. 45.
20. John D. Montgomery, "Scientific Politics for Second-Class Statesman," review of Warren F. Ilchman and Norman Thomas Uphoff's *The Political Economy of Change, Public Administration Review,* Vol. 32, No. 3 (May/June 1972), p. 264.
21. Stanley B. Botner, "PPB Under Nixon," *Public Administration Review,* Vol. 32, No. 3 (May/June 1972), p. 255.
22. William E. Nelson, Jr., *Black Politics in Gary: Problems and Prospects* (Washington, D.C.: Joint Center for Political Studies, Vol. 1, No. 3, March 1972).

1973 (33:543-552)

PART IV

Intergovernmental Finances: Federal Aid and Fiscal Dependency/Interdependency

Intergovernmental finances have been and continue to be a salient feature of American federalism. It has been the basis and impetus for many intergovernmental relationships. Permeating intergovernmental finance are issues such as inter-level dependency and interdependency, program centralization and decentralization, grant-in-aid evolution and devolution. The six articles in this section can examine only a limited number of issues and aspects of intergovernmental finance. A broad-gauged introductory selection is followed by three articles—one on each of the major types of federal aid: categorical, block, and general revenue sharing. Also included are two articles that address specific and problematic aspects of grants-in-aid.

Professor Daniel J. Elazar of Temple University shows the intimate relationship between finances and politics. They are, for most purposes, the opposite sides of the same coin. Contained in Elazar's exploration are analyses of the consequences of federal aid and descriptions of three theories of federal influence in providing intergovernmental aid. Elazar also offers observations on the notable rise in the intergovernmental sharing of revenues and expenditures.

The article by Gilbert and Specht was published in 1973 but it deals with a competitive categorical grant program in the late 1960s, the heyday of grantsmanship. It describes the operation of the Model Cities grant program. Particular emphasis is placed on the selection process—the competitiveness, complexity, and the subjectiveness (politics) of award criteria in categorical grants. A simplified and "inexpensive" grant rating method is proposed—one that contains less "subjective" criteria for determining potential performances of applicants.

The third selection reviews the development and operation of the first major block grant to state and local governments, the Omnibus Crime Control and Safe Streets Act of 1968. Douglas Harman, currently the City Manager of Alexandria, Virginia, provides an overview of the block grant concept and of the entry of the national government into law enforcement.

Harman explores the multiple and varied political conflicts emanating from this new national role and from the block grant approach to intergovernmental aid. He correctly predicted in 1970 that the LEAA Block grant foreshadowed "future patterns of intergovernmental relations in other grant fields," but that the device is likely to be "successfully introduced into only a limited number of policy fields."

Professors David A. Caputo (Purdue University) and Richard L. Cole (The George Washington University) reported in 1975 on the use of general revenue sharing (GRS) monies in cities with populations over 50,000. They analyzed the functional distribution of GRS funds as well as allocations between existing and new programs. Their survey-based findings show that GRS had noticeable perceived impacts on city tax rates but resulted in limited effects on social service programs. The most prominent impact of GRS, however, was the general satisfaction of city officials with the program.

Robert D. Newton of National Science Foundation discusses various administrative issues of federal assistance programs. Of particular concern are issues relating to: (1) management requirements and standards for monitoring, reporting, directing and approving grants and (2) roles and responsibilities in federal assistance transactions. He suggests that the Federal Grant and Cooperative Agreement Act of 1977 established a framework which permits a resolution of these and other concerns about the administration of federal assistance activities. Newton makes a case for drawing clear distinctions among three types of intergovernmental fiscal transactions: (a) contracts, (b) cooperative agreements, and (c) grants.

The concluding article in this section was written by Eugene S. Sunshine, an administrator in New York State government. Drawing on his experience with the New York State energy program, he outlines a strategy for dealing with a major by-product of the current era of retrenchment—unsuccessful grant applicants. He also describes the reactions of unsuccessful grant applicants to this strategy in New York state. The "minimizing of disappointment," according to Sunshine, requires special and concerted efforts because the negative consequences of inaction "are too severe to be left to happenstance."

The six articles included in this section explore significant issues and aspects of intergovernmental finance. The first provides a contextual framework for the section. The next three reflect programmatic grant-in-aid developments. The last two address special problematic aspects of aid programs. Together these articles demonstrate the diversity, complexity, and dynamism of this dimension of intergovernmental relations.

DANIEL J. ELAZAR

Fiscal Questions and Political Answers in Intergovernmental Finance

This article is devoted to the political analysis and understanding of certain fiscal questions affecting federal-state-local relations in the United States today. This seemingly obvious point must be made at the outset because it is too easy, when dealing with fiscal questions, to substitute economic for political answers. Perhaps the most prominent example of this is the oft-encountered tendency to assess the respective policy roles of the various American governments by ascertaining what share of the total expenditure they contribute to the funding of specific programs. This shorthand but often misleading view is frequently encountered in the mass media where local programs are presented as federal ones on the assumption that the source of the funds also indicates the locus of political control, a view that has been refuted time and again by studies of a whole host of intergovernmental programs.

In recent years there have been a number of studies of intergovernmental financing in the United States which have attempted to assess the economic impact of various kinds of intergovernmental fiscal relationships, devices, and arrangements, with varying degrees of success.

If the economic impacts are hard to assess, the political ones are even more difficult. For one thing, they cannot be derived from the easily available quantitative data. Rather, they require sophisticated probing beneath the surface and examination of specific cases in light of the development of intergovernmental collaboration over the nearly two centuries that have elapsed since the founding of the Republic.

The issue is further complicated because, even if the impacts are not identical, in many cases they coincide. For example, it is of both political and economic significance that state and local expenditures combined exceed federal expenditures for domestic civil purposes by a ratio of approximately two to one. The radical increase in the number of federal grant programs since 1953 and the amount of federal funds allocated to those programs since 1964 are also significant in both respects. By the same token, so are the changing ratios of support in specific programs. Consequently, we cannot be too careful in avoiding the use of economic tests of significance to draw political conclusions that may not be warranted when the political evidence is given primacy.

There are a number of apparent trends in intergovernmental fiscal relations which are easily recognizable:

1. While all governmental spending is rising, the federal share of total state and local expenditures is increasing at an even faster pace.
2. Direct federal-local relations in funding specific programs are also increasing.
3. State aid to localities, through grants and revenue sharing, is increasing even more rapidly than federal aid.
4. Special state, local, and state-local financing arrangements—in the form of special districts or authorities—continue to be created, expanded, or simply maintained at existing levels.
5. More government programs are being financed intergovernmentally and are involving all planes of government.

At the same time:

1. While federal tax collections continue to dominate the revenue field, the share of governmental revenues raised by the states and their local subdivisions is actually growing.
2. The impact of state-local expenditures on the economy seems to be growing faster than state-local revenues.
3. Overall the fiscal role of the states in domestic matters is growing faster than that of any other government.
4. Local government's role as the handler of public funds is increasing even as its role as a source of funds has declined precipitously.
5. Whereas the federal role in spending money is necessariy of a piece and the states' roles are becoming increasingly similar, local governments are developing highly differentiated roles depending on the purposes for which they have been created and the populations they serve.
6. Perhaps the greatest impact of federal activity on the states and localities comes from direct federal expenditures for defense contracts, social security benefits, agricultural subsidies, and, now, Medicare, rather than from the federal share of more orthodox cooperative programs.

The Consequences of Federal Aid

The share of federal funds in state and local budgets is not in itself an indicator of the degree of federal control over programs. The southern states have continually ranked high in proportion of their budgets derived from federal sources (averaging 21.1 percent in 1968), yet, as we all know, they are willing—and generally able—to resist "federal control" more forcefully. The western states also rank above the national average (21.5 percent minus Alaska and Hawaii; 23.1 percent plus Alaska and Hawaii) in the proportion of their budgets derived from federal sources, yet they are no more subject to federal control than New Jersey (12.1 percent) or Massachusetts (14.6 percent).

The historical record tends to confirm this. In recent years the federal government has provided an average of 17 percent of state budgets through transfers of payments; and in excess of 30 percent in one or two states. In Minnesota, from the time it achieved statehood in 1858 to the turn of the century, the federal share of the state budget ranged from 17.9 to 56.3 percent, usually hovering around 30 percent. Today the state receives approximately 25 percent of its funds from federal sources. There has probably been little fundamental change in the power relationship between Minnesota and Washington in the past 100 years, but if anything, federal control over Minnesota's governmental activities was less a century ago than today.

The extent of federal control is largely determined through the political process. This means that most intergovernmental arrangements tend to be the immediate products of pragmatic decisions. Typically, such decisions reserve a substantial role for the states and localities because the political system and the public philosophy supporting it strongly reinforce the principle of noncentralization.

It has been argued that, even acknowledging the central role played by the states and localities in determining how federal money should be spent, the very fact that there is federal money available operates as a distorting influence causing the states and localities to spend their resources on programs that are desired by Washington in order to gain the federal grants. It is questionable whether this was ever true, if only because of the widespread nationwide consensus that has supported the great grant programs, usually from their very inception.

If federal aid for highways has tended to pull in a major share of state matching funds, all the evidence shows that highways are extraordinarily popular at the state level, that they would be popular regardless of the amount of federal funds available, and that if federal funds were reduced more, state and local resources would be allocated for road building even at the expense of other programs. Even the public welfare programs, though they are much less popular than highways with the taxpaying public, are supported on all planes of government by the general agreement that they must be continued, and federal funds make better state services possible. The truth is that the publics of the states are the same people who endorse (at times begrudgingly, it is true) the principle of federal action to relieve the less fortunate.

Today, the argument that federal funds skew the state and local expenditures is even more difficult to substantiate because the wide variety of federal grants makes the situation more comparable to a smorgasbord than to a set menu. With somewhere between 190 and 1,400 different grant allocations to choose from (the figure depends on how they are counted), no state or locality takes advantage of all the federal funds potentially available to it. Rather, each must pick and choose and thereby gain a measure of flexibility in putting together a "package" suitable to its particular needs.

If the share of federal funds is not, in itself, an indicator of the degree of federal control or even influence over programs, it does function to turn public attention to Washington. Given the limited amount of attention the public is apparently willing to focus on relatively dull questions of who provides what public services and how, and the even more limited space or time that can be devoted to such questions in the newspapers or on radio or television, it is not surprising that what generally gets to be reported are discussions in Congress or actions of the President. Nevertheless, this does a disservice to the programs in question as well as to the state and local governments by neglecting to show how the latter make crucial decisions in very important fields.

This problem is exacerbated by the fact that the prestigious national mass media focus attention on state and local actions only in time of crisis and invariably at times when some state is doing something contrary to national policy or national sentiment. Governor George Wallace of Alabama attracted attention almost every time he gave a speech outside of his own state, yet few of the "new breed" of governors, such as Shapp of Pennsylvania or Lucey of Wisconsin, not in the running for the presidential nomination, could get national attention for progressive action in their states.

As public attention is turned toward Washington, it becomes easier for people who would like to transform federally aided programs into federally controlled ones to do so. Thus the focus on Washington may come to be used both as an excuse and a vehicle for increasing federal control along with the federal dollar.

Three Theories of Federal Aid

To a greater degree than is normally acknowledged in our desire to emphasize American "pragmatism," it is possible to conclude that the nature of federal influence in federally aided programs depends upon the theory of the federal role implicit in those programs as structured by Congress, held implicitly by those who administer the programs, or pervading the country at the time. Three fundamental if implicit theories of federal aid can be identified. It is possible to trace all three theories back to the earliest days of the Republic.

1. The Federal Government-as-Servant Theory

First put in concrete form by John C. Calhoun, this theory holds that federal aid is legitimate, but only insofar as it is used to further state objectives in the national interest. Under this theory, Uncle Sam becomes a conduit, utilizing the superior revenue-raising powers of the federal government to funnel money back to the states and their subdivisions without dictating the uses to which the aid is to be put beyond setting certain very broad limits (e.g., that the funds be used for education or internal improvements) and, at the most, requiring an accounting for the honest use of the funds so transmitted. Most revenue-sharing proposals fall into this category.

While this theory was first popular among southern nationalists, every section of the country and every segment of the political system has espoused it at one time or another. Today the spokesmen for the major cities propound it most aggressively.

This theory is more than a claim that the states have a right to federal assistance to maintain programs tailored entirely to suit their own needs. Ultimately it rests on the idea that there is a strong convergence of national and local interests in meeting public demands so that the states or their subdivisions will use the money in ways consistent with national goals. Though this theory is frequently discussed disparagingly today, as lacking a degree of federal "muscle" deemed necessary by some, the historical record shows that when and where it has been tried, it has generally worked well.

2. The National Uniformity Theory

Those who espouse this notion generally hold that the goal of federally aided programs should be to establish uniform conditions throughout the country. In general, they espouse federal aid to states and localities only because they recognize the constitutional or political difficulties in obtaining direct federal management of such programs, or recognize the administrative values of decentralization. Far from viewing Uncle Sam as a conduit, they hold that federal funds should be utilized to minimize state and local discretionary action. They do not look upon the states or localities as political systems with legitimate goals of their own. In fact, they view state and local differences as residual phenomena, holdovers from another age or reflections of unhealthy deviations from national norms.

Alexander Hamilton comes closest to being the classic spokesman for the national uniformity theory. Since his day and, more particularly, since the New Deal, it has been widely held by those with particular programmatic interests who operate on the premise that national uniformity will eliminate problems of clashing interests in securing their programmatic goals. In fact, there is considerable evidence that those programs which have been shaped according to this theory also have the most administrative and political problems.

3. The Local Right—National Interest Theory

Those who espouse this position are prepared to acknowledge the existence of a substantial measure of legitimate distinctiveness in the states and localities and to affirm their constitutional right to preserve that distinctiveness. At the same time, they are equally prepared to recognize the existence of a national interest in securing the implementation of certain programs or the establishment of certain nationwide standards. They view federal aid as a means to accomplish both ends.

Those who espouse it generally favor the shaping of federal transfers of payments to reflect a certain broad national policy that also represents a consensus of state and local views in significant ways. Under this theory, basic federal standards are established for each transfer program, but in such a way that the states and localities are given considerable leeway for discretionary implementation of the programs by right.

The first great American statesman to formally elucidate this theory was Albert Gallatin, a great and too-little-recognized architect of the American system. Since the days of Gallatin, it has been enunciated in every generation in terms appropriate to the times and has been enormously influential in the shaping of cooperative programs because it implicitly suits the consensus of interests that usually underline such programs.

Use of the Theories

Carried to their logical extremes, these three theories are incompatible, but, in fact, they may and usually do function simultaneously to influence the system of federal aid as it has evolved, primarily because they are rarely made explicit and, hence, are not in a position to be pushed to their limits. This is particularly true because individuals who represent each of the three positions may come to tactical agreement on the structure and functioning of specific programs, either out of necessity or because the practical expressions of their theories in particular cases coincide. Still, it is quite clear that the impact of federal transfers is quite different when one theory or another becomes dominant.

In the 19th century, there is some evidence that most federal aid to the states and localities was justified on the basis of the first theory. Thus, federal standards were usually justified as being necessary to assure proper handling of the transfers from a purely technical standpoint and were not considered to be devices to foster explicit national policies even where, in fact, that is just what they were doing. The perceptive political leaders of the time understood this and were content to justify their practices using such theories.

Until very recently, 20th century aid programs have generally been justified through an implicit reliance on the third theory. The federal role has come to be a more positive one as Congress and the federal administration have assumed the responsibility for developing national standards of varying breadth and intensity while at the same time reaffirming the primary role of the state and local governments in the domestic sphere. As in the 19th century, there was a great gap between the verbalized theory of federal-state relations and the implicit theory used to make the federal system function while meeting the demands of the times.

Most recently, there has been an increasing demand in some quarters for the reorganization of federal aid programs in line with the principles of the second theory. In those quarters, the importance of the national view is considered to far exceed any need for state and local differentiation no matter how legitimate. They are willing to acknowledge state and local primacy, even in constitutional terms. In some programs this viewpoint has gathered considerable momentum. If its thrust were to grow, the effects of the increase in the amount of federal funds transferred to the states and localities would be quite different and would be of momentous significance for the noncentralized system of government which America has chosen to maintain.

Contradictory Trends in Federal-Local Relations

Much is being made today of the increase in direct federal-local relations in funding various programs. While it is true that such relations have been increasing steadily since the 1930s and at an accelerated pace in the last several years, they are not as unprecedented as most people believe. From the earliest days of the Republic, there has been a tendency for the largest cities in the several states to seek direct ties with the national government. This was true even when the cities themselves were relatively small, so long as they were substantially larger than any other local governments within their respective states. The principal concerns that led the cities to Washington in the 19th century were those related to the promotion of commerce: the improvement of the rivers and harbors; the construction of canals, roads, and railroads; the extension of postal services; the provision of proper customs and immigration facilities; and in some cases, harbor defense. In their day, programs in these fields had all of the impact and stimulated all of the interest that urban redevelopment programs do in ours.

In this spirit, the city council of Richmond, Virginia, lobbied before Congress long, hard, and successfully in the generation prior to the Civil War for the assignment of the U.S. Corps of Engineers to improve navigation on the James River and the appropriation of federal funds for the work. The cooperative program that emerged from their efforts was an informal one whereby the U.S. Engineers not only undertook the work but contracted with the city to provide the equipment, thus transferring enough federal funds to Richmond to enabled it to acquire equipment which it could continue to use after the congressional appropriations for direct federal activity had run out. The Richmond case was typical. In Boston, the city fathers went so far to secure federally financed harbor improvements as to constitute a Harbor Improvement Board whose membership included such federal authorities as the U.S. Customs officials in the Port of Boston.

Despite rhetoric to the contrary, this is the pattern that has persisted into the 20th century. The large cities have, in most cases, been encouraged to turn to Washington by their states, if not openly, at least by tacit agreement that the states would use their limited resources of money, time, and manpower to service smaller urban and rural places, while their great metropolitan centers would complement their efforts by doing similar work themselves. In this respect, the states are behaving no differently from when they encourage certain of their functional agencies such as the highway or welfare departments to pursue negotiations with their federal counterparts, in effect utilizing the cities as agents of state interests as much as autonomous entities.

It is only in relatively recent times that the cities have taken advantage of their political muscle to seek federal aid in competition with their states, actively opposing state involvement in programs in which the states were ready to assume responsibility. This new trend is partly a simple consequence of the growth in size of the very largest cities in the country to the point where their horizons tend to be bounded by their own metropolitan areas, while, at the same time, their resources have increased to enable them to function as well as many states. Partly it also reflects the competition between those interests which are rooted in the very largest cities and those rooted outside of them.

This city-state competition for the federal dollar is particularly strong where the great cities—the six with a million or more people and perhaps another ten that stand just below the million mark—are involved. These great cities are presently at the height of their political power even though, by objective criteria, they have passed their peak. Today cities of over a million represent less than 10 percent of the total population of the United States, while close to 60 percent of all Americans live in cities or communities of less than 50,000 population. Furthermore, the proportion of the nation's population in the former is declining while the proportion in the latter group grows. In this respect, the great cities' recent acquisition of political power parallels that of the agricultural interests in the past. The latter gained power in the 1930s, a generation after they had passed their peak strength and were then able to saddle the country with a number of programs of questionable utility in solving basic agricultural problems.

In fact, however, the great cities do not necessarily otain the largest share of the federal aid distributed to the localities, and certainly do not have a majority of the projects supported with such aid. Cities of all sizes have been sharing in the expansion of federal aid for urban improvements. But, with the smaller cities, even those in metropolitan areas as most of them are, there is a significant difference: they must rely upon their states for technical assistance in obtaining and utilizing federal aid to a far greater extent than their larger sisters.

Herein lies the trend of the future. Even as metropolitanization of the country increases, the great cities continue to decline. The new centers of local power are in the suburbs and exurbs that are rapidly becoming complete cities in their own right. Increasingly, federal-local relations will be with those communities as much as with the central cities. If present trends continue—as in all likelihood they will—these communities will become increasingly detached from their central cities as they develop more sophisticated economic and social bases of their own without recourse to "downtown."

This trend is likely to accelerate to include the medium-sized and small cities outside of the great metropolitan areas. It is possible that these communities may well come to rely on federal funds to an even greater extent than the big cities. Even today, the federal share of big city budgets tends to be small. But, at the same time, the smaller cities will have less independent political muscle and are likely to rely more heavily on their states for political as well as financial support. This is already evident in many states.

Program Versus Project Grants

To date, federal aid has reached the states and localities in two different ways. Federal aid to the states has generally been programmatic, that is to say, it is oriented to supporting particular kinds of programs, e.g., the highway program, welfare program, mental health program, and the like. Federal aid to localities, on the other hand, has been project oriented, designed to support individual projects of a highly specific nature. In fact, where new general aid programs have been developed, they have generally been channelled through the states, whereas when project grant programs are established, they tend to be passed directly to the localities, sometimes with state involvement, but, even so, they are usually shaped through direct federal-local negotiations.

On one hand, the project grant system has placed an even greater premium on local initiative than more traditional aid programs, rewarding local energy on a case-by-case basis. In other respects, it has led to greater federal power in determining local use of federal funds, since each project must be approved by the appropriate federal agency before it is funded.

Significantly, the project system has led to the tremendous log jams at the federal level which are now attracting so much attention, since the federal agencies are forced to screen projects from all over the country without any intermediary agency to assign priorities or limit the flow of requests (which invariably exceed the funds available). While attempts have been made to reduce these log jams through devolution of decision-making responsibilities to regional offices, the character of the American political system means that communities refused at the regional level turn to their representatives in Washington to reopen the issue, thus bringing matters up to the highest decision-making level in any case. In this respect, all arguments about the political virtues of noncentralization aside, the project system violates certain cardinal administrative tenets that were maintained in the more traditional grant-in-aid program whereby the states were given the last word in determining which local projects should be funded and were able to handle the pressures more easily.

The really new "Great Society" grant programs emphasized project grants. Consequently, there has been a great proliferation of problems of allocation and coordination in recent years, leading willy-nilly to greater federal control, even where such control is not intended by Congress or the federal administrative authorities. Herein lies a major problem whose resolution will determine much of the future impact of federal funds on state and local operations.

The Hidden Dimension: State Aid to Localities

Frequently overlooked in considering the changing character of public finance in the United States is the increased state role in financing local government. In fact, there has been a greater shift in the fiscal balance between the states and localities than between the federal government and the states since the beginning of the 20th century (when figures first became available on a consistent basis).

By and large, the states provide aid to their local subdivisions through programmatic grants and revenue sharing. To date, they have made little use of project grants except in the conservation and road construction fields. Revenue sharing is the most important device, primarily because of the tremendous share of total state-local expenditures devoted to education, where the states are relied upon to provide substantial assistance while assuring maximum local control over the schools. This has led to the development of formulas for distributing aid on a per-pupil basis with minimal standards demanded by the state in return for the funds.

Though superficial examination of the situation would seem to indicate that the more focused aid provided by the federal government has had more impact on the localities than the more general aid given by the states, this is by no means certain. In truth, no adequate studies of the relative impacts have been made, but a careful look at the situation would no doubt indicate that, in those fields in which state aid has been substantial, state aid has had at least as great an impact as federal aid. The states, without setting the kinds of specific detailed requirements often demanded by the federal government, have been able to combine technical assistance and professional standards with money to enable the localities to utilize the first and establish the second. It is likely, given the general consensus on behalf of common goals that exists in the United States, that this kind of aid is sufficient to accomplish a great deal with a minimum amount of red tape or political dislocation.

The states' role in providing revenue for their localities is found to increase, given all the tendencies of the day. The very dispersal of population into smaller political units at the local level, coupled with the genuine and legitimate reluctance of those units to merge, adds to the necessity for state activity in the fiscal field. In fact, the states will undoubtedly have to assume new roles in tax and assessment equalization in order to reduce some of the worst inequities that are already seen to be by-products of the present system of complex local governmental jurisdictions.

Special State-Local Financing Arrangements

In this regard, it is important to consider the continuing development of special state and local financing arrangements, usually through special districts at the local level or authorities where the state is directly involved. Whatever their drawbacks, such special financing arrangements serve very distinctive purposes which are intricately tied to the character of the American political system. Since our political system places a premium on the ability to negotiate in order to achieve a share in the compromises that become programs at any and all levels of government, the first requisite for any interest is to have the best possible seat at the negotiating table. When this necessity to have a good (meaning legitimate) seat is combined with the usual intense competition for limited funds and the American predilection for limiting the activities of government, the special district or the state authority has an obvious appeal to those who are interested in achieving new public goals.

In essence, the special district allows specialized local interests to obtain a guaranteed position for a particular program in the constellation of governments and a guarantee of a certain amount of revenue for its maintenance as well. In a somewhat different vein, the authority device not only allows the states to gain a say in certain predominantly local matters, but offers a way to achieve inter-local coordination in a situation where the fragmentation of local government prevents concerted action by local decision alone.

The conditions which promote special financing arrangements do not appear likely to diminish. In fact, there is some indication that these special state and local arrangements actually increase the autonomy of state and local interests in dealing with the federal government by concentrating energy at key points, protecting that concentration, and then letting the authorities or districts negotiate with their federal counterparts.

The disadvantages of this approach have frequently been noted—even exaggerated. There are, however, some real advantages as well. In terms more familiar to the game of poker, the existence of special government institutions is a means of paying the ante that gives interests a right to sit in on the game, a license to negotiate and bargain with other governments and the interests they represent. Once the ante is paid, the possibilities of coming out ahead are substantially equalized for all players, thus allowing local governments to serve local interests and not just administer national programs.

Intergovernmental Grants: The Reasons Why

Herein lies the key to the growth in intergovernmental sharing of revenues and expenditures. On one hand, local governments are prevented by circumstances (in the form of rising costs) from relying on exclusively local revenues for paying the ante as much as they had in the past, and must seek outside aid while turning to structural devices to protect their interests in cooperative efforts. On the other hand, the states and particularly the federal government frequently gain their right to sit in on games previously considered exclusively local by contributing needed funds to them. Indeed, they frequently are able to start new games with their funding powers. But even when they start a new game, they can do so only by setting up another table and inviting those who are constitutionally entitled or politically able to participate in the great game of government in the United States to sit at it.

Sharing, then, is a way to maximize the chances of all three planes of government plus public and private nongovernmental interests to participate in the public decision-making process and in the shaping of life in these United States. Typically, all decisions involve a wide range of actors drawn from all the relevant governments and interested private parties, regardless of the precise sharing of fiscal responsibility. The American political system as a whole is designed to encourage this kind of widespread participation in the decision-making process. In fact, a kind of circularity prevails. The complexities of federalism offer many points of access for influencing decisions. The decisions that emerge reflect the many pressures that have come into play and offer something for most of those involved in the process. Among the consequences of such decisions is the reinforcement of the system as it exists through the encouragement of the actors who feel reasonably satisfied with the rewards it offers them.

1972 (32:471-478)

NEIL GILBERT and HARRY SPECHT

"Picking Winners": Federal Discretion and Local Experience as Bases for Planning Grant Allocation

Federal grant allocation procedures often rely upon the granting authority's technical ability to judge the merits of different applicants as a basis for selecting those to be funded. The rationale for such selection procedures, how these procedures are organized, and their results are the general issues of concern in this study. The specific context in which these questions are addressed is the Model Cities Program. Cities were chosen to receive initial planning grants for this program through an intricate selection process developed by HUD. The fundamental assumption of this selection process was that by using expert judgments made by federal staff, HUD could "pick winners"; that is, they could select those applicants who would be most likely to achieve Model Cities Program objectives better than could be done by random choice, first-come-first-served, or some other system of selection. By comparing the federal ratings given to applicants with measures of actual program outcomes, we attempt to estimate the extent to which this assumption provides a useful guide for grant allocation policy.

The Model Cities Program Selection Process

The Demonstration Cities and Metropolitan Development Act of 1966 called for a comprehensive approach in combined physical and social planning to attack the problems of urban decay and human strife affecting large sections of cities throughout the nation. For the cities selected, participation in the Model Cities Program was expected to last approximately six years. The first year was to be devoted to planning, the product of which was a Comprehensive Demonstration Plan (CDP). The CDP was to designate the specific content and objectives of programs to be implemented in the following action year and to set the general framework for programs over a continuing five-year period.

The first major task in launching the Model Cities Program was to select the cities that were to receive planning grants. All cities were eligible to submit applications for grants. By May 1, 1967, the deadline for submissions, 193 cities had applied. Six months later, on November 16, 1967, the first 63 cities to receive grants were announced, and 12 more were named during the spring of 1968. In all, 75 cities were selected from the original 193 applicants for first-round funding. The cities and towns chosen had populations ranging in size from approximately 2,300 to 8,000,000.

In applying for these first-round planning grants the cities followed a 51-page Program Guide prepared by HUD.[1] The Guide stated that applications should include an analysis of the social, economic, and physical problems of the proposed Model Neighborhood Area (MNA). The size of model neighborhoods was not stipulated, but it was suggested that the MNA should be a sizable, cohesive, primarily residential area, and "at least part hard-core slum in which low-income families are concentrated."[2] In addition to the problem analysis, applications were to specify proposed program approaches and goals related to identified problems, the anticipated administrative and planning structure for the Model Cities Program, and a work program for producing the CDP. The Guide stressed that programs "should be truly comprehensive, both in range and completeness of the activities proposed and in the resources brought to bear."[3] The suggested list of Model Cities Program components included: physical improvement, housing, transportation, education, manpower and economic development, recreation and culture, crime reduction, health, social services, and public assistance. Finally, the Guide noted that proposed planning structures should provide "mechanisms for a flow of communication and meaningful dialogue between the citizens of the area and the demonstration agency" as well as opportunities for residents to participate actively in planning and program implementation.[4] The form and substance of this statutory requirement for "widespread citizen participation" was not clearly stated in the Guide.

As suggested above, preparing the application for a planning grant was no simple matter. In effect the cities were asked to submit a "plan to plan." Willmann notes that Philadelphia, which submitted a 350-page proposal for a planning grant, was "an outstanding example of the kind of planning necessary for model city activity."[5] From HUD's perspective, putting the application together was an initial test of a city's potential for meeting the more extensive planning and program objectives that would be required of cities participating in the Model Cities Program. It was from this perspective that an intricate and costly project was established to review and compare applications for the purpose of awarding the first-round Model Cities planning grants.

The procedure for choosing among applicants was called the Planning

Grant Review Project (PGRP). The PGRP was a systematic attempt to analyze and evaluate all of the applications submitted. Initially, applications were reviewed and commented upon or rated by members of each of the agencies expected to be engaged in funding demonstration projects—HUD, Department of Justice, Department of Health, Education, and Welfare (HEW), Office of Economic Opportunity (OEO), and the Departments of Labor, Transportation, and Commerce. Following this review, there was a preliminary interagency review committee meeting in which decisions were made either to defer the application or to move it to an advanced review, at which point the final funding recommendation was made. Based upon the final recommendations, HUD made the selection of cities to be funded, subject to White House approval.

Of course, the final selection of cities was not a purely technical matter based on expert judgments of capability. Political considerations also played a role in this process. At the very least, a wide geographical spread among the chosen cities was politically desirable. And there is reason to believe that in some cases more stringent political constraints were operating. For example, only nine of the first 63 cities chosen were represented in the House of Representatives by Republicans. Five of the cities chosen were in the districts of Administration supporters on the House HUD-Independent Offices Appropriations Subcommittee.[6] One of these cities, Smithville, Tennessee (population approximately 2,300), was represented by the Subcommittee's chairman. Later, this city received a substantial action grant for the first program year. Asked to explain Smithville's good fortune, former HUD Secretary Wood said, "Smithville is a very small place, but there are those who love it."[7] Similarly, James notes that although Albuquerque, New Mexico, officials spent only six days preparing their application, they were confident that Senator Clinton Anderson would not be refused, and they were right.[8]

On the other hand, Charlotte, North Carolina, was selected despite the fact that its congressman was one of the most vigorous House opponents of Model Cities. This suggests that, as with many federal allocations, the Planning Grant Review Project (PGRP) may be seen as an effort to exercise discretion and technical expertise within broad political boundaries of choice. Another interpretation is possible. That is, the PGRP was simply an elaborate device to rationalize predetermined political choices. If this was the case, it was not a very imaginative effort from the viewpoint of efficiency. For, as shall be seen, a tremendous amount of time and money went into this selection procedure.

In the PGRP there were two main dimensions along which applicants were evaluated by each federal agency. These dimensions were conceived of as a "capability analysis" and a "functional analysis." The capability analysis was primarily an evaluation of the applicant's general capacity for meeting Model Cities' objectives as judged by experience and performance in related programs. For example, a typical HEW capability report is summarized thus:[9]

> [The applicant] rated above average in ability to develop, execute, and support a coordinated MN program. Communications across organizational lines, with client groups and individual citizens has been effective and maintained. County schools enjoy excellent leadership and history of cooperative enterprise. There has been a "creative" response to a potentially overwhelming Cuban refuge problem. Schools, public welfare and state Vocational Rehabilitation all rated better than average.

HUD's capability reports were the most systematic. They were usually based on input obtained from HUD regional staff which rated the city's experience and performance in the areas of urban renewal, public housing, relocation, workable program, and equal opportunity.

The functional analysis focused upon the substance of the application. Reviewers sought to evaluate the quality and coherence of the problem analysis, program approaches, and objectives. For example, the following comments are reported in the staff summary of an advanced review:[10]

> Though he says *goals* and objectives are clearly stated, Washington reader is left with impression that the city feels there is little wrong with its past performance and that the trouble lies with the people who need changing more than the structures in which they live (a comment bearing more on problem analysis than on goals, priorities, program strategy, and approach). Regional reviewer sees lack of concreteness in problem analysis reflected in goals and program approaches; cites absence of priorities and program strategy.

In addition, the proposed planning structure was carefully reviewed with an eye on the applicant's translation of the citizen participation requirement into operational procedures. Some cities rated high on this criterion, as exemplified by one review statement that "the applicant presents a thoughtful and innovative proposal designed to place power to plan and implement the program in the hands of neighborhood."[11] Other cities appeared to miss the mark, as suggested in the following comment:[12]

> [The applicant] proposes a minimal citizen participation mechanism which can only be characterized as tightfisted. Not only does the Mayor have total control over who shall be appointed to the citizen participation panel, but the panel itself does not participate in policy making as prescribed by the law and is limited to "discussing and reacting" to ideas presented to it by the city. Additionally, the average resident is barred from being considered for appointment because the majority of citizens seats will go to property owners.

Of the various agencies involved in the PGRP, HEW conducted the most systematic functional review of applications by means of a rating scale on which reviewers gave cities numerical scores. The HEW analysis of applications was divided into five areas: objectives, methods of reaching goals, innovative approaches, administrative machinery, and problem analysis. Each of these areas was rated on a 1-5 scale and the area ratings were weighted differentially according to HEW's estimates of their importance. The average score given to cities was 60 out of a possible 100 points.

As this description suggests, the PGRP was a costly and time-consuming operation. It required that high-level officials of various federal agencies read numerous applications, comment on them in writing, and discuss them in committee meetings. The process required that HUD make some decisions based upon the information, opinions, and data gathered. The knowledge, experience, and expert judgments of the professional staff of many different agencies was utilized in a concerted effort to exercise federal discretion fairly, systematically, and intelligently. The objective of all this activity was to select the 75 cities from among 193 applicants that appeared most likely to be able to carry out the planning process envisioned by HUD and to implement plans after they were approved. Recognizing that, without the PGRP, about 29 of the 75 cities finally selected through PGRP would probably have been chosen anyhow by simple random selection, it is useful to ask whether this monumental effort made any difference. In an attempt to shed some light on this question, the federal ratings given applicants in the PGRP are compared with measures of performance. Before examining the results of this analysis, we will briefly review how PGRP ratings and performance indicators were operationally defined.

Planning Grant Review Project Ratings

The PGRP ratings were taken from the Review Committee Summaries on each city. With the exception of the HEW numerical functional ratings, these ratings were in the form of qualitative statements on selection criteria. To transform these qualitative data to quantitative ratings in order to make statistical comparisons, the documents on each city were independently reviewed by three coders with instructions to rank the city from poor to excellent based upon the PGRP qualitative judgments on the following four selection criteria:[13]

1. *Overall Capability:* a rating of the city's potential for planning and implementation according to HUD guidelines based on prior experience in related programs.
2. *HEW Functional Rating:* the numerical rating that HEW staff gave each city according to the formula they developed for analyzing applications.

3. *Citizen Participation:* a rating of how well the city was expected to implement citizen participation in the planning process based on the structure described in their application.
4. *Technical Quality:* an overall rating of the technical quality of the city's application.

One major caveat is in order. That is, interpretation of the findings is limited in a significant way because our comparative analysis deals only with those cities that were finally selected to participate. We do not have PGRP ratings for the rejected cities and we have no evidence about how the rejected cities might have fared in terms of the performance criteria. More than half of the cities that applied for first-round funding were rejected, presumably in most cases because they received lower ratings in the PGRP than those cities that were selected. But there is no way to judge whether these cities with the presumably lower PGRP ratings would have also ranked lower in program accomplishments had they received grants. Thus, what this analysis focuses upon is the PGRP's ability to estimate the relative potential for performance among the seemingly best of the applicants; that is, it makes comparisons among those that were not rejected. In this sense it may be that our data reveal how well the PGRP could rank those cities within the "winner's circle," assuming a degree of accuracy in the initial rejections. If this is the case, then even a moderate degree of success should be considered quite impressive.

Performance Indicator

The Model Cities Program had multiple goals framed in such terms as: citizen participation, coordination, innovation, comprehensive planning, and delivery of services. HUD did not operationally define the specific content of these objectives. Some of the objectives pertained to the planning process, others to the substantive character of the Comprehensive Development Plan, and others to implementation. And, as James has suggested, these objectives are not necessarily consonant.[14] Hence, in order to make comparative judgments of the cities' performances it was necessary to make a selection from among a wide variety of objectives. In line with the HUD-stated Model Cities objectives we selected five indicators of performance. The following is a brief discussion of the rationale for selecting these indicators, the operational definitions used, and the sources of data.

1. *Degree of Citizen Influence in the Planning Process.* One of the major performance criteria used by HUD to evaluate the planning process was the extent to which local citizens were involved in decision

making. In this regard the planning process was not simply perceived as a means; it was also an end, valued in its own right.

To obtain measures of this indicator, interviews were conducted with HUD personnel in Washington, D.C. ("deskmen"), who were responsible for managing and maintaining relationships with city and regional staff; each of the interviewees had direct responsibility for programs in from 12 to 30 cities within a region. These HUD officials were asked to rate each of the programs under their jurisdiction along a five-point continuum of citizen influence on decision making, ranging from "weakest" to "strongest," as it appeared during the last quarter of the planning period. A second set of ratings of degree citizen influence was obtained through a content analysis of the "briefing memos" on each program that were prepared by HUD regional staff ("leadmen'). Here, each program was ranked along a three-point continuum ("weak," "moderate," and "strong" citizen influence) by three raters; judgments were accepted only for the cases in which at least two of the three ratings were in agreement. The two sets of judgments (deskmen interviews and analysis of briefing memos) were correlated and demonstrated a high degree of association (Gamma .667). The deskmen interview ratings were then collapsed into a three-point continuum (1,2 weak; 3 moderate; 4,5 strong) and again correlated with the ratings of the content analysis of briefing memos. This time the degree of association between the two sets of judgments was very high (Gamma .769). We selected the collapsed interview ratings of the deskmen as the indicators of the strength of citizen influence on decision making in the planning year.[15]

2. *Overall Quality of the Comprehensive Demonstration Plan.* The quality of the Comprehensive Demonstration Plan (CDP) was another dimension of performance upon which cities were judged. For this study we selected two rather broad criteria by which to make some relative assessments of CDP quality. The first criterion is based on judgments of HUD deskmen who were asked to evaluate the overall quality of the CDPs, produced by the cities in their regions. Interviewees were not asked to rate every city, but rather to select those cities that produced the plans they considered "best" and those cities that produced the plans they considered "worst."

3. *Percent of CDP Budget Composed of Categorical Funds.* The second criterion of quality of the CDP is the proportion of categorical funds (as a percent of the total CDP budget) that was included in the plan for the first program year. The proportion of categorical funds anticipated in the budget is employed as an indicator of "quality" of the plan in the sense that it reflects a city's performance with regard to the mobilization and coordination of resources. One of the objectives in

the methods of financing the Model Cities Program was to provide a form of seed money (i.e., supplemental funds from HUD) to attract and coordinate outside sources of funding, primarily categorical monies. To the extent that a CDP demonstrated the city's ability to muster a large proportion of outside resources, or at least get them down on paper, we infer that it comes closer to satisfying the coordination and mobilization of resources objectives than a CDP that contained a small proportion of categorical funds.[16] Data on the categorical component of the CDP budget were obtained by a survey conducted under the sponsorship of the U.S. Conference of Mayors of all the Model Cities programs.

4. and 5. *First Program Year Expenditures for Service Delivery, and Per Capita First-Year Program Expenditures for Service Delivery.* The ultimate test of a city's performance was its ability to implement plans and to deliver services. Among other things, this involved spending the supplemental funds allocated for their first action year which followed the completion of the CDP and its approval by HUD. As it turned out, spending the money (i.e., program implementation) was more difficult than many cities had anticipated. As of April 1971, only 38 percent of 65 cities that had completed their first action year had been able to spend 50 percent or more of their supplemental budgets. The criteria we selected to compare performances in this area are simple and straightforward—the percent of supplemental funds spent by each city at 12 months, and the amount of supplemental funds spent at 12 months per capita. These indicators do not tap any of the qualitative aspects of service delivery which might be measured along various dimensions (e.g., *Who* was served? How *efficient* were services? How *effective* were services? etc.). To obtain such specific qualitative measures of program implementation would require resources far in excess of those available for this study. Similar to the other performance criteria, the indicators employed to measure service delivery are, at best, approximations of the subtle and complex phenomena they represent. Data on supplemental funds spent for the first program year were obtained from HUD's accounting offices.[17]

Findings: PGRP Selection Criteria and Program Performance

To what extent did the four PGRP ratings of cities' potential for program implementation correspond with the actual performance of the cities in terms of the five performance criteria? An approximate answer to this question may be found by examining the relationships between PGRP ratings and ratings on performance criteria shown in Table 1. The general pattern of findings in Table 1 indicates that the results were mixed but on the whole not very encouraging with regard to the accuracy of PGRP ratings of the applicants' potential for satisfying the various objectives of the Model

TABLE 1
Correlations between Planning Grant Review Project Ratings and Performance Indicators (Gammas)

Performance Indicators	PGRP Ratings			
	(1) Overall Capability	(2) HEW Functional Rating	(3) Citizen Participation	(4) Technical Quality
1) Citizen influence in the planning process	.377	.290	.454	.154
2) Overall quality of the CDP	.091	.211	.305	.178
3) Percent of CDP budget composed of categorical funds	–.453	–.332	–.121	–.222
4) First program-year expenditures	–.321	.173	.002	.036
5) Per capita first program-year expenditures	–.426	–.185	–.098	–.162

Cities Program. In 45 percent of the cells correlations are in the negative direction, in which cases the high PGRP ratings of potential are associated with low performance ratings. Thus, for example, cities that were rated high on overall capability based on PGRP staff assessments of their prior experience actually tended to perform worse with regard to the acquisition of categorical funds (Gamma –.453) and spending in terms of the percent of supplemental funds (Gamma –.321) and per capita supplemental funds (Gamma –.426) than cities that were judged to have low capability. Only 25 percent of the cells show moderate positive correlations between PGRP ratings and performance, with the remaining cells showing positive correlations that are low or negligible (i.e., less than .200).

The sharpest distinction that emerges from these findings is that PGRP ratings are most strongly and consistently associated in a positive direction with performance ratings of citizen influence in the planning process. Indeed, the strongest positive correlation in Table 1 is between PGRP ratings of potential for citizen participation and the performance ratings of citizen influence (Gamma .454). And the second strongest correlation is between PGRP ratings of overall capability and performance ratings of citizen influence (Gamma .377).

These findings suggest that the PGRP gave special emphasis to assessments of the applicants' plans for citizen participation and the applicants' capacity for implementing this particular objective. The findings apparently reflect the staunch commitment to citizen participation objectives of the HUD administrative staff responsible for the Model Cities Program during this period. (The Model Cities Administration was staffed largely from outside of HUD. A number of personnel from the Office of Economic Opportunity, which was a major initiating force of the citizen participation movement in the 1960s, had transferred to the Model Cities Program anticipating that this program was where the Administration would concentrate its urban thrust.) The emphasis placed upon citizen participation is confirmed by evidence from other sources which indicate that first-round planning grant awards were often accompanied by stipulations that the city spell out or strengthen its provisions for resident participation in Model Cities planning.[18]

A Simplified Alternative

The first-round Model Cities could have been selected by a variety of methods utilizing assumptions similar to those on which the PGRP ratings were based. We will conclude our analysis by presenting one example of a simple and inexpensive alternative method for the quantitative rating of applicants and the results obtained when ratings generated by this alternative approach are compared with performance ratings. Our major purpose in presenting this alternative is to illustrate the possibilities of simplified measures and at the same time to provide a comparative set of measures against which the relative utility of PGRP ratings can be assessed. We do not offer it as a substitute for a PGRP-type of selection method or even as a necessarily desirable approach to the selection problem.

In the PGRP, overall capability ratings were based on qualitative judgments of the applicants' past experiences in related program areas. The assumption was that these were judgments of the quality of past program experience, including the knowledge, skill, commitment, agency linkages, and other characteristics that would be relevant to an assessment of a city's potential to successfully implement the Model Cities Program.[19] And it was believed that the differential quality of these experiences could be assessed accurately enough to be a useful tool in the selection process. Another approach is simply to assume that the length of experience in related program areas (e.g., urban renewal) will reflect the development of knowledge, skills, and other characteristics prerequisite for the Model Cities Program; i.e., the longer a city has been operating a related program, the earlier it submitted an acceptable application for that program, and the more time it has had to learn from and to integrate its experience.[20] Based on this assumption, estimates of capability can be derived by calculating the number of years prior to 1967 that applicants had been operating programs in related areas.

For the purposes of this illustration, Public Housing and Urban Renewal were selected as related program areas. (Both programs received emphasis in HUD capability ratings in the PGRP.) The applicants' ranks on length of experience in these programs were correlated with performance ratings, the results of which are shown in Table 2.

The data in Table 2 show that of the ten relationships between performance indicators and applicants' length of experience in the two programs, only four are in the expected positive direction. Similar to the findings in Table 1, the strongest positive correlations are with citizen influence (Gammas .563 and .231) and the other positive correlations are with CDP ratings (Gammas .117 and .060). If we compare the length of experience in urban renewal (Table 2) with the overall capability rating (Table 1), both of which are based on the same assumption, little difference is found in either the direction or the strength of associating with performance indicators. The largest difference obtained is in regard to citizen influence, where the length of experience (Gamma .563) has a stronger relationship than the overall capability ratings (Gamma .377). In fact, for citizen influence, the performance variable with which the PGRP as a whole was best correlated, none of the PGRP ratings has a stronger correlation than the length of experience in urban renewal. This suggests that if applicants were selected mainly on the basis of their potential for developing active citizen participation in the planning process, length of experience in urban renewal as a selection criterion would have produced as good, if not better, results than

TABLE 2
Correlations between Length of Experience and Performance Indicators (Gammas)

	Experience in Urban Renewal and Public Housing	
Performance Indicators	Number of Years Between First Approval for Urban Renewal Program and 1967*	Number of Years Between Initial Occupancy of Public Housing and 1967**
1) Citizen influence in the planning process	.563	.231
2) Overall quality of the CDP	.117	.060
3) Percent of CDP budget composed of categorical funds	–.288	–.141
4) First program-year expenditures	–.372	–.099
5) Per capita first program-year expenditures	–.562	–.446

*Source of data: *Urban Renewal Directory*, December 31, 1967, U.S. Department of Housing and Urban Development.

**Source of data: *Consolidated Development Directory*, Report S-11A, June 30, 1967, U.S. Department of Housing and Urban Development.

the array of qualitative judgments actually employed. We do not mean to suggest that urban renewal programs were distinguished for the amount of citizen participation they encouraged. There is much evidence to the contrary.[21] Rather, the assumption is that, over time, cities engaged in urban renewal activities develop a pool of professionals skilled and experienced in dealing with citizen groups (sometimes undermining and deflating participation) and, with the proper incentives from HUD, these skills can be converted to the task of encouraging citizen participation.[22]

Conclusions: Manifest and Latent Functions of Selection Procedures

Before attempting to derive some general meaning from these results, let us summarize a number of related points that have been made in this study.

A. In terms of the process:

1. The PGRP was an elaborate and costly exercise in federal discretion that involved various personnel of different departments.
2. Though it was an elaborate process, the PGRP was not very precise in the sense that it lacked an explicit systematic procedure for weighting the variety of qualitative inputs and setting priorities among different objectives.
3. In addition, the PGRP selection process was not an exercise in discretion based on purely rational or technical judgments of capability. Some number of applicants apparently were selected on the basis of political favor, the quality of their submission notwithstanding.

B. In terms of outcome:

1. The ratio of applicants to program slots available was such that more than one-third of the applicants selected through the PGRP probably would have been chosen by simple random selection.
2. When the various capability ratings of the cities selected to participate in the program are compared with measures of performance, evidence to support the PGRP ratings in terms of their ability to differentiate potential levels of performance is generally weak, except with regard to citizen participation.
3. The employment of inexpensive and simply constructed measures of the cities' prior experience would have produced estimates of performance generally equivalent to those that emerged from the array of qualitative judgments employed in the PGRP decisions.

Given the constraints, the probabilities of random selection, the somewhat imprecise quality of PGRP measures and decisions, the lack of congruence between PGRP ratings and certain types of performance, and the availability of alternative means for "rational" selection, there is little to justify the PGRP in terms of its manifest function. That is, the time and money spent on this type of selection process do not seem warranted in light of the program outcomes. The PGRP was not especially accurate in "picking winners" with regard to the various HUD objectives. For the one objective, citizen participation, with which PGRP ratings correlate most strongly, a simple and inexpensive alternative rating procedure (length of experience) produced similar results. It is possible, as suggested earlier, that the PGRP was developed as a means of cloaking what were essentially political choices in the guise of technical rationality. If this were the major underlying function served by the PGRP, it would certainly be difficult to justify all the energy and expense incurred. More creative and less expensive procedures might have been developed. At the very least, fewer agencies could have been involved.

Was PGRP merely an example of "bureaucratic aggrandizement" whereby federal staff creates a process that exaggerates the power and importance of their judgments and decisions? The evidence tempts the observer to make such an interpretation. It is likely that to some degree the process rewarded those involved with an inflated sense of importance. But the significance of this self-serving function should not be overestimated. The federal staff in the PGRP generally were in the business of making judgments and allocating funds. In this sense the PGRP did not represent a special opportunity to which they responded with excessive zeal.

There is another interpretation of the latent function served by the PGRP that applies directly to program needs, rather than to the needs of politicians or personal aspirations of federal staff. That is, one primary function of this elaborate process may be seen not as a mechanism for selection, but as a strategy to lay the groundwork for program coordination at the federal level. From this perspective the PGRP provided HUD an opportunity to engage the support of other federal agencies in the Model Cities enterprise. Whether intended or not the review of applications and various interagency staff meetings served as a socialization process for the different actors that would be called upon to participate once the program began operations. The involvement of these other agencies at this early stage was a means not only of gathering judgments on selection, but also, and perhaps more importantly, a means for developing common frames of reference and obtaining commitments to the program. It may be assumed that coordination among federal agencies is difficult to attain under any circumstances. But it is more likely to occur in a program in which these agencies play a major role at the start by participating in the meaty and difficult task of selecting beneficiaries, than in a program which delays their participation to the implementation stage. If this is the case, it follows that the imprecise nature of the PGRP was also functional inasmuch as it allowed each participating agency to imagine that they exercised more influence than was probably the case.

Finally, and perhaps most germane from an administrative viewpoint, the PGRP may also be interpreted as a means to promote specific policy objectives. The Model Cities Program was established to achieve varied, sometimes conflicting objectives, such as coordination of resources, citizen participation, service delivery, and so forth. While no formal set of priorities among these objectives were designated in the legislation, analysis of the PGRP suggests that in judging applicants, special emphasis was placed on assessments of their potential to achieve citizen participation in the planning process. In this manner, an element of policy determination based on agency established priorities is introduced to the program through the design and administration of its selection procedures. Assessed on the basis of these latent functions, the utility and efficiency of selection processes like the PGRP may be more substantial than appears when such processes are judged only according to their stated purpose.

Notes

1. U.S. Department of Housing and Urban Development, *Improving the Quality of Urban Life: A Program Guide to Model Neighborhoods in Demonstration Cities* (Washington, D.C.: U.S. Government Printing Office, December 1966).
2. *Ibid.,* p. 6.
3. *Ibid.,* p. 8.
4. *Ibid.,* p. 14.
5. John B. Willmann, *The Department of Housing and Urban Development* (New York: Praeger Publishers, 1967), p. 113.
6. "CQ Fact Sheet on Model City Grants," *Congressional Quarterly Weekly Report,* Vol. 25 (December 1, 1967), pp. 2455-2458.
7. *New York Times,* July 13, 1969, p. 49.
8. Judson L. James, "Federalism and the Model Cities Experiment," paper delivered at the 1970 Annual Meeting of the American Political Science Association, Los Angeles, Sept. 8-12, 1970 (mimeographed), p. 17.
9. Interagency Review Summary, May 12, 1967, U.S. Department of Housing and Urban Development, Model Cities Administration.
10. Staff Summary—Advanced Review, June 1, 1967, U.S. Department of Housing and Urban Development, Model Cities Administration.
11. Staff Summary—Advanced Review, n.d., U.S. Department of Housing and Urban Development, Model Cities Administration.
12. Staff Summary—Advanced Review, June 1, 1967, U.S. Department of Housing and Urban Development, Model Cities Administration.
13. For additional methodological details on the development of these rating scores, see Neil Gilbert and Harry Specht, *The Model Cities Program, A Comparative Analysis of Participating Cities: Process, Product, Performance and Prediction*

(Washington, D.C.: U.S. Government Printing Office, 1973), pp. 36-37.

14. For an in-depth analysis of Model Cities objectives see James, *op. cit.*
15. It should be noted that these two sets of ratings were not, strictly speaking, independent measures. The deskmen we interviewed were familiar with information contained in the briefing memos, and their judgments of citizen participation were undoubtedly influenced by this information. What this indicator represents is a fairly consistent "federal perspective" on what happened in the Model Cities Program. In some respects this allows for as clear a view of the Model Cities Program nationwide as could be hoped for. The deskmen were close enough to a number of programs for a long enough period of time to be able to make informed comparative judgments, and yet removed enough from these programs (as compared, for example, to local CDA staff or citizen participants) to allow these judgments to be made with a reasonable degree of objectivity.
16. This is not meant to infer that a city with a high proportion of categorical funds in its plan was able to implement its plan for mobilization and coordination of resources any more successfully than other cities.
17. We did obtain general qualitative judgments of program implementation in interviews with the HUD officials. There was substantial agreement between these qualitative judgments (programs considered to be of the "highest quality" and the "lowest quality") and the percent of funds spent for six months (Gamma .552) and for 12 months (Gamma .459).
18. See, for example, Roland Warren, "Model Cities First Round: Politics, Planning, and Participation," *Journal of the American Institute of Planners,* Vol. 35 (July 1969), pp. 245-252; Marshall Kaplan, Gans and Kahn, *The Model Cities Program: A Comparative Analysis of the Planning Process in Eleven Cities* (Washington, D.C.: U.S. Government Printing Office, 1969); and James, *op. cit.*
19. This assumption recognizes that over the last decade cities have used, for example, urban renewal programs not only to secure federal funds for themselves, but also to create, outside the city's regular department structure, a cadre of professional talent that could be employed in various capacities. "The best local renewal authorities," Wilson observes, "became generalized sources of innovation and policy staffing and their directors became in effect deputy Mayors (and sometimes more than that)." See James Q. Wilson, "The Mayors vs. the Cities," *The Public Interest,* Vol. 23, No. 3 (Summer 1969), p. 30.
20. The length of time that a city has operated urban renewal and public housing programs has been used in other studies as an indicator of the "speed of community innovation." See Michael Aiken and Robert Alford, "Community Structure and Innovation: The Case of Public Housing," *American Political Science Review,* Vol. 64, No. 3 (September 1970), pp. 843-864; and Michael Aiken and Robert Alford, "Community Structure and Innovation: The Case of Urban Renewal," *American Sociological Review,* Vol. 35, No. 4 (August 1970), pp. 650-665.
21. For example, see Peter M. Rossi and Robert Dentler, *The Politics of Urban Renewal* (New York: Free Press, 1961), pp. 287-288; James Q. Wilson, "Planning and Politics: Citizen Participation in Urban Renewal," *Urban Renewal:*

People, Politics, and Planning, Jewel Bellush and Murray Haustnecht (eds.) (New York: Anchor Books, 1967), pp. 287-301; and Scott Greer, *Urban Renewal and American Cities* (Indianapolis: Bobbs-Merrill, 1965), p. 37.

22. For an analysis of how skills and linkages that arise out of prior experience in related programs may be employed for developing structures for community participation, see Neil Gilbert, *Clients or Constituents* (San Francisco: Jossey-Bass, Publishers, 1970), pp. 42-68.

1974 (34:565-574)

B. DOUGLAS HARMAN

The Bloc Grant: Readings From a First Experiment

In its simplest form, the bloc grant is an unconditional grant from the federal government to state governments which can be used for any proper purposes in broad functional areas. However, the concept of the bloc grant widely discussed today includes program requirements and other restrictions. Despite these restrictions, it is different from the categorical grants which establish narrow programs directed toward specific objectives and delineated by specific federal guidelines.

Development of the Bloc Grant Concept

The first Hoover Commission discussed the bloc grant in its 1949 report. It proposed that a system of bloc grants be established based upon broad functional categories, such as highways, education, and public health as a way of reducing the fragmentation in categorical grants.[1] Little was done to implement this recommendation. In 1955 the Kestnbaum Commission considered the question of making federal assistance to states available in the form of unconditional bloc grants, but it concluded that unconditional grants would not insure compliance with national objectives. Therefore, it concluded that categorical grants should be continued.[2]

Twelve years after publication of the Kestnbaum report, the Advisory Commission on Intergovernmental Relations found that the grant-in-aid system lacked flexibility and needed an overhauling. Although it concluded that categorical grants should be retained, the Commission recommended that a "new federal aid mix" was needed, and urged the utilization of bloc grants to consolidate categorical programs.[3]

On April 30, 1969, President Nixon asked Congress for authority to consolidate existing grant programs. Further support of this goal is found in two bills pending before Congress, the Intergovernmental Cooperation Act of 1969 (HR 7366) and the Grant Consolidation Act of 1969 (HR 10954). Both call for consolidation of federal assistance programs which are in the same or closely related functional areas.

Administrative Goals

Governmental records and special studies as well as the background literature on problems of categorical grants-in-aid identify the administrative goals of the bloc grant approach.[4] The basic goal is simplification of grant-in-aid procedures in order to make federal assistance more effective and useful to state and local officials. In addition, four specific goals can be identified:

(1) *Comprehensive planning and program development for broad functional fields.* A major goal of the bloc grant is to promote comprehensive planning for functional fields and to allow the recipient governments flexibility in meeting the needs which they identify.

(2) *Promotion of uncomplicated intergovernmental relationships.* An advantage of the bloc grant, according to its supporters, is the reduction of the number of major participants. This is expected to result from the channeling of funds from the federal government to the 50 states rather than from the national government to hundreds of state, local, and private sources.

(3) *Elimination of federal control and domination of the grant-in-aid program.* This goal suggests the transfer of administrative and review responsibilities from the federal government to state governments, or the sharing of these responsibilities. The bloc grant seeks to shift program control to a level of government closer to the problem areas.

(4) *State authority to allocate funds.* This goal requires relative freedom on the part of the state to implement its comprehensive program plans and places states in the position of making grant allocations to local governments as well as to private groups.

The administrative politics of the law enforcement assistance program reveal, however, that several sets of political factors make law enforcement assistance much more complicated than the goals suggest. While the bloc grant approach changes the administrative and political relationships inherent in categorical grants, it also results in competition among federal, state, and local officials to achieve control over administration of the program and allocation of funds.

Congress Enacts a Bloc Grant

The first bloc grant program to receive a great amount of political attention was the 1968 Safe Streets Act.[5] This act, because it is directed toward a critical urban problem and forms the basis for federal assistance in law enforcement, has become an important political test of the bloc grant approach.

The 1968 Safe Streets Act established the Law Enforcement Assistance

Administration (LEAA) in the Department of Justice to implement the bloc grant assistance program. The Safe Streets Act authorized $100,111,000 for fiscal year 1969, and Congress appropriated $63 million for fiscal year 1969. The following year, Congress appropriated nearly the complete amount authorized, $300 million. It is possible that if current interest in law enforcement continues the program may grow to nearly a billion dollars in coming years.

In order to facilitate administration of the program, the Safe Streets Act requires each state to establish a planning agency under the authority of the governor. It further requires that the planning agency develop a statewide comprehensive law enforcement plan for the allocation of action grant funds to the state and local governments. The state agency must distribute 40 percent of the planning funds and 75 percent of the action funds to units of local government or combinations of local units, with the remainder going to the state government. Direct grants are available under the legislation to local governments if the state fails to seek funds under the act. However, all states applied for and received funds. Eighty-five percent of the federal funds were allocated in fiscal year 1969 to the states according to population, with the remainder allocated at the discretion of LEAA.

Implementing Law Enforcement Assistance: The Politics of the Federal Role

Although the federal role in a bloc grant program superficially appears to be a simple one, examination of the LEAA state assistance programs indicates that the federal government plays complex roles with many political dimensions. The federal agency in a bloc grant program is caught between countervailing political pressures. Although some of these cross pressures may be peculiar to this initial, precedent-establishing grant program, the LEAA experience indicates that future urban bloc grant programs will be subject to heavy political pressures and to varying interpretations by federal administrators.

Two Views of the Federal Role

During the debate over the 1968 Safe Streets Act, Attorney General Ramsey Clark became one of the principal spokesmen against bloc grants. As a result, the Democratic leadership of the Department of Justice favored strict interpretation of the federal mandate with strong requirements imposed upon state governments. Indications of this position are found in the detailed program guidelines written for the states.

Although the Republican Administration inherited the program midway in its first year, its orientation differed from the previous Administration through emphasis upon a more modest federal role. LEAA Administrator Charles H. Rogovin voiced this position at the Senate hearing on his nomination.

> LEAA does not intend to attempt to control the development of law enforcement reforms in the states and cities. It has the authority to rule on the "comprehensiveness" of state plans, but LEAA does not have the power to approve or disapprove specific projects within a state plan. The states should set their own priorities and design their own programs. The role of LEAA is to assist them with their projects. There is no intention of directing the manner in which the states must respond.[6]
>
> The Republican administrators hold that under the bloc grant approach state governments should provide the leadership and be responsible for making the program successful.

Political Cross Pressures

One of the most important political dimensions of this bloc grant program is the cross pressure generated by state and local public interest groups. Because of the significance of this early bloc grant program, the organizations representing state and local governments have been keenly interested in its development. The representatives of the cities have a vested interest in proving that the bloc grant approach fails to achieve meaningful results and does not direct funds to the cities. The representatives of the states wish to demonstrate that the bloc grant has been a successful experiment. Six organizations have been responsible for the pressures placed upon the development and administration of the LEAA program: the U.S. Conference of Mayors (USCM), the National League of Cities (NLC), The Urban Coalition, Urban America, Inc., the National Association of Counties (NACO), and the National Governors' Conference (NGC).

The USCM and the NLC are the chief Washington spokesmen for the cities. These two organizations oppose the bloc grant. In March 1969 the League of Cities published a scathing attack on the bloc grant aspects of the LEAA program which argued that:

> . . . the Safe Streets Act, as currently administered by LEAA and most of the states, will fail to achieve Congress' primary goal of controlling crime in the streets of urban high crime areas. Instead of focusing dollars on the critical problems of crime in the streets, local planning funds are being used to finance third levels of bureaucracy as a matter of state administrative convenience.[7]

NLC held that regional planning was diluting the role of cities in the planning process and that rural areas were receiving a disproportionate amount of federal funds. It also criticized the weak representation of cities on state planning agencies and the failure of LEAA to require states to give city policy-making officials stronger roles.

Big city mayors strongly criticized the LEAA program at the June 1969 annual meeting of the U.S. Conference of Mayors. Vice-President Spiro Agnew's attempt to convince them that state administration of programs was preferable to creation of more federal bureaucracy was not particularly successful, and they adopted a resolution against bloc grants.

The Urban Coalition and Urban America, Inc., published their evaluation of state planning in June 1969. After examination of planning in 12 major urban states, they concluded that planning was being carried out largely by "a small number of professionals" with limited representation from the poor and minority groups. In addition they felt that states were planning for the three traditional segments of the criminal justice system: police, courts, and corrections, without concern for th needs of innovation in the whole system.[8] In conclusion, the report urged LEAA to demand considerable detail from state agencies about their action plans as a way of insuring that meaningful changes would be accomplished. The significance of this report and that of the NLC is that they demanded a stronger federal role in supervising state agencies.

The National Association of Counties also published an analysis of the LEAA program which mildly criticized the LEAA program for not involving local policy-making officials. While the NACO study identified some problems, it recommended only minor changes.[9] The stake of counties in the bloc grant approach helps explain their response. Counties tend to have a better relationship with state governments than do cities, and under regional planning, they often serve as the planning districts.

The National Governors' Conference achieved a significant victory when Congress transformed the LEAA program into a bloc grant because that action made the states the focal point for law enforcement assistance. Therefore, it is to NGC's benefit to have the program operate smoothly and without major controversy. Accordingly, NGC has devoted a great deal of attention to the administration of law enforcement assistance and to helping governments strengthen their programs. While NGC has sought to protect the program from its critics, it has worked to keep federal control over state activities to a minimum and to insure against erosion of state discretion under the bloc grant approach.

One indication that the city groups have influenced the administration of the program was LEAA's decision to allocate some of its 15 percent discretionary funds to the 11 largest cities in the nation. This decision meant that the big cities would each receive $100,000. LEAA officials admit that this allocation was an effort specifically designed to reduce the dissatisfaction of the cities. However, soon after the award's announcement, the governor of Utah, representing the National Governors' Conference, complained that the grants were a deviation from the bloc grant approach. The cities were also unhappy because they were required to gain approval of state agencies before spending their funds.

LEAA's Memorandum Number 12 reflects city criticisms of state planning. It admitted that there had been "considerably less direct pass through to major local units of local government than had been anticipated." The memorandum warned the states to take "special care in planning for city needs and to document the acceptability of their approaches to local governments. The city lobby has, however, been less than successful because there is little interest in Congress in changing law enforcement assistance into a categorical grant program.

Guidelines as a Source of Control

Effects of interest group pressures are found in the LEAA guidelines. The guidelines direct state and local government participation in the bloc grant program, and thereby serve as a critical device in the exercise of federal control. By requiring the states to comply with detailed instructions, the federal government increases its supervisory powers. The Democratic Administration's original guidelines called for close federal supervision of state planning and expenditures of funds. At that time LEAA wanted both to have membership on state planning agencies determined according to the ratio of state and local expenditures in law enforcement, and to set specific ratios of representation from functional fields, such as police, courts, and corrections.

The National Governors' Conference felt that the LEAA approach at that time denied states important powers which the bloc grant approach was intended to give. Spokesmen for the Conference claimed that suggested guidelines represented a reduction of state flexibility which would make the program unworkable. Although the guidelines were further changed, the ones prepared under the Democratic Administration went well beyond the LEAA legislation in specifying details of the state programs.

While the legislation merely requires that membership on the state planning agencies must be representative of "law enforcement agencies of the state and the units of government within the State," LEAA lists seven categories of persons necessary to constitute this balanced representation. They are: (1) representation of state law enforcement agencies; (2) representation of units of general local government by elected policy-making or executive officials; (3) representation of law enforcement officials or administrators from local units of government; (4) representation of each major law enforcement function, police, corrections, and courts; (5) representation of the field of juvenile delinquency control; (6) representation of community or citizen interests; and (7) representation that "offers reasonable geographical and urban-rural balance'' and regard for the incidence of crime.[10]

It is significant that one of the first major actions of the Republican-appointed LEAA administration was to publish a simplified set of guidelines for state comprehensive plans.[11] The new guidelines were designed to expedite state planning, and they represented a decision at the federal level to assent to fewer controls over state activities. Despite this shift, the federal government still maintains a set of guidelines which outline many aspects of state law enforcement planning.

Special Conditions and State Plans

A way federal officials impose their will on state agencies is by refusing to approve state plans until special conditions have been met. Thus, state and local officials may be required to agree to stated arrangements as a condition for the receipt of funds. Elements subjected to special conditions have included state administrative practices, pass-through provisions, analysis of existing law enforcement system, review procedures, and reporting requirements. The ability to review such matters even in a bloc grant places federal officials in strategic position to exercise authority over state and local activities.

Before making the action grant allocations to individual states, the federal officials make decisions on what they consider acceptable plans and whether conditions are to be attached to plans. California, the first state to submit its plans, immediately raised the question of how much program detail the states were obligated to provide the federal government. The California planning director felt that his plan would be an important test which would determine whether LEAA would accept comprehensive plans which presented broad criteria for states to use in deciding specifically how money would be used, rather than listing projects.[12] Following the submissions of state plans, federal and state officials negotiated over their acceptance. Although the results of these negotiations were a compromise between the desire of federal officials for program details and the desire of state officials to maintain large degrees of flexibility, LEAA exercised its authority to place a total of 29 special conditions on the action grants awarded to the states in 1969. Of these, approximately two-thirds were demands for additional program detail. For example, California must submit additional information on all its program information. Several special conditions required states to prepare plans for specific areas of the law enforcement system, such as corrections, courts, and organized crime. Some special conditions required changes in state organization. West Virginia, for example, must add state officials to its supervisory body.

Imposition of special conditions came after negotiations had failed to achieve the changes in state programs desired by LEAA officials. In this sense, the establishment of the special conditions was the political tool used by LEAA to obtain greater program information that state officials desired to give and to force state officials to make changes. Since states must agree to these conditions before federal funding becomes available, the special condition is a strong device for achieving federal control in this bloc grant program.

Federal-State Conflict

From the standpoint of the federal officials, special conditions and guidelines are merely devices to insure state compliance with legislative requirements and to implement national standards in law enforcement assistance. State officials view the program from a different perspective. They see Congress' passage of the bloc grant program as an indication that they will be subject to fewer federal controls than under categorical grants.

Some state planning directors fear that LEAA desires for program information will lead to a loss of state flexibility and an increase in federal control. In response to a questionnaire on the LEAA program, a few state directors contended that the purpose of the bloc grant was to provide funds to the states to be spent according to their general plans, with few or no strings attached by LEAA. One state director said, "LEAA is increasingly asking for more and more detailed plans which is really defeating the bloc grant approach!" Another state director pleaded that states are in no position to provide detailed program information because the state effort was directed toward the development of a general plan which would provide the criteria and rationale for judging local project requests.

The extent and nature of the federal agency's powers is one of the basic issues in a bloc grant program. What is at stake is whether the federal government or the states have primary responsibility to insure that the general or national purposes of the program are satisfied. Although Congress emphasized the bloc grant aspect of LEAA's program and the Republican administrators of LEAA are oriented toward a modest federal role, federal oversight of state planning and allocation of funds remains strong. There are strong tendencies on the part of federal agencies to exercise the power to establish and maintain national standards even under a bloc grant program. One reason for this tendency is found in congressional behavior.

Congress and the Bloc Grant

In addition to the cities, Congress also puts pressure on federal administrators and some of these force LEAA to review closely state and local activities. While Congress may demand a small federal staff because the federal role appears to be limited, it may at the same time require the federal agency to account for all funds spent at the state and local levels. The LEAA program experienced this type of congressional pressures when Congressman John J. Rooney (D-NY), chairman of appropriations subcommittee reviewing its budget, took the position that the agency could function with "six persons and a checkwriter."

> *Mr. Rooney:* I thought all you needed was somebody to see to it that the checks are sent to the right addresses and that one of the people knows how to run a checkwriter.
>
> *Mr. Rogovin:* I think it goes beyond that, sir.
>
> *Mr. Rooney:* I don't think so. I don't think it was ever intended that we would create another hierarchy. I thought this would be a function of the Department of Justice to get this money out.
>
> *Mr. Rogovin:* It was, sir. There is a responsibility, one, to follow it. It has to be ascertained that the money is properly spent.
>
> *Mr. Rooney:* I think we will have to have a real understanding on that.[13]

Congress, as seen in the above testimony, can demand that federal offices administering the bloc grant remain small and have a limited ability to supervise state activities.

While Congress may limit federal staff size, it may also hold the federal officials fully accountable for expenditures at the state level. In the hearings on the 1970 LEAA budget, Congressman Rooney criticized specific grants which financed the painting of District of Columbia police vehicles and purchased Italian motor scooters. The power of the appropriations committee in reviewing bloc grants programs is great and can extend to the details of state expenditures.

The federal role in the LEAA bloc grant program is complex and is affected by many pressures demanding at the same time both expanded and diminished powers. While the Democratic and Republican leaders of Law Enforcement Assistance Administration may have had differing opinions about the extent of federal involvement appropriate under this program, the political pressures brought upon LEAA moderated both positions. Although the bloc grant concept was intended to reduce federal control and transfer responsibilities to state governments, the federal government's role in law enforcement assistance remains strong because of the pressures of Congress and urban organizations. The state and local relationships in the bloc grant approach provide further evidence of the administrative complexities and political competition involved in this type of grant-in-aid system.

State-Local Politics and the Bloc Grant

State and local intergovernmental politics constitute a crucial arena in a bloc grant program. Under the bloc grant, state governments have important powers over planning and utilization of funds. If past relations between states and cities had been close and had involved many joint efforts to solve problems, the state role might not cause objections. Unfortunately, states and cities have a long history of conflict, and the bloc grant inherits the distrust and suspicion of earlier state-city clashes.

Before analyzing state-local relations, it is necessary to identify the sources of the data used in this section of the study. The author prepared, and the International City Management Association (ICMA) distributed, two questionnaires on law enforcement assistance during June 1969. ICMA sent one to the directors of state law enforcement planning agencies and the other to the chief administrative officials of the 859 cities with a population of 25,000 or more. All 50 state agencies responded; 637 cities (74 percent) returned questionnaires.[14] In addition to analyzing the above data, the author systematically examined the administrative elements of the 50 state law enforcement plans.

The Heritage of State-Local Relations

Many political factors explain the difficulties found in state-local relations, including malapportionment of legislatures, debt management conflicts, restrictive laws governing cities, and state failure to give attention to urban problems. Table 1 drawn from the ICMA survey reflects the attitudes of the cities toward state governments. These tables indicate that 45 percent of the responding cities feel that state governments are seldom or only occasionally sympathetic or helpful in coping with urban problems; 55 percent believe that the states are usually or always sympathetic or helpful. The chart shows that attitudes towards state actions differ according to the size of the city. Almost 60 percent of the officials from cities with a population of 100,000 or more hold a negative opinion of state governments' activities in urban problems; a smaller percentage of medium and small cities (populations of 25,000 to 100,000) share that attitude. When the attitudes of the largest cities are compared with those of the smallest, we find that 35 percent of the cities with more than 500,000 population feel the state governments are seldom helpful, while only 13 percent of the cities with 25,000 to 50,000 population view the states in such a negative way.

The lack of state assistance to cities in urban problem fields probably explains the negative opinion held by many cities toward state governments. Many states have been more oriented toward rural interests than toward those of urban areas. Urban bloc grants required state governments to

TABLE 1
City Identification of the Actions and Attitudes of State Government Toward Urban Problems

	No. of Cities Reporting	State Government Seldom Sympathetic and Helpful		State Government Occasionally Sympathetic and Helpful		State Government Usually Sympathetic and Helpful		State Government Nearly Always Sympathetic and Helpful	
	%	No.	%	No.	%	No.	%	No.	%
Total, all cities	580	77	13	183	32	216	37	104	18
Population group									
Over 500,000	20	7	35	4	20	6	30	3	15
250,000-500,000	23	2	9	13	57	6	26	2	9
100,000-250,000	80	10	13	33	41	28	35	9	11
50,000-100,000	156	19	12	46	30	60	39	31	20
25,000-50,000	301	39	13	87	29	116	39	59	20

administer federal programs to cities, an unfamiliar role for many state governments.

State Power and Representation of Interests

The governor has in most states the power to determine membership on the state law enforcement agency. Although governors must comply with the general membership provisions of the LEAA guidelines, state officials have the ability to shape the character of the state agency through allocating representation to large and small cities, political parties, professional disciplines, and regions of the state.

The most important dimensions of representation on state agencies are: (1) the proportion of state and local officials, (2) the functional composition of the board according to professional fields, and (3) the number of general policy and elected officials as contrasted to professional experts. Development of a reasonable system of representation is not an easy task within the constraints of the number of officials on these agencies. The median number of persons on state planning agencies is 17, with a range extending from a low of five to a high of 50. The first quartile is 17 and the third is 27.

The dilemma faced by state officials is that there is no correct formula for representation of interests. One state planning director commented that, "This subject appears to be related to who views the composition," and noted that his agency received complaints about the representation given local elected officials, minority groups, private agencies, criminal justice agencies, and geographical areas. Another director explained, "The main difficulty is having a balanced representation and still having a body with the size that can be worked with. Getting everyone represented means having a convention instead of a meeting."

The amount of state and local representation on supervisory agencies has great implications for the administration of law enforcement assistance. Despite the key role played by the state government in administration of this program, 40 percent of planning funds and 75 percent of action funds are intended for local governments according to pass-through provision. Local government associations have taken keen interests in this matter and have urged states to give greater representation to local governments and their policy officials. Forty-three percent of the persons serving on all state law enforcement agencies are from local government, 35 percent from state government, and the remainder citizens. These are averages and state agencies vary significantly in the amount of state and local representation. The distribution of the percentages of state representation is as follows: $Q_1 = 29$ percent, $Q_2 = 36$ percent, and $Q_3 = 45$ percent. All except three states above the third quartile have agencies with 50 percent or more state officials. Nine states are in this category. In one state (Alaska) the strong state official domination can be explained by the small number of cities. The other states (Virginia, South Dakota, New Jersey, Indiana, Idaho, North Dakota, North Carolina, and Rhode Island) have agencies dominated by state officials despite the large amounts of funds which local governments are to receive under this program.

The percentages of local official membership does not perfectly mirror the percentages of state representation, since the number of citizens varies in each state. The distribution of local representation is: $Q_1 = 38$ percent, $Q_2 = 43$ percent, and $Q_3 = 50$ percent. Variation in crime problems among cities complicates the issue of city representation in state law enforcement planning. In general, serious crime problems are concentrated in the densely populated central cities, not the suburban jurisdictions or small towns. Federal guidelines only require representation of local governments and do not specify governments with serious crime problems. Therefore, governors are free to select officials from low-crime areas.

Since the LEAA program is still in its first year and states are only now making subgrants to local governments, it is difficult to determine the policy effects of state domination or the character of local representation. Analysis of the allocation of funds will be required in order to establish relationships between the amounts of state and local representation and the grants approved by state agencies. Despite the inability to complete this analysis now, the representatives of local governments are probably correct that the amounts and character of state and local representation does have a great effect upon the type of grants made by a state government.

The report of the Urban Coalition and Urban America, Inc., criticized state agencies for being dominated by functional specialists and professional law enforcement officials with the exclusion of "residents of poor and minority neighborhoods, where the problem of crime is most intense." Although citizens compose 22 percent of the total agency membership, few of these individuals have central city backgrounds or come from minority groups. New York is one of the few states to include specifically minority representatives on the state agency.

The assertion that professional law enforcement officials control the planning process also has some validity. The distribution of public safety officials on state agencies is as follows: $Q_1 = 16$ percent, $Q_2 = 23$ percent, and $Q_3 = 30$ percent. These percentages do not, however, include officials from corrections and courts, and their inclusion would increase the percentages of persons from professional criminal justice positions. Using strictly the public safety figures, the states with the largest proportions of public safety representation are: Tennessee = 47 percent, Colorado = 39 percent, South Dakota = 38 percent, Arkansas = 36 percent, and Minnesota = 34 percent. These states, it can be argued, are heavily influenced by the viewpoints of policemen, state patrolmen, and sheriffs. States with low percentages of public safety officials, such as Delaware with 13 percent, are probably less affected by public safety perspectives than the ones with large percentages of police officials.

In response to criticisms about functional domination of state agencies, many federal and state officials take the position that the main purpose of the LEAA program is to provide support for law enforcement agencies and that professional competence is the principal goal of the program. Citizen participation, according to some officials, is largely unnecessary. Others take the position that innovation must be one of the major purposes of law enforcement assistance and that nonpolice members are necessary to achieve innovation.

The number of elected policy officials is a third issue about the composition of state law enforcement agencies. The NLC report argued that mayors, county commissioners, and city councilmen were necessary because of their understanding of "the general policy implications of particular law enforcement improvement programs. . . ." Police officials and law enforcement planners, the NLC report held, lack understanding of the political and financial implications of their proposals.

Elected policy officials from both state and local governments make up about one-fifth of all members of state agencies. The distribution is as follows: $Q_1 = 13$ percent, $Q_2 = 19$ percent, and $Q_3 = 24$ percent. It can be argued that this amount of representation for elected policy officials is insufficient in most states. Furthermore, the above percentages include both state and local elected officials. It is significant that there is a higher percentage of elected officials among state officials than among local officials serving on state law enforcement agencies. The median percentage of elected policy officials among state officials is 25 percent; among local officials it is only 13 percent. This breakdown seems to provide additional support to the NLC conclusion that there has been weak representation from local policy makers.

While an advantage to the bloc grant is that each state government can form its own representational system in response to its criminal justice needs, important groups or interests may be overlooked. Supporters of the bloc grant claim that there is nothing wrong with giving governors discretion over appointments because they are elected by entire states. Critics argue that it is unrealistic to expect governments to appoint representatives of the large cities and minority groups which need to be heard and have close involvement in the serious problems of urban crime. Strong federal control over state appointments would be required in order to change the present system, and the bloc grant approach reduces the amount of federal supervision possible.

Regional Planning and City Interests

The League of Cities, Urban Coalition, and Urban America, Inc., criticized regional law enforcement planning for failing to address the crime needs of large cities. Representatives of city interests are sensitive to the regional planning process because it helps establish the degree to which urban and rural areas, as well as large and small cities, are involved in the law enforcement program.

Forty-one of the 50 states used regions in 1969 for planning purposes and as a geographic base for allocating planning funds. Approximately half of those states utilized from five to eight regions. Seven of the states using regions established planning districts exclusively for law enforcement planning; the remainder used combinations of state planning districts, economic development agencies, councils of governments, regional planning agencies, counties, and cities. Twenty-four state governments allocated planning funds among the various regional planning bodies strictly upon the basis of population. The other states divided planning money through minimum funding formulas and also took into account population differences and variations in crime problems.

The League of Cities identified two consequences resulting from the distribution of planning funds according to regional districts. In some cases the use of regions provided too much funding to rural and low-crime areas. For example, California's allocation system resulted in Los Angeles receiving only 2.3 cents per capita while a rural region received 58 cents per capita. Regional planning may also result in inconsequential sums of money for rural districts. As an example of this, the NLC report cited a rural district in Nebraska given $864.70, an amount insufficient to support meaningful planning.[15] As long as the federal guidelines suggest geographic balance in planning and states continue to use regional bodies, low crime, non-urban areas will probably receive more than they would under allocation formulas based on the presence of crime.

Strong arguments, however, can be made for statewide regional planning. California, for example, with more than 400 units of local government and 58 counties, would have difficulty planning without its system of 11 regions. Furthermore, crime can be viewed as a phenomenon which crosses jurisdictional boundaries and necessitates planning for areas larger than any single political unit.

Despite the controversy surrounding regional planning, regional bodies have few powers. Their principal role is to study crime problems and to make recommendations to the state supervisory agency. While regional units receive planning funds, they do not necessarily play an important part in deciding where the action money will be spent within their district. Only three states claim to allow regional bodies to make final decisions on action money allocations. This system of allowing regional officials to plan but not allocate funds for their areas may eventually lead to serious disputes with the state supervisory agency. In cases of such disagreement, the state agency holds the decision-making powers.

State Allocation of Funds

One of the most striking political features of the bloc grant is that state governments make the actual decisions about how much money specific cities and counties will receive. The strong role played by state officials in deciding how federal law enforcement assistance will be divided among the many competing jurisdictions stands in sharp contrast to the weak role played by states in direct federal-local programs.

One of the sensitive administrative issues about fund allocations concerns state services which may be considered as part of the local percentage of federal funds. Under the LEAA program, the state is supposed to receive the concurrence of the local governments for state services, such as a state-run academy for police officials, which take a portion of the local government's funds. This issue raises the question of who within the local government has the authority to give local approval of such arrangements. Allowing a police chief or even a city manager to waive a city's right to federal funds would be a questionable practice since they are elected policy-making officials. The early experience with the LEAA program indicates that the pass-through provision can lead to many complications resulting from state and local efforts to maximize their potential resources.

The representative composition of the state supervisory agency becomes critical in the process of allocating funds. Analysis by regional planning task forces and priorities in state plans may have less influence on the allocation of funds than will the political and functional representation on the state agency. A state agency with little or no central city representation might view the big city crime problems as relatively unimportant and focus resources on statewide and interjurisdictional needs instead. In addition, heavy representation from public safety officials can result in an emphasis upon purchasing police equipment and little attention upon the needs for innovations.

Newark's place in New Jersey's law enforcement planning system is an example of one of the dilemmas in state fund allocation for urban problems. New Jersey's state law enforcement planning agency has no one from Newark on its governing board although it includes small town and county officials, several state officers, and citizens. The state has eight planning regions, and population is the basis for distribution of planning money. Although the incidence of crime is a factor in allocating funds, some Newark officials fear that they will not receive the support they deserve as a result of their serious crime problems. The city is in state region I, a region which also includes Jersey City, another city with serious central city crime problems. Even if Newark's views were accurately presented at the regional level, the regional body is only advisory to the state body which has weak central city representation. On the other hand, if Newark had as dominant a role as the city argues it should have, it is possible that resources would not be available to support a comprehensive statewide distribution of funds. As a result of those problems, state officials have altered the administrative system to allow more direct relationships with large cities. But the conflicts between statewide goals and central city desires remain a difficult issue.

The matching arrangements are complex in a bloc grant program. The federal government supports several categories of activities according to different levels of matching, ranging from 95 percent to 50 percent federal matching money depending upon the particular category of program activity. In addition, state and local governments must divide the federal funds available according to the pass-through formula. Because state governments set priorities and allocate grants to local governments, the ability or interest of the local unit to provide its required matching money may not be determined until late and only through revisions in its budget. The issue of who speaks for the city becomes important at this time, and the lack of policy officials in the planning process may become a serious problem. A city police chief, for example, may put his jurisdiction on record as requesting federal funds for construction of a new law enforcement facility. The city council, however, may refuse to provide the 50 percent matching money because of financial pressures or disagreement over priorities. A similar problem can occur at the state level. Since law enforcement planning is closely tied to the governor, conflicts between governor and the state legislature can lead to refusals by the legislature to provide the needed matching funds for state projects. Such a struggle in Nebraska, for example, put that program in serious jeopardy and disrupted planning activities.

State-local relations are perhaps the most critical feature of the bloc grant. The early experiences with the LEAA program indicate that state officials must become sensitive intergovernmental diplomats if they are to handle successfully urban bloc grant programs. Otherwise, cities and state governments will not be able to achieve the administrative cooperation necessary under this grant-in-aid approach.

Conclusion

The bloc grant is an important device with significant support in the Nixon Administration, Congress, and state governments. It is possible that Congress will apply the bloc grant idea to many existing fields of grant-in-aid assistance in the coming years. Although it has been heralded as a reform measure designed to correct problems found in categorical grant programs, there are political and administrative complexities in bloc grants not anticipated by the bloc grant proponents.

The administrative goals of this form of grant-in-aid included comprehensive planning, uncomplicated intergovernmental relationships, elimination of federal controls, and state allocation of funds. While some of these goals have been partially achieved, the bloc grant has caused great amounts of intergovernmental competition and has generated significant political cross pressures from important groups. The bloc grant has not brought about uncomplicated intergovernmental relations or eliminated federal controls. The network of intergovernmental relations in the LEAA program are complex because all of the governmental units involved in it want to maximize their powers. States want as much flexibility and as few regulations as possible. Large cities, on the other hand, want strict federal controls which will force states to allocate more power and funds to them. The federal government is caught in the middle of these pressures. Although the Republican Administration is committed to strengthening state governments, the LEAA administrators must necessarily take responsibilities for their program before the powerful committees of Congress and respond to the pressures of the local government associations.

Controversy surrounding this program have been particularly acute because the greatest crime problems are found in central cities, and the bloc grant is not an administrative device capable of funneling large amounts of money directly into cities. When the objective is to address an urgent urban need, the bloc grant may not be a satisfactory system. There is a significant conflict between the goals of fighting immediate urban crime problems and a grant-in-aid system dominated by state governments. If Congress had intended to develop a system of aiding the large cities with serious crime problems, a direct, categorical grant system would have been appropriate. In this instance, Congress has another principal objective: the transfer of grant-in-aid powers to state governments and the promotion of interjurisdictional law enforcement planning. In this sense, the big cities lost their battle in Congress.

There are important consequences to the use of the bloc grant in urban problem fields. One of the most important in law enforcement assistance has been the institutionalization of patterns of intergovernmental competition and conflict for federal funds. While competition may foster desirable changes in the criminal justice system, an important test of the bloc grant will be the degree of cooperation among cities, states, and the federal which can be achieved despite such competition.

In the final analysis, the ability of state governments to apportion funds wisely and to respond to urban needs will determine the success or the failure of the bloc grant. The early experience with the Safe Streets Act indicates that some states are capable of administering such an important program. However, other states because of antiquated constitutions, weak executive leadership, and rurally oriented bureaucracies may not effectively fulfill their responsibilities. Judgment as to the number of state governments possessing sufficient capabilities in law enforcement and criminal justice must wait until several funding cycles have been completed. Despite some achievements in law enforcement assistance, variations in competency among state governments as well as patterns of city-state conflict may lead to the conclusion that the bloc grant mechanism can be successfully introduced into only a limited number of policy fields.

Notes

1. Commission on the Organization of the Executive Branch of the Government, Overseas Administration, Federal-State Relations, Federal Research, Report to Congress (Washington, D.C.: U.S. Government Printing Office, March 1949), p. 31.
2. Commission on Intergovernmental Relations, *Report to the President* (Washington, D.C.: U.S. Government Printing Office, June 1955), p. 121.
3. Advisory Commission on Intergovernmental Relations, *Fiscal Balance in the American Federal System,* Volume I (Washington, D.C.: U.S. Government Printing Office, October 1967), p. xxi.
4. Some of the important studies include: ACIR, *Fiscal Balance. . . , op. cit.;* Daniel J. Elazar and Ellis Katz, "The Law Enforcement and Criminal Justice Assistance Act of 1967" (Philadelphia: Center for the Study of Federalism, January 1968); W. Brooke Graves, *American Intergovernmental Relations: Their Origins, Historical Development, and Current Status* (New York: Charles Scribner & Sons, 1964); Selma J. Mushkin and John F. Cotton, *Functional Federalism: Grants-in-Aid and PPB Systems* (Washington, D.C.: State-Local Finances Project of the George Washington University, 1968).
5. Omnibus Crime Control and Safe Streets Act of 1968, Public Law 90-351, 90th Congress, HR 5037, June 19, 1968.
6. Committee on the Judiciary, U.S. Senate, "Report of Proceedings on Nomination of Charles H. Rogovin and Richard W. Velde," unpublished record of hearing held on March 12, 1969, p. 3.
7. National League of Cities, *Analysis of State Administration of Planning Funds Allocated Under the Omnibus Crime Control and Safe Streets Act of 1968* (Washington, D.C.: NLC, March 18, 1968), p. i.
8. The Urban Coalition and Urban America, Inc., *Law and Disorder: State Planning Under the Safe Streets Act* (Washington, D.C.: The Urban Coalition and Urban America, Inc., June 1969), p. 24.
9. National Association of Counties, *National Urban County Survey of Crime Control and Safe Streets Act of 1968* (Washington, D.C.: NACO, April 10, 1969).
10. U.S. Department of Justice, LEAA, *Guide for State Planning Agency Grants*

(Washington, D.C.: U.S. Government Printing Office, November 1968), p. 8.

11. U.S. Department of Justice, LEAA, "Comprehensive Plan Outline and Format for Action Grant Applications—Fiscal Year 1969" (Washington, D.C.: LEAA, 1969).
12. Statement by Kai R. Martensen, executive director, California Council on Criminal Justice, personal interview, April 9, 1969.
13. Committee on Appropriations, House of Representatives, U.S. Congress, *Hearings on Departments of State, Justice and Commerce, The Judiciary and Related Agencies* (Washington, D.C.: U.S. Government Printing Office, 1969), p. 1040.
14. Detailed analysis of the survey findings are presented in International City Management Association, "The Safe Streets Act: The Cities' Evaluation," *Urban Data Service,* Volume I, No. 9 (September 1969).
15. National League of Cities, *op. cit.,* p. 12.

1970 (30:141-153)

DAVID A. CAPUTO and RICHARD L. COLE

General Revenue Sharing Expenditure Decisions in Cities Over 50,000

General Revenue sharing has been returning federal revenues to state and local governments since November 1972. By June 30, 1974, over $14 billion of the $30+ billion to be distributed by 1976 had been sent back to various governmental units.[1] Despite the research and speculation which has occurred concerning the impact of revenue sharing funds on governmental expenditures and services, there is still a need for information on how and for what purposes the general revenue sharing funds have been allocated.[2] This symposium article summarizes the results of a survey dealing with general revenue sharing decisions and city officials' attitudes toward general revenue sharing.[3] These findings are then compared with other available studies to indicate the general trends and patterns which characterize general revenue sharing decisions.

In January 1974 the chief administrative officers in all cities over 50,000 were sent a questionnaire requesting information about the proportion of Entitlement Period 4 (July 1, 1973, to June 30, 1974) general revenue sharing funds allocated to various functional categories. In addition, the respondents were asked to differentiate among operating and capital expense items and the use of funds for new or existing programs. A second section asked the respondents to indicate their attitudes and opinions about the revenue sharing program and its general impact. The January 1974 survey was similar to a March 1973 survey conducted by the authors.[4] In addition, the Office of Revenue Sharing's report, *The First Actual Use Reports,* which is based on an entirely different data source, provides information concerning initial spending decisions.[5] Despite the widespread interest in general revenue sharing, to our knowledge, these are the only sources of data indicating how funds have actually been spent for other than a preselected subsample of recipient units of governments. In addition, attitudinal data are also scarce. In sum then, the data presented here provide the most complete summary of decisions reached in cities over 50,000 population regarding Entitlement Period 4 general revenue sharing allocations.

Table 1 summarizes the number of cities in each category sent questionnaires and the number responding. The overall response rate of 53 percent is acceptable; it should be noted that cities over 500,000 and under 50,000 had response rates less than the overall response rate. Even in these cases, however, response rates were sufficiently high to permit generalizations from the data supplied by the respondents.

Expenditure Decisions

Table 2 indicates the spending patterns for responding cities during Entitlement Period 4 and the budgetary year prior to general revenue sharing. Law enforcement (16.3 percent), fire protection (15.3 percent), street and road repairs (12.5 percent), environmental protection (13.2 percent), and recreation and parks (10.9 percent) received 68.2 percent of the total general revenue sharing funds. Note the small percentage of funds allocated to transit systems, code enforcement, salaries, and undetermined categories. It would appear that local decision makers may have reached similar conclusions concerning the pressing needs of their communities.

A separate analysis was done comparing the proportion of general revenue sharing funds spent for capital and operating purposes. For Entitlement Period 4, 52 percent of total general revenue sharing funds were spent to meet operating expenses, while 48 percent was spent for capital purposes. This nearly even distribution between operating (52 percent) and capital (48 percent) expenditures varies sharply with the Office of Revenue Sharing's report, *The First Actual Use Reports,* finding that similar size cities expended approximately 70 percent of their funds for the first three entitlement periods for operating expenditures.[6] However, that report showed

TABLE 1
Distribution and Rate of Questionnaire Return: 4/10/74

Classification	No. of Cities Surveyed (A)	Cities Reporting No.	Cities Reporting % of (A)
Total, all cities	409	216	53%
Population group			
Over 500,000	26	13	50%
250,000-500,000	30	21	70%
100,000-250,000	98	60	61%
50,000-100,000	255	122	48%

TABLE 2
Distribution of Entitlement Period Four General Revenue Sharing Funds

Expenditure for:	General Revenue Sharing Expenditures* 1974 (N=216) %	Prior Budgetary Expenditures* 1971 (N=216) %
Law enforcement	16.3	12.6
Fire protection	15.3	9.4
Building and zoning code enforcement	.7	NA
Environmental protection (sewage, pollution, sanitation, etc.)	13.2	11.8
Transit systems	2.9	NA
Street and road repair	12.5	11.6
Social services for the poor, aged, and minority groups	2.8	1.1
Health services	2.8	3.7
Recreation and parks	10.9	6.9
Public building renovation	3.9	3.7
Supplementing municipal salaries	1.1	NA
Libraries	2.2	1.9
Other	11.3	37.3
Undetermined	4.1	NA
Total	100.0	100.0

*Source: 1974 data from questionnaires returned. 1971 budgetary expenditures calculated from data in Table 5, U.S. Bureau of the Census, *City Government Finances in 1970-1971* (Washington, D.C.: U.S. Government Printing Office, 1972).

that cities planned to spend greater portions of their fourth entitlement period checks for capital purposes. If this trend to increased capital expenditures is in fact supported by spending patterns in future years, it would warrant the contention that, initially at least, many of the larger cities had to use general revenue sharing funds to meet a very real local fiscal crisis, but that as the crisis subsided, they were able to use a larger proportion of their general revenue sharing funds on capital expenditure items.

Another important comparison is between the proportion spent for services which are traditionally associated with and provided to low income groups in urban areas. In these cities, social and health proportions do not seem to be increasing drastically in the amount or percentage of revenue sharing funds received. In fact, a comparison with the data in the *First Actual Use Reports* indicates a slight percentage decline in health expenditures in cities of similar size.[7] While it is too early to conclude that these program recipients will not benefit from programs directly funded by general revenue sharing funds, it does indicate that they have so far been unsuccessful in gaining favorable access to the allocation process. The implications of this could be significant if other social service programs are phased out.

Finally, it appears that there may be a general decline in the percentage of funds allocated to public safety (law enforcement and fire protection) categories, even though that category still dominates. When compared with the *First Actual Use Reports,* this trend is clear.[8] In addition, the percentages allocated for street and road repair, environmental protection, recreation and parks, and municipal salaries have increased.[9] This would indicate that priorities may have been clearly set and are being followed.

Another area of interest to researchers dealing with the impact of general revenue sharing is the innovative use of the funds. Are new programs and personnel being provided by the funds or are they in fact going into already existing programs where additional funds may be needed? Table 3 provides some insights on this question.

General revenue sharing funds are being used largely to support existing programs rather than beginning new programs. Existing programs received the largest proportion of general revenue sharing funds in the fire prevention (82.3 percent), building and code enforcement (76.7 percent),

TABLE 3
Use of Fourth Entitlement Period
General Revenue Sharing for New and Existing Programs by Function*

	Revenue Sharing Used For:		
Function	Existing Programs	Both Equally	New Programs
Law enforcement	76.4%	4.7%	18.9%
Fire prevention	82.3	5.3	12.4
Building and code enforcement	76.7	0.0	23.3
Environmental protection	69.1	6.4	24.5
Transit systems	60.9	8.7	30.4
Street and road repair	76.1	8.0	15.9
Social services	45.8	6.8	47.4
Health	66.7	7.4	25.9
Parks and recreation	55.6	6.5	37.9
Building renovation	71.1	0.0	28.9
Libraries	62.0	6.0	32.0
Financial administration	66.7	7.0	26.3
Other	51.7	5.0	43.3

*This table based on 1974 survey data. Functions not listed were too seldomly selected for meaningful comparisons.

law enforcement (76.4 percent), street and road repairs (76.1 percent), and building renovation (71.1 percent) categories. New programs received more than 25 percent of the total general revenue sharing funds spent in the social services (47.4 percent), other (43.3 percent), parks and recreation (37.9 percent), libraries (32 percent), transit systems (30.4 percent), building renovation (28.9 percent), financial administration (26.3 percent), and health (25.9 percent) categories. Based on related research we have done, it appears that cities over 50,000 are beginning to allocate a larger proportion of general revenue sharing funds to new programs.[10] This is additional support for the contention that cities, if their individual fiscal crisis subsides, may increase the proportion of general revenue sharing funds allocated to new programs. It is also important to point out that the proportion spent for new programs in the social services category exceeded that spent for existing programs. The point is clear; general revenue sharing has not been used primarily to initiate new programs, but it has made innovation possible and it appears that the trend may be towards increased funding of new programs. This may have important political and social implications for American cities and for those groups competing for the funds. It could also result in the development of new and different urban programs.

Administrative Needs

Before ending this discussion, one additional point needs to be raised. In our 1973 survey, the respondents were asked to indicate the number of full-time personnel assigned to general revenue sharing. Eighty-five percent of the cities had no full-time personnel, 11 percent had one to two assigned, and 4 percent had two or more assigned.[11] This question was repeated this year, and we found that 90 percent of the cities had no full-time personnel, 8 percent had one, and 2 percent had two or more full-time personnel devoted to general revenue sharing. This indicates that cities have not considered it important to develop specialized staff personnel to deal with the general revenue sharing programs. It also indicates that one of the main arguments by those who support the program apparently is true: general revenue sharing does not require a large local bureaucracy or preoccupation with administrative matters for its implementation. We explore these expenditure decisions in greater depth in chapters 4 and 5 of our *Urban Politics and Decentralization: The Case of General Revenue Sharing.*

In addition to determining what expenditure categories received allocations, our study also provides information on the impact general revenue sharing has had on local tax rates and public hearings. Tables 4 and 5 summarize the aggregate returns for these questions; wherever possible the 1974 results have been compared with the 1973 results.

TABLE 4
Effect of General Revenue Sharing on Tax Rate

	Allowed for Reduction	Prevented Increase in Rate	Reduced Amount of Rate Increase	No Effect
1974 (N=210)	25 (12%)	75 (36%)	36 (17%)	74 (35%)
Long range (N=206)	5 (2%)	56 (27%)	98 (48%)	47 (23%)

Table 4 indicates that general revenue sharing has had a marked effect on local tax rates. Note that only 35 percent of the respondents felt that general revenue sharing funds had no immediate effect on tax rates, while the largest number of respondents (48 percent) indicated that the funds had either prevented or reduced the amount of a tax rate increase. These findings again support the contention that the fiscal crisis facing many American cities was positively affected by general revenue sharing funds. While it would be a mistake to assume that general revenue sharing funds alone were responsible for the stabilization of tax rates, it cannot be dismissed as an insignificant factor.

Table 4 also summarizes the respondents' attitudes towards the long-range effect of general revenue sharing on tax rates. This table indicates that

TABLE 5
General Revenue Sharing Decisions and Public Hearings

	Public Hearings Held			
	Yes	(%)	No	(%)
1973* (N=195)	96	(49)	99	(51)
1974 (N=203)	119	(59)	84	(41)
	Public Hearings to be Held in the Future**			
	Yes	(%)	No	(%)
1973* (N=199)	75	(38)	75	(38)
1974 (N=205)	104	(51)	101	(49)

*Source: Table 5/5, *1974 Municipal Year Book,* p. 98.

**1973 question included an undecided option which was chosen by 49 respondents or 24 percent of the respondents. Thus the 1973 percentage adds to 100 percent when these respondents are included.

few officials believe that general revenue sharing, in the long run, will allow for actual reduction in the tax rate (2 percent), but even more officials (75 percent) believe general revenue sharing will prevent or reduce the rate of increase. It is also observed that fewer officials (23 percent) believe general revenue sharing, in the long run, will fail to have a noticeable effect on the cities' tax rates. General revenue sharing, based on Table 4, is not seen as a "cure all" for the economic problems of the cities, but as a useful resource in meeting the many service demands they face.

The procedures used by cities to decide the allocation of their revenue sharing funds are important and deserve careful attention. Table 5 summarizes the responses to the questions of whether the cities held public hearings on revenue sharing decisions during the past year and whether public hearings are anticipated in the future. It is important to note that a larger percentage of respondents held public hearings concerning Entitlement Period 4 funds than in 1973. The 10 percent increase can be attributed to numerous factors, but certainly one which may have had an impact would have been the fact that cities had more time in 1974 to set up and hold public hearings since there was more lead time on the funding. Of course, an additional factor may be that citizen groups have become more active and forceful in their attempts to influence revenue sharing decisions and that an increase in the frequency of public hearings is one result of that activity.

Another interesting aspect of Table 5 is the increase in the tendency to hold public hearings in the future. There is a 13 percent increase in favorable responses from 1973 to 1974, but only 104 cities indicate they will hold public hearings in the future, while 119 actually held them in 1974. This is similar to the 1973 experience where 96 cities (49 percent) held public hearings in 1973, but only 75 cities (38 percent) responded "yes" to holding public hearings in the future. While one should be cautious about drawing conclusions based on such a small shift, it is possible that cities may be experiencing disillusionment with public hearings as a means of obtaining public sentiment concerning general revenue sharing allocations. If this trend continues, it will be interesting to note what mechanism, if any, for public input will be utilized. The reactions of public groups as well as governmental decision makers will determine the adoption or continuation of public hearings during the general revenue sharing allocation process.

Categorical Grant Programs

Another critical area to many cities is the effect of general revenue sharing funds on various categorical grant programs and the total amount of federal revenues coming into a community. Table 6 indicates the probability that general revenue sharing funds will be used to fund model cities and various OEO and urban renewal programs if such categorical grant programs are phased out or reduced. Note that from 1973 to 1974 there was in fact an increase (20 percent to 30 percent) in the propensity to allocate general revenue sharing funds to these programs. While the increase is not drastic, it is consistent and may indicate that these programs will fare better in terms of revenue sharing allocations at the local level than was anticipated. Again, this may be a function of increasing activism on the part of citizen organizations attempting to influence revenue sharing expenditures. On the other hand, less than a third of the cities indicated they would support the programs with general revenue sharing funds in both years; thus the major conclusion must be that these programs will not fare well if left to local budgetary processes. The implications of this are many and far reaching, but are probably most important for lower income and non-white elements in the cities involved. The end result may be a very serious curtailment of services which these programs provided unless the recipients are able to bring greater pressure to bear on the participants in the local budgetary process.

Officials' Satisfaction and Attitudes

Related to this question is a broader one of the effect general revenue sharing funds will have on total federal funds to the community. As was the case in 1973, most of the respondents (66 percent) felt general revenue sharing would not lead to a net increase in federal funds. In fact, a lower percentage (34 percent to 43 percent) of respondents felt that general revenue sharing funds would increase total federal funds in 1974 than in 1973. These findings indicate that city officials did not see general revenue sharing as the first of many federal programs providing them with increased revenues. It appears that they were much less optimistic in that respect and that their

TABLE 6
Allocation of General Revenue Sharing Funds to Model Cities, Urban Renewal, or OEO Programs*

	Definitely Yes	Probably Yes	Uncertain	Probably Not	Definitely Not
1973** (N=147)	3 (2%)	26 (18%)	59 (40%)	44 (30%)	15 (10%)
1974 (N=142)	8 (6%)	32 (23%)	55 (38%)	36 (25%)	11 (8%)

*Only asked of cities receiving these types of category grant assistance.

**Source: Table 5/5, *1974 Municipal Year Book,* 1974, p. 98.

TABLE 7
Long-Run Effect of General Revenue Sharing Funds on Total Community Funds

	Greatly Increase	Increase Somewhat	Little or No Effect	Decrease Somewhat	Greatly Decrease
1973* (N=180)	22 (12%)	55 (31%)	41 (23%)	34 (18%)	28 (16%)
1974 (N=193)	21 (11%)	45 (23%)	51 (26%)	53 (28%)	23 (12%)

*Source: Table 5/8, *1974 Municipal Year Book,* p. 99.

pessimism about increased federal funds has increased slightly in the last year.

Despite this continued and even increased feeling that general revenue sharing would not lead to increased federal funds, Table 8 demonstrates that satisfaction for the program has increased in the past year. Ninety percent of the 1974 respondents (compared with 78 percent in 1973) indicated they were either somewhat (28 percent) or very satisfied (62 percent) with the program, while only 6 percent of the respondents indicated dissatisfaction. In addition, the number of undecided declined (from 13 percent to 4 percent) substantially from 1973 to 1974. This indicates that support for the program increased even though the respondents did not feel it would lead to substantially more federal revenues. The result of this may be a well-organized lobbying effort to influence the renewal legislation discussion during the present congressional session. It is obvious that general revenue sharing is quite popular with local officials.

TABLE 8
Evaluation of General Revenue Sharing

	Very Satisfied	Somewhat Satisfied	Undecided	Somewhat Unsatisfied	Very Unsatisfied
1973* (N=199)	92 (46%)	64 (32%)	26 (13%)	12 (6%)	5 (3%)
1974 (N=195)	121 (62%)	55 (28%)	7 (4%)	10 (5%)	2 (1%)

*Source: Table 5/14, *1974 Municipal Year Book,* p. 101.

Conclusion

The final assessment and evaluation of general revenue sharing and its impact in cities over 50,000 must await additional time and decision making. Despite this, there are several major conclusions which emerge from this study.

First, general revenue sharing expenditures continue to be concentrated in a very few categories. In fact the concentration of expenditures into a few categories increased sharply during Entitlement Period 4. This would indicate that many cities are indeed allocating general revenue sharing expenditures for a narrow range of categories.

Second, health and social service programs normally associated with low-income or socially disadvantaged groups have not received a large proportion of general revenue sharing funds. Such programs may receive additional funds in the future as other aspects of the local fiscal or political situation permit. This concern over the lack of general revenue sharing funds for social programs will be a major point in the upcoming legislative debate over the renewal of general revenue sharing.

Third, general revenue sharing funds have gone, to the largest extent, to support already existing programs and have not been widely used to develop new and innovative programs. This will be a widely discussed point in the upcoming legislative debate.

Fourth, general revenue sharing has not drastically affected the tax rates prevalent in American cities over 50,000 but the funds have helped to stabilize the rates. It appears that the fiscal crisis claimed by many cities in the early 1970s may have been alleviated somewhat in the past few years, but the problems of providing city services in an inflationary economy may make the impact of general revenue sharing funds on local tax rates even more marginal.

Fifth, probably the most important impact of general revenue sharing funds may well be the general satisfaction of city officials with the program and the apparent increase in that satisfaction as the program continues. It would appear that local officials will indeed be united in their support of general revenue when renewal legislation is considered in 1975. This fact is supported by Mayor Moon Landrieu's statement, in testimony before the Senate Government Operations Subcommittee on Intergovernmental Relations in June 1974, that "the single overriding message we (the nation's mayors) are determined to leave with this committee, and to leave with the entire Congress, is that the nation's cities continue to be 100 percent united in their support of the general revenue sharing program."[12]

Finally, given the strong support expressed in this statement and indicated by our respondents, the debate over the renewal of general revenue sharing will deal with specific changes and recommendations in the program rather than deciding to leave it as it is or eliminate it. Certainly President Ford's statements in the fall of 1974 indicate his support of the program and his unwillingness to eliminate or reduce it as an anti-inflationary measure. The results of the up-coming legislative debate will have far-reaching significance for officials and individual citizens in the nation's cities. Hopefully our findings will cast additional light on the general revenue sharing program and its impact on urban America.

Notes

1. For a detailed discussion of the legislative history of general revenue sharing, see "Congress Clears Nixon's Revenue-Sharing Plan," in *1972 Congressional Quarterly Almanac* (Washington, D.C.: Congressional Quarterly, Inc.), pp. 636-652. Also useful are Richard E. Thompson's, *Revenue Sharing: A New Era in Federalism?* (Washington, D.C.: Revenue Sharing Advisory Service, 1973), and the legislation itself, Public Law 92-512.
2. The best available summary of the various research attempts investigating general revenue sharing is found in *Compendium of Research in Progress* (Washington, D.C.: National Planning Association, 1973).
3. The 1974 survey was part of our joint research effort investigating the impact of general revenue sharing funds in cities over 50,000. This research is fully summarized and the important theoretical and empirical points pertaining to general revenue sharing and urban politics developed in David A. Caputo and Richard L. Cole, *Urban Politics and Decentralization: The Case of General Revenue Sharing* (Lexington, Mass.: D.C. Heath/Lexington, 1974).
4. For a detailed discussion of the 1973 survey see David A. Caputo and Richard L. Cole, *General Revenue Sharing: Initial Decisions* (Washington, D.C.: International City Management Association, December 1973), and David A. Caputo and Richard L. Cole, "Initial Decisions in General Revenue Sharing," *1974 Municipal Year Book* (Washington, D.C.: International City Management Association, 1974), pp. 95-102.
5. David A. Caputo and Richard L. Cole, *Revenue Sharing: The First Actual Use Reports* (Washington, D.C.: Office of Revenue Sharing, March 1974).
6. *Ibid.*, Table 7, p. 25.
7. *Ibid.*, Table 8, pp. 29-30.
8. *Ibid.*
9. *Ibid.*
10. Caputo and Cole, *Urban Politics and Decentralization, op. cit.*, chapter 5.
11. Caputo and Cole, *Revenue Sharing: The First Actual Use Reports, op. cit.*, Table 1, pp. 4-5.
12. Moon Landrieu, "Statement to the Senate Government Operations Subcommittee on Intergovernmental Relations," June 11, 1974, p. 1.

1975 (35:136-142)

ROBERT D. NEWTON

Administrative Federalism

Background

The creation of the assistance programs of the 1960s was accompanied by spectacular innovations in policy, which must now be followed by a period in which the federal system is organized to make possible the achievement of the goals which have been established.[1] That period of organization requires innovation in administration that, while it perhaps can never be as spectacular, will be equally historic.[2]

Focusing on administrative or management purposes and processes is not easy. Much attention is given to program purposes and objectives. There are thousands of programs. Much less attention is given to program and project implementing methods and processes. There are fewer of those. They are inherently less interesting, but they hold the key to developing the system that is needed. That is so because those methods and processes can be described independently of the multitude of functional or activity program specialties whose objectives they implement.

The Commission on Government Procurement proposed and the federal government has now enacted legislation requiring the use of concepts of federal/non-federal procurement and grant-type assistance relationships that establish a framework for the basic system that is needed.[3] This framework of program implementing alternatives recognizes different federal purposes, procurement and assistance, and separates assistance relationships into types based on federal involvement during performance of projects or activities. This framework will facilitate management choices and will permit a systematic analysis of federal purposes in terms of the specifics of (1) how they are implemented (management requirements and standards for monitoring, reporting, directing and approving) and (2) the resources utilized (who does what) to serve the objectives of federal programs. The resulting system will enable and require the executive branch to manage assistance relationships in a more conscious and consistent fashion. Being independent of functional or activity distinctions, it should facilitate obtaining answers to the who-does-what-and-why questions asked by operating managers and students of federalism. It will also make federal/non-federal relationships more visible to those with political and oversight interests and responsibilities.

Administrative Federalism

"Administrative federalism"[4] would be an appropriate term to describe the proposed system. The use of this term might foster communication among practitioners, who are often not fully aware of the relevance of subjects such as federalism and intergovernmental relations to what they do, and students of federalism and intergovernmental relations, who are often not fully aware of the various assistance and procurement methods and processes that constitute the operational means used to accomplish program purposes and objectives.

The proliferation of complex assistance programs requiring federal agency intervention or participation has not been matched with either systematic modification of traditional grant or procurement contract methods or by the development of appropriate new methods to accommodate the relationships established to implement these programs. The confusion that now exists is attributable in large measure to the inconsistent use of grant, contract, and other instrument designations. Grants and other instruments are used in what should be procurement situations and procurement contracts are used in some assistance situations. More importantly, "grants" are used indiscriminately in situations in which there is federal preemption of assumption of management control, in situations in which there is federal operational involvement, collaboration or cooperation, and in situations in which there is little or no federal involvement during performance.

The lack of systematic connections among instrument designations and relationships encourages *ad hoc* and unsystematic application of resources in many of the thousands of programs and hundreds of thousands of projects and activities. Management planning and program implementation tend to be chaotic. If we are successfully to reduce this confusion, the framework which would order relationships must recognize the need for accommodating existing relationships by deliberate modification of the traditional grant/contract dichotomy and clear definition of the alternatives proposed.

To accomplish the proposed restructuring of the traditional grant/contract dichotomy to provide the needed program and project implementing methods, we propose the following[5] as a framework for a system of administrative federalism, seen from the perspective of the program purposes of the federal agencies:

	Contracts	Cooperative Agreements	Grants
Federal roles	(1) "Purchaser" or (2) "Manager" of some assistance relationships	(3) "Partner" or "Active Supporter"	(4) "Patron" or "Passive Supporter"
Primary responsibility	Federal	Shared	Recipient
Type of federal involvement	Whatever involvement is necessary consistent with federal procurement regulations	Use of program or administrative standards requiring substantial review and/or approvals during performance and/or Substantial operational involvement during performance to approve specific decisions, subawards, or provide guidance or technical assistance and/or Participate as coworkers or otherwise collaborate	Use of program and administrative standards requiring little or no involvement during performance
Right to redirect or change within scope	Unilateral federal right to change or redirect	Shared right to change or redirect	Recipient right to change or redirect

Grant-type relationships will be established when (a) the federal purpose is to support recipients in carrying out functions which serve national objectives for which the federal agencies have responsibilities, and (b) the recipient has primary responsibility for managing the federally-supported project or activity, thus, there will be little or no federal involvement during performance. The projects or activities will be carried out in accordance with approved proposals and administrative standards. The federal agency will monitor performance of the projects or activities only to the extent necessary to keep generally informed of progress and to assure compliance with applicable standards.

Cooperative agreement-type relationships will be established when (a) the federal purpose is to support or stimulate recipients to carry out functions which serve national objectives for which the federal agencies have responsibilities, and (b) recipients and the federal agencies share responsibility for or collaborate in the management or the conduct of projects, including performing specific roles and responsibilities, coordinating and integrating the project with related projects or activities, and assuring that the results of the work will be acceptable for the purposes intended. The federal role will be to monitor the work to provide necessary advice and assistance of a management, coordinating, or technical nature and to be actively involved by approving specific decisions and subawards or otherwise being involved as stipulated by the terms of the cooperative agreement.

Procurement contract-type relationships will be established when (a) the federal agencies are procuring products, services and studies required primarily for direct federal use, including the procurement of services or facilities for use by third parties; and (b) the federal role will be that of a purchaser or buyer who establishes a specific requirement or specification and judges acceptability of the product or service against the requirement or specification. The federal agency will monitor the work to the extent necessary to assure timely and satisfactory performance. It will reserve the right unilaterally to change the work and, if appropriate, to terminate it for default.

Procurement contract-type relationships[6] may also be established to serve assistance purposes when an agency determines, for example, that accomplishing project or activity objectives requires that a federal agency assume the role of a manager responsible for coordinating or integrating the particular project or activity with related projects or activities and for determining the acceptability of the work being performed or the product produced. To convey the federal right to exercise "control," the federal agency will reserve the right unilaterally to stop, change, or redirect the work. The federal agency will also monitor the work to assure adequate project management, including approving major decisions and subawards.

The foregoing alternative methods of project or program implementation can be abstracted in decision-tree form as follows:

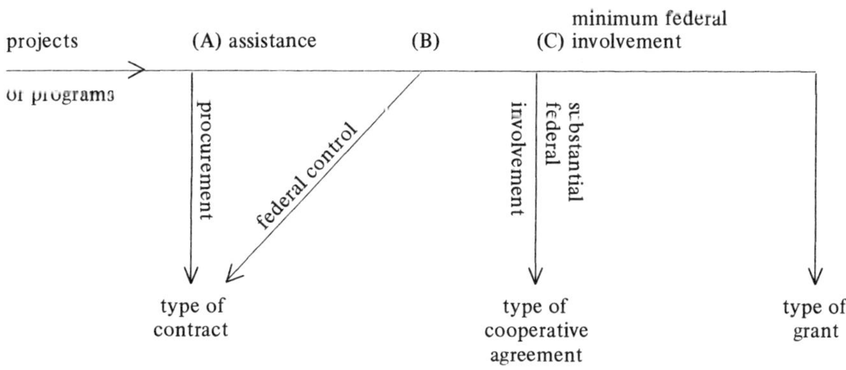

At the program or transaction level, Decision (A) separates procurement relationships from assistance relationships. Decision (A) requires an answer to the question of whether the purpose of the relationship is primarily to support or stimulate an activity which serves general public purposes *or* is primarily to acquire a product or service for direct federal use. Decision (B) separates assistance relationships in which the federal agencies intend to exercise "control" from all other assistance relationships. Decision (B) requires examination of reasons, if any, why the federal agency should control or manage a proposed project or activity to the extent of needing to change or redirect the work. This decision turns on factors such as program intent and resources, how the project is related technically or managerially to other projects, the novelty or complexity of the project and the capacity of the performer. Consideration of factors such as these should yield a decision on where primary responsibility for managing the project and for acceptability of the work should lie, with the federal agency or with the recipient of an award. Decision (C) separates grants from cooperative agreements. It turns on whether the reasoning that resulted in Decision (B) indicates that, although the federal agency does not need to accept contract responsibilities, it does need to be substantially involved during performance of the activity. A cooperative agreement relationship would differ both in character and degree from the usual grant relationship in which the federal role is the establishment of requirements or standards with a routine review of performance to assure compliance with them. It would entail active federal monitoring of and participation in the activity to assist, to approve specified decisions, milestones, subawards, or to be otherwise involved in ways specified in the cooperative agreement. In the cooperative agreement relationship the federal agency and the recipient share responsibility for or collaborate in the management of the activity. In the grant relationship the recipient is responsible for the management of the activity.

Implications and Conclusions

The federal government has not been notably successful in accomplishing federal assistance objectives outlined by the Congress. We do not have adequate institutional means to accomplish stated objectives. To be sure, the stated objectives may be unclear and the consequences of realizing them unperceived. Nonetheless, the fact that the means by which objectives are sought may not be well suited to their realization surely contributes to some failures to achieve them as well as to difficulty in determining the reasons for success or failure.

The proposed framework for a system of administrative federalism was developed from the perspective of federal purposes and intents. It can also conceptualize recipient responsibilities. For example, a state finds itself, figuratively speaking, with the federal government above and units of local government and other organizations and institutions below. While the federal agencies assume roles of buyers, grantors, and the initiators of other types of agreements, the states, being between levels of government, play a larger number of roles. A state may be a federal grantee and a grantor in its own right; it may be a seller to the federal government, but a buyer of supplies and services from industry and others; and it may both initiate collaborative arrangements and respond to initiatives from others. The federal agencies may control through a contract, support via grant, or participate through a cooperative agreement. The states perform these same functions and also find themselves at the receiving ends of each of these relationships.[7] This being the case, administrative federalism should also aid the states, as well as other public and private institutions and organizations, in understanding and managing the networks of relationships in which they find themselves.

When elaborated and used, a system of administrative federalism will provide not only a means but also an inducement to more effective management. There is a need for performance incentives in governmental and other "nonprofit" systems. Units of government are not subject to the incentive of the "bottom line" that assures dollar-effective performance in those industries that are price competitive. A system of alternatives that requires systematic role decisions in federal/non-federal relationships and exposes the structure and results of those decisions to public view may provide new incentives to the effective and efficient operation of public activities.

Administrative federalism has considerable potential for illuminating planning, budgeting and evaluation processes and techniques. These processes and techniques usually stop short of using data at the project or activity level because, except for procurement relationships, there are inadequate conventions for describing and prescribing what happens at these levels. Administrative federalism can provide comparative operating level detail on program management or implementing alternatives that could greatly enhance planning, budgeting, and evaluation processes and techniques.

A system of administrative federalism can facilitate the intelligent devolvement of federal authority. Revenue sharing and block grants are looked upon as means of devolvement. Categorical programs are looked upon as an alternative requiring federal responsibility to assure adequate performance. The difference of opinion among those who prefer one or the other of these approaches may occur because devolvements tend to be made in terms of broad functional or program categories of transactions. Quite possibly decisions on devolvement are being made at too high a level of both program and project aggregation to permit informed judgments on which projects or classes of projects should be devolved. A framework which facilitates devolvement at the project level will complement the use of block grants and general revenue sharing.

Because "operations constitute policy,"[8] and operations are scattered across the federal bureaucracy, initiatives for systematic reform of the federal assistance system must come from the Executive Office of the President or the Congress. The Congress should provide guidance for the executive departments and agencies on the nature and extent of the federal role. The Congress should express alternative federal roles more clearly and consistently in the multitude of program authorizations it enacts. The executive should provide, through the Office of Management and Budget or otherwise, systematic guidance on the implementation of federal programs.

In passing the Federal Grant and Cooperative Agreement Act of 1977 the 95th Congress has established a framework that will (1) permit systematic role decisions in federal/non-federal relationships; (2) accommodate both the shifting of maximum responsibility to recipients of federal awards and the rationalizing of the significant amount of federal intervention that became necessary in the 1960s; and (3) provide federal program managers with realistic project and activity implementing alternatives.

This framework requires definition of the federal "grant" in a way that provides an alternative to considering grants as a form of "administrative contract."[9] The federal intervention and strings that characterize the "contract state" have been proliferating in federal grant programs. That trend can be reversed. Doing so requires recognizing clear differences in kind between the contract and the grant. It also requires recognizing necessary federal involvement in cooperative agreement-type relationships. An institutionally accepted framework which expresses these alternative relationships will focus attention on role decisions. Systematic public consideration of role decisions is necessary to maintain the balance in our federal system.

Notes

1. See Chapter 1 of James L. Sundquist and David W. Davis, *Making Federalism Work* (Washington, D.C.: The Brookings Institution, 1969).
2. *Ibid.*, Sundquist and Davis, p. 278.
3. U.S. Commission on Government Procurement, *Report of the Commission on Government Procurement,* Vol. 3, Part F. "Federal Grant-Type Assistance Programs" (Washington, D.C.: U.S. Government Printing Office, December 1972). The basic Procurement Commission concepts are discussed in Robert D. Newton, "Towards an Understanding of Federal Assistance," *Public Administration Review,* Vol. 35, No. 4 (July/August 1975), pp. 372-377. They also are illustrated in Robert D. Newton, "Contracting Under Grants: The Need to Define the Federal Role," *Public Contract Law Journal,* Vol. 9, No. 1 (June 1977), pp. 35-44.

4. The term "administrative federalism" was first suggested to me by James D. Carroll of Syracuse University.
5. These concepts are contained in PL 95-224, the Federal Grant and Cooperative Agreement Act of 1978, signed into law by President Carter on February 3, 1978. See *Report of the Committee on Government Operations, United States Senate, to Accompany S. 431, to Distinguish Federal Grant and Cooperative Agreement Relationships From Federal Procurement Relationships, and for Other Purposes,* 95th Congress, First Session, Report No. 95-449 (Washington, D.C.: U.S. Government Printing Office, 1977).
6. "Assistance contract" would be an appropriate designation for this relationship.
7. Many states are hampered by inadequate statutory authority to enter into grant-type relationships, forcing the creating of unnecessarily complicated relationships as funds pass from one tier to another. The type of broad authority for the federal executive agencies contained in PL 95-224 would be of significant use to many states.
8. Richard P. Nathan, "The Administrative Presidency," *The Public Interest,* No. 44 (Summer 1976), p. 42.
9. See the discussions of the "administrative contract" and its relations to accountability and control in Bruce L. R. Smith and D. C. Hague, editors, *The Dilemma of Accountability in Modern Government: Independence versus Control* (New York: St. Martin's Press, 1971).

1978 (38:252-255)

EUGENE S. SUNSHINE

Minimizing the Disappointment of Unsuccessful Applicants in Grant Programs

Today's climate of diminishing funds for many federal grant programs generally means fewer program beneficiaries. Less funding also means that a larger number of disappointed applicants is generated. These unsuccessful applicants—such as school districts, recipients of fuel assistance payments, local governments, or public housing authorities—are receiving either no assistance from the grant programs or less than they received in the past. Depending upon the degree of their perceived or real financial need, these individuals or institutions may hold a sense of disappointment ranging from mild distress to outrage. Certainly, no one will be pleased at receiving less than before or nothing at all.

With the dispensing of increased disappointment comes the strong likelihood of political fallout for the federal government—the president, Congress, and federal agencies—since it is obviously politically desirable to increase, rather than decrease, the number of program beneficiaries. But are the potential political liabilities limited to the federal government when federal grant programs are reduced? Not necessarily. Many such grant programs are wholly or partially administered by state and local governments that may well share the dangers of political fallout because of their association with program implementation. Their susceptibility probably grows as block grants replace multitudes of categorical grants, resulting in more state and local discretion in the use of federal funds and a blurring of where the funds originated and what level of government is responsible for their diminution.

The Dangers

For a state agency, the potential political fallout from being a part of dispensing large amounts of disappointment is insidious. The disappointment spurs the unsuccessful applicants to voice their discontent to state legislators, the governor's office, and interest groups representing their causes. It could also result in law suits costing time and money and inflicting political damage even if the agency wins in the court. Those who hear the complaints could well develop negative impressions of the involved state agency that would pervade their overall attitude toward and opinion of the agency. (Obviously, generating dissatisfied constituents is not a way for an agency to endear itself to officeholders or interest groups.) Reasonableness plays little part in this sequence of events; perception and the fact that the agency is the closest and most visible reason for the disappointment often count the most and overshadow the fact that the root of the problem is the diminished federal funds.

Any negative feelings—regardless of their cause or legitimacy—held by officeholders for an agency may damage, and certainly will not help, an agency's budget in the state's appropriation process, as well as its legislative initiatives and relative standing in intra-executive department tiffs between agencies. The extent of the damage will vary, but it may manifest itself in serious ways and affect agency activities that have absolutely nothing to do with the federal grant program the agency is also administering.

Because of the potential political fallout from administering a diminished federal grant program, it is very advantageous for a state agency to acknowledge the dangers as early as possible, and then formulate and undertake mitigating actions. Presented below, in the context of a federal grant program administered by the New York State Energy Office, are examples of mitigating actions that can be taken by an agency. Discussing these actions as they relate to a particular program affords an opportunity to illustrate and describe them clearly and fully. While the actions are not inclusive and applicable to all grants, they are very relevant to federal programs administered at the state or local level for which a competition of funds occurs among a large audience.

Program Description

The New York State Energy Office administers a statewide federal energy conservation grant program for public and non-profit schools, colleges and universities, hospitals, certain types of public care institutions, and buildings owned by local governments (hereinafter referred to as the "Institutional Energy Conservation Grant Program"). Matching federal grants are made available to these institutions from the U.S. Department of Energy (DOE) pursuant to Title III of the National Energy Conservation Policy Act of 1978. The matching grants are available for detailed energy conservation studies of buildings and, in some instances, for the design and undertaking of energy conserving capital improvements in buildings.

Under elaborate federal regulations governing program administration, DOE essentially has responsibility for formally determining which institutions receive grants, issuing grant award notices, and making payments to grant recipients. The New York State Energy Office, like other state energy offices involved in implementing this program, has responsibility for: disseminating program information; assisting grant applicants in completing application forms; reviewing and ranking grant applications against evaluation criteria; making specific (building-by-building) grant award recommendations to DOE; and, monitoring the use of the grants subsequent to their award by DOE. (In the program's history, DOE has made very few changes from the New York State Energy Office's recommendations in awarding the grants and this fact is known by grant applicants.)

The program operates annually, i.e., the state and DOE receive grant applications and award grants according to a specified schedule once a year. Each year's activities constitute a different grant cycle, and through 1982 four grant cycles have been conducted. In each of the grant cycles, federal grant funds requested exceeded funds available by an average ratio of almost four to one. In total, $137 million has been requested in grant applications, and only $37.5 million has been available and ultimately awarded over the four grant cycles.

It is evident from the numbers that "dispensing disappointment" has historically been a major factor in this grant program. This "disappointment" factor was especially prevalent in the 1982, or fourth grant cycle, when available federal funds were about a third of the average awarded in each of the program's first three years while demand remained substantial.

Suggested Actions

1. *Form and Use Advisory Committees.* The establishment of advisory committees by a government agency to guide the administration of a program is too often merely window dressing to satisfy public participation requirements. Sometimes they are even intended by the agency and perceived by their members as such. Advisory committees, however, can make valuable contributions and provide important third party credibility to an agency's administration of a grant program.

For the Institutional Energy Conservation Grant Program, several advisory committees were formed representing the major building sectors eligible for the grant program. For example, one such committee represented public schools and consisted of individuals from the State School Boards Association, State School Business Officials Association, State Department of Education, and the New York City Board of Education. Another committee represented hospitals and consisted of representatives from such organizations as the Hospital Association of New York State,

Blue Cross and Blue Shield, the State Chapter of the American Society for Hospital Engineering and the State Department of Health.

Securing and being responsive to as much program planning advice from advisory committees as practicable is, of course, always recommended because it may enhance program administration. But following such a policy can also be advantageous because it leads to advisory committee members being well informed about the program. They will learn about the program's funding constraints, the agency's methods of program outreach, and details of application ranking.

If the committee members are convinced that the grant program is fairly and otherwise properly administered, this judgment will be communicated to the institutions they represent and, most importantly, will partially blunt the disappointment of grant applicants who receive no funds. Their expressed sentiments will help immeasurably to communicate the message that the program was run equitably and that the underlying cause for many institutions failing to receive grant funds was not the fault of the state, but the insufficient amount of federal assistance. Considering that the interest groups, such as those represented on advisory committees, are among the first line recipients of complaints from disappointed grant applicants, it is extremely important that they be believers in the state's administration of the program and understand the limitations of the state's authority.

2. *Spread the "Program Work" Widely.* Certain to fuel the flames of a disappointed grant applicant is the memory of having to struggle to learn about the program in the first place and having difficulty in getting quick and thorough answers to questions when the applicant was completing the application forms. In the Institutional Energy Conservation Grant Program, numerous vehicles are used to ensure that all eligible institutions (prospective grant applicants) know about the program and its requirements and can easily receive help in applying for the funds. Regarding the dissemination of program information, emphasis is placed on reaching each eligible institution through multiple means. For example, in the case of public schools, word is spread through a direct mailing by the agency to the chief executive officers of school districts and also through announcements contained in the publications of the State Education Department and the school boards and business officials associations. The operating theory is that at least one channel will be successful in communicating the information to the right personnel.

Methods used to help institutions in the application process include conducting regional briefing sessions on completing the application forms and related issues, and making staff available to aid institutional representatives on a one-to-one basis over the telephone and in person.

The negative side of operating a thorough program outreach operation is that it will produce more grant applications than a less extensive effort would have generated and will ultimately add to the number of unsuccessful grant applicants. This result is an unavoidable consequence. The general program and agency credibility rests on ensuring that equal opportunity to secure grants is maintained for all eligible institutions; achieving equity necessitates all eligible institutions knowing about the program. Furthermore, in all of its communications with eligible institutions, the agency can advise and then remind the institutions about the limited federal funds and the severity of the competition for them, which helps set the stage should they ultimately become unsuccessful grant applicants.

3. *Establish, Publicize and Adhere to Objective Ranking Criteria.* Probably nothing will enrage and disappoint grant applicant more, and guarantee adverse results for an agency faster, than a prevailing belief that the grants were awarded on a less-than-objective basis. If such a belief exists, agency success in offsetting potential political fallout will be dealt a severe blow simply because it will make accepting disappointment very difficult for grant applicants. (It is one thing to lose in a fair game; it is another thing to lose in a game where others are benefiting from special treatment.)

In the Institutional Energy Conservation Grant Program, specific grant application ranking criteria were established and publicized early in the program and are adhered to in actual practice. To the maximum extent possible, the criteria were designed to minimize subjectively in their use so that how the applications ranked against each criterion was generally straightforward and not open to much discretion. Examples of the criteria are: the average payback of the proposed energy conservation measures (i.e., the time it takes for the measures to pay for themselves in energy savings); the type of energy to be saved by the proposed measures (oil has top priority); and, the extent to which an institution applying for funds has already reduced its energy consumption. Use of a numerical scoring for each criterion reinforces the ranking system's objectivity and provides a relatively easy means for an applicant to compare its application to others.

4. *Provide "Good News" to State Legislators.* In each grant cycle of the Institutional Energy Conservation Grant Program, at about the same time grant award recommendations were made by the New York State Energy Office to DOE and before grant applicants were informed by the agency of the status of their applications, letters are sent to every state legislator by the agency informing them of the institutions recommended for grants in their districts. The purpose of the letter is to enable the legislator to share the "good news" with the successful institutions in his/her district. The letter also enables the agency to reiterate grant application ranking procedures,

and describe how federal funding limitations prevented the agency from being able to recommend grants for more applicants.

Having received the "good news" and been reminded about the most relevant program and funding information, the legislators are more likely to view the disappointment of unsuccessful grant applicants from their districts in light of the limitations imposed on the administering state agency. Successfully communicating this kind of complete program message to state legislators is critical to minimizing the political fallout from dispensing large amounts of disappointment because legislators, of course, must and will regard the complaints of their constituents quite seriously. The more the legislators know and understand about the program, the more probable it is that the complaints they hear from the unsuccessful applicants will be viewed in their proper context.

5. *Pay Particular Attention to Unsuccessful Grant Applicants.* Unsuccessful grant applicants will never be fully satisfied with any explanation as to why they did not receive grants; their disappointment prevents this from happening. Nevertheless, special efforts should be made by the administering agency to explain to these applicants why they were unsuccessful and to be fully responsive to their post-notification inquiries. Such efforts will constitute a statement to the unsuccessful applicants that the agency cares about their disappointment and understands its importance. They also support the applicants' understanding that the grant determinations were made equitably and objectively because the agency is demonstrating a real willingness to share the details of the application ranking results with unsuccessful applicants. Any agency actions perceived to be a runaround will have the exact opposite effect.

In the Institutional Energy Conservation Grant Program, the New York State Energy Office takes a few basic steps along these lines. At the same time successful applicants are informed that they have been recommended for grants to DOE, each unsuccessful applicant is sent a personal letter from a senior agency official. The letter explains the reasons for the agency's inability to recommend grant funds for the applicant, emphasizing the volume of applications versus the availability of very limited federal funds. The letter also cites the numerical ranking of the particular application and the ranking of the last application that was recommended for funding. This information enables the unsuccessful applicant to understand how close the application came to being recommended for grant assistance.

Upon receiving these letters, the unsuccessful applicants sometime desire additional information on the reasons for their grant determinations. These requests, oftentimes resulting in meetings with the heads of the applicant institutions (e.g., president of a university) and their elected state legislators, need to be responded to quickly and thoroughly. At these meetings, the agency often provides a detailed breakdown of how the application specifically scored against each of the ranking criterion. The same information is mailed upon telephone inquiries from applicants. In providing this information, the agency also explains how the application could be improved or strengthened if the institution intends to submit it again in future grant cycles. This is accomplished by discussing specific alternative ways that the application's score could be increased for some or all of the criteria. For example, in some instances, deleting a particular conservation measure from an application may shorten the average payback for the remaining measures being proposed, thereby enhancing the strength of the application, since the average payback of the conservation measures proposed is the paramount ranking criterion. In another situation, it may be possible to delete a proposed measure that would save natural gas, leaving only oil-saving measures that would enable the application to rank better.

6. *Encourage Organizations Representing Program Eligible Institutions to Lobby for Federal Appropriations.* Many state agencies spend considerable effort lobbying Congress for appropriations for their programs. Sometimes this is accomplished directly by agencies, and/or through a state's Washington office and the National Governors' Association. The more aggressive state agencies closely track the life of a program appropriation from the introduction of the president's budget to enactment of the appropriation by both houses of Congress. At key points along the way, the agency may send letters and telegrams or make phone calls to appropriate individuals or present testimony before congressional committees, all to obtain or increase the size of an appropriation.

In this effort, the New York State Energy Office has actively sought the assistance of the various state associations representing institutions eligible for the Institutional Energy Conservation Grant Program. Since virtually all of these associations are on the agency's program advisory committees (discussed above), access to these groups is excellent. Experience indicates that the associations are generally very willing and able to lobby in Congress, oftentimes with or through their national associations.

Their lobbying contributions have been important factors in influencing congressional actions. In addition, an agency's attempt to enlist association help in lobbying demonstrates the agency's own aggressiveness and care for the program as well as its high regard for the associations and their members as effective program advocates.

Reaction of Unsuccessful Applicants and Others

While a specific evaluation has not been conducted to determine whether the actions described above, either collectively or individually, were directly responsible for minimizing disappointment and political fallout, there is evidence suggesting that the goal is being accomplished and that the actions are contributing factors. The evidence is as follows:

- Most unsuccessful grant applicants reapplied for funding in subsequent grant cycles. This can be interpreted as an indication that these applicants maintained their regard for the program and its administration since they were willing to spend the time and money to try again. Many such applicants ultimately were successful in securing grants because they needed the advice provided by the agency and strengthened their applications.
- Many unsuccessful applicants, state legislators, and other interested parties availed themselves of the opportunity to find out why particular applications were not recommended for funding, however, the agency is not aware of any individual who concluded this process feeling that the ranking system was rigged or that the program was otherwise poorly administered. This observation suggests that agency efforts to employ objective application ranking criteria and pay particular attention to unsuccessful applicants succeeded in making a contribution to minimizing disappointment.
- Over the entire course of the program, state appropriations to enable the agency to administer the grant program have always been enacted at the desired levels. This indicates that legislators generally are supporters of the program and do not hold bad feelings about the agency's administration of it.

  In addition, there has never been an indication that the grant program has adversely affected the perception held by outsiders of any agency program. To the contrary, several state legislative initiatives have been introduced in the past several years proposing energy conservation programs and assistance for the types of institutions covered by the grant program and other building sectors as well. Many of these initiatives, offered by the governor and legislators, envisioned a prominent role for the agency in program administration based, at least in part, on the agency's reputation established in operating the grant program.
- Many of the associations representing eligible institutions provided very positive formal testimony about the agency's management of the grant program before the State Energy Office Review Commission, an independent body established pursuant to the State Energy Law to conduct a "sunset audit" of the agency. Examples of such associations are the State Commission on Independent Colleges and Universities and the State School Boards Association. The Commission's report, issued in November 1981, specifically praised the agency for the national recognition its operation of the grant program had attained. The

Commission's report also complimented the agency for undertaking one of the actions described above when it cited the agency's aggressive outreach effort in informing all eligible institutions about the grant program to ensure a wide distribution of grant funds.

Conclusion

Diminishing funds for many federal grant programs could cause political fallout for state and local agencies involved in administering the programs and associated with dispensing larger amounts of disappointment to unsuccessful grant applicants. For a state agency, the dangers of political fallout are insidious and can adversely affect an agency's budget in the state's appropriation process, as well as its legislative initiatives and other matters of agency concern. A state agency should acknowledge the dangers as early as possible and undertake mitigating actions which include: forming and using advisory committees; spreading the "program word" widely; establishing, publicizing, and adhering to objective ranking criteria; providing "good news" to state legislators; paying particular attention to unsuccessful grant applicants; and, encouraging organizations representing program eligible institutions to lobby for federal appropriations.

These actions all require concerted efforts to be successful although most do not require substantially more than "good government" practices. The potential negative consequences of not undertaking the actions are too severe to leave to happenstance.

1982 (42:479-483)

PART V

The Management of Intergovernmental Implementation: Coordination and Cooperation, Complexity and Conflict

The 1970s represented a shift in attention to the management of intergovernmental relations. This shift accompanied but was not synonymous with the beginning of the "third new federalism." Concern for intergovernmental management and the third new federalism were, in part, responses to the "topsy-turvy" growth of grants and other assistance programs. First, the demands of implementing rapidly expanding grant-in-aid programs from the second new federalism placed severe strains on the management capacity of all levels of government. Second, limited management capacity aggravated what William Carey called the "gap between policy design, program definition and effective delivery." These factors, in turn, generated substantial apprehension among officials about the ability of governments to manage the implementation of intergovernmental policy.

Intergovernmental *management* provides a conceptual framework for addressing concerns relative to the implementation of intergovernmental programs. This framework emphasizes an action-based, problem-solving orientation to interjurisdictional exchanges, combined with guidance on how to cope with and direct networks that include numerous intergovernmental actors and entities. In short, intergovernmental management involves the development of tools for guiding the actions of policymakers on how to cope constructively with the problems they face. The articles selected on this topic convey the apprehension that has surrounded the implementation of intergovernmental programs. However, they also reveal the emphasis placed on coordination and cooperation amid an environment that is often permeated with complexity and conflict.

The article by William Carey, at the U.S. Bureau of the Budget in 1967, provides a starting point for this section. Noting that the "public business is in a stage of exceptional fluidity . . ." he argues for more innovation and experimentation in public administration. He also calls for a balance between the philosophical and clinical approaches to governmental problem solving. Above all, Carey insists that public administration has a responsibility to help "society order its purposes and its resources in relation to meanings. . . ." He sees creative federalism (the second new federalism) as a positive step in this direction because it is the "beginning of a theoretical formulation of intergovernmental and public-private partnership in approaching actions."

Professor Lawrence C. Howard of the University of Pittsburgh discusses the need for top-level managers trained in intergovernmental management. He suggests that the missing ingredient of intergovernmental policy initiatives was the absence of an administrative cadre trained in intergovernmental management. Professor Howard envisions the necessary intergovernmental training of managers occurring through the joint effort of government and schools of public affairs. He also proposes a national policy for intergovernmental executive development.

The third selection is the executive summary of the Study Committee on Policy Management Assistance. It addresses questions of how the national government can assist in improving state and local government management. Three elements of management are delineated: policy management; resource management; and program management. These categories provide a basis for priority-setting in offering management assistance to states and local governments.

The fourth article in this section is by Professor Catherine H. Lovell of the University of California (Riverside). Professor Lovell approaches the coordination of federal grants from a community-level, bottom-up perspective. She identifies three general methods of program coordination: (1) orchestration from above, (2) self linking among functional professionals, and (3) the meshing of the grants from below. Data are presented to exemplify the use of these methods in eight communities and the impact of block grants on each method is described.

The article by Thomas J. Mikulecky, City Manager of Bartlesville (Oklahoma), is an overview of his strategy for intergovernmental relations. Inclusive in this strategy are ways local managers can improve their grantsmanship. Crucial for the design and implementation of his intergovernmental strategy is said to be an ability to comprehend technical material, creativity in program development, an appreciation of what motivates others, and goal orientation. Implicit in each of these is the presence of the diplomacy necessary to "cultivate the faith and friendship of counterparts at other levels of government."

The sixth article is by Donald F. Kettl of the University of Virginia. It examines aspects of the relatively "new approach" to program implementation—contracting out. Using the city of Richmond, Virginia as an example, Professor Kettl describes the impact of this new approach on local administration. The most obvious impact was an increase in administrative cost. Another was the new status and role for non-city agencies. This "fourth face of federalism'' is highly significant for the intergovernmental system because it encourages neighborhood, non-profit, and other non-city organizations and individuals to become active in the intergovernmental arena.

The concluding article in this section was co-authored by Richard C. Kearney (University of South Carolina) and Robert G. Garey (Oak Ridge Associated Universities). Kearney and Garey examine the important role and partial resurgence of the states as political actors in national-state relations in the regulation of radioactive wastes. Major points of conflict in the system are discussed and a principal conflict is the question of the ''states' right to determine for themselves whether they will participate in any future federal waste program.'' The authors note a strong potential for the development of a ''contentious federalism'' in waste management and similar policy areas.

Articles in this section typify crucial issues in the management of intergovernmental implementation. Among the most prominent are issues of coordination and cooperation as well as complexity and conflict. A related and pervasive theme present in the section is an applied, problem-solving, action bias. The content of the articles exemplify management as the process of getting things done in an intergovernmental context.

WILLIAM D. CAREY

Intergovernmental Relations: Guides to Development

Despite the pretentiousness of this topic, I do not plan to pontificate about the new federalism. Like most people, I see the future with fewer certainties than I had when the grass was green and the grain was yellow. My view is that the public business today is in a stage of exceptional fluidity, and because of this the public manager's first responsibility is to have an open mind, and his second is to want passionately to understand the meanings—not the forms—of his changing world. Even the term "public administration" itself is a handicap to the extent that it conjures up a catechism of rights and wrongs that instruct us on how to do our work.

The hard and terrible truth is that we age and cling to axioms and Bible texts while the ground under us shakes and trembles. Politics and government—like humanity—have their own cycles and each generation must develop its own wisdom. The difficulty is that it is so much easier to retain than it is to forget, and I sometimes think that the memory system of public administration is so strong that it will be the death of innovation and experimentation. If so, the times will pass it by and we may find that public administrators are relegated, in John Gardner's phrase, to being mere tenders of the public machinery, while the decision-makers are a baffling breed with whom we can no longer communicate. All of which heresy is by way of suggesting that it is time for public administration to hold a Vatican II of its own.

We can approach the problems of government today both philosophically and clinically. What we must be careful about is to see to it that the clinical approach does not drive out the philosophical, because nothing transcends the need to ponder the uses of responsibility. I dwell on this because I have been in Europe meeting with representatives of 14 nations. Even as they respect our capacity to excel in economics and technology, they wonder if we really have any awareness of our power and responsibility. They see our economy advancing at an incredible rate that is taking us in just a few more years to a trillion dollar annual level. And looking at us, they wonder if we have the compassion and restraint to administer all this for good.

We are not very well organized to answer such questions. Nor am I prepared to leave them entirely to government. I think they must engage the centers of thought, rather than the engines of action. The really great questions are philosophical—as they have always been when great changes have attacked and overrun order and social structures. Public administration has a responsibility, in my view, to help a society to order its purposes and its resources in relation to *meanings,* and not merely to needs, opportunities, and institutional forms.

Dimensions of Government

Government today certainly is motivated to address the problems of society more than at any time in the past. We have no shortage of objectives or enthusiasm. But there is a gap between policy design, program definition, and effective delivery that accuses all of us. It would be tragic if great ideas should fail—should be picked to pieces by criticism—for want of imagination in getting them to work. "Creative federalism" is not just a catchy slogan. It is the beginning of a theoretical formulation of intergovernmental and public-private partnership in approaching actions.

Administration

First, there is the *administrative* dimension. It relates to how we effectively manage complex undertakings which are increasingly multiagency, multiprogram, and multijurisdictional. To take an illustration, the President has directed that pilot tests be made, in 14 urban ghettos, of comprehensive multipurpose neighborhood centers, with the objective of concerting scattered service programs for greater combined impact on people who are in trouble. At least four major departments and agencies of the federal government will usually be involved, with from 10 to 20 grant-in-aid components to be synchronized and state and local agencies and community action groups to be tied in.

This is a formidable undertaking. It begins with defining the concept of a multipurpose neighborhood center, and this is not easy. Then comes the question of how to identify the needs and desires of the neighborhood you are trying to help, and who in the community speaks for the neighborhood. In short order you find yourself up against the problem of sorting out what we choose to call "power structures" and probing the sensitive nerve of city and county politics. Meanwhile, back home there is the job of converting a couple of dozen bureau chiefs to believe in the generic idea of a multipurpose center, to agree on setting aside program funds, and to send the right signals to lower-echelon functionaries. While this is going on, delegates from the four departments are engaged in marathon negotiations to agree on guidelines and ground rules and to settle such momentous questions as whether the mayor or the federal team calls the turn, whether the community action agency is to run the center or simply "participate" (whatever that means), and whether the bricks and mortar or the services come first.

I have said enough, although I could say a great deal more, to suggest that the grandeur of the undertaking quickly breaks down in practice to the bumps and grinds that are the not-so-exotic realities of administration. It is futile to look for short cuts or straight-line solutions, because "people problems" are not the straight-line variety. More and more, administration means starting from scratch to assemble systems of services engineered to explore and test feasibility and effectiveness. It is *improvisation*—a term that is not found in many treatises on public administration; it is applied research, if the phrase makes you less nervous. It comes to the same thing. Harvey Sherman came close to it in his new book about concepts of organization, which he titled *It All Depends.*

What I think we must do is recognize that network administration has arrived as a way of doing government's business, and that it will affect and alter all the doctrines we have been brought up to believe in. The administrative dimension of creative federalism is frankly empirical, high-risk administration applied to institutional arrangements that are rather rigid and not likely to become flexible.

Information

Next, there is the *information dimension.* It is not too much to say that a fully developed society bent on rationalizing its social investments needs an efficient information system in order both to select its goals and to formulate workable strategies to accomplish them. We are prolific in collecting data but inadequate in transforming it into information. We are ingenious in devising creative models and "demonstration projects" but pathetically inept in evaluating them and in transferring the learning dividend into an incremental gain in program terms. We are generous in funding prodigious expenditures to rectify social disaster areas but mindless when we are faced with reasonable questions as to what we have to show for it in terms of altering root conditions. The problem is one of imbalance between the shares of effort and money going into gathering data versus producing meaningful information which can then be assembled into some mechanism of social reporting. Fortunately, thoughtful scholars are beginning to hammer on these points.

Analysis

The third dimension is the *analytical* one. This is the job of defining the problem that exists and formulating alternative approaches in order to select the one most likely to produce the most for the least cost. Now this is not simply sophistication for its own sake. It comes as close as we can get, in the public sector, to analyzing problems of choice with the tools used in the private sector. It is an effort to be rational and systematic in designing public—or if you will, social—investment so as to optimize the returns, not in financial yields but in terms of social gains.

When the federal budget was only $3 billion a year, perhaps it did not matter too much how wisely we designed our public investment. But when the federal budget on a cash transactions basis is in the range of $175 billion, it matters very much what we do, why we do it, and how we do it. We cannot afford mistakes on this scale, particularly since we pay twice for what we do—for the investment itself and for the foregone opportunities that we passed up in order to make it.

Moreover, systematic analysis of problems of choice is our best defense against incremental budgeting—the process by which new commitments are invariably piled on top of a base which is taken for granted. If we know that our taxing system as it now operates will produce an additional $35 billion in new revenues over the next five years, assuming reasonable economic growth, it seems possible to weigh in advance the choices among tax reduction as a stimulant, on the one hand, and a whole spectrum of innovative social investments, on the other. In any event, the state of the art has brought us to the point where we now recognize that government *can* analyze problems of choice, and shape strategies for social investment, and it is my belief that this discovery will have deep effects upon managerial processes in the 1970s. I do not claim that the economics of choice will supplant the politics of choice, but the one will certainly illuminate the other, even though for as long as I care to look ahead public decision-making will remain a misty mixture of compassion and calculation.

Delivery

The fourth dimension is that of *delivery.* For example, we spend tens of billions of dollars in this country on medical research and medical care, and it is probable that the mind of man has never witnessed a more inefficient delivery system. The doctors are massed in the cities but not in the ghettos. The handful of medical schools are unable to generate adequate numbers of physicians. Once a doctor is licensed he is in business forever, regardless of whether his knowledge is obsolete in ten years. The medical care system is structured on the basis of every-man-for-himself, instead of organized so that skills are assembled in a sufficient critical mass to cope adequately, and at acceptable costs, with demand.

On another front, our social services are also fragmented so that welfare is colored blue, mental health green, family counselling orange, job placement red, and so on down the long, weary list. Again, we are right up against the problem of how to arrange government services so that they reach out to those who need them most, and deal with their needs effectively rather than with a glancing blow or at best a partial solution.

Geography

Next, there is the *geographic dimension,* and here I am speaking of the area or spatial aspect of planning and operations. We see evidence of the problem when we observe the maze of planning enterprises afoot all around us, functional planning in 57 varieties, propped up here and there with valiant attempts at comprehensive planning on a county, multicounty, statewide, or regional basis. We are using up our scant supply of qualified planners faster than they can be turned out. We are pyramiding planning upon planning. We are trying to plan without adequate data bases.

On the operating side, every federal agency has its own dogmatic convictions as to what administrative areas should look like. We have 12-region systems, 10-region systems, 7-region systems; we have area systems and no regions; we have district systems. Within these various area structures, field offices are located without rationality and for reasons that seemed good 20 years ago. We simply do not understand the geographic dimension of creative federalism, and we have no criteria to go by. Yet, the geographic dimension is unavoidably linked to two of the other dimensions that I have discussed: the administrative and the delivery dimensions.

Innovation

Lastly, there is the *innovative* dimension. This is the terrain of lively ideas and trial approaches. We see it in the proposal for revenue sharing, for block grants, for pre-financing of joint federal-state undertakings. It takes another form in the President's directive that heads of agencies must consult on program and administration with elected heads of state, county, and city governments. It emerges in the formation of multijurisdictional consortiums like the councils of government and the multicounty community action agencies. We find it in the stimulus toward neighborhood corporations based on self-determination around a legal personality in the urban ghetto. We see it in the Model Cities approach to the re-creation of viable urban complexes, and in the action of three federal departments in jointly funding the University of Minnesota to study the problems and technology of creating and operating a completely new self-sufficient city. We see innovation in the new regional education laboratories, in the heart-cancer-stroke centers, in the Public Television Act, in the drive for intergovernmental personnel mobility, and in the Chapel Hill Institute on State Programming for the 70s.

What it all adds up to is a disturbing question as to whether public administration as we understand it, research it, teach it, and practice it even begins to match the propensity of political action to recognize and respond to crisis conditions. Politics may turn the wheels, but administration must furnish the traction.

1968 (28:22-25)

LAWRENCE C. HOWARD

Executive Development: An Intergovernmental Perspective

> The paradox of both distrusting and burdening government reveals the lack of a conscious philosophy of politics. It betrays some unresolved inner conflict about the interaction of government and society. We have not adjusted our thinking about government to the overwhelming facts of modern life, and so carry over old mental habits, traditional school book platitudes and campaign slogans as to the role, the purpose and the methods of government (20, p. 2).
>
> John Gaus, *Reflections of Public Administration*

This 1945 quote from John Gaus provides a framework for the suggestion that executive manpower be developed—at least in part—in an intergovernmental framework. Aside from bringing significant numbers of federal, state, and local top managers together, it is urged that the training be done in large urban centers as a way to help program implementation. We must demonstrate that the government is a *single* interactive system and not a series of layers. Public and private training resources, particularly the comprehensive graduate public affairs schools, should be fully used as a way of clarifying the urban public-private meshing of national domestic programs.

Much attention is now being given to the training and development of executive manpower by several elements in the public administration community. Of special interest are studies completed and underway in the National Academy of Public Administration, and the proposals being drafted and considered within the U.S. Civil Service Commission (73). The comments and questions raised in this paper offer the argument that these studies and proposals be extended to an executive manpower development approach that is deliberately intergovernmental in form and scope.

John Gaus, who was quoting from a 1930 lecture by Felix Frankfurter, sets the intergovernmental framework. His approach emphasizes the art of politics and is shared by many others, in particular, Campbell (11), Cleveland (16), McLean (41), Sherwood (57), Stone (63), and Sundquist (65).

Perhaps the most fervent advocate of an intergovernmental perspective beyond the work of Rand (19), the George Washington University group (46), ACIR (1), and CED (12) is President Richard M. Nixon. In Philadelphia on the occasion of signing the State and Local Fiscal Assistance Act of 1972, the legislation known as General Revenue Sharing, he said (49):

> They came here in the 18th century to establish the Federal system. We return here in the 20th century to renew the Federal system.
>
> They came here to create a balance between the various levels of government. We come here to restore that balance.

The Need for Executives with an Intergovernmental Perspective: The Distrust and Burdening of Government

The federal system is in crisis!

Many scholars have addressed this problem. Sundquist (65, p. 3), for example, cites the mounting citizen needs which have called forth *national purpose* programs reflecting the coalescence of a national society. National programs have brought with them complex mechanisms for both citizen and professional accountability. The crisis is a product of the federal government's inability to get the required action of legally independent and often reluctant state and local units. Coordinate action is not occurring.

State and local incapacities are also well documented. Ford Foundation support, for example, has gone to speed reapportionment, strengthen legislatures, help in constitutional reform, support chief executives, aid county reform, underwrite regional councils, and especially work on the fiscal aspects of federalism (19). All this underlines that the Washington initiatives have encountered incapacities in the states.

A general theme permeating the crisis is public distrust of the very government they burden. Again, hardly any one has presented the problem as clearly as the President: "Most Americans today are simply fed up with government at all levels" (6).

Since these burdens on government will only increase, one approach to regaining public confidence is through providing services that people perceive as responsive to their needs. John Gaus, looking back to 1789 or ahead to the '70s, comments, "The point I would urge, is that no problem which affects our local communities or national strength can be resolved, or seriously attacked, in this country unless the resources of every level of government operating in a given area are mobilized to supplement (not supplant) each other" (20, p. 80).

Questions:

1. Must a response to the nation's ills be as intergovernmental as these commentators suggest?
2. Could the federal government be reorganized to support intergovernmental interdependence?
3. Is public distrust of government new, or is this a continuing bucolic now somewhat magnified by contemporary problems?

A probing of these questions suggests the need for more executives, from all levels, with intergovernmental perspectives. Quoting Sundquist again,

> In the final analysis, the managerial question is very much an intergovernmental issue. State and local officials do not manage in the splendid isolation of their own geographical bailiwicks. Federal administrators cannot function without State and local officials, and these administrators in turn must operate with a continuing awareness of the prerogatives of other levels of government. The effective State or local manager is one who learns to work effectively within the intergovernmental structure, and Federal agencies will contribute to his effectiveness by encouraging and supporting his efforts to do so (65, p. 271).

Unresolved Inner Conflicts

The manner in which public managers and executives are trained—or not trained—has come under increasing criticism. Training at all levels of government is said to be unsatisfactory.

Perhaps the most comprehensive critique of federal executive development comes from those who know the supergrades best, and from the incumbents themselves. It is from a substantial knowledge base that Sherwood at the Federal Executive Institute (57), Berlin from the Executive Inventory (7), Beck from the Bureau of Training (38), Jones consulting in OMB (70), and agency heads now required to complete training guidelines —reiterate the inadequacies (30).

Again, the President's voice is the clearest (48):

> . . . the Government's executive manpower systems have shown increasingly evidence of weakness. The present arrangements have grown up over the years without any comprehensive plan. The resulting complexities and rigidities have reached a point at which it is now futile to try to patch the present structure further . . . reforms are essential.

Criticism of the inadequacies of executive development are at least as great at the state and local levels. Examples can be found in the writings of

Bailey (4), Campbell (10), Keane (34), and Sanford (55), and in CED Policy Statements (12). Managerial incapacities loom large as scholars have attempted to unravel the intergovernmental fiscal snarl described by Mushkin (46), ACIR (1), and Brookings (8) studies. There is an almost unbroken lament since the 1962 Municipal Manpower Commission (45): the management crisis of state and local government is acute. Bahl *et al.* (3), in a recent issue of *PAR,* point to fresh problems, almost uncontrolled increases in pensions and fringe benefits which reflect the poor performance by public executives in collective bargaining. The emerging demands for increasing productivity will surely make the tasks of state and local executives still more difficult.

Some remedies for these problems are well known. On one point most commentators agree, there is too little training for too few emerging managers and almost no continuing education for executives at any levels of government. Moreover, the turbulence of social and technological environments makes training on a continuing basis a necessary part of program implementation. A body of knowledge and skills to nurture executive leadership are available, but the fact is they are little used.

Opposition to systematic training at the federal level is silent but effective with minor exceptions in select agencies like IRS, State, and the military.

Questions:

1. Why does executive development have such a low priority?
2. If there is an anti-training policy, where is it articulated?

Partial answers to these questions may be found in Gaus' "unresolved inner conflicts." These interagency conflicts about executive development come out in criticisms by observers largely outside government. Business groups, like CED, have specifically addressed the need for White House leadership for executive development at the federal level (27). The need for an orderly approach to career development has been sought by professional associations like ASPA (2), and urged by close observers of the public scene like Leach (35), Macy (37), Millett (42), Mosher (44), and Vaughn (66), to mention only a few recent statements.

Unresolved inner conflict in government appears to be a major reason executive development has received so little support. One could cite several examples: internal conflicts in OMB; conflicts between the EEOC and line agencies, between Washington and the field, between HEW and HUD, or between state capitols and large urban centers. Inevitably, some of the criticism centers on the USCSC. The persistence of the apparent personnel approach to management, the understandable and legally required preoccupation with "merit," which at times appears to be at odds with their responsibility to foster equal employment opportunities at all levels and especially at the executive level, represents a clear problem area (9). Some critics are saying that the administration of IPA by USCSC so far has meant a preoccupation with the personnel function and consequently little understanding of its intergovernmental possibilities. Perhaps most unfortunate is the reluctance to extend the "public executive" mantle to include the social responsibilities increasingly assumed by executives in the private sector. A clear statement of what the USCSC sees ahead in intergovernmental executive development would be particularly helpful.

Questions:

1. Is the federal training priority lost in the conflict within or between agencies?
2. Why is there so little federal support for executive development for state and local government, and almost no programs aimed at understanding problems intergovernmentally?
3. Is the program content of in-house government training efforts unresponsive to the emerging need for public executives with an intergovernmental perspective?
4. Why have training programs put so little stress on the education of the public executive, many of whom are in the private sector?

"Getting it all-together" is one purpose of the current federal effort. It is therefore somewhat surprising that the need for federal/state/local executive interdependence has gone virtually unnoticed. OMB has been at least on notice. "Didn't the White House know," asked Stone (62), "that the provisions of Title IX [of the Higher Education Act] were the other half of the Intergovernmental Personnel Act?" Given the small size of HUD fellowships (100), where is any real federal initiative? Why so little support for research, development, and training to make revenue sharing work? Why has the government at all levels failed to come to grips with the "administrative problems of federalism?" (64).

The Lack of a Conscious Philosophy of Politics

The paradox of citizen demands for service accompanied by increasing conflicts in government brings out the need for a more conscious sense of politics; as McLean has remarked, the need for more "general awareness of the changing role of government and of the environment in which public servants must work" (40).

The political ecology of government is undergong complex changes. One change too little understood is the nationalization of urban concerns. This means, say Stone (63), Sundquist (65), Mushkin (46), Sacks (10), and

Howard (25), that it is on the urban scene that the federal and state programs must be meshed. Urbanization is so pervasive that the federal and state programs increasingly are only offers of money with accompanying statements of constraints. Program development and administration are pushed down to the urban and community level where increasingly citizens demand to participate. In the absence of a conscious philosophy of politics, Moynihan's "Maximum Feasible Misunderstanding" has proliferated. In essence, the New Federalism is a groping toward a national urban and regional policy.

Questions:

1. What limits do urban problems and the demands by citizens to participate put upon budget making as the focal point of national coordination and control?
2. How are public executives made aware of the new urban focused politics?
3. How is the public interest to be related to private objectives and resources in their multinational context?

The politics of administration is brought out in comments by Morris (43), Staats (60), and McKinney (39) who see new patterns of accountability in which the public is doing its own auditing. Consumer interest groups, like Common Cause and Nader's Raiders (66), have surfaced. And the political choices may get harder, for Campbell predicts the issues ahead will not only be adjusting resources to priorities, but equally the task of finding new resources in a situation of shortages (10).

The President repeatedly has articulated his politics of bringing decision making in government closer to the people (17). His reelection suggests that the people generally endorse this desire. It is not clear, however, how that philosophy of politics finds its way into patterns of implementation. One could argue that the missing ingredient in the New Federalism is a cadre of executives trained to put the President's words into effect.

Preparing Intergovernmental Public Executives: From Campaign Slogans to the Methods of Government

Plans for executive development are currently under active discussion in Washington (73). Each starts from the premise that the present approach to executive development needs some modification. This paper is in agreement with these urgings that the government better utilize its senior-level civil servants as a means of putting program into effect. Needed, however, is a much-enlarged training and educational program with an intergovernmental perspective if the policy priority is to make the federal system work.

The move for common training for top federal, state, and local public servants has begun to gain momentum. Some congressional authorizations are in the Federal Personnel Training Act, the Intergovernmental Cooperation Act and the Intergovernmental Personnel Act. Senator Muskie (65) and John D. Rockefeller, III, (53) have offered specific suggestions for strengthening the federal presence in the region, and the FEI National Board has asked for 50 state and local officials annually to have scholarships at Charlottesville. Wynia (70) and Howard (25) have specifically called for intergovernmental training facilities to be established in the regions. The clearest operating example of a cooperative intergovernmental personnel training program, however, is the tiny Intergovernmental Affairs Fellowships (IGAF) program under the sponsorship of the Comptroller General (47).

Questions:

1. In the light of the acknowledged need of the federal government to train nearly 60,000 federal managers and executives, would it be possible to increase that number to 100,000 by mixing in a substantial number of state and local officials (38)?
2. Under what present or future authorizations could further intergovernmental training be undertaken? Could the IGAF format be expanded?

Suggestions as to the content of training designed to make the federal system work can be drawn from the reflections quoted here from John Gaus (20), and from more contemporary statements by public figures like Macy (36, 37), Millet (42), and Webb (58, 69). Four additional areas appear essential in an intergovernmental approach to executive development: (a) executives must come to know their environment of operation well and in output terms, (b) they must be acutely attuned to the new accountabilities which may be more process in nature and less fiscal or program in form (39), (c) the insights available from development administration must be systematically tapped (18), and finally, (d) a multinational perspective must come to have a much more prominent place in executive development.

This education in environmental accountabilities needed by an intergovernmental public executive can draw much from Harlan Cleveland's ideas on the ecology of administration (14, 15, 16):

> . . . leadership is collective, away from the more formal, hierarchical, order giving way of doing business and towards the more informal, fluid workways of bargaining, brokerage, advice, and consent. . . .
>
> [The public executive needs] a sense of responsibility for the situation as a whole.

The Role of Public Affairs Schools in Executive Development

If intergovernmental executive training is conducted in urban centers around problems in program implementation it will provide a great opportunity and challenge to the university. The comprehensive graduate schools of public affairs with departments devoted to urban affairs, public administration, economic and social development, and international affairs should be able to make a substantial contribution (18, 25). These schools are also actively expanding their public service internship requirements. It is clear that better interaction between public executives and the public affairs academicians is mutually beneficial (26).

Questions:

1. What changes in curriculum, perspective, and teaching methods must these schools make to provide the intergovernmental executive with appropriate preparation?
2. What are the available resources to assist in this transformation?
3. How can a government-academic dialogue on public policy questions be sustained?

Shortly after John Gaus finished his *Reflections of Public Administration,* he wrote a chapter in a volume called *The Public Service and University Education* (40, p. 19). In concluding the introduction for the volume, editor Joseph E. McLean wrote:

> There is a critical lack in the federal service of men with those qualities usually associated with the higher grades of the British civil service, men who have breadth of experience, maturity of personality, and a capacity to deal with large matters of state.
>
> There is currently no program to develop such men, nor are there well established posts at the top of the American public service for career men of these qualities. The responsibility for developing such a program rests with the highest level of government . . . we must define a system a) that will be in harmony with American traditions, and b) that will aim at a high level of intellectual and personal capacity. . . .
>
> Much remains to be done by government if it is to meet its share of the responsibility for providing the conditions under which a democratic career service may be developed and under which our democratic system may be preserved. The universities, also, share in this over-all responsibility.

As an approach to a solution, McLean (41, p. 5) originated the marble cake concept of government:

> Most of us think of our federal system as having three layers of government—federal, state and local—with each layer assigned definite functions and responsibilities. And many of us believe that a specific service or function belongs exclusively to one layer of government . . . most of us fail to realize that this layer cake is much more like a marble cake. There are too many combined activities—administrative, financial and political—which blend throughout the cake and ignore the layers . . . almost any public problem you can mention today involves all of the so-called "layers" of government.

As a matter of fact, some of the services and functions necessitated by rapid urbanization and by our intensified use of ocean space involve an international layer as well. Three years ago the Stratten Commission warned us that "the most serious barriers to effective state action are the conflicting and overlapping Federal, State, and local laws and regulations which attempt to control certain coastal zone activities as well as the lack of suitable laws and regulations for other activities of equal importance" (71). The Commission noted a consistent growth pattern in the nation's coastal population since 1850. By 1960 45 percent of the nation's population was living in coastal counties. Increasingly greater demands on ocean uses and resources are the result. As dwellers on the shores of New York Bay, the Baltic Sea, Lake Erie, and the Mediterranean Coast know already, the use of oceans and lakes as waste disposal units makes them unfit for recreation and fishing. Cities are growing up on the shores of underwater oil and gas fields. As the demand for fossil fuel continues to grow, nations fence off increasingly large ocean areas for their own use to protect important sources of food and minerals. Sometimes international conflict results. The nation's stake in its coastal zone and in the world ocean for its health, its food, and its fuel require intergovernmental action at the global level (72).

Surely deliberate executive development in an intergovernmental context is an idea whose time has come.

Toward a National Policy on Intergovernmental Executive Development: Topics for Further Discussion

Some answers to the questions raised in this paper may come through sustained dialogue between public affairs scholars and government practitioners about an intergovernmental policy and strategy for the education and training of public executives. The action program that emerges should result in a strengthening of state and local government.

There is a large role for the federal government. Fundamental is the need to clarify what the role should be in setting national standards, attending to the multinational character of domestic urban ills, and in providing financial and technical support. Implementation will probably have to be done regionally in the context of what Sundquist has described as a "differential approach to Federal-State relations" (65, p. 270). The universities, and particularly graduate programs in public affairs, should play a major role in helping to relate government policy to its larger ecology.

Needed now are guidelines as to the outcomes executive development should serve. Discussion might begin around the following ten points.

Executive development with an intergovernmental perspective should:

1. Provide deliberate support to intergovernmental delivery systems.
2. Tie training to the implementation of affirmative action plans.
3. Promote mobility meaningful for individuals and for the public service.
4. Utilize available knowledge about how increments of manpower relate to regional development.
5. Result in models for career-long education programs with options.
6. Support quasi-public and private education and training resources as a means to supplement public faciities.
7. Establish continuous evaluation of training as a means to improve management in government, particularly at the regional level.
8. Address executive leadership to making public programs more accountable to clients and to the general public.
9. Relate the public service to private endeavors and to the relevant multinational environment.
10. Result in programs capable of reaching at least 100,000 public executives annually.

Cleveland has set forth the more fundamental knowledge and attitudes that the future executive should have. These perspectives on the public interest, he urges, must reflect a deepened understanding of American democratic thought: a sense of welfare, a sense of equity, a sense of achievement, and a sense of participation (14).

References

1. Advisory Committee on Intergovernmental Relations, *Measuring the Fiscal Capacity and Effort of State and Local Areas,* 1971.
2. ASPA Program for Executive Development, *Public Administration Review* (September/October 1971).
3. Bahl, Roy W., *et al.,* "Intergovernmental and Functional Aspects of Trends in Public Employment in the United States," *Public Administration Review* (November/December 1972).

4. Bailey, Frank H., "State Manpower and Training Needs," *Civil Service Journal* (April/June 1970). The poor manpower position of the states is discussed, as is how the grant in aid program tends to create "have" and "have not" pockets in states.
5. Bayton, James A., and Richard L. Chapman, *Transformation of Scientists and Engineers into Managers* (Washington: NASA SP-291, 1972). A detailed look at the problems of preparing bench scientists and engineers for managerial roles which stresses the importance of personal role redefinition.
6. Beckman, Norman, "The Public Literature of Reorganization: The more change. . . ," *The Bureaucrat* (Spring 1972). Despite the President's clear statements, not much change is found.
7. Berlin, Seymour S., "The Federal Executive Service," *Civil Service Journal* (April/June 1971). Addresses the problems in the executive service and the comprehensive manner in which FES would respond to them.
8. The Brookings Institution: George F. Break, *Intergovernmental Fiscal Relations in the U.S.* (1967); Jerome Rothenberg, *Economic Evaluations of Urban Renewal* (1967).
9. For a statement of what IPA is doing see: Robert E. Hampton, "The Intergovernmental Act: Front Line for Strengthening Government Services," *State Government* (Autumn 1972). For the EEO problem, see "Remarks by William H. Brown, III, Chairman, Equal Employment Commission," presented before IRS Executive Development Group, Arlington, Virginia, June 19, 1972. For the demerits of merit, see David H. Rosenbloom, "Equal Employment Opportunity Another Strategy," and Rosaline Levenson, "The Merit Principle in Municipalities—Strengthened or Eroded," *Personnel Administration* (Autumn 1972).
10. Campbell, Alan K., and Seymour Sacks, *Fiscal Patterns and Governmental Systems* (New York: The Free Press, 1967). The concern with tax "effort" reveals the integration of government at the local level.
11. Campbell, Alan K., "Fiscal Outputs: Determinants and Policy Consequences," *Public Administration Review* (November/December 1968). Campbell has placed the fiscal problem in a somewhat larger political context in his "Old and New Public Administration in the 1970s," *Public Administration Review* (July/August 1972).
12. Committee for Economic Development, *Reshaping Government in Metropolitan Areas* (New York: CED, 1970). The project leader for this study was Alan K. Campbell. The policy statement provides guidelines for redesigning the present organization of metropolitan areas on a two-tier basis. Relevant earlier statements are *Modernizing State Government,* July 1967, and *Modernizing Local Government,* July 1966.
13. "Characteristics of the Federal Executive," *Public Administration Review* (March/April 1970). Details taken from the November 1969 Executive Inventory prepared by the Bureau of Executive Manpower of the USCSC.
14. Cleveland, Harlan, *The Future Executive: A Guide for Tomorrow's Managers* (New York: Harper & Row, 1972). The condition, qualities, and purposes of the executive are presented.

15. ______, "The Growing of Public Executives," in *Improving Management for More Effective Government* (Washington, D.C.: GAO, 1971).
16. ______, "The American Public Executive: New Functions," in James C. Charlesworth (ed.), *Theory and Practice of Public Administration: Scope, Objectives and Methods,* The American Academy of Political and Social Science, October 1968. Shows how the business of the public executive has always been to bring people together to make something happen in the public interest.
17. Cohen, Michael, "The Generalist and Organizational Mobility," *Public Administration Review* (September/October 1970). Study of supergrades contrasting those who have worked in one department with those who have worked in two or more. The mobile groups tend to be the generalists.
18. Dunn, W. N., *A Multidisciplinary Introduction to Development Analysis: Readings, Cases and Materials* (Pittsburgh: Graduate School of Public and International Affairs, University of Pittsburgh, 1972), mimeo. Treats of the meaning and analysis of development using political and social materials to supplement economic approaches. A comparative approach is employed throughout.
19. Ford Foundation, *The Near Side of Federalism, Improving State and Local Government,* text by Jeanne R. Lowe (January 1972). The works of Rand and others are reported.
20. Gaus, John, *Reflections of Public Administration* (Birmingham: University of Alabama Press, 1947). Treats the philosophical aspects of public administration.
21. Haas, Frederick C., *Executive Obsolescence,* American Management Association, Inc., Research Study 90, 1968. The problems of obsolescence, its causes, and the ways it can be identified and counteracted are offered.
22. Hampton, Robert E., "Rededicating Ourselves to Merit Principles," *Personnel Administration and Public Personnel Review* (July/August 1972). Defense of the merit system particularly against pressures for quotas.
23. ______, Statement on Nader Reports, *Civil Service Journal* (October 4, 1972).
24. ______, "The Essence of IPA," *Civil Service Journal* (April/June 1971).
25. Howard, Lawrence C., "From Institutionalized Inadequacy to Executive Development: Toward a Broader View of Executive Training," addendum to Annual Report to Chairman, USCSC, prepared by the National Advisory Board of the Federal Executive Institute, October 1972. The emphasis is on the need for training around problem areas in urban community settings.
26. ______, "Participation and the Delivery of Health Care Service," *Public Administration Review,* Special Issue (October 1972).
27. *Improving Executive Management in the Federal Government,* CED, July 1964. Policy statement deals with the need for more effective management of the 8,600 public executives. Recommendations are offered to meet problems of selection, development, compensation, and utilization of key political and career groups.
28. *Improving Management for More Effective Government,* 50th Anniversary Lectures for the United States General Accounting Office, 1921-1971.
29. Ink, Dwight A., "A Management Crisis for the New President: People Pro-

gram," *Public Administration Review* (November/December 1968). The socially oriented federal departments can't administer up to their programs. An eight-point plan is advanced to strengthen management, cut red tape, and streamline our response to the urban crisis.

30. ______, "People in Public Service," *Civil Service Journal* (April/June 1970). Stresses the importance of intergovernmental management for the effective execution of social programs.
31. Jackson, Henry M., "Excellence in the Public Service," in *Achieving Excellence in Public Service,* American Academy (August 1963).
32. Jones, Roger W., "What the FES Package Will Do," *Public Administration Review* (July/August 1971).
33. Katz, Saul M., "A Model for Educating Development Administrators," *Public Administration Review* (November/December 1968). An educational plan based upon needed substantive knowledge, methodologies, and grasp of development administration.
34. Keane, Mark E., "Quality Manpower in the Cities," *Civil Service Journal* (April/June 1970).
35. Leach, Richard H., "Federalism: Continuing Predicament, *Public Administration Review* (March/April 1971). This is a review article on 10 major works in this area.
36. Macy, John W., Jr., "A Perspective—Quest for Quality, *Annals* (August 1963). Macy formerly was with the USCSC.
37. ______, "To Decentralize and to Delegate," *Public Administration Review* (July/August 1970). Reflectiong on leaving the public service.
38. *Managerial and Executive Development Needs in the Federal Service and Recommended Actions for Meeting the Needs,* United States Civil Service Commission (October 1972). Outlines of a training policy and how it can be executed. James Beck is the chairman of the Staffing Committee that prepared the report.
39. McKinney, Jerome, "Some Thoughts on Accountability and Executive Training in the Federal Government," GSPIA Memo 1972. McKinney urges that the central task of the public executive is the "management of accountability" which he calls "process accountability." In essence the higher the GS level, the more the focus is on steering the organization by comparing program outcomes with program intensions. Since many program outcomes are indeterminate, surrogates must be invented to stand for what the outcomes are thought to be. At the same time, McKinney urges the pushing of the audit function down all the way to the client or consumer who is the only person or group really able to judge the value of the outcome. The executive who does well in his/her management of accountability will attend closely to those processes that make the organization responsive. Beyond motivations of efficiency or effectiveness, the executive will seek to make the program the servant of those it serves, because only in this manner can the public effort tap the private sources needed to achieve the outcomes it seeks. The ideas are compatible with those advanced by Robert T. Golembiewski, *Men, Mortality and Management* (New York: McGraw-Hill, 1965).
40. McLean, Joseph E. (ed.), *The Public Service and University Education* (Prince-

ton: Princeton University Press, 1949). Aside from assessing the personnel needs of government and the role of the university in the education of public servants. This value also evolved at education for senior civil servants in periods of emergencies, and in the international arena, and compared British and America's experience.

41. McLean, Joseph E., *Politics Is What You Make It* (New York: Public Affairs Pamphlet, 1952).
42. Millett, John D., "Will Out Governmental System Get Bigger and More Pervasive?" In *Achieving Excellence in Public Service, Annals* (August 1963).
43. Morris, Thomas E., "A Dilemma for Federalism," *The GAO Review* (Summer 1972). The dilemma is general revenue sharing offering state and local government more freedom at the same time that members of Congress and program administrators are demanding greater accountability.
44. Mosher, Frederick C., *Professional Education and the Public Service: An Exploratory Study,* Final Report of OEO Research Project at Berkeley (April 1968). Public professions exert increasing influence on public policy, yet a clear approach to their education has not yet been defined.
45. Municipal Manpower Commission, *Governmental Manpower for Tomorrow's Cities* (New York: McGraw-Hill Book Company, 1962). Assesses the acute shortage of administrative, professional, and technical manpower at the urban level.
46. Mushkin, Selma J., and John R. Cotton, assisted by Gabrielle Lupo, *Functional Federalism: Grant-in-Aid and PPB Systems* (Washington, D.C.: George Washington University, 1968). Comprehensive study of the fiscal interdependence of the national government, the states, and local committees through the instrumentality of grants-in-aid, with some suggestions for reforms.
47. Intergovernmental Affairs Fellowship Program for 1972 and 1973, Director's Report, USCSC, Bureau of Training, mimeo. IGAF is a 10-week work/study mobility assignment system around the problem of grants administration. In 1973 host governments are to be available at every level. To date 55 middle-level federal civil servants have participated.
48. Nixon, Richard M., Message to Congress Proposing the Federal Executive Service, February 2, 1971, *Public Administration Review* (March/April 1971).
49. ——, Statement on the Signing of the State and Local Assistance Act of 1972, Philadelphia, October 20, 1972.
50. On the Federal Executive Service Proposal, George A. Graham, "The FES Package Won't Do"; Roger W. Jones, "What the FES Package Will Do," *Public Administration Review* (July/August 1971).
51. Rehfuss, John A., "Executive Development: Executive Seminar Center Style," *Public Administration Review* (September/October 1970). The operations of these centers is reviewed and generally endorsed.
52. Richter, Anders, "The Existentialist Executive," *Public Administration Review* (July/August 1970). His writing grew out of an eight-week stay at FEI where he found philosophical existentialism relevant to public administration.
53. Rockefeller, John D., III, "Needed: A Fresh Approach for the Public Service," speech given December 1968 at Princeton.
54. Rosenbloom, David H., "Equal Employment Opportunity: Another Strategy,"

Personnel Administration and Public Personnel Review (July/August 1972). Instead of ranking those certified, the author calls for a "pass principle strategy."

55. Sanford, Terry, *Storm Over the States* (New York: McGraw-Hill, 1967). The focus is on strengthening governors.
56. Schultz, George P., "Views on Improving Management for More Effective Government," in *Improvement of Management for More Effective Government.*
57. Sherwood, Frank P., *Executive Development and the Federal Executive Institute, Selected Papers,* U.S. Civil Service Commission, Federal Executive Institute, Charlottesville, Virginia, September 1971. Essays on needs, theories, and problems in executive manpower development at federal, state, and local levels, along with a comprehensive statement of the FEI approach.
58. Staats, Elmer B., "Managers of Tomorrow, Toward the Year 2000," *Civil Service Journal* (October/December 1969).
59. ______, "New Problems of Accountability for Federal Programs," in *Improving Management for More Effective Government,* 50th Anniversary Lectures of the U.S. GAO.
60. ______, "Problems in Revenue Sharing," *GAO Review* (Summer 1972). Concern about the President's accountability vote for the electorate.
61. Stahl, Glenn D., "Do Present Public Servants Approach the Ideal?" in *Achieving Excellence in Public Service,* American Academy, 1963.
62. Stone, Donald C., "Letter to James Hester," *Public Administration Review* (March/April 1970). The correspondence with OMB Associate Director Arnold Weber and Director George P. Schultz pushed hard for support of Title IX of the Higher Education Act. The problem of inadequate support for public executive training was also reviewed in National Association of Schools of Public Affairs and Administration, Circular #18, May 19, 1971.
63. ______, "Making the Federal-State-Local System Manageable," background paper prepared for the Committee on the Improvement of Management in Government, CED, November 1970. Unfortunately this excellent study remains unpublished.
64. ______, "An Agenda for Advocates," *The Bureaucrat,* Vol. 1, No. 1 (Spring 1972). Reviews the agenda the public affairs profession should push.
65. Sundquist, James L., with the collaboration of Davis, David W., *Making Federalism Work* (Washington, D.C.: The Brookings Institution, 1969). The focus is on program coordination at the community level.
66. Vaughn, Robert, *The Spoiled System, A Call for Civil Service Reform,* with Introduction by Ralph Nader (Washington, D.C.: Public Interest Research Group, 1972). Bristling attack on the practices of the U.S. Civil Service Commission is presented as unfair to employees and unhelpful to the general public. To be read in conjunction with:
67. Statement of the Honorable Robert E. Hampton, Chairman of the USCSC, before the Subcommittee on Investigations of the Committee on Post Office and Civil Services of the House of Representatives, on the Operations of the Civil Service Commission, October 4, 1972. The refuting statement includes "An Analysis of the Nader Reports Recommendation."

68. Webb, James E., "Leadership Evaluation in Large-scale Efforts," in *Improving Management for More Effective Government* (Washington, D.C.: GAO, 1971).
69. ______, "What Kinds of People Are Needed for an Adequate Government in the Future?" in *Achieving Excellence in Public Service* (Philadelphia: A symposium sponsored by the American Academy of Political and Social Science, August 1963).
70. Wynia, Bob L., "Executive Development in the Federal Government," *Public Administration Review* (July/August 1972). Some of the flaws in the present system of "training" federal executives with recommendations for change. Roger Jones is quoted by Wynia for his recommendation for changes in federal government training. Jones is also the chairman of the National Advisory Board of the Federal Executive Institute.
71. *Our Nation and the Sea—A Plan for National Action,* Report of the Commission on Marine Science, Engineering and Resources (Washington, D.C.: U.S. Government Printing Office, January 1969).
72. For some international consequences of intensified ocean and coastal zone usage, see Cheever, Daniel S., "Marine Science and Ocean Politics," *Bulletin of Atomic Scientists* (February 1970), p. 29.
73. Three proposals are currently circulating in Washington on the subject of executive development: *Transformation of Scientists and Engineers into Managers,* James A. Bayton and Richard L. Chapman (Washington, D.C.: NASA Contract, Scientific and Technical Information Office, 1972); *Managerial and Executive Development Needs in the Federal Service and Recommended Actions for Meeting the Needs* (Washington, D.C.: U.S. Civil Service Commission, October 1972); and *Report of the National Advisory Board of the Federal Executive Institute,* 2nd draft, November 7, 1972.

    The Bayton/Chapman study is based on earlier work by Floyd C. Mann, L. F. Urwick, and Rensis Likert. It utilizes 610 interviews of GA 13-16 personnel in NIH and NASA. The report calls for specialized training to overcome anti-management attitudes and work patterns that are common among persons trained in scientific disciplines. The transitional program from the scientific to the management role is felt to be particularly critical. Training in what are called "personal skills" would make up an important part of the needed preparation for organizational leadership.

    The USCSC, so-called M-5 proposal was prepared by the Committee on Staffing of the Commission. The background information was drawn from ongoing Bureau of Training studies of management and executive needs in the federal system. A questionnaire, utilizing ranked attributes, was distributed to two levels of supervisors. The resulting proposal called for a governmentwide program to train managers and executives. To meet this need, a strategy is offered to give priority to persons coming into managerial roles for the first time. Additional attention would be given to other executives and managers toward serving a group numbering some 60,000. The proposed training would focus upon management and organizational topics with considerable attention to exercises in leadership development. The USCSC would play the key role in providing or approving training programs.

The Advisory Board of the FEI offers a general review of executive development programs at Charlottesville. On the whole, the report applauds what has been done. Attention is focused mainly on the internal operation of the Institute and its continuing problems in getting participants and financial support. A variety of new initiatives are identified, particularly the need to assure greater participation by state and local officials in the residential program.

1973 (33:101-110)

VOLUME II OF THE STUDY COMMITTEE ON POLICY MANAGEMENT ASSISTANCE, "STRENGTHENING PUBLIC MANAGEMENT IN THE INTERGOVERNMENTAL SYSTEM"

Executive Summary

As the nation approaches its bicentennial, it is confronted with a quite different set of problems than it has faced in the past. Resource scarcity, environmental concerns, changing values about work and the quality of life, for instance, do not lend themselves to simple national solutions. They are complex problems that take diverse forms in different regions, states and communities.

In recognition of the changing nature of domestic problems, the past four administrations have, by action and words, sought to place greater responsibilities on state and local government for allocating federal funds and tailoring their use to meet local needs.

This trend toward devolution and decentralization of federal programs is most clearly represented by the enactment of general revenue sharing and a number of block grant programs such as the Safe Streets Act and the Comprehensive Employment and Training Act, as well as by a series of less publicized actions such as grant consolidations and the establishment of Federal Regional Councils. Meanwhile, the primary mode for delivery of federal domestic programs is still categorical assistance. Categorical assistance programs, now numbering some 1100, also rely heavily on state and local government for their administration. Thus, the federal government has imposed heavy demands on the public management capacity of state and local governments which are already under severe strain from pressures of their own locally-mandated service responsibilities.

While demands upon them for services have risen dramatically, their tax base has not grown in proportion. In some cases, it has declined. Inflation and recession have also contributed to their fiscal instability.

The Challenge to State and Local Management. Taken together, the pressures on the political leaders of state and local government represent a formidable management challenge. What they are being asked to do with limited authority and generally brief tenures is to provide—from a highly complex and nonharmonious mix of programs, fiscal sources and administrative entities—an integrated package of services tailored to the special needs of their jurisdictions.

Some states and localities have made significant progress in upgrading their management capacity through the adoption of home rule charters, professionalization of top management staff, development of program-performance budgets, and numerous other innovations.

Most, however, have an extremely limited ability to plan and direct on a long-term basis for the total needs of their particular jurisdiction. The usual management style is the functional approach—presiding over a fractionalized set of programs with little attention to the whole. The jurisdictional approach—which requires integration of needs analysis, goal setting, long-term planning and evaluation with daily operations—is usually beyond their existing management capacity.

The principal responsibility for remedying this management deficiency rests with the states and localities themselves. But lower levels of government do not operate in a vacuum; they are heavily influenced by the actions of the federal government. This report addresses the question of how the federal government can assist in improving state and local government management.

Priorities for Management Assistance. In seeking to determine priorities for public management assistance to state and local government by the federal government, the Committee found it useful to distinguish among three different elements of management:

1) *Policy management*—the identification of needs, analysis of options, selection of programs, and allocation of resources on a jurisdiction-wide basis.
2) *Resource management*—the establishment of basic administrative support systems such as budgeting, financial management, procurement and supply, and personnel administration.
3) *Program management*—the implementation of policy or daily operation of agencies carrying out policy along functional lines (education, law enforcement, etc.).

Relatively greater progress has been made in program management. This can be attributed both to state and local government efforts to professionalize their line operating staffs and to the manner in which federal categorical programs are structured along program lines to assist them. This is not to say that the management of operating departments is optimal or even adequate in all jurisdictions, or that federal assistance is not needed along program lines.

But the greatest needs of state and local officials are the proper tools and resources for policy and resource management: in short, for managing their jurisdictions as a whole—both by integrating the maze of functional, vertically structured programs, and by assuring that, taken together, these programs are meeting community needs effectively and efficiently.

Ironically, the functional approach of federal activities which has assisted in improving state/local program management has been partially responsible for the deficiencies in policy and resource management. For by establishing or strengthening functional specialists and bureaucracies at these levels, federal programs frequently bypass the governors, mayors, county executives, legislative bodies, and chief administrative officers who perform policy and resource management. Today, these top-level officials find themselves at a loss to understand the maze of program operations within their jurisdictions for which they are, nonetheless, politically accountable. Furthermore, they lack the professional staff and management systems either to integrate and coordinate these programs or to assure that they meet community needs.

Similarly, deficiencies have arisen in resource management not because administrative systems have deteriorated, but because they have lagged behind while the size and complexity of state and local government has mushroomed.

Line-item budgeting systems, for instance, may be adequate for less complex operations, but do not provide the information required for analyzing performance or comparing relative needs among programs; and accounting systems designed to meet legal state reporting requirements do not provide the information necessary for financial control, pinpointing responsibility and assessing performance.

The principal need therefore, is to strengthen the hands of top elected officials and administrators.

Strategy for Federal Action. Based upon its analysis of state and local management and how the federal government impacts upon it, the committee recommends a three-part strategy for federal action:

1. Reorienting federal domestic programs, in order to minimize the administrative burdens on state and local government and the conflicts with local priorities.
2. Expanding and coordinating federal public management assistance specifically aimed at strengthening the overall management capacity of state and local governments that desire such assistance.
3. Improving the federal government's machinery for conducting intergovernmental business in order to bring about more effective state and local participation and liaison in accomplishing the two objectives stated above.

These three recommendations are discussed in summary here and in detail in succeeding chapters.

1. Reorienting Federal Programs to State and Local Needs (Chapter II)

Federal programs have impeded state and local management in three ways.

First, federal assistance is fragmented, making it difficult to administer and use. Of the 1976 total of $55.6 billion in federal aid to state and local government, only $13.4 billion was in block grants and revenue sharing; the remainder was distributed through 1100 categorical grant programs. In the health area alone, 10 federal agencies administer 230 separate programs. The Comptroller General of the United States recently noted the "substantial problems that occur when State and local government attempt to identify, obtain, and use Federal assistance to meet their needs."

Second, the regulation, guidelines and practices governing categorical assistance programs frequently have been confusing and unresponsive to local needs and priorities. A recent survey of 868 cities found only one in four that felt federal agencies adjusted their programs to local conditions more than occasionally. Mayor Richard Lugar of Indianapolis cautioned: "If Congress had any idea of what a horrendous monstrosity the administration of these hundreds of billions of dollars has been, they would look more kindly on the deficiencies of local governments."

Governor James Holshouser of North Carolina put the matter more bluntly: "The best thing the Federal government could do to help State and local government would be to get some of the regulations out of our hair and let us do our job."

Third, federal domestic assistance often goes directly to non-governmental or special-purpose agencies, bypassing key state and local decision-makers and thereby weakening their authority and management capacity. For example, federal assistance to official agencies of the city of Richmond, Virginia in FY 1970 totaled $18.3 million; in the same year, there were 29 federal programs for non-governmental organizations in Richmond totaling $12.3 million, or equivalent to roughly two-thirds of the official agencies' allocation.

The former executive vice-president of the National League of Cities, Allen E. Pritchard, said that this process of creating bureaucracies outside the scope of local governments makes it "impossible for a mayor and a city council to make realistic policy."

By the mid 1960s, the federal government began to recognize the need for simpler, better coordinated delivery of its programs more closely tailored to state and local needs. As a result, both the executive and legislative branches took a number of initiatives to:

- devolve decisions on allocation of resources and the design of specific program packages to state and local government (e.g., revenue sharing, block grants, procedures for review by elected officials of federal grant applications within their jurisdictions).
- decentralize federal program development and administration (Department of Transportation's National Transportation Study process involving governors of each state; the Department of Housing and Urban Development's Annual Arrangements providing for local chief executive officers' approval of HUD-funded programs in their jurisdictions; and the establishment of 10 Federal Regional Councils comprising the major domestic assistance agencies).
- simplify the administration of federal programs (standardizing grant requirements, shortening grant processing time and joint funding arrangements).

Despite these efforts, which have achieved some significant impacts in bringing about greater involvement of state and local elected officials in federal program design and in lightening their administrative burdens, the federal government has fallen short of even the most minimal criteria for establishing genuine partnerships with state and local governments for the design and execution of its domestic assistance programs. Therefore, the Committee RECOMMENDS:

1) The federal government should, in its domestic assistance programs, continue moving in the direction of revenue sharing, block grant, grant consolidation and other funding devices that allow state and local government leaders more flexibility in allocating resources and coordinating the delivery of services and benefits within the framework of more clearly-stated national objectives to be accomplished by the assistance programs.
2) Federal agencies should encourage, in any performance or evaluation criteria for domestic assistance, the accomplishment of basic national legislative purposes and the development or enhancement of state and local management structures necessary to carry these out, rather than creation of detailed administrative guidelines that constrain state and local flexibility.
3) Grant notification and review procedures for state and local leaders should be expanded to cover all major domestic assistance or grant activity within their jurisdictions relevant to the management of the jurisdiction and the federal government should contribute to the cost of such review procedures.
4) Greater supervision should be exercised within federal agencies to ensure compliance with recent federal requirements for standardized and simpli-

fied grant application and administration procedures.

5) Federal agencies should more fully utilize integrated planning, awarding and monitoring of federal grants based on the experience of the Integrated Grant Administration Program and Joint Funding Simplification Act, HUD's Planned Variations and Annual Arrangements, DOT's Unified Work Program Requirements and Intermodal Planning Groups and other arrangements that promote state and local participation in program formulation, administration, and evaluation.

2. Expanding and Coordinating Public Management Assistance (Chapters III and IV)

The federal government is concerned about the management capacity of state and local governments for two reasons.

First, it depends on them for the delivery of many of the services financed by federal domestic programs (e.g., waste water treatment, welfare, health care, law enforcement), that is for the accomplishment of agency missions.

Second, if devolution and decentralization of government authority in the federal system are to work, state and local governments must become sophisticated enough in their management to confront the new complex problems and interrelationships in our society. They must learn how to work cooperatively with each other on metropolitan, state and regional bases and to draw on outside sources of expertise, including the federal government.

Constraints on State/Local Management Capacity Building. Some states and localities are rising to the challenge. But in general, their top elected officials and administrators find it difficult to strengthen their own management capacities for two reasons:

First, their budgets are constrained fiscally and politically. The International City Management Association points out that in deciding whether to add another policeman or another managerial person, officials choose a policeman 99 times out of 100.

Second, when managers seek assistance through management consultants, universities and other external sources in the private sector, it is typically a band-aid operation and not an integrated, on-going effort to build long-term capacity. The short terms of elected officials and sensitivities to assistance from outside ''experts'' have militated against the latter approach.

Federal Efforts to Fill the Gap. In FY 1974, federal assistance to states and local management totalled $512 million, or about one percent of total grant assistance, administered through 80 programs run by 41 agencies. Of the total, 87 percent focused on functional areas (law enforcement, health, etc. for program management; only $79 million or 13 percent addressed policy or resource management needs.

Of the $79 million in assistance for policy or resource management, only half specifically addressed general management needs (the bulk went for physical or land-use planning).

Only two federal programs focus on across-the-board management needs of state and local government: the Department of Housing and Urban Development's "701" Planning and Management Program; and the Intergovernmental Personnel Act. These and numerous other resources within the federal government could be used to assist or encourage state/local management improvement, such as training, research and development, and public service employment.

The Committee found strong support for increased emphasis on policy and resource management in federal assistance programs. However, it also found considerable reservations among state and local elected officials in advocating federal assistance for the policy and resource management functions. These involve understandable concerns about possible federal encroachment into local policy matters or the imposition of particular management structures or processes. These concerns must be taken into account in the design of such assistance. The Committee, therefore, RECOMMENDS:

1) The federal government should strongly reaffirm its commitment to public management assistance for state and local governments.
2) The federal government should initiate a joint effort with key state and local elected officials and their representatiaves to develop a policy and strategy for delivery of public management assistance embracing the three functions of policy management, resource management, and program management.
3) Public management assistance should reflect the diversity and variation of state and local governments' management needs and should be tailored to the needs of each recipient unit through the development of joint federal/recipient needs assessment processes.
4) Such assistance should also provide incentives for more intensive state government efforts to (a) strengthen, through financial and technical assistance, local governments' management capacity and (b) remove institutional constraints (such as those on the organization, structure, finances and personnel of local government).
5) The designers of an expanded and coordinated public management assistance effort should build on current federal strengths in technical assistance and capacity building and should consider strengthening the capability of user-oriented, non-federal resources such as state community development agencies, public interest groups, university public service institutes and programs, and professional association.

6) As an interim strategy, federal agencies should substantially increase their level of investment in policy and resource management assistance relative to program management assistance and monitor and evaluate the response of state and local elected leaders to this investment.
7) The federal government should develop a more adequate information base on agency activities relating to public management assistance that can be used for planning and evaluation of programmatic efforts as well as for disseminating information on objective evaluations of projects and techniques that state and local officials view as successful.

3. Federal Machinery for Improved Intergovernmental Management (Chapter V)

The intergovernmental frictions associated with federal domestic programs and the importance of strengthening state and local management have been recognized for many years. The remedies prescribed above have frequently been debated; and on many, consensus already exists. The difficulty is achieving sustained action in the appropriate directions.

Perhaps the key missing element has been formal machinery in the federal government for making on-going adjustments in federal policy toward state and local government, and for persevering in the implementation of policy changes.

Only one agency is charged with a strictly intergovernmental mission: The Advisory Commission on Intergovernmental Relations. For all its outstanding work, however, ACIR is confined to research and recommendations. The temporary interagency committees and presidential commissions assembled to deal with intergovernmental problems also have lacked implementing power, or the organizational status and staff to goad others to action.

If the federal government is to develop the capacity for ongoing analysis and improvement of public management at all levels of government, responsibility for conducting intergovernmental business should be clearly assigned to key agencies.

The Committee is not necessarily recommending that new agencies be established for this purpose. For the most part, the basic elements of such machinery are now in place in the form of the Domestic Council, the Office of Management and Budget, the Undersecretaries Group for Regional Operations, and the Regional Councils. The Committee, therefore, RECOMMENDS:

1) A policy focal point should be designated in the Executive Office of the President, with responsibilities for overall direction, coordination, and

evaluation of intergovernmental policy and programs, including capacity building components.

2) A separate management focal point or mechanism should be provided within the Executive Office of the President to oversee the implementation of intergovernmental policies and to assure the development of effective intergovernmental processes.
3) Each federal domestic agency should clearly assign functional responsibility for: obtaining state and local inputs into agency program development; integrating the planning, management and assessment of capacity building programs within the agency; promoting integrated and effective R&D utilization, technical assistance and training activities in each agency; and providing a contact point for state and local officials.
4) The intergovernmental role of federal field operations should be administratively strengthened by:

- increasing consultation with federal field staff in agency policy and program formulation.
- further strengthening of the role of the Federal Regional Councils in intergovernmental relations.

Strengthening public management at all levels of the federal system is not a task susceptible to standardized, across-the-board solutions. For this reason, the Committee firmly believes that a long-term effort to improve intergovernmental management must systematically involve state and local officials in a partnership with the federal government.

The Committee has attempted to analyze salient management needs in the intergovernmental system and to construct an outline for initial action.

The situation clearly calls for superior capacity to manage at the local level, supported by flexible programs and resource availability from higher levels of government. But improved intergovernmental management will require more than adjusted administrative machinery. Equally, or perhaps more important, it will require a commitment from the highest levels of government to make it work. It will also require a change in attitude at all levels of government to recognize the vital importance of management by jurisdiction and of devising practical arrangements for the national, state and local governments to work *together* utilizing the unique strengths of each, to meet the challenge of America's third century.

1975 (35:700-705)

CATHERINE H. LOVELL

Coordinating Federal Grants from Below

Federal block grants, in contrast to categorical grants, were designed to give recipient governments increased flexibility to spend money as they wish. Under the traditional categorical grant form, money is awarded to local governments for specific projects or programs and is limited to the narrowly defined activities outlined in an approved grant application. Under the new block grant form, money is allocated to local governments in accordance with a statutory formula and may be used, largely at the recipient government's discretion, in a variety of activities within the broad functional area as long as certain general guidelines are followed.

The new form places the responsibility on local governments to tailor grant uses to meet local needs. One of the most important consequences of the new flexibility is the freedom it has given to the recipient jurisdictions to integrate various grants as they wish, enabling them to maximize impact on local target areas by meshing federal grants with each other and with other state and local programs.

Coordination among federal grants had been viewed, until the advent of the new federalism, as almost exclusively a federal government problem. As grants proliferated in the 1960s, cries for improved coordination among them proliferated also.[1] New mechanisms for coordinating the actions of the granting agencies were proposed and tried at the national level. Coordinating authority was assigned to various departments and agency heads by either executive order or statute. For example, the Economic Opportunity Act of 1964 directed the director of the Office of Economic Opportunity (OEO) to assist the president in coordinating the anti-poverty efforts of all federal agencies.[2] Similarly an Executive Order in 1966 authorized HUD to assist the president in achieving maximum coordination of the various federal activities which were to affect urban community, suburban, or metropolitan development.[3] Numerous other major coordination attempts were also made in the 60s.[4]

Concurrent with these attempts to coordinate programs by function among the federal agencies, attempts at coordination by geographical area were being tried. Interagency coordinating councils such as the Federal Regional Councils (FRCs) and the Title II Commissions were established. The FRCs were created to coordinate the regional directors of the major federal grant-in-aid agencies in each of the 10 federal administration regions. The Title II Commissions were developed to bring together representatives of those governments and agencies with an interest in river basin development.[5] Bodies such as the Appalachian Regional Commission, the Delaware River Basin Commission and the Title V Commissions for regional economic development also based on geographical area were developed.[6]

Both the functional and geographical coordinating devices recognized the complexities of our federal system and the difficulties inherent in the attempts at central coordination, so actual programmatic coordination was based almost wholly on systems of mutual adjustment among agencies. Adjustments such as joint committees, common planning frameworks, agency agreements, agreed consultation procedures, designated liaison roles, task forces of various kinds, and negotiated arrangements for conducting day to day operations were tried.

Most of these federal coordination attempts were less than successful. First, granting agencies have few incentives to coordinate; and second, they failed to recognize that the ultimate purpose of coordination is to harmonize and link programs and projects at the point of impact in the local communities where programs have to be carried out. Not only must federal grant programs be interrelated at the point of impact, but they must be related to state grant programs and to the local jurisdiction's own public programs and private endeavors. Thus, successful coordination and implementation can usually only take place in the community where the programs will be carried out because of the diversity of needs and purposes in the various local communities.

Some leading architects of the new federalism recognized both the failures of past national coordination attempts and the variety in needs and purposes for programs among local communities. They believed that only by decentralization and devolution of federal programs could the various programs be coordinated in ways useful to the local communities.[7] The new federalism policies reduced the emphasis on coordination among the agencies and programs at the federal level and emphasized, instead, decentralizing strategies and aids to local communities to strengthen their coordination capacities. The block grant device was a key to their devolutionary strategy because it gave recipient jurisdictions the responsibility for integrating the various programs, plus the increased flexibility to enable them to do it.

Considerable research has been conducted on the fiscal and political impacts of the block grant programs, but little research has been done on whether or not the block grant flexibilities have, in fact, led to more coordination among grant programs. The research described here concentrated on that question. It examined the experiences of eight local jurisdictions in different parts of the country in coordinating them with categorical programs, with state grants, with voluntary programs, and with the jurisdiction's own programs.[8] The governments studied were Rochester, New York, and its surrounding metropolitan county of Monroe; St. Louis, Missouri, and the contiguous suburban county of St. Louis; Phoenix, Arizona, and Maricopa County which includes Phoenix; and Huntington Beach, in Southern California, and its surrounding Orange County. The research, conducted in the fall of 1977, was based on interviews with policy-involved officials and community organization leaders.

The block grant programs examined were General Revenue Sharing, the Housing and Community Development Act, the Comprehensive Employment and Training Act, and the Law Enforcement Assistance Administration authorized by the Omnibus Crime Control and Safe Streets Acts, and Title XX of the 1974 Social Security Act Amendments.[9]

General Revenue Sharing (GRS) comes to all general purpose local governments according to an allotment by statutory formula with virtually no programmatic conditions. The Housing and Community Development Act (CD) allots funds to large cities and urban counties by statutory formula which may be spent for many purposes as long as they: 1) contribute to the elimination of slums and blight and blighting influences, 2) eliminate conditions that are detrimental to health, safety, and public welfare, 3) conserve and expand housing principally for those of low and moderate income, 4) expand and improve the quality and quantity of community services principally for persons of low and moderate income, 5) use land and other natural resources rationally, 6) reduce the isolation of income groups within communities, and 7) restore and preserve properties of special historical, architectural, or aesthetic value.

The Comprehensive Employment and Training Act (CETA) provides funds to communities by formula based on need (high unemployment and population) which must be spent to hire and train the economically disadvantaged, the unemployed, and the under-employed. The Title XX amendments to the Social Security Act (Title XX) transfers the planning and priority setting processes for the provision of adult and child social services to states and local governments, to provide social services for people to become or remain economically self-supporting, socially self-sufficient, and to protect them from abuse, neglect, exploitation, and inappropriate institutionalization. The Law Enforcement Assistance Administration (LEAA) is designed to reduce and prevent juvenile delinquency, crime and recidivism, and to improve the criminal justice system. Allocations are made to local governments under Title XX and LEAA through local government consortia or various state-local forms which vary from state to state. All five of these block grant programs transfer design responsibility for specific activities to the local jurisdictions.

Coordination in the Local Jurisdictions

Three general types of coordination methods for linking grants with each other and with other funding sources were found in the local governments studied. The first type may be referred to as "orchestration from above," the second, "self-linking among functional professionals," and the third, "meshing the grants from below."[10] Experiences in the jurisdictions with each of the three types are described below.

As a guide to this discussion Table 1 may be helpful. It displays the jurisdictions studied, the three coordination methods, and a few examples of funding source linkages. All jurisdictions, to some extent at least, used each of the coordination methods. The scope of the linkages accomplished through each method varied from place to place and over time. The most comprehensive linking activity discovered was being done by the community-based organizations "meshing the grants from below."

The descriptions of coordination by each of the three methods given in the following pages are not exhaustive for each jurisdiction. Since space limitations do not permit the inclusion of all the findings, only a few examples are presented to illustrate my main finding that there is a great deal of coordination among various federal grant programs going on at the local level and that these programs are also being coordinated with state programs and with the jurisdiction's own programs, both public and private.

Orchestration from Above

Orchestration from above involves explicit planning processes and ad hoc project development. Local governments have long been accustomed to doing "multi-pocket budgeting"; the managers in the jurisdictions are extremely skillful at mixing funds from multiple sources to accomplish their various purposes.[11] Since more than a third of the incomes of local governments comes to them in many different pots from the federal and state governments, most jurisdictional managers have developed methods for integrating the funds through the use of various centralized planning processes such as goals projects, needs and resource assessments, capital planning, budgeting procedures, and other hierarchical controls. The managers have also become skillful at integration on ad hoc, project-to-project bases in which the various revenue sources are blended by them to meet the needs of particular projects.[12]

TABLE 1
Examples of Revenue Source Linkages by the Various Coordinating Methods

	Coordinating Method		
Jurisdiction	**Orchestration from Above**	**Linking by Functional Specialists**	**Meshing from Below**
Counties			
Orange			Free Clinic meshing HEW categorical funds, Title XX City tax revenues, CETA, United Way.
Monroe		Department of Social Services linking funds from Title XX, Council on Aging, other categoricals, LEAA, GRS, United Way in a multi-service center.	
St. Louis	Mayor orchestrated Washington University low income housing linked CD, CETA, local tax revenues, state redevelopment funds, local developer money.		
Maricopa			Indian Center meshing CETA, Title XX, Older American Act, HEW categorical funds.
Cities			
Huntington Beach	City Council discussed GRS, CD, and CETA together relating their uses to the city plan.		
Phoenix		Salt River project linking CD, CETA, Department of Agriculture, other categoricals, state funds, and local tax funds.	
Rochester	City leadership created Multi-service Centers by linking CD, CETA, Title XX, Older Americans Act, LEAA and local tax funds.		
St. Louis			Community Corporation linked CETA, CD and funds raised from community festival to aid elderly people repair homes.

Several of the jurisdictions in our study used formal, explicit planning approaches, based on capital planning programs that rank needed capital projects and relate them to the various grant sources. The city of Huntington Beach now coordinates grants with the city's physical and social master plan. The council considers general revenue sharing, community development, and manpower funds together, and relates allocations of the funds to the city plan. Using the plan as the reference point, the Council decides on the projects and programs to be funded with the various grants. The city manager's office, too, now relates the resource possibilities to the city's goals in an explicit way in the budgetary process. All these approaches came about after the implementation of block grants.

Phoenix now utilizes an interdepartmental task force headed by the Office of Community Services to develop long-range plans to integrate various grant resources with other funds. The city utilizes needs and resource assessments as part of this planning process, and has moved away from the shotgun approach previously used on applications for categorical grants to a more targeted approach using categorical grants to fill gaps in their plans. As one official explained, "Once a need is established and a commitment to it is accepted, we aggressively try for a categorical grant to mesh with the block grant money to attack the need."

Orange County has utilized an extensive social needs assessment using a Delphi process to identify county needs and to interrelate the various grant programs. In Rochester, the city council and the manager together began a goals identification program aided by a citizen survey, and they plan to continue to use this process. These planning activities may have happened without the impetus of the block grants, but many officials feel that having the new options and responsibilities provided by the block grants gave them an added impetus for integrated planning.

Formal planning approaches on a jurisdiction-wide basis are, however, not the most common coordination method. It is more common to integrate various sources of money on a project-by-project basis, through the leadership and ingenuity of top administrators. A former assistant to the mayor of St. Louis said that the block grant form enabled St. Louis to integrate multifaceted kinds of programs with all the grants feeding into, and orchestrated by the mayor's office. One such project, a low income housing development near Washington University, was put together in the mayor's office by coordinating multiple funding sources. Under the state redevelopment law, tax abated property was obtained, private developers built the houses, the streets were installed with CD money and the remaining public works infrastructure was built by CETA employees supervised by regular city workers.

Since the advent of block grants, Rochester has established multiservice centers by linking the various block grants with categoricals. CD funds are used to renovate facilities, and various other grant funds pay for running the services in them—e.g., day care is paid for with Title XX funds, nutrition for the elderly is paid for with Council on Aging funds, drug programs are done with LEAA funds, and overall staffing is supported by CETA funds. St. Louis County, too, has established multi-service centers by linking CD and CETA with various categorical grant funds to establish facilities and furnish aging, youth, and health programs. Neighborhood preservation efforts in older suburban communities along the city fringe are orchestrated by linking together small cities and the neighboring unincorporated areas in a coordinated approach using various grant funds, particularly CD and CETA, combined with regular county services in the target areas.

In all of the cases described above the impetus for coordination and coordinative direction comes from top management and elected officials. Orchestration from above is on the increase but remains the least used coordinating strategy in the jurisdictions studied. Orchestration from above depends on the personality and talent of the chief executive, or one of his top-level executive subordinates, and the drive to take advantage of the opportunities. With multiple pots of flexible money, the chief executive's office has a lot of room to operate—but the executive has to want to put things together and has to have the imagination, drive, and ingenuity to do it.

Linking by Functional Specialists

A second mechanism for coordinating the multiple sources of money is informal linking among the various functional department specialists. This kind of linkage does not occur in any planned way but takes place primarily through communication, sharing of information, and exchanges of ideas.[13] Every official when asked about coordination among grants described the self-linking process. An administrator in the Monroe County (New York) Department of Social Services described linking as it happens in the human services area. In staff meetings, in planning meetings with nongovernmental service organizations, and in meetings about specific problem areas, information is exchanged, needs are spotlighted, and the working professionals get to know where money might be available to fill in a special need. They work together, often in special task forces, to tap the various grant sources and put programs together.

In Huntington Beach, California, the manager said that department heads' meetings and normal hallway conversations provide the vehicles for exchange of information. Because the city is growing so rapidly, demands for service development are constantly heavy, making each department masterful at finding all sources of money to do the things they have to do.

Department heads have strong incentives to get as much from each pocket as they can and to join with other departments to maximize services. The department specialists do not wait for the generalist officials to put things together—they actively seek out the various grant funds on their own and do their own meshing. Officials in all the other jurisdictions described similar dynamics. The consensus was that a great deal of grant meshing jurisdiction-wide is done in the day-to-day work of the functional professionals.

Informal intergovernmental linking among jurisdictions (e.g., city and city, city and county) has enlarged greatly under the block grants. Several kinds of newly formalized intergovernmental mechanisms have been developed to coordinate grant programs or to actually manage individual grants. All of the counties have entered into cooperative agreements on community development with their smaller cities, towns, and villages. CETA is run by interjurisdictional consortia in two of the eight jurisdictions while in the remaining six, the jurisdiction which is the prime sponsor subcontracts with the other jurisdictions. LEAA is run in most of the areas by multijurisdictional councils, and in all the areas these criminal justice councils subcontract to police or other departments in neighboring jurisdictions. Title XX funds are allocated by a council of governments in one jurisdiction and in the others, various kinds of intergovernmental contracting occurs. In one of the jurisdictions, GRS has been used explicitly to stimulate intergovernmental cooperation by making grants of GRS funds contingent upon such cooperation.

There has been a marked expansion of coordinating groups to provide opportunities for both intra- and interjurisdictional self-linking among the various functional specialists. Area clearinghouses, councils of social agencies meeting jointly with governmental people, and ad hoc project groups have proliferated, and a great deal of coordination through these channels now takes place. Although informal channels still facilitate most of the linking, these kinds of coordinating groups are becoming more important and institutionalized.

Meshing the Grants from Below

Coordination of grants at the neighborhood level has been almost totally unnoticed in the literature, yet it has been extensive and effective. This kind of coordination clearly has been enhanced by the block grant form. In the eight jurisdictions included in this study, hundreds of community-based organizations are providing services on a year-to-year basis piecing together various sources of funding to fill out their budgets. The community-based organizations all agree that their opportunities for meshing the various fund sources to implement programs has been enlarged by the flexibility of the block grants, and by the fact that the local jurisdiction rather than the federal government now has control over allocation. Most of the community-based organizations do not depend on federal grants alone but combine the federal funds with state and local funds, private donations, and fees from clients. The following examples are typical of the sorts of meshing activities done by numerous organizations in each of the jurisdictions.

In Rochester, a settlement house, whose purpose is to assist individuals living in a rapidly deteriorating black and Spanish-speaking area, has been supported traditionally only by community fund raising and allocations from the United Community Chest. Several years ago the settlement house was given an abandoned appliance factory by private donors. Last year, the staff was able to get CD funds to renovate the building to accommodate a day and evening child care program, a job training program, and family and personal counseling programs. They also obtained a CETA grant from the city to conduct job skills training for 50 parolees, and 24 CETA-funded positions from the city so they could hire people to help with the renovation of deteriorating homes in the area. The materials for the renovations were paid for with CD funds. In addition, they obtained Title XX funds to run child care programs and a categorical grant under the Older Americans Act to do a foster grandparent program. A skills training program for younger adolescents who had just had their first encounter with the law was funded by the State Division of Youth on a dollar-for-dollar matching basis, and another job training program for young people was paid for by LEAA funds.

The director of the settlement house described his job as "splicing a lot of wires." He explained that over the last three years since block grants were initiated he had been able to tap a lot of resources that he could not tap before since the city and county just did not have the funding flexibility provided by the block grants. "If we had to go to Washington to do this meshing," he said, "it would be just too hard; we'd lose our sense of timing. Here we can coordinate one grant office with another and splice it all together." In putting it all together, his staff and the neighborhood leaders have lobbied extensively with the city to get the two allocations of CD money and the CETA money, and, as a consequence, they have become more politicized and much more knowledgeable about local government.

The Rochester Regional Council on the Aging, a multi-purpose agency, has been equally resourceful. Its basic minimum subsistence budget is funded by the community chest and a small guaranteed stipend from county tax funds. Ingenious coordination of various grant programs has amplified their activities. City CD funds provided for the renovation and equipping of a large, privately donated building which has become a center for senior citizens. The city provides CETA positions for two full-time and two part-time counselors, and county CETA funds pay for one full-time and four part-time counselors and office workers. Another CETA grant supports a program to train active elderly people to do home visitations to shut-in elderly people. Several titles of the Older Americans Act pay for an outreach program, a nutrition program, and various other special activities. An ACTION grant supplies the money to organize a retired volunteer program, and a VISTA grant pays a worker to oversee volunteers who aid handicapped senior citizens. LEAA is funding the materials cost of a program to install safe locks on the doors of senior citizens' homes, city financed CETA employees are installing the locks, and city police are inspecting the homes for other safety problems. A new LEAA grant to do safety training with the elderly is expected to come through soon. The money for an ombudsman program for nursing homes comes from a state grant. A Title XX application for other social service programs is in the works.

A neighborhood program in St. Louis also demonstrates the meshing possibilities but on a much more modest scale. Residents in an old, relatively stable, middle-income, white neighborhood in the downtown area are attempting to forestall deterioration. Through a volunteer community corporation they have been running an annual community festival to raise money for a series of projects to revive the neighborhood. Last year the Community Corporation applied to the city for funds for 50 summer CETA jobs so that they could hire teenagers from their own neighborhood to work in their local hospital and to help with maintenance work on houses owned by elderly citizens who have problems in keeping up repairs. This year the Community Corporation applied for a small CD grant to help pay for the repair materials. The community members want to keep their projects small and to keep them focused on the very special needs of their immediate neighborhood. They like the opportunities provided by CETA and CD to mesh grant funds with their own funds to run programs they can control themselves.

Two final examples come from Orange County, California. The first, a free clinic located in Laguna Beach, provides medical and dental counseling, information and referral, and legal aid. It gets $50,000, which is half of its budget, from the county's General Revenue Sharing funds. It obtained $3,000 from a subcontract of HEW funds through the county Department of Health, and another $24,000 in Title XX funds through the state Department of Health, the Title XX agent in California. It gets $2,000 from the city of Laguna Beach and $3,600 in VD funds from the county of Orange. From the city/CETA Grant it got $5,000 towards one CETA employee. The rest of their funds come from patient donations, community groups, and the United Way.

A Dental Abuse Clinic, located in the city of Cypress, put together $42,000 in General Revenue Sharing funds from the county with $6,000 from the city of Cypress general fund, $1,200 from another neighboring city, $20,000 from the state Office of Narcotics and Drug Abuse, $9,000 in state supplied mental health funds, $10,000 from an LEAA grant subcontracted through the police department, $8,000 for a CETA staff member, free rent from the city, and client donations. Together, all of these pieces combine to pay for a $100,000 annual program.

As we can see from the examples, linking by community-based organizations takes energy, time, and entrepreneurial skill. No two organizations put programs together in exactly the same way, yet all are developing expertise in splicing together the various grant sources. What is of particular interest to this discussion of grant coordination is the contribution that the decentralized block grant form is making to the potential for meshing by community organizations. All of the organization directors, without exception, lauded the block grant flexibilities and the "closeness to home" of the money as facilitators of their meshing possibilities. All spoke of the advantages of the flexibilities in enabling a great variety of programs individually tailored to the needs of specialized clientele and neighborhood problems.

Conclusions

Projects funded from multiple grant sources have proliferated in both quantity and variety. In each of the jurisdictions by one or another of the three coordination methods the various block grants are being linked with each other and are being meshed in innovative and diverse ways with federal categorical and block grants, state grants, and the jurisdictions' own funds, both public and private. All of the various actors in the process, from mayors to neighborhood groups, piece resources together to accomplish their diverse ends. The flexibility given to the local jurisdictions by the block grants has been essential to these integrating processes. The wide diversity in local uses of funds illustrates the potential for tailoring projects to meet specific community needs when there is enough flexibility in the sources of money to make the tailoring possible.

Of the three coordination methods described, overall jurisdiction-wide planning or centrally-directed coordination in any formal sense is the least used. Linking of the various sources of funds takes place most often on an ad hoc, project-by-project basis either through informal negotiations among the various functional departments or through the linking mechanisms exemplified by the actions of the community organizations.

It is apparent that coordination of federal grant programs at the local jurisdiction level by one or a combination of the three methods is a viable alternative to attempts at coordination by the federal government. There are strong incentives to coordinate at the local level since desired programs can be accomplished through the integration of the various sources of money.

On the other hand, there are strong incentives for the granting agencies not to coordinate at the federal level, even if that were possible, because coordination by federal granting agencies are due partially to agency fears of loss of independence or domain, but they also reflect the strength of the particularistic interests which press on each Washington agency to represent the accumulated demands of its particular clientele. The dynamic to mesh the grants at the recipient level is powerful; the dynamic to coordinate at the granting level does not exist.

Coordination of the grant programs by the recipients does not, however, reduce the federal granting agencies' ultimate control or national program design responsibilities. Obviously, federal programs are intended to achieve certain national policies and one of the goals of federal grant designers, always, is to develop programs with the least likelihood of recipient subversion. An important question, therefore, is whether or not the increased flexibility given to local jurisdictions by the block grants has encouraged the recipient jurisdictions to subvert federal intentions. On the basis of this study there is some evidence to show that it has. For example, in each of the jurisdictions some CETA positions were being used to fund people who did not meet the income guidelines as strictly interpreted. In most of the communities, a small part of CD funds were being used to pay for projects that were already planned in the jurisdictions' own capital budgets, and regular police activity got LEAA funds in some jurisdictions. What must be considered, however, is whether or not such transgressions are substantially greater under grants with flexibility than under the more targeted, "controlled," categorical programs, and whether or not the advantages attendant to the new flexibility make up for the diversion possibilities.

A further question that is especially pertinent in light of the findings described here is whether or not under the new flexibility so much fragmentation is taking place in the recipient jurisdictions that there is no real impact on the jurisdictions as a whole or on the substantive goals of a particular block grant. The Brookings Institution research on CD in over 60 jurisdictions has found some, but not extensive evidence of a "spreading effect" in allocations to local projects within the recipient jurisdictions.[14] The spreading effect, according to that research, results from the political necessity for some sharing of grant money among various political subdivisions (councilmanic or supervisorial districts, for example). This sort of fragmentation is mitigated by the opportunities described in this article for coordination of one grant with another to make smaller, dispersed projects more effective.

Only time and careful monitoring will be able to test whether or not a series of smaller, multi-purpose programs designed locally and dispersed throughout communities will have more effective impact than larger, jurisdiction-wide programs.

The fundamental question remains: can the local jurisdictions, and even the neighborhoods, be allowed the flexibility to coordinate and integrate resources to meet specific needs in their communities without diminishing the intent of the individual grant programs? Our findings would suggest yes. In fact, when grant forms facilitate local ingenuity, national intentions are likely to be enhanced since national program goals will be implemented through mechanisms that fit the diverse capabilities of service providers in the local communities where programs have to be carried out. Fundamental to the successful implementation of national policy goals is the continuation and enlargement of sufficient flexibility in federal grants so that local decisions about activities are possible and combinations of programs can be tailored to meet local needs. The evidence from these eight cases suggests that the local political and community institutions have the capacity to link the programs together in highly effective ways.

Notes

1. For a discussion of the principal coordination attempts of the '60s see: James Sundquist, *Making Federalism Work* (Washington, D.C.: The Brookings Institution, 1969).
2. Economic Opportunity Act of 1964, Sections 2, 6, 11, 605 (a) (b).
3. "Coordination of Federal Urban Programs," Executive Order 11297, August 11, 1966, Section 1.
4. Examples of these coordination attempts include instructions to the Department of Agriculture to coordinate federal programs affecting agriculture and rural area development, "Coordination of Federal Programs Affecting Agricultural and Rural Area Development," Executive Order 11307, September 30, 1966; instructions to HEW, OEO, and Labor Department to coordinate all programs and activities related to training of the unemployed, Economic Opportunity Act of 1964 (as amended in 1967), Section 637(a); instructions to the Department of Labor to coordinate manpower planning, "Cooperative Area Manpower Planning System," Executive Order 11422, August 15, 1968, Section 1(a), 2(c); instructions to the secretary of commerce to promote coordinated regional economic development programs, "Regional Economic Development," Executive Order 11386, December 28, 1967; and the creation by President Nixon of an Urban Affairs Council to coordinate programs and provide a forum for the discussion of interdepartmental problems that cut across agencies, described in Richard H. Leach, *American Federalism* (New York: W. W. Norton, 1970).
5. For a discussion of the various attempts at coordination by geographical area see: Martha Derthick, *Between State and Nation* (Washington, D.C.: The Brookings Institution, 1964).
6. *Idem.*

7. For a brief, yet thoughtful discussion about how the new federalist philosophy was to be operationalized see: *Strengthening Public Management in the Intergovernmental System* (Washington, D.C.: Executive Office of the President, 1975).
8. Expenses for the research were paid by the Brookings Institution. A more extensive discussion by the author of the impacts of the new federalism grants on the local governments will be included as a chapter in Richard Nathan (ed.), *America's Changing Federalism* (Washington, D.C.: The Brookings Institution, 1979).
9. We included Title XX (of the Social Security Act Amendments) and the Law Enforcement Assistance Act in the research even though both programs are, in effect, block grants to the states. They were included because in many cases the funds are passed down to the localities in block form with substantial spending flexibility.
10. The three types of coordination relate to Charles Lindblom's and Robert Dahl's conceptualization of general types of coordination processes. They are discussed in Charles E. Lindblom, *The Intelligence of Democracy* (New York: The Free Press, 1965), and Robert A. Dahl and Charles E. Lindblom, *Politics, Economics, and Welfare* (New York: Harper and Row, 1953). The first type of coordination, "orchestration from above," in its purest form is clearly Dahl's and Lindblom's central coordination type in which decision makers adapt to one another on instructions from a central decision maker. The second type, "self-linking among the functional professionals," is akin to partisan mutual adjustment in which no central mind or decision maker exercises any coordinating responsibility. This type of coordination takes place through mutual adjustment characterized by a variety of bargaining, information sharing and other relationships in which not every program is adjusted to every other program, yet which results in decisions which are intelligently related.

    My third type, "meshing the grants from below," is close to coordination through the market mechanism which is a highly developed process for coordinating interdependent actors without their being deliberately coordinated by a central coordinator, without rules that assign to each actor a position relative to all others, and without a dominant common purpose. For Lindblom and Dahl, since the market coordination is powered by diverse self-interests it is a form of coordination through mutual adjustment of partisans in the market, and is, therefore, one form of partisan mutual adjustment. For our purposes since meshing the grant from below involves quite a different set of processes than self-linking by the functional professionals, we discuss them as two different types.
11. For the term, "multi-pocket budgeting," I am indebted to David O. Porter, David Warren, and Teddie Porter, *The Politics of Budgeting Federal Aid: Resource Mobilization by Local School Districts* (Beverly Hills: Sage Publications, 1973).
12. As an example see the extensive discussion of how local governments are coordinating public and private resources to stimulate local economic growth in National Council for Urban Economic Development, *Coordinated Urban Economic Development* (Washington, D.C., 1978).

13. Organizational literature for some years has described this type of informal linking. See for example, Rensis Likert, *New Patterns of Management* (New York: McGraw-Hill, 1961). The newer intergovernmental relations literature also discusses the negotiating, information sharing roles of local government administrators. See, for example, Deil S. Wright, *Understanding Intergovernmental Relations* (Belmont, Calif.: Wadsworth Publishing Co., 1978).
14. Richard Nathan, et al., *Decentralizing Community Development* (Washington, D.C.: The Brookings Institution, 1977).

1979 (39:432-439)

THOMAS J. MIKULECKY

Intergovernmental Relations Strategies for the Local Manager

The intensity of problems in our cities has become a matter of national concern. This had led to growing interdependence of governmental agencies at each level on the powers, capacities, and resources of the others. Hardly a function of local government can be found which is not in some way aided or regulated (or both) by another governmental agency.

In this context, concerns for "sovereignty" of local decision making are simply irrelevant and obsolete. Attitudes of local independence are negotiable matters. What is important for the manager to realize is that interdependence is present and unavoidable, and that the only real options have to do with the extent to which the city wishes to commit to a higher degree of interdependence.

This article is an overview of a strategic approach to intergovernmental relations. It is concerned with the ways in which local managers can promote the use of resources of other governmental agencies to improve the quality of city life and to cope more effectively with regional, state, and national agencies. The focus will be on the process of grant financing, the response to federal regulation, and metropolitan governmental reorganization.

I.

The extent of national involvement in traditional areas of municipal responsibility is well documented. Local officials select grant programs which coincide with the needs for additional financing of a priority program or project. But additional criteria are also commonly used due to the fact that the formal process of identification-application-approval-implementation is seldom followed. The key to successful intergovernmental funding is the informal diplomacy that is carried out from the earliest stages on through completion of the undertaking.

To be established early is how closely objectives coincide. Are the national objectives tied to the possible grant the same as the local objectives to be achieved, or must the local project be skewed in such a way as to make it eligible? And is the extent of the skew required desirable or at least tolerable? It is presumed that some degree of flexibility exists within each agency and that negotiating room can be found. The extent of negotiability and therefore flexibility in program design will determine whether an application for assistance is worth the preparation time and costs.

There are several key elements in this process. The first is that the local government ought not to distort its objectives and procedures for the sake of acquiring the needed revenue. Only when the national objectives have been examined and found to be of value is it appropriate to seek assistance, and then to determine whether these programs are compatible with what is right and proper locally. Too often local government units have succumbed to the pressure of participation for political reasons, such as the prestige of being a city which utilizes a specific program. But it is also possible to "fit the square peg in the round hole" by "massaging" either the federal program or the local objective in order to acquire the needed support. This does not necessarily involve the sacrificing of important objectives or procedures, but may require a skillful program design and application writing process in which the objectives of all affected and involved governmental units can be achieved compatibly if not in the same order of priority. Intergovernmental management on the local level involves skilled program design in its initial stages, coupled with a highly persuasive presentation to funding agencies and those agencies responsible for regional and state reviews and comments.

A second aspect of intergovernmental grantsmanship is diplomacy. Local governments have sought in vain for federal and state assistance, only to be turned down for lack of credibility. Federal agencies have rejected applications from local governments because of their lack of faith in the management system into which their funding was to be injected. The parallel of intergovernmental relations within the American federal system and international relations among the foreign nations is striking. Cultures are often no less foreign to one another between the local government and a distant federal regional office. Values of the primary actors are often as different as they are across the Suez Canal or the Pacific Ocean. The lesson we learn from this divergence is that diplomacy is no less needed in the intergovernmental sector than it is in the international sphere. The manager, like the delegate, is required to cultivate and exercise the same level of finesse and appreciation for the values of others. Experience reveals that those managers who have taken the time to cultivate the faith and friendship of their counterparts at other levels of government and have utilized the same informal diplomacy as characterizes the international arena, have found a reward in a more trusting, cooperative effort, increased intergovernmental funding, and a valuable technical working relationship as well as collaborative problem solving.

The local manager responsible for the design and implementation of the intergovernmental strategy will rank the following additional skills as uppermost requirements:

1. An ability to comprehend an adequate level of technical material in such fields as housing or water quality, and being conversant, authoritative, and respected among technicians, yet not so narrow as to be unable to coordinate and appreciate technical detail in other related areas.
2. Creativity in program development, writing, and cross-the-table persuasion with the capability to take often inconsistent national, state, and local objectives and show how they can and should be used to accomplish a specific program or project. This also implies the need to be flexible when faced with a possible impasse in discussion.
3. An appreciation of what motivates other governmental or bureaucratic "cultures" and a capacity to appeal, stimulate, and work within the framework of these cultures as sensitivity and expediency might dictate.
4. A goal orientation, utilizing systems and processes for achievement, and the ability to organize tasks and timetables to illustrate goal attainment.

The increasing and necessary intensity of relations among governments in particular functional areas requires that the manager maximize these qualities. The fact that agencies have become interdependent requires that each manager be the leader in the diplomatic skills of intergovernmental relations.

II.

Minimizing the adverse impact of national and state regulations on local policy and administration has become a more recent objective of the intergovernmental manager. This condition results from the fact that our national government and its component elements have realized that it is not possible to solve all the problems of urban areas through the funding of categorical programs. An alternative is a system of nationally contrived and administered regulations. These regulations prevail in nearly every part of life, but the local manager sees them more frequently in the areas of environment, health, equal employment opportunity, and housing. To face up to the reality of this stage in the evolution of our federal system is to recognize that this national arrogance will not go away with any sudden realizations of local intelligence or any sudden shift in public policy.

The regulation game must be played by all actors at each level of government. If regulations are to achieve their intended purpose without adversely affecting local operations, managers should participate in their design and implementation rather than letting them be written and imposed by national level agencies in a vacuum. When advertised regulations appear in publications such as the *Federal Register,* local managers individually and collectively can make a tremendous impact when their voice is heard in favor of less regulation, or regulation which is more compatible with local objectives. Few local managers really learn how to lobby effectively in the federal bureaucracy, much less in the Congress. Those who have learned to penetrate the bureaucratic maze have found a marvelously simple process in which people can be isolated and responsibility pinned down.

III.

Public managers can look at their private corporate counterparts and find organizations which change to accommodate the need to move products or to secure a greater profit. Then why are the public agencies by comparison so inflexible to change and reorganization? The reasons are found in part in the interest group influence in local government; those who have ties to the specific service or the manner in which it is delivered resist reorganization. However, public agencies can achieve greater economies and efficiencies through reorganization of functions, not only within their agencies, but also among their various agencies. Reorganization of governmental functions in urban areas and in self-contained counties should be high on the local agenda in the next decade, and it will require a level of diplomatic skill and persuasion not yet experienced or realized among most managers.

Each population center is unique in its political culture, its propensity to accept change, and the governing style or structure that is most appropriate. But citizens everywhere have the right and reason to demand tax savings and improved efficiencies in service delivery. The task is to identify what functions and services are presently offered by which agencies, to determine the distribution of responsibility, and then to compare objectively the alternative methods of reorganization of responsibility in terms of the traditional values of efficiency, economy, and responsiveness to citizen needs. With this information we are ready to decide whether the existing governmental structures are worth retention in their present form. Or is it more desirable to consider a process of change in which the structures may be altered, greater collaboration or cooperation planned, and perhaps greater collaboration or cooperation planned, and perhaps greater economies of scale achieved? Of course this is a process that is easily delayed because to face up to it is to provide a threat to political prerogatives and "turf."

Recently in the Colorado legislature, for example, representatives on a powerful local government committee killed a bill which would have allowed the voters to decide whether a limited function metropolitan council should be formed. The proposal lost because of the metropolitan county commissioners who saw their already impotent authority threatened, and because it was an election year when change was not supposed to occur.

Local governmental reorganization requires the manager to take a fresh and detached view of the arrangement of functional responsibilities among local jurisdictions. He or she must return to the basics of his or her training and ask hard questions of economy and efficiency which might suggest recommendations that are at odds with sacred local policies. This is the stage at which planning begins, for the long-term objectives may be politically unrealistic in the short run. "Planting the seed" of subtle ideas in the right places and then designing a strategy of moves over a period of time may be the most effective approach. That long-term objective could be consolidation or a multi-functional contractual system, or a totally new and unique form of government. The short term may be only a modest step in that direction.

IV.

Intergovernmental relations is a dynamic *process* that is subject to an infinite number of private and public influences. When the process works well and the individual participants contribute maximally, problems of growth are contained, conflicts resolved, decisions made, and adjustments occur in the distribution of power and responsibility within the federal structure. When the process functions minimally, primarily because of limitations of the individuals involved, conflicts result in agencies becoming jealous of their prerogatives or adopting an authoritarian attitude. In short, the evolution of the American federal system and its ability to cope with inevitable change are direct results of the effective individual contribution to the process of intergovernmental relations by sensitive and skilled managers.

What has been presented here is the very preliminary beginnings of a strategy of intergovernmental relations for the local manager. It demands a higher level of diplomatic skill than we have developed or considered necessary in the past. It also demands that the intergovernmental responsibility cannot be completely delegated away to an assistant or a line department head. Intergovernmental relations affect the viability of local governments at the very core, and are therefore the proper focus of our priority attention if we want to be good at what we do.

1980 (40:379-381)

DONALD F. KETTL

The Fourth Face of Federalism

The 1970s brought a new face to federalism, a collection of private and semi-public groups and agencies that moved into a full partnership with the national, state, and local governments in administering federal policy. This fourth face of federalism emerged from the decade's new breed of intergovernmental grant programs. Richard Nixon promised a "New Federalism" of guaranteed grants, fewer federal rules, and more discretion for state and local governments on what project could receive support. It was in general revenue sharing for all state and local governments and in manpower and community development programs, mainly for the cities, that this "new" federalism bore fruit. It was fruit, however, that the cities found difficult to pick, for the programs proved complex to administer.

Two programs—the Comprehensive Employment and Training Act, enacted in 1973, and Community Development Block grants, established a year later—became important sources of both revenue and services for local governments. CETA allows recipients, mostly large cities,[1] wide discretion in establishing their own manpower training and public service employment programs. CD gives cities a nearly free rein in choosing projects for housing rehabilitation, development, and public services.[2] Both programs have relatively simple application requirements and both programs leave most of the responsibility for deciding how best to administer local projects in local hands. It was as a solution to the administrative question that the fourth face of federalism emerged.

Very few—if any—cities had extensive experience in organizing and running manpower and community development programs before the 1970s. Most of the mayors' complaints during the Great Society, in fact, were that the federal government was bypassing city hall in dealing directly with clients like neighborhood groups or in providing money to quasi-municipal bureaus like redevelopment agencies that often resisted local control. CETA and CD ended that era by delivering the money directly to city hall along with the federal government's directive to go forth, plan wisely, and administer well.

This was a formidable charge. In the medium-sized city of Richmond, the city government collected $9 million from CETA and $7 million from CD in fiscal year 1979, 10 cents for each dollar of the $156 million it collected from local sources. The two programs were to pay for a wide variety of services: job training, public service jobs, housing rehabilitation, downtown economic development, and many more. Moreover, the city faced a choice: Should it attempt to run directly each of the more than 100 projects? Or should it use other groups in the city? If the city ran all the programs directly, from where would the needed expertise come? If it contracted the projects out, how could it ensure that the projects were run well and were pursuing the city's goals?

For many cities, including Richmond, the choice was contracting out the direct administration of many projects to non-city agencies. As we shall see by examining the case of Richmond, that choice raised a fundamental problem of accountability for the use of the federal government's money. As the recipient, the city government had to ensure that the federal government's requirements were met. Because the city served only as the conduit for much of the money, it faced the challenge of ensuring that the non-city agencies met both federal requirements and local policy goals without interfering excessively with how those non-city agencies ran their projects. Richmond, as did many of her sister cities, solved the problem by creating new (and apparently permanent) municipal agencies to oversee the work of these non-city groups. The new city agencies in turn developed formal ties with the non-city groups. The result was a new set of bureaucratic arrangements that lifted these non-city groups into a new intergovernmental arrangement, an arrangement that added a fourth face to federalism.

Contracting Out

Richmond's city council assigned responsibility for CETA and CD to a new Department of Developmental Programs.[4] A wide collection of agencies had run earlier categorical programs, but the unified planning and reporting requirements of the new programs argued for central coordination, and the council decided to house both programs in a single agency. The department, however, runs few of the city's CETA and CD projects itself. Although other city agencies run many projects, most are contracted out to non-city agencies. In the 1978-79 fiscal year, for example, non-city agencies spent 63 percent of the CD funds and 64 percent of the CETA funds. As City Manager Manuel Deese explained, "The more you get involved and try to play the federal game, the more you have to go outside [city agencies]."

Some of the non-city agencies are neighborhood groups spurred on by the political support the neighborhoods gained during the 1970s. The Great Society's confrontation between city hall and city neighborhoods, often fueled by federal grants that bypassed city governments and were channelled directly to the neighborhoods, slowly gave way to closer (if not always pacific) ties.[5] National interest groups representing the neighborhoods struggled to win representation by an assistant secretary in the U.S. Department of Housing and Urban Development and battled their way into recognition by Jimmy Carter's domestic policy staff. "First the neighborhood organizations got the attention of City Hall and now they've got some funding," William A. Whiteside, director of the urban reinvestment task force explained. "It is a natural progression from a militant stand to get resources to a constructive role once you have the attention and the funds."[6]

Other groups are varied non-profit organizations. Some, like Opportunities Industrialization Centers from previous manpower programs and social service agencies from the Model Cities program, received funds under the categorical programs that preceded CETA and CD. Many of these agencies fully expected to continue receiving funds under the new programs. National interest groups, representing some of these agencies managed, furthermore, to have provisions inserted into the CETA legislation to ensure that programs of "demonstrated effectiveness" be given "due consideration" for continued funding.[7]

Yet, other groups are quasi-city agencies like the Richmond Redevelopment and Housing Authority and the city school board, agencies responsible to the city council but not answerable to the city manager. The redevelopment agency had some old projects whose completion demanded continued funding, but Richmond went beyond past patterns of funding in giving money to non-city agencies.

Four factors shaped the choices for this strange assortment of administrative agencies. First, Richmond city officials wanted to avoid building the programs permanently into the city's bureaucracy. If the city had created, for example, a new agency to administer directly all of the city's CETA training programs and the federal government later reduced or eliminated the program, the city might face the dilemma of either laying off a large number of city employees or of funding the projects from local revenue. Cycles alternating between federal pleas for rapid spending and federal warnings of funding cuts made city officials very wary of building the programs permanently into the municipal bureaucracy. City officials were reluctant to assume direct responsibility for programs that the federal government might not later support.

Second, previous federal programs had created a large and powerful constituency for continued community-level funding. As one manpower official explained about CETA:

> First, when CETA started, there was very heavy emphasis [from the Department of Labor] on the fact that we had to do business with the people who had been doing business before with the feds. Second, the nature of city politics dictated that we had to keep these people happy.[8]

Most of these agencies, from the Community Action Program Agency to the Redevelopment and Housing Authority, depended on federal funds for their existence. Any attempt to change the pattern of funding would have stirred up loud howls from entrenched organizations.

The changing nature of Richmond politics also deeply affected these organizational decisions. As CD and CETA arrived in Richmond, the city was in the midst of a dramatic change in community power. A shift from at-large to district representation on the city council gave blacks their first city council majority, and they elected one of their number as the city's first black mayor. Before the change, the white council majority had no desire to jeopardize an already precarious position by antagonizing black community leaders with a change in funding strategy. Moreover, after the blacks gained the majority, their one-vote edge left no room for dissension. Particularly in the CETA program, the community-based organizations were enjoying support that made a dramatic reorganization unthinkable.

Finally, for some of the projects, particularly in the CD program, non-city agencies were the city's only alternative. The Richmond Redevelopment and Housing Authority, for example, had worked for years on the city's redevelopment program. For the redevelopment projects continued under the CD program, the authority was the only agency in the city with the expertise to make the projects work. Dismantling the agency would have meant destroying much needed expertise.

Federal Control of Federal Grants

The use of non-city agencies, however, complicated the city's management of the projects. As the grant recipient, the city was responsible to the federal government for ensuring that each program's requirements were met regardless of who eventually operated the projects. With more than 100 non-city agencies operating CETA and CD projects, the city (through the Department of Developmental Programs) had to devise procedures to make sure that all agencies spending federal money followed federal rules.

Despite earlier promises of few federal strings, both CETA and CD acquired a complicated collection of regulations. Some of these regulations were designed to guarantee that early charges of program abuses could not recur. Monitors of both programs in the first few years had found trouble wherever they looked: tales of CD funds used to build tennis courts and marinas (instead of housing for the poor), as well as corrupt hiring practices in CETA projects. Charges of abuse and outright fraud were legion.[9] In many cases, however, the allegations turned out to be baseless, and even when there truly was fraud or abuse, no one knew how large the problem actually was.

The very hint of abuses, however, rendered this question moot. The Department of Housing and Urban Development began taking a much closer look at CD applications and insisting that cities document the extent to which each project would benefit the poor. In the CETA program's 1978 annual renewal, Congress put limits on how long CETA participants could work and how much they could be paid. In addition to supervising local applications more closely to ensure that local governments fulfilled their federally-defined obligations to the poor, the federal government also began to conduct far more stringent monitoring. As one Richmond official explained, "They are requiring us to have a mechanism to substantiate the fact that we are benefiting low and moderate income people."

At the same time, the federal government was adding an ever-increasing number of general, crosscutting requirements to intergovernmental grant programs. These rules, totalling 59 by one U.S. Office of Management and Budget count in 1980,[10] required all grant recipients to examine the environmental impact of any projects they planned, to guarantee that they would not discriminate in the use of the funds, to keep their books in a prescribed manner, to pay workers at prevailing wages, and on, and on.

All of these actions created a complicated mix of federal controls: extensive regulations detailing what had to be done; application reviews to determine whether the cities were meeting the regulations; and monitoring procedures after program execution to see if the cities had complied with the regulations' requirements. As Richmond's assistant city manager, A. Howe Todd, explained, "Here we are five or six years down the program with HUD, and HUD is putting the screws on. I see more and more constraints being put on us, making it more and more costly for us to comply with their requirements."

The result was that the cities had to assemble an enormous mass of data to keep the federal agencies satisfied that all of the standards were being met. As Richmond Finance Director Jack Lissenden explained, "Their [the federal agencies'] monitoring is much more demanding than anything we've ever had before, even the categorical grants." The federal agencies, Lissenden said, were now sending armies of inspectors to examine the books for days, where before they might have sent one investigator to review the records for a few hours. Complicating the city's record-keeping task, furthermore, were frequent changes in those items the federal agencies wanted the cities to measure. One city official pointed to recent federal regulations in the CD program that required the city to determine the beneficiaries by income and sex for projects such as sidewalk cuts that make it easy for wheelchairs to pass over curbs. Another city official complained about HUD's requirement of keeping program records available for public inspection in a "file":

> The regulations always call for having all the information in a file. A file to me is the four drawers out there in a cabinet. But for the field man, a file means one folder. I've had to change my filing system three times. Now, I'm back to the system I used at the beginning of the program.[11]

"The diversity and complexity of the things we are doing to satisfy the federal government's demands is getting worse," one Richmond CETA official complained. He pointed out that, after quarreling with the U.S. Department of Labor for a year, he finally had to lease a word processing computer just to collect the information needed to satisfy the department's data demands. The burdens of collecting the information, the official concluded, are not all that oppressive, but they are time-consuming. "They are getting to be nit-picking," he complained. "They are capturing a lot of statistics that aren't useful. They should be asking, 'Is anything useful happening down there?' "[12]

Through all of these regulatory changes, the federal government has subtly drawn power back to Washington. This centralization has come in rules about both the substance of programs (who must be hired or what projects must be funded, for example) and about the procedures that local governments must follow (such as what public hearings must be held and what environmental effects must be examined). The federal government has required the collection of more information on more kinds of problems by more cities than was ever the case in the categorical programs.

Managing Contracts

No matter who ultimately spent the money, the federal government held the cities accountable for adherence to the regulations. The cities, thus, had to guarantee that each non-city agency receiving federal money met the federal rules and that each agency could supply the city with proof of compliance. Furthermore, the cities naturally had their own ideas of what benefits should come from the projects and the non-city agencies had goals of their own. The programs were thus encumbered with four layers of accountability: accountability to the federal government for general, cross-cutting requirements; accountability to the federal government for specific program requirements; accountability to city officials for individual project goals; and accountability to those who ultimately received the fruits of the projects—usually the clients of the non-city agencies—for the quality of the services.

Richmond's contracting-out policy sought to guarantee that the city could supply the federal agencies with the answers they wanted and that the non-city agencies would provide the services the city desired. The task of extracting adequate performance for the non-city agencies, however, proved difficult. Many of the CETA and CD agencies were new to the grant business, and even for those that were not, past experience was no guarantee of present capacity. City officials charged that the federal government had not overseen community-based organizations very closely in the earlier categorical programs: "Private non-profits [non-profit organizations] can get away with a little more than governments can," one city official remarked.

Furthermore, city staff members agreed, the use of non-city agencies has often raised problems of competence. "Going to a non-city agency," one city official said, "the chances are very good that they wouldn't have the capacity to manage a project." Even basic skills like accounting for petty cash and maintaining adequate financial records, according to some city officials, are often absent. If basic operations proved troublesome, the pursuit of project goals was therefore often an elusive business. The city has faced, first, task of factoring its general program goals into projects the non-city agencies could handle, and then the job, sometimes overwhelming, of making the agencies both productive and accountable.

To meet these needs, Richmond has relied (as have many other cities) on drafting detailed and often lengthy agreements. For city agencies conducting CD and CETA projects, these agreements take the form of countersigned memorandums; for non-city agencies, the agreements are formal contracts. These agreements spell out the administering agency's role in detail: its budget, detailed by activity such as land acquisition costs, training expenses, and administration; its responsibilities, described by the nature of the project and a "milestone chart" that indicates when each step of the project is to occur; and its reporting requirements, defined in sufficient detail to allow the city to follow the project's substantive progress and to enable the city to collect the information needed to satisfy the federal government. These agreements provide the city with its most important means of control, extracting promises from the operating agencies about exactly what is to be done in which ways. As one official explained, "We have no control over these agencies except through the contract. The only time we can dictate to them is when they are in violation of the contract."

Relations between the city government and most agencies operating CETA and CD projects, therefore, have revolved around accountability through paperwork. A written agreement details what will be done when. Periodic reports describe what has been accomplished toward the city's objectives. Other reports describe beneficiaries of the projects by income, sex, and so on, to help the city satisfy the federal government's demands. The city government, particularly its Department of Developmental Programs, serves as a contract manager, administering projects that previously would have been managed from separate field offices of separate federal agencies.

Effects on Local Administration

Department of Developmental Programs Director Aaron Knight is frank about the importance of federal grants for his agency: "The agency wouldn't exist without federal money." Of the department's 60 employees in the 1979-1980 fiscal year, only 16 (27 percent) were paid from city revenues. Federal grants—principally CETA and CD—paid the salaries of the other 44 workers. These grants, thus, have been responsible for the creation of a large—and now apparently permanent—city agency whose mission it is to service federal grants.

The federal grants, in turn, have spawned a network of *ad hoc* arrangements that have scrambled the city's traditional administrative organization. In the CD program, a multi-agency task force cuts across the city's regular departmental boundaries to deal with the problems that often occur in non-city agencies. The CETA program has a very different administrative structure. The city's CETA program is part of the Richmond Area Manpower System, a consortium formed by Richmond and four nearby counties.[13] Richmond receives most of the jobs, has half of the votes on the consortium's governing board, and administers the program for the consortium through the Manpower Bureau of the city's Department of Developmental Programs. These arrangements have tangled the lines of accountability still further, for that department serves as the staff arm for the regional CETA program at the same time it operates as the umbrella agency for administering the city's CETA projects.

The bureaucratic arrangements for the administration of CETA and CD in Richmond, thus, are intricate and convoluted. They exist to satisfy the fragmented demands of different federal programs, but they have produced unusual arrangements. The CETA projects come to Richmond's citizens through the U.S. Department of Labor, the regional consortium, the city's Department of Developmental Programs, and numerous contractors, most of which are non-city agencies. The CD funds flow from the U.S. Department of Developmental Programs (in part) and the city's Department of Planning and Community Development (in part), as well as to the task force (in part), and, finally, to the program's contractors who, again, are mostly non-city agencies.

The two programs have fostered the creation of a new agency, a new regional consortium, formal agreements among city agencies, and a network of non-city agencies officially doing the federal government's business under local direction. All of this is overlaid upon a city bureaucracy that, of course, works in different ways under different rules toward different local goals.

The result is a bureaucratization of the federal aid function in Richmond. Large agencies have been created to manage the myriad projects and to service the federal government's demands for information. Existing ties among city agencies have been scrambled as a different, federally-oriented bureaucracy has been overlaid over locally-oriented agencies. The number and complexity of the projects, furthermore, have created formal ties between city hall and many private, quasi-public, and neighborhood-based agencies that now depend on good administrative relations with city officials to ensure the continued flow of federal aid. The federal programs have, thus, created a large network of intricate relationships that channel aid to local agencies, with the city of Richmond acting as the administrative intermediary between the federal government, with its money, goals, and requirements, and the non-city agencies, with their own disparate agendas.

Richmond city officials do not seem particularly annoyed about their new role. They grumble about conflicting or unclear demands from federal agencies, they dislike rearranging their files regularly, and they complain about the paperwork required. However, the city's administrative officials have been willing to meet nearly any requirement for the aid, provided the requirements are clear.

More important is the increase in the administrative costs. More local staff people are preparing environmental assessments, equal opportunity and fair housing plans, contracts, monitoring reports, performance reports, and financial audits; more contractors are filing reports to tell the city what they are doing and to help the city keep the federal agencies happy. There is, of course, nothing wrong with using a share of any grant for overhead costs to ensure adequate management control; but three points are significant.

First, more of these requirements are in effect now than ever before. For example, nearly all of the 59 general requirements that come with most federal grant programs are mandates established in the last 15 years; 35 of these (59 percent) were ordered during the 1970s.[14] The federal government itself pays nearly all of the costs for complying with these regulations, and, thus, they do not place a large financial burden on local governments. The regulations have, however, increased the level of "overhead costs" in the federal aid system: more money must be spent to comply with these requirements, and less money, consequently, is available for services.

Second, these requirements are more and more the responsibility of local governments rather than the federal government. Before Richard Nixon's New Federalism, for example, the federal government performed the environmental reviews now required of local governments. The programs transferred the administrative burden for complying with these "overhead" requirements into local hands. Local officials had to develop new areas of expertise; environmental reviews, planning for equal opportunity and fair housing, and so on, and they had to develop a contracting system to ensure that those who actually spent the money met the requirements.

Finally, the programs have inserted city hall as the formal intermediary between the federal government and the non-city agencies. This happened, of course, because of complaints in the late 1960s that city government officials were being excluded from important decisions that intimately affected their communities. In the 1970s, the pressures for administrative expedience and for neighborhood power gave non-city agencies a continuing but different role. City officials controlled the non-city agencies by contract, and the friction-filled days of the Great Society grew into the formal, institutionalized (but not always placid) relationships of the New Federalism.

The Changing Face of Federalism

The clear thrust of this movement is to resolve the city hall-neighborhood conflicts of the 1960s while capitalizing on the intensity of concern that first spawned the controversies. HUD's first assistant secretary for neighborhoods, Geno Baroni, explained, "There are some groups that raise hell and some groups that get involved in development. The thrust of the urban partnership is to get those [latter] groups and put them together with local government and the private side" to improve their own areas.[15] To a large degree, CETA and CD have succeeded. Years of experience gradually soothed the initial raw feelings between Richmond and its contractors.

These programs, however, have brought an important change to the basic function of the city. Cities, as Douglas Yates has argued, have traditionally been service providers.[16] Even as the federal government gradually relied more on outside organizations to perform its basic functions and the states struggled to define their role in a changing intergovernmental system, the cities were in the front lines providing direct services like police, fire, and sanitation. Local governments, of course, overwhelmingly still provide most of their services directly.[17] The two grant programs signal an important change in this tradition, for they have moved local government a short step from direct provision of services to management of contracted services. This not only means a change in some of what local governments do, but also a shift in who does it. Accountants, contract specialists, environmental engineers, and equal opportunity experts have moved into a key role in helping to govern urban America.

At the same time, the complicated administrative networks that manage CETA and CD have simultaneously streamlined and muddied the problem of accountability. By channeling the grants through local elected officials, the federal government has identified mayors and city councilors as those ultimately responsible for local projects. By encouraging such a complex administrative web, the programs simultaneously have made it more difficult to determine both what is going on and who is responsible for doing it. This paradox of accountability has only encouraged a basic regulatory approach to grant programs that has grown through the 1970s. Faced with confusion over program administration, federal agencies have retreated back into increasingly complex rules that seek to frame the basic administrative patterns of the programs.[18]

Perhaps most importantly, the programs have also led to formal, regular ties between city hall and a wide assortment of neighborhood, nonprofit, and other non-city organizations. These ties have enabled the cities to specify with greater detail the conditions under which these agencies would receive federal funds. At the same time, these programs have led to more and more formal arrangements between the city and others, non-city local groups, arrangements that through the 1970s have strategically built the non-city groups into a fourth face of federalism.

Notes

1. Cities and counties with a population of more than 100,000 receive CETA funds as "prime sponsors." States receive grants for those areas not covered by local prime sponsors. For a description of the history and issues in the CETA program, see U.S. Advisory Commission on Intergovernmental Relations, *The Comprehensive Employment and Training Act: Early Readings from a Hybrid Block Grant* (Washington, D.C.: U.S. Government Printing Office, 1977).
2. On the CD program, see U.S. Advisory Commission on Intergovernmental Relations, *Community Development: The Workings of a Federal-Local Block Grant* (Washington, D.C.: U.S. Government Printing Office, 1977).
3. For some examples, see the author's *Managing Community Development in the New Federalism* (New York: Praeger, 1980).
4. Richmond has a council-manager form of government.
5. For a look at the tensions of the Great Society programs, see Daniel P. Moynihan, *Maximum Feasible Misunderstanding: Community Action in the War on Poverty* (New York: Free Press, 1970).
6. Quoted by Rochell L. Stanfield, "The Neighborhoods—Getting a Piece of the Urban Policy Pie," *National Journal* (April 22, 1978), p. 624.
7. See U.S. National Commission for Manpower Policy, *Community Based Organizations in Manpower Programs and Policy* (Washington, D.C.: U.S. Government Printing Office, 1977).
8. Interview with Richmond city official.
9. See, for example, Raymond Brown *et al.*, *A Time for Accounting: The Housing*

and Community Development Act in the South (Atlanta: Southern Regional Council, 1976); and U.S. General Accounting Office, *Administrative Weaknesses in St. Louis' Comprehensive Employment and Training Act Program* (March 2, 1979).

10. U.S. Office of Management and Budget, *Managing Federal Assistance in the 1980s* (Washington, D.C.: U.S. Government Printing Office, 1980), p. 20.
11. Interview with Richmond city official.
12. Interview with Richmond city official.
13. The four counties are New Kent, Charles City, Goochland, and Powhatan; they form an outer ring around Henrico and Chesterfield, the two counties surrounding and immediately adjacent to Richmond. Henrico and Chesterfield counties chose to form their own consortium.
14. U.S. Office of Management and Budget, *Managing Federal Assistance in the 1980s, Working Papers* (Washington, D.C.: U.S. Government Printing Office, 1980), Vol. 1, p. A-2-11.
15. Quoted by Rochelle L. Stanfield, "The Neighborhood Movement—What Price Success?" *National Journal,* November 18, 1978, p. 1863.
16. Douglas Yates, *The Ungovernable City: The Politics of Urban Problems and Policy Making* (Cambridge, Mass.: MIT Press, 1977).
17. See Donald Fisk, Herbert Kiesling, and Thomas Muller, *Private Provision of Public Services: An Overview* (Washington, D.C.: The Urban Institute, 1978).
18. See the author's "Regulating the Cities," *Publius* 11 (Winter 1981), forthcoming.

1981 (41:366-371)

RICHARD C. KEARNEY and ROBERT B. GAREY

American Federalism and the Management of Radioactive Wastes

The American system of federalism[1] has been a topic of philosophical, legal, and political debate since Madison, Hamilton, and Jay authored *The Federalist* papers almost 200 years ago. Although most observers have considered the federal bargain struck by the Founding Fathers a happy and productive one, there have been times when the viability of the system has been severely threatened—the Civil War being the most extreme example. In general, American federalism has been characterized by cooperative relationships between the governmental partners, highlighted by occasional conflictual behavior spawned within the political and economic context of the times. This paper will describe what appears to be the basis for a reshaping of the federal-state relationship through an examination of what has proved to be a particularly contentious policy area—radioactive waste management.

Federal Relations in the United States

While federalism has been "a much-used and much-abused term,"[2] it is possible to trace the historical development of various conceptualizations of the relationship between the national government and its constituent units. Many of the earlier scholars concentrated on the legalistic parameters of American federalism, especially the formal hierarchical division of power and authority between the national and state governments.[3] The term "dual federalism" was descriptive of the notion that both levels of government enjoyed their own constitutional domain, with powers not explicitly granted to the national government residing with the states through the Tenth Amendment. When conflict ensued from a clash of interests, the U.S. Supreme Court would serve as arbiter in separating functions into their proper position in the "layer-cake" of governmental authority.[4]

Although some scholars have continued to perceive the American federal system in terms of a separation of powers,[5] Supreme Court decisions and other developments beginning with the 1930s persuaded Grodzins, Elazar, and other observers to reject "layer-cake" federalism in favor of a model of "marble-cake" federalism, in which policy decisions are perceived as made and implemented through cooperative arrangements at various levels of government.[6] Government functions were not seen to be separate, but rather blended in a complex mosaic depending upon the policy area under consideration. This model of national-state relations has continued to dominate the literature of federalism, although various permutations of the "cooperative federalism" model have been described, including the "Creative Federalism" of the 1960s Great Society programs and the "New Federalism" of the early 1970s.[7]

Regardless of which descriptive rubric is employed, there is widespread consensus that the balance of federal power, albeit sometimes with slips and lurches, has gradually shifted in favor of the national government.[8] According to Reagan and Sanzone,[9] ". . . we have now arrived at the point in our constitutional history when no sphere of life is beyond the reach of the national government." In judicial terms, Article VI, Section 2 of the U.S. Constitution (the so-called Supremacy Clause) has outweighed the Tenth Amendment (the Reserve Clause) as a result of a consistent propensity of the Supreme Court since the Chief Justiceship of John Marshall to favor national supremacy over the rights of the states. As indicated earlier, however, there have been occasional setbacks to the steady accrual of power at the national level, even at the behest of the Supreme Court.[10] Moreover, in certain instances the states have held forth in open conflict against the national government, in effect invoking the doctrine of interposition by placing themselves between their citizens and what they perceive to be an unjust action by the national government.[11] Such state actions were targeted at national civil rights and desegregation policies during the early 1960s and, more recently, in the general policy area of energy, natural resources, and the environment.[12]

Is there a resurgence of the states, those subnational units which have been referred to as "political obstacles," "fallen arches," and "weak sisters" of the federal system? Perhaps not for all of the states, and certainly not in all policy activities, but a "new States' Rights"[13] has appeared in some contexts. In the Western portion of the United States, for example, federal-state conflict over the exploitation of coal, oil shale, and other energy resources,[14] federally imposed air quality standards, water projects,[15] and severance taxes has been intensifying, even though state demands for greater policy roles have not been entirely accommodated.[16] National-Western state conflicts also have developed over land-management and reclamation decisions, especially those involving surface mining reclamation.[17] Other states have clashed with the federal government over the regulation, storage, and disposal of hazardous chemical wastes[18] and various types of radioactive wastes. Most of these policy areas hold certain attributes in common: they are extraordinarily complex; they have been indecisively dealt with by the federal government; and they involve perceptions of inequity. The following discussion will focus on the management of radioactive wastes—the policy field which has perhaps bred more federal-state conflict than any other since the battle over desegregation in the South, and which, in conjunction with other energy and environmental policy areas, may force a reconceptualization of the system in terms of "contentious federalism."

Radioactive Wastes: Background

Radioactive waste is generated from the nuclear weapons program, commercial nuclear reactors, medical applications, and various research programs. While the greatest quantity of existing radioactive wastes has been produced by the military, the more toxic commercial nuclear wastes are accumulating rapidly. Generally, wastes may be categorized as high-level, low-level, and transuranic. High-level wastes are extremely toxic for as long as 400,000 years, as their radioisotopes have long half-lives. These constitute the most troublesome nuclear wastes because they must be isolated from people and the environment for such long periods of time (permanently, for all intents and purposes). Low-level wastes consist of radioactive clothing, tools, equipment, and other materials from the weapons program, commercial reactors, hospitals, and research facilities. They are of low toxicity and have short half-lives. Transuranic wastes are produced from the fabrication of plutonium for nuclear weapons and the reprocessing of spent nuclear fuel. These are not as toxic as high-level wastes, but they must be isolated for very long periods of time.

Waste management policy varies in accordance with the toxicity of the material and its source. Military high-level and transuranic wastes are the sole responsibility of the federal government; they are stored primarily at federal facilities in Washington (Hanford), South Carolina (Savannah River Plant), and Idaho (National Reactor Testing Station). Low-level military wastes are disposed of at these or other federal sites or at commercial disposal locations.[19] Considerable secrecy surrounds the disposition of defense related high-level wastes, which presently are treated as a matter related to the national defense and national security.

Low-level commercial radioactive wastes have been disposed of in several locations across the United States, including Barnwell, South Carolina; Maxey Flats, Kentucky; Sheffield, Illinois; Beatty, Nevada; Hanford, Washington; and West Valley, New York. At the present time, however, only three facilities are receiving low-level wastes: Barnwell, Beatty, and Hanford. High-level commercial wastes are produced in the form of spent nuclear reactor fuel from the 70 operating nuclear power plants in the United States and a number of plants overseas.[20] Until 1977 this spent fuel, which today is the primary responsibility of utility companies, was intended to be reprocessed to recover uranium and by-product plutonium; remaining wastes were to be solidified and stored at a federal repository.[21] President Carter deferred the commercial reprocessing option in April 1977, however.[22] Thus, decisions had to be made concerning what to do with the approximately 60 tons of spent fuel being generated and stored on site at nuclear power plants each year.

Radioactive Wastes and Early Federal-State Relations

Federal-state relations in the nuclear waste policy area were, until the mid-1970s, characterized by a hierarchical model of layer-cake federalism elegant in its simplicity. Under the Atomic Energy Act of 1954, the federal government dominated policy making in all phases of the commercial nuclear fuel cycle (from mining, development and fabrication of the fuel, and its use in reactors, to storage or disposal of spent fuel and low-level wastes). This act gave the Atomic Energy Commission (AEC) a dual mandate to promote development of the nuclear fuel industry and to regulate and license the industry to control radiation health and safety hazards. Under amendments to the act in 1959, the AEC was authorized, at its discretion, to enter into an "agreement" with any state to turn over to that state regulation of small quantities of radioactive materials, and wastes of low radioactive intensity.[23] State regulatory standards were required to be compatible with federal standards, and the AEC retained the right to abrogate its agreement with any state whose standards were not in compliance. The AEC maintained sole regulatory authority over the siting and operation of nuclear reactors and the storage and disposal of especially hazardous, highly radioactive materials such as spent fuel.

This simple model of nuclear waste policy making, in which federal regulatory actions precluded any actions by the states outside the narrow authority delegated to some in "agreements," was accepted by officials at all levels of government for two reasons. First, state legislatures were convinced that any regulatory efforts by them would be struck down as unconstitutional encroachments on federal prerogatives. This assumption was supported by the courts in the early 1970s, when the federal government successfully challenged some state programs designed to regulate the radiation health and safety effects of nuclear facilities. The landmark case was the 1971 *Northern States Power Company vs. Minnesota*[24] decision in which a federal circuit court affirmed that Minnesota could not force a commercial nuclear reactor to meet state radioactive pollution standards that were stricter than those set by the AEC. The decision was guided by the doctrine of "federal preemption," based on the constitutional principle (Article VI, Section 2) of the supremacy of federal law over state law when the two conflict.

Second, state governments had no technological reasons for challenging the federal government's management of nuclear wastes. Through the 1950s and early 1960s, state governments were concerned almost exlcusively with the benefits of nuclear production of electricity. Furthermore, the nuclear industry-federal government complex, which was responsible for waste management, considered the disposition of spent fuel and other wastes from commercial reactors and the weapons program to be a problem of much less eminence than that of increasing the production of electricity and nuclear warheads. It was believed that the waste problem would be easily dispensed with once the accelerating advance of nuclear technology brought the inevitable solution.[25] The lack of attention to the waste end of the nuclear fuel cycle by the AEC through the 1950s is described by the General Accounting Office (GAO) as being a product of "expediency" and of confidence in the certainty of a technological "fix" surfacing before the problem became critical:

> Little budget or management attention was given to addressing permanent disposal of the resulting nuclear waste (from the weapons program). The Atomic Energy Commission believed the disposal problem was technically solvable and could be addressed at some future time. As a result, decisions on nuclear waste management were based on short-term expediency rather than long-term management. Beginning in the late 1950's, the expansion of the commercial nuclear power industry prompted the Atomic Energy Commission to *begin* research programs to develop safe, long-term storage or permanent disposal methods.[26]

To the degree that high-level nuclear waste disposal was even an issue, the confidence within the AEC and the Congressional Joint Committee on Atomic Energy that a satisfactory technological solution to the problem would evolve from the federal research and development program was paralleled by an equal confidence among the general public. There was almost universal agreement in the United States through the early 1960s that the "tremendous success" of the Manhattan Project would carry over into commercial nuclear research, and that solving the problem of high-level waste disposal was only a matter of time.[27] Moreover, since the federal government alone could afford the costs of nuclear technology development, and had, since the 1940s, employed (along with corporations such as Union Carbide which did its research) most of the non-university nuclear scientists, state or local governments had little of the capital or human resources necessary to challenge the AEC's optimistic predictions that nuclear waste problems would be solved.

Conflict in the Federal System

As indicated earlier, the policy fields which today are characterized by federal-state conflicts tend to involve complex issues, indecisive federal responses, and perceptions of inequity. The complexity of radioactive waste management first became publicly evident during the environmental movement of the 1960s which began to challenge the assumption that American technology was capable of or could be trusted to find solutions to major environmental problems.[28] Reluctant industries had to be "forced" through a series of clean air, clean water, and other environmental protection acts during the early 1970s to begin confronting the "negative externalities" of industrial production which society had been sustaining.[29] After success with major legislation early in the decade, and perhaps capitalizing on the growing distrust of government in general after the war in Vietnam, the Pentagon Papers, and Watergate, environmentalists began to focus increasingly during the mid-1970s on the economics[30] and hazards of nuclear power and nuclear waste. The problem had entered what Downs refers to as the "issue-attention cycle" and reached the state of "alarmed discovery."[31]

Most important, the 1970s brought a series of revelations of technological setbacks and failures in the management of high-level nuclear waste which for the first time caused defections among some nuclear scientists from the profession's technological fix doctrine.[32] The AEC's experience at its Hanford, Washington storage facility for high-level military wastes, where "a total of 18 separate leaks have been detected in which 450,000 gallons of (radioactive) liquid entered the environment" since 1956[33] provided an important example of the inadequacy of either the storage technology itself or its implementation. Perhaps the greatest technological setback, however, was the AEC's failure to demonstrate that spent fuel and solidified high-level liquid wastes could be safely isolated and disposed of in underground salt deposits. An ill-fated AEC project near Lyons, Kansas, first intended as an "experimental" undertaking, but later upgraded to a "demonstration repository" in 1970,[34] was strongly criticized by the director of the Kansas Geological Survey and other scientists. Their main concerns were "that not enough was known about possible radiation damage to the salt, about waste cannister movement in the salt, about retrievability," and about the mathematical modelling of the process of heat transfer.[35] Moreover, previous mining ventures in the Lyons area had made the salt dome permeable. These objections, plus the apparent disregard for the opinions of the Kansas scientists by the AEC, "provided a basis for political opposition" by Kansas representatives, senators, and the governor, who sought to stop the project.

Criticism of the "legacy of secrecy" surrounding the atom since the early years of World War II began to mount. Many believed "that the public is not being informed of the real risks involved in nuclear energy and, in particular, of the hazards involved with nuclear waste management."[37] There were two primary sources of this criticism. First was the fact that the federal government in general—and the AEC in particular—had "made numerous decisions concerning the development and siting of nuclear facilities without the effective participation of the people whose lives will be affected."[38] Under the doctrine of federal preemption there appeared to be little role for public participation in nuclear waste decision making. A second source of the increasing hostility directed toward the federal government and the AEC concerned the issue of credibility. A technological fix for the disposal of high-level wastes has not been forthcoming, even though investigation of the Lyons site and others had commenced as early as 1963.[39]

In 1974, the AEC was abolished. Its regulatory functions were assumed by the Nuclear Regulatory Commission (NRC) and its nuclear research and development duties were placed within the Energy Research and Development Administration (ERDA). It soon became apparent that ERDA had learned little from its predecessor's past mistakes, as the agency began drilling operations to determine the suitability for nuclear waste disposal in Michigan without informing that state's elected officials or citizens.[40] Recently, the mounting criticism, abetted by the Freedom of Information Act, has forced the Department of Energy (DOE) (which absorbed ERDA) to be more open in its decision making. Nonetheless, the credibility problem remains because of continuing technological difficulties in storing or disposing of high-level wastes. The once promising Waste Isolation Pilot Project (WIPP), for example, in which high-level wastes would be vitrified, encased in concrete, and stored in New Mexico salt formations, was terminated with respect to spent fuel because of serious concern expressed by some scientists about the geological feasibility of the project, and because of subsequent political opposition in New Mexico and elsewhere.[41]

The continuing nonappearance of a demonstrated technological fix for the complex matter of the storage or disposal of spent fuel and other high-level wastes, combined with the aborted Lyons and WIPP projects and the absence of a coherent long-term national strategy for radioactive wastes, created the impression of a rudderless ship of state. The layer-cake model of federalism collapsed, becoming patently inaccurate in its description of federal-state relations in radioactive waste management. When federal goals *were* enunciated, frequently they seemed to conflict with earlier policy statements. Several congressional and executive branch actions in the second half of the 1970s seemed to contradict previous expressions of national intent that presumably were still in force. Specifically, two competing policy objectives emerged to bring about conflicts between and among levels of government in the nuclear waste policy field. These objectives were (1) the original goal of Congress and previous administrations to occupy the nuclear policy field exclusively, including the regulation of nuclear wastes (except for the limited authority over low-level wastes delegated to some states under agreements); and (2) the goal of consultation and concurrence with the states initiated by the Carter administration.

Vestiges of the layer-cake model survive through the 1954 Atomic Energy Act and the 1974 Energy Reorganization Act which grant the NRC broad regulatory authority over high-level nuclear waste facilities, including establishing general radioactivity standards consistent with guidelines of the Environmental Protection Agency and "licensing and regulating long-term high-level waste storage or disposal facilities."[42] From the federal authority of the 1954 and 1974 acts and other specific mandates, the U.S. Department of Energy is charged with "building and operating facilities for long-term storage and/or disposal of both Federal Program and Commercial high-level wastes. . . ," including spent fuel.[43] Regulation of the transportation of nuclear waste is delegated to the U.S. Department of Transportation (DOT) under the Hazardous Materials Transportation Act (HMTA) of 1976. The regulations necessary to implement this act, currently under review, will outline requirements for routing radioactive wastes and delineate advisory roles of state and local governments in devising routes. Meanwhile, the NRC, under general authority granted by the Atomic Energy Acts and the Energy Reorganization Act, has published interim rules on foreign and domestic spent fuel transportation, including planning and control of routes to avoid major urban areas and requirements for prior notification of all jurisdictions along the routes of each shipment.[44]

No formal state role, other than an advisory capacity for certain transportation decisions, is provided in these various activities concerning the shipment, storage, and disposal of high-level radioactive wastes. Nonetheless, the late 1970s witnessed a storm of state legislative actions to oversee, regulate, restrict, set conditions for, and even ban the shipment of highly toxic nuclear wastes, and the establishment of radioactive waste facilities within state borders.[45] The stumbling indecisiveness of the federal government had served as a cue for state and local government intervention.[46]

A formal state role, however, was granted in the consultation and concurrence policy announced by the Carter administration—in direct conflict with federal preemption. The problem with selecting and licensing high-level waste storage or disposal facilities by DOE and NRC, quite simply, is that the facilities must be located within *some* state. Few citizens or state officials are opposed to waste facilities *per se,* and most agree that they are necessary, but a majority in each state seem to be opposed to locating sites within their own jurisdictions. Similar opinions are held in opposition to the establishment of major waste transportation routes through local communities. An increasing proportion of the public apparently is becoming unconvinced that the radiation from wastes can be safely contained by the federal government.[47]

Because of this political reality, and a sense of urgency in the executive branch to "do something" about high-level waste (and especially spent fuel) before the administration's program to increase the country's reliance on nuclear power was derailed, President Carter commissioned the Interagency Review Group (IRG) of 14 federal agencies to make "recommendations for a long-term waste management policy and programs to implement it."[48] Along with several technological recommendations, the IRG, in its October 1978 draft report, "emphasized the 'cooperative federalism' approach and explicitly rejected federal preemption and state veto proposals"[49] in an effort to head off a potential constitutional crisis. To implement this plan for a federal-state partnership in nuclear waste policy making, the IRG recommended a strategy shown to be effective in other policy fields—a web of connections between federal agencies and the states. To bind the national and state governments together, the IRG suggested establishment of an Executive Planning Council whose membership would consist of several governors and representatives of DOE and other federal agencies. The Executive Planning Council's purpose would be to establish a set of procedures, always with the consultation and concurrence of the states, to be followed in choosing sites for waste facilities.

In mid-February 1980, President Carter issued an executive order implementing the IRG's proposal for an Executive Planning Council. Termed the "State Planning Council" (SPC), the organization is composed of 18 members including governors, state representatives, two local government officials, an American Indian representative, and the heads of the Departments of Energy, Interior, Transportation and the Environmental Protection Agency. It is chaired by Governor Richard Riley of South Carolina.[50] The executive order does not directly address the matter of a state veto power over SPC recommendations for the siting of waste facilities.

The policy of consultation and concurrence has floundered over the question of the right of a state to "veto" a federal decision to locate a waste facility within its borders, which is, of course, a logical extension of the right of non-concurrence. The right to concur without the right to refuse to concur clearly is a rather empty privilege. But the obvious consequence of a consultation and concurrence policy permitting state vetos would be to thwart any federal waste program which would require locating or licensing a new high-level waste storage or disposal facility inside one of the states. If states are to have the right not to concur with federal plans to establish commercial spent fuel or high-level liquid waste sites within their borders, and state or local governments are to have the right to restrict or reject the transportation of wastes through their jurisdictions, it is highly unlikely that any facilities will become operational or that the necessary transport routes will be allowed in many areas of the country. Thus, state veto power is not compatible with the notion of cooperative federalism, and it certainly is not in keeping with the doctrine of federal preemption. These simple political facts are summarized succinctly by the GAO as follows:

> Apparently, there are only a limited number of sites in a few States which are suitable for a permanent repository. Under the . . . DOE (consultation and concurrence) policy it appears that if each of the States were to object to any site selected in that State, none would be available for establishment of the repository. In such circumstances, if DOE is to exercise its authority to establish waste storage facilities, it would have to abandon its policy and choose a location without regard to the States' objection (as it is legally free to do).[51]

As indicated earlier, the lack of coherent federal policy direction in the exceedingly complex field of radioactive waste management provoked many state and local governments to take legislative actions designed to set forth their own role in the growing controversy over what to do with these wastes and where to do it. It is here that perceptions of inequity become important in explaining the aggressiveness of the sub-national governments.

The principal nuclear waste policy decisions affecting the states are (1) the siting of one or more "permanent" repositories for spent fuel and (2) the location of one or more "temporary" away-from-reactor storage ponds to hold spent fuel from overloaded on-site pools until permanent storage or disposal can be implemented. While the federal policy thrust seems to be in the direction of the states "sharing the burden" on a regional basis, national efforts in the management of radioactive wastes have been perceived by many state officials as inadequate, inept, overly secretive, and inequitable. With this lack of confidence has come a redefinition of the nuclear waste issue from a technical, scientific perspective to a more symbolic, political conception, with an increase in the level of conflict surrounding policy decisions.[52] Expansion of the nuclear waste issue to a larger public is not surprising, given the ambiguous nature of the matter, its lack of a clear policy precedent, and the long-term importance of impending federal policy decisions.[53]

As the radioactive waste policy discussions have shifted from the arcane terminology of the scientific community to the symbolic phraseology of the political arena,[54] three emotionally charged political symbols have become especially salient to interests which hope to induce or encourage state officials to resist proposed federal actions: alleged threats to the health and safety of citizens living in proximity to waste storage facilities and transportation routes; the labelling of those states considered most likely to host waste facilities as "nuclear waste garbage dumps"; and "states rights," or the right of states to determine for themselves whether or not they will participate in any future federal waste program.

Since the impacts of most proposed nuclear waste policies are characterized by highly concentrated costs and widely distributed benefits,[55] the thrust of the states' rights issue is to parry the perceived inequities of the health and safety and "garbage dump" concerns. The away-from-reactor (AFR) storage facilities previously favored by DOE and the Carter administration, for example, would be situated in one or two states,[56] but would possibly receive spent fuel shipments from the 25 other states which benefit from the electricity generated by nuclear reactors. Thus, host states would be compelled to bear an inequitable share of a "national solution to a national problem."

The federal quest for suitable locations for AFR facilities and permanent repositories for spent reactor fuel has resulted in a plethora of actions by state and local governments seeking to opt out of the process. As described above, legislative action has been the most frequent strategy. Other states, however, have managed to strike separate "deals" with the federal government. For example, when former DOE Secretary Schlesinger was negotiating with New Mexico officials to acquire the Carlsbad salt deposits for the Waste Isolation Pilot Project plan, he gave "assurance that the state would have veto power over the project";[57] similar assurances were delivered to the governor of Louisiana in 1978.[58] More recently, the state of New York signed a 17-year agreement with DOE for the solidification of some 600,000 gallons of high-level liquid wastes at the West Valley site, after which the wastes will be moved to a permanent, federally owned location. Meanwhile, New York has final veto power over other uses of the facility (such as for AFR storage).[59]

While the states as a whole have strongly asserted themselves in nuclear waste policy making, it is clear that they are not united in a common front, as the individual scrambling to avoid being tagged as a high-level waste "host state" indicates.[60] The major interstate focus of conflict has been on the management of low-level wastes, however. Until recently, low-level wastes were shipped by rail or highway to the six primary burial facilities mentioned earlier: West Valley, New York; Sheffield, Illinois; Maxey Flats, Kentucky; Hanford, Washington; Beatty, Nevada; and Barnwell, South Carolina. Because of a variety of problems at the various sites including leakages, public opposition, and corporate financial difficulties, West Valley closed down in 1971 (abandoning 600,000 gallons of radioactive wastes to the State of New York); Maxey Flats terminated operations soon thereafter; Sheffield closed its doors to waste in 1978; and during late 1979 the Beatty and Hanford facilities also closed down intermittently. About 50 percent of the nation's low-level commercial wastes are currently being buried at the South Carolina location.

These sites did not close because of any reduction in the amount of low-level wastes being generated in the United States. Indeed, the quantity is increasing rapidly, and is expected to approach 20 million 55-gallon drums by the year 2000.[61] Rather, the sites were shut down because of containment and other waste management problems, and because of growing public opposition to the apparent inequity of a few states storing what all states, at least to some extent, produce, and what all states in theory could store within their own jurisdictions. Resistance on the part of the governors of the three states which had operating facilities in mid-1979 (South Carolina, Nevada, and Washington), however, led to an agreement "to mutually ban any violator of laws, rules, or regulations concerning the packaging and/or transporting of low-level nuclear wastes."[62] In addition, the governor of South Carolina announced a more than 600 percent increase in disposal fees and a substantial curtailment in the quantity of wastes to be allowed into the Barnwell burial grounds. As inventories of low-level wastes began to accumulate at universities, hospitals, and commercial reactor facilities, the federal government was forced to open five of its own sites to low-level wastes.

Officials and citizens of the three low-level waste host states applied increasing pressure on Congress and the Executive Branch during 1980: Beatty was closed down on several occasions, the governor of South Carolina threatened to shut down the Chem Nuclear Systems site in Barnwell unless Congress passed a law calling for regional facilities for low-level wastes,[63] and the state of Washington passed an initiative which banned storage of out-of-state low-level wastes except from medical facilities and from states which agreed to develop their own disposal sites. Faced with the possible closure of many medical and research facilities which had limited on-site storage capacity, the federal government finally responded with legislation (HR 8378) in December 1980, which authorizes regional state compacts for the disposal of low-level wastes, and permits host states to refuse shipments from other states as of January 1, 1986.

The actions of the three low-level waste host states clearly were directed both at the federal government and at the states which had refused to take care of their own low-level radioactive wastes. The concept of regional sharing of the low-level waste burden was supported by the National Governor's Association and the National Conference of State Legislatures, who agreed that this was a matter which state government could deal with effectively, given the proper congressional delegation of authority. The low-level waste initiative of the host states is important, because it is one of the few such state actions which has been proactive in nature rather than obstructive.

Throughout the history of federal-state relations, ". . . the most spectacular examples of the power of the states . . . tend to reflect obstructionism."[64] Because of the constitutional foundations of the pact between the national government and the states, and the propensity of the federal courts since the late 1800s to favor the National Supremacy Clause over the powers "reserved to the states" under the Tenth Amendment, the states frequently have found themselves in the position of accepting national policy initiatives and directives in their entirety or rejecting them with an accompanying sacrifice of federal grant-in-aid dollars. When states have refused to drink at the federal trough or otherwise opposed national policy over some matter of "principle," they have appeared "obstructive" to many observers. Images of Southern governors standing on the schoolhouse steps in an effort to block federal desegregation policies come readily to mind. More recently, states have seemed obstructive in their opposition to the national 55-mile-per-hour speed limit; air and water pollution control standards; abortion, pornography, and school prayer decisions of the federal courts; the protection of defendants' rights; and other national policies set forth by Congress or the courts. Most observers of the American federal system would agree that such obstructionism is the major source of political leverage held by the states in view of the power of federal preemption of conflicting state and local policies. Furthermore, as often as not, obstructive tactics are effective, at least in the short term, especially where noncomplying subgovernments cannot be disciplined through a cutoff of federal funding.[65] In this sense, the doctrine of interposition "lives."[66]

While the states have been successful in working through their own executive, legislative, and judicial branches to thwart national policies with which they disagree, there is evidence that at least in some policy fields, such as low-level nuclear waste management and other energy and environment-related concerns, the states are acting in a progressive manner in confronting the problems which face them, and insisting on "the right to participate more actively in making national policies which more adequately promote and protect what they perceive to be in their interests."[67] It has been a major point of this article that such state activity seems to be most common in those policy areas characterized by complexity, federal indecisiveness, and questions of equity, with the management of radioactive wastes being the major case in point.

Conclusions

When the production of electricity from commercial nuclear reactors commenced during the 1950s, the promise of nearly unlimited benefits with minimal costs seemed almost too good to be true. Congress made the production of nuclear power a matter of high national priority, entrusting (until recently) both the production and almost exclusive regulation of the nuclear industry to a single federal agency, and targeting billions of dollars to entice private firms into splitting the atom for profit. Until recently, one major issue was often overlooked or given short shrift—the problem of how to dispose of the radioactive wastes which are a by-product of nuclear energy. Today, it is becoming increasingly apparent that the radioactive waste problem is the potential Achilles heel of the entire nuclear industry. Furthermore, the issue has brought about a period of intense conflict in federal relations in the United States. Radioactive waste management has been in a constant state of policy flux for the past several years, making it difficult to predict the final resolution of the waste problem, if indeed there ever will be one. Several major policy issues remain unresolved, however, and undoubtedly will be addressed within the next few years by the Reagan administration.

1. The low-level waste problem. This may have been eased, at least in the short term, by congressional enactment of the bill permitting regional interstate pacts for the burial of commercial wastes. Negotiations already have begun in several regions of the country.[68] The only apparent unresolved difficulty, assuming additional states agree to serve as regional hosts for low-level wastes,[69] involves the disposition of defense and other military low-level wastes.

2. Away-from-reactor storage of spent fuel. Although the immediacy of the problem is subject to debate,[70] it is clear that unless new storage space is provided somewhere within the next few years, reactor shutdowns will occur. A proposal which has enjoyed support in Congress entails DOE taking title to spent fuel after payment of a fee to utilities, and storing the fuel assemblies at one or more regional facilities[71] which would be built by DOE or purchased as an existing site. An alternative policy would be to retain spent fuel at reactor sites and permit the construction of additional storage space where required. This is the position favored by many of the states and most environmental groups, as the *status quo* would be maintained while potential transportation problems would be postponed.

3. Reprocessing of spent fuel. If the reprocessing option is reinstated, there will be some mitigation of the need for interim storage of spent fuel at AFR sites, although at least one such facility might still be procured.[72]

4. Long-term (permanent) storage or disposal of high-level wastes. The question of how to resolve the back end of the nuclear fuel cycle has generated an almost incredible variety of policy suggestions, from rocketing the wastes toward the sun to burial at sea or on some isolated island.[73] A consensus seems to be developing in Congress that demonstration projects for the geologic disposal of high-level wastes should be undertaken and, depending upon the results, a final "technological fix" should be selected.[74]

Other related policy issues must also be resolved, including (1) the disposal or storage of uranium mill tailings,[75] (2) whether or not defense and commercial wastes should be dealt with as one, (3) the need for federal licensing of waste facilities, and (4) the retrievability of buried spent fuel. According to a transition team report, the Reagan administration favors reprocessing, demonstration projects to support selection of a long-term storage strategy for high-level wastes, the policy separation of defense and commercial wastes, and no licensing for defense waste facilities. Other positions have not as yet been clarified, including the matter of AFR facilities as interim storage sites.

The American federal system has been remarkably flexible in adapting to changing social, economic, and technological conditions; however, the choices confronting the nation and its subgovernments have become exceedingly complex, "more numerous . . . more interrelated than ever before in history."[76] In some cases, the responses of the national government have not been particularly commendable, farsighted, or decisive. In policy areas which are characterized by active public interest, the clash of political symbols, and salient questions of equity, there has been a reassertion of state concern and interest to the point where some have perceived the development of a new states' rights. Deil Wright, among others, has observed this phenomenon, noting that the state legislatures, for instance, "now seem to be making their influence felt more vigorously in (the federal system) than at any time in the past century," by becoming increasingly assertive and competitive with the federal government.[77]

There have been other such periods in the history of American federalism. All have involved conflict between the national government and its subgovernments. All have ultimately been resolved in favor of the federal government, as it has centralized its powers throughout the economic and political arenas. Indeed, that may also be the final outcome of this present "divided and contentious time"[78] in federal-state relations.

Recently, however, certain states have emerged from policy conflicts with the national government savoring the taste of victory. Wyoming and Utah led the way in rejecting federal supremacy in mined land reclamation;[79] Colorado and Montana have increased their control over water policy'[80] and more than half of the states have opted out of any significant national role in resolving the problems of radioactive waste. In these and other policy areas it is clear that any conception of a hierarchical model of federalism "stumbles on the rock of local autonomy,"[81] and the conventional operating model of cooperative federal-state relations is being supplanted by the rise of contentious federalism.

Undeniably, the management of high-level radioactive wastes, like other energy and environment-related policies, requires coordination at the national level. The consultation and concurrence policy of the Carter administration recognized this basic fact, while also granting some voice to the states. But the critical question of state veto rights has not been answered satisfactorily.[82] Until congressional legislation contends with this issue head-on, federal-state conflict over the management of radioactive wastes will continue unabated.

Notes

1. "Federalism" is treated in this paper primarily in terms of the relationships between the national government and the states. State-local and interstate relations receive due attention, but "all the permutations and combinations of relations among the units of government," which Wright labels as "intergovernmental relations" are not the major focus. For discussions defining federalism and intergovernmental relations see Deil S. Wright, *Understanding Intergovernmental Relations* (North Scituate, Mass., 1978), pp. 16-19; Parris N. Glendening and Mavis Mann Reeves, *Pragmatic Federalism* (Pacific Palisades, Calif.: Palisades Publishers, 1977), pp. 6-8; Roxann Rothman, "The Ambiguity of American Federal Theory," *Publius* (Summer 1978), pp. 103-122.
2. Wright, p. 19.
3. See Edward S. Corwin, *National Supremacy* (New York: Henry Holt and Co., 1913).
4. The role of the court as "umpire" of the federal system was established in the famous case of *Marbury v. Madison* (Cranch 137 [1803]) and based on Article VI of the Constitution.
5. See K. C. Wheare, *Federal Government* (3rd ed.) (New York: Oxford University Press, 1953); William H. Riker, *Federalism* (Boston: Little, Brown, 1964).
6. Morton Grodzins, "The Federal System," in *Goals for Americans* (Englewood Cliffs, N.J.: Prentice-Hall, 1960), pp. 265-282; Daniel J. Elazar, *American Federalism: A View from the States* (2nd ed.) (New York: Crowell, 1972).
7. "Creative Federalism" of the Lyndon B. Johnson years in the White House stressed new, direct relationships between the national government and the state and local governments and nongovernmental entities.

   The "New Federalism" of the Nixon years emphasized a shift in program and spending authority toward the subnational governments.
8. See James L. Sundquist, *Making Federalism Work* (Washington, D.C.: The Brookings Institution, 1969).
9. See Michael D. Reagan and John G. Sanzone, *The New Federalism* (2nd ed.) (New York: Oxford University Press, 1981); Glendening and Reeves, pp. 98-100.
10. The major anomalous court decision is *National League of Cities v. Usery* (96 U.S. Supreme Court 2465; 1976) in which the Supreme Court held that Congress could not extend minimum wages, maximum hour and overtime pay provisions to state and local employees under 1974 amendments to the Fair Labor Standards Act because they would impair the effective functioning of these government systems. (But see *Maryland v. Wirtz* 1392, U.S. 183 [1968].) Legislative action favoring states' rights includes Section 14(b) of Taft-Hartley,

which permits state prohibition of certain security arrangements to preempt federal legislation.

11. The concept of interposition originally was set forth in the United States by Jefferson and Madison in the Kentucky and Virginia Resolutions of 1799, in opposition to the Alien and Sedition Acts. While the doctrine usually is associated with John C. Calhoun and the Southern states' opposition to abolition measures, it has been invoked more frequently by non-southern states, in matters unrelated to slavery or other racial issues. See Glendening and Reeves, pp. 110-112.
12. Timothy Hall, Irvin L. White, and Steven C. Ballard, "Western States and National Energy Policy," *American Behavioral Scientist* 22 (Nov./Dec. 1978), pp. 191-212.
13. *Idem.*
14. *Ibid.,* p. 198; James L. Regens, "Energy Development, Environmental Protection, and Public Policy," *American Behavioral Scientist* 22 (Nov./Dec. 1978), pp. 175-190.
15. Richard H. Leach, "Federalism: A Battery of Questions," *Publius The Federal Polity* 3 (Fall 1973), pp. 32-37; Larry E. Moss, "Federal Water Development: Imperial Edict or Federal-State Partnership?" *Publius* 9 (Winter 1979), pp. 127-140.
16. Hall, White, and Ballard, pp. 204-206.
17. Donald C. Menzel and Terry D. Edgemon, "The Struggle to Implement a National Surface Mining Policy," *Publius* 10 (Winter 1980), pp. 81-91.
18. Rae Tyson, "The Intergovernmental Cleanup at Love Canal: A First Crack at 'The Sleeping Giant of the Decade,' " *Publius* 10 (Winter 1980), pp. 101-109.
19. Because low-level wastes have relatively short-lived periods of radioactivity, they can be safely disposed of by being sealed in protective containers and buried in the ground at federal and state approved and monitored sites.
20. High-level wastes are defined by NRC as those generated in the processing of spent fuel; however, for the purposes of this paper high-level waste is defined to include unreprocessed spent fuel. Foreign spent fuel is being shipped to the U.S. through Portsmouth, Virginia to the Savannah River Plant as a result of President Eisenhower's "Atoms for Peace" program and President Carter's nonproliferation policy. Approximately 10,000 pounds of foreign spent fuel enter the U.S. annually through Portsmouth from West Germany, Sweden, France, Great Britain, and other nations. Some of this spent fuel is reprocessed at Savannah River Plant.
21. See Alfred R. Light, "The Hidden Dimension of the National Energy Plan: Executive Policy Direction in Nuclear Waste Management," *Publius* 9 (Winter 1979), pp. 172-175.
22. The Carter reprocessing moratorium continued a policy originally set forth by President Ford in 1976. Nonproliferation and the prevention of plutonium from being acquired by bomb-making terrorists were given as the primary reasons for deferral. It should be noted that the reprocessing of spent fuel results in a reduction of high-level wastes, but produces a large volume of transuranic wastes with equally long-lasting and dangerous radioactivity.
23. There are approximately 25 "agreement" states.

24. *Northern States Power Co. v. Minnesota,* 447 F. 2nd 1143 (1971). See Laurence H. Tribe, "California Declines the Nuclear Gamble: Is Such a State Choice Preempted?" *Ecology Law Quarterly* 7 (1979), pp. 679-729. Several recent federal district court decisions have affirmed federal preemption in the nuclear waste field. For example, a court held that a California statute providing that no nuclear power plant be certified until a finding by a state commission that a federally approved technology for the disposal of high-level wastes exists, was declared unconstitutional (*Pacific Legal Foundation v. State Energy Resources Conservation and Development Commission,* 472 F. Supp. 191 (S.D. Cal 1979). Also Washington State's referendum banning out-of-state waste shipments was overturned by a federal district court in June 1981.
25. Daniel S. Metlay, "History and Interpretation of Radioactive Waste Management in the United States," in William P. Bishop, *et al., Essays on Issues Relevant to the Regulation of Radioactive Waste Management* NUREG-0412 (Washington, D.C.: U.S. Nuclear Regulatory Commission, 1978), p. 10.
26. U.S. General Accounting Office, *The Nation's Nuclear Waste: Proposals for Organization and Siting* EMD 79-77 (Washington, D.C., 1979), pp. 3-4 (emphasis added).
27. R. Freeman, "Aspects of Public Policy for Innovation," in G. Boyle, *et al.* (ed.), *The Politics of Technology* (New York: Longmans, 1978).
28. For example, see Jacques Ellul, *The Technological Society* (New York: Knopf, 1964).
29. Barry Commoner, "Social Aspects of the Environmental Crisis," in Boyle, *et al., The Politics of Technology.*
30. For a look at "how an elaborate structure of artificial incentives has buttressed this ailing industry from the world of harsh economic realities," see Gregory A. Daneke, "The Political Economy of Nuclear Development," *Policy Studies Journal* (Autumn 1978), pp. 84-89.
31. Anthony Downs, "Up and Down with Ecology: The Issue-Attention Cycle," *The Public Interest* 28 (Summer 1972). Downs contends that a public environmental crisis does not reflect a suddenly changed condition so much as it reflects the operation of a systematic cycle of increased public attention to an ongoing situation. The issue-attention cycle has five stages through which issues may pass: the pre-problem stage, alarmed discovery and euphoric enthusiasm, realization of the cost of significant progress, gradual decline of intense public interest, and the post-problem stage.
32. See, for example, Steven Harwood, Kenneth May, Marvin Resnikoff, Barbara Schlenger, and Pam Tanes, *Decommissioning Nuclear Reactors* (Buffalo: New York Public Interest Research Group, 1976); "Nuclear Power: A Declaration (To the President and Congress of the United States) by members of the American Technical Community" (Cambridge, Mass.: Union of Concerned Scientists, August 6, 1975).
33. Metlay, "History and Interpretation of Radioactive Waste Management." According to Willrich and Lester, "Since the beginning of operations at the Hanford site, up to 43 million curies of beta emitters and 192 kilograms of plutonium have been carried into the soil in 140 billion gallons of liquid effluents." Additional leaks have occurred at the federal government's Savannah

River Plant, some of which posed a threat to local sources of drinking water. See Mason Willrich and Richard K. Lester, *Radioactive Waste Management* (New York: The Free Press, 1977), pp. 17-18.

34. Metlay, "History and Interpretation of Radioactive Waste Management," pp. 4-6.
35. *Idem.* For further discussion of the growing scientific doubts about the feasibility of geological waste disposal, see Luther Carter, "Nuclear Waste: The Science of Waste Disposal Seen as Weak," *Science* 200 (June 9, 1978), pp. 1135-1137; and Lorna Salzman, "The Five Thousand Centuries of Nuclear Garbage," *Business and Society Review* 26 (Summer 1978), pp. 9-15.
36. Metlay, pp. 4-6.
37. Dorothy Zinberg, "The Public and Nuclear Waste Management," *Bulletin of the Atomic Scientists* (January 1979), pp. 34-39. For other criticisms of AEC secrecy, see Walter C. Patterson, *Nuclear Power* (London: Penguin Books, 1976); and H. Peter Metzger, *The Atomic Establishment* (New York: Simon and Schuster, 1972).
38. Richard A. Watson, "Goals for Nuclear Waste Management," in Bishop, *et al., Essays on Issues Relevant to the Regulation of Radioactive Waste Management,* p. 86.
39. Ida R. Hoos, "The Credibility Issue," in Bishop, *et al., Essays on Issues Relevant to the Regulation of Radioactive Waste Management,* pp. 20-30.
40. For a description of the "blundering insensitivity" of ERDA (later DOE), see John Abbots, "Radioactive Waste: A Technical Solution?" *Bulletin of the Atomic Scientists* 35 (October 1979), pp. 12-18.
41. WIPP was planned in the mid-1970s as an experiment involving transuranic military wastes, high-level military wastes, and spent fuel from commercial reactors. On the recommendation of the IRG report, however, and as a result of growing public opposition by New Mexicans, the program is scheduled to proceed with military wastes only; this does not require licensing by the NRC. See U.S. General Accounting Office, *The Nation's Nuclear Waste: Proposals for Organizing and Siting.*
42. U.S. General Accounting Office, *The Nation's Nuclear Waste: Proposals for Organizing and Siting.*
43. *Idem.*
44. The NRC has no authority over the transportation, storage, or disposal of defense-related wastes; see Light, "The Hidden Dimension of the National Energy Plan," p. 171.
45. State and local government actions include rejecting consideration for federal storage or disposal sites within their jurisdictions, banning the transportation of nuclear wastes, and requiring transport or siting permits. For summaries of state and local actions, see the U.S. Nuclear Regulatory Commission, Office of State Programs, "Information Report on State Legislation" (Washington, D.C.: U.S. Nuclear Regulatory Commission, 1977-1980), and Robert B. Garey and Richard C. Kearney, "State Policies on Nuclear Waste Transportation and Storage," *Texas Business Review* (Sept./Oct. 1980), pp. 249-255.
46. While this article focuses on federal-state conflicts in the nuclear waste field, it should be noted that many local governments have, through legislative actions,

interposed themselves between the national government and the health and safety concerns of their citizens. For example, at least 15 counties and municipalities have enacted ordinances restricting the routing of radioactive waste shipments through their jurisdictions. When the HMTA regulations are adopted, these actions may be ruled "inconsistent" and preempted in a DOT hearing or by a federal court. Meanwhile, unless state or local provisions are held to restrict interstate commerce, they operate effectively in restricting transport. (For an example of model local legislation, see New York City Health Codes, Art. 175, Sec. 175.111.) One interesting possibility is the scenario of various local governments opting out as host jurisdictions for nuclear facilities *within* an individual state. See Laura M. Lake, *Environmental Mediation: The Search for Consensus* (Boulder: Westview Press, 1980), p. 9.

47. See Dorothy Zinberg, "The Public and Nuclear Waste Management," *Bulletin of the Atomic Scientists* (January 1979), pp. 34-39.
48. *Report to the President by the Interagency Review Group on Nuclear Waste Management October 1978 Draft* (Springfield, Va.: National Technical Information Service, 1978).
49. Light, "The Hidden Dimension of the National Energy Plan," p. 183.
50. It should be noted that the election of President Ronald Reagan could eliminate the SPC from any potential influence over radioactive waste policy decisions. A Reagan transition team has recommended that Democratic Governor Riley be removed from the chairmanship of the SPC, whose mandate expires in October 1981. It is also considered likely that the SPC charter will be allowed to expire on the same date.
51. Of the numerous bills introduced in Congress during 1980, none which proceeded through the committee process granted states an absolute veto power over facility siting. The issue of state authority in nuclear waste decisions has been a major stumbling block to legislative compromise, however. Toward the end of the 1980-81 lame duck session, the controversy appeared to focus on whether one or both Houses of Congress should be required to affirm any state's objections to housing a permanent waste repository, and whether or not consultation and concurrence should also apply to the siting of an away-from-reactor facility.
52. See E. E. Schattschneider, *The Semi-Sovereign People* (New York: Holt, Rinehart and Winston, 1960), for a discussion on publicity and problem redefinition as critical aspects of changing the level of conflict.
53. See Roger W. Cobb and Charles D. Elder, *Participation in American Politics: The Dynamics of Agenda-Building* (Baltimore: Johns Hopkins Press, 1972), pp. 110-129.
54. See Murray Edelman, *Politics as Symbolic Action* (Chicago: Markham Publishing Co., 1971).
55. See James Q. Wilson, "The Politics of Regulation," in James W. McKie (ed.), *Social Responsibility and the Business Predicament* (Washington, D.C.: The Brookings Institution, 1974), pp. 135-168. Other environmental protection policies impose concentrated costs and diffused benefits including the Water Quality Act of 1965, the Clean Water Restoration Act of 1966, and the Water Quality Improvement Act of 1970. See Wilson, pp. 143-144 for other examples.

56. The most frequently mentioned sites are Barnwell, S.C., West Valley, N.Y., and Morris, Illinois.
57. DOE also assured New Mexico and New York that waste repositories would not be sited there unless the states concurred.
58. R. F. Keller, acting comptroller general of the U.S., letter to John D. Dingell, chairman, Subcommittee on Energy and Power, House of Representatives, U.S. Congress, June 19, 1978.
59. Kristine Moe, "West Valley's High-Level Nuclear Waste to be Gone by 1977, Larocca Says," *Buffalo Courier-Express* (Nov. 13, 1980), p. 3.
60. According to Elazar (*American Federalism,* p. 34), ". . . few issues confronting the American people have so great an impact on the states as to unite their people in a common front . . . in most cases, issues will lead to conflicts dividing the states as well as the Nation."
61. See Luther Carter, "The Radioactive Waste Inventory," *Science* (1978).
62. Testimony of Governor Richard Riley of South Carolina before the House Subcommittee on Energy and Production, November 7, 1979.
63. "Riley Hints at Closing Nuke Dump," *The State* (Columbia, S.C., December 12, 1980), Section D, pp. 1, 4.
64. Elazar, p. 60.
65. Sundquist, p. 12.
66. Glendening and Reeves, p. 111.
67. Hall, White, and Ballard, p. 192. It should further be noted that, "as likely as not the (obstructive) power of the state is used to advance projects commonly considered in the public interest as against what might be called federal shortsightedness" (see Elazar, p. 60).
68. For instance, representatives of nine states held discussions in South Carolina during January 1981, and several western states may finalize a regional pact by the end of 1982. See *Nuclear Waste News* (Feb. 12, 1981), p. 3.
69. This should not be a foregone conclusion, as substantial political hurdles must be surmounted in convincing a local government to accept low-level waste disposal in its jurisdiction.
70. See, for example, General Accounting Office, *Federal Facilities for Storing Spent Nuclear Fuel—Are They Needed?* GAO (June 27, 1979).
71. This was the basic intent of the proposed Spent Fuel Act of 1979 and subsequently proposed legislation in 1980.
72. Reprocessing removes usable plutonium and uranium from spent reactor fuel, leaving a residue of high-level liquid wastes. Although the West Valley reprocessing facility operated for a short time, at present no other commercial reprocessing of spent fuel is underway. The Barnwell Nuclear Fuels Plant (BNFP) in Barnwell, S.C. was originally intended for use as a massive reprocessing center, and the Reagan Administration Nuclear Energy Transition Team proposed that BNFP fulfill its initial purpose through a revival of the reprocessing strategy. It is considered unlikely that BNFP will be purchased by DOE, however; the asking price of the owners and expenditures for completion of the facility seem prohibitive during a year of across-the-board cutbacks. Furthermore, President Reagan has professed a desire for the private sector to manage reprocessing.
73. See, for example, Guna S. Selvadoray, Mark K. Goldstein, and Robert N.

Anderson, "Finding a Site to Store Spent Fuel in the Pacific Basin," *Nuclear Engineering International* (September 1979), pp. 44-47. *Radioactive Waste Technology Newsletter* (August 1980), p. 2, reports that the National Aeronautics and Space Administration and DOE have contracted with Boeing to study the concept of rocketing nuclear waste into space.

74. Demonstration projects by DOE already have begun in New Mexico (under the WIPP program, with defense waste) and on the Hanford Reservation in Washington. See "Legislation," *Nuclear News* (January 1981), pp. 94-95.
75. See William Sweet, "Unresolved: The Front End of Nuclear Waste Disposal," *Bulletin of Atomic Scientists* (May 1979), pp. 44-48.
76. Frederick C. Mosher, "The Changing Responsibility and Tactics of the Federal Government," *Public Administration Review* (November/December 1980), p. 545.
77. Wright, pp. 233-237.
78. Kai Lee, "Energy Politics and Energy Policies," *Public Administration Review* (January/February 1976), p. 115.
79. Hall, White, and Ballard, pp. 204-205.
80. *Ibid.,* p. 206.
81. Sundquist, p. 117.
82. Interestingly, a quite similar problem has characterized nuclear facility siting decisions in the federal system of West Germany. During May 1979, the government of the state of Lower Saxony vetoed national government plans to construct a reprocessing and waste disposal facility at the town of Gorleben. Two years earlier, court decisions in two other West German states held that construction on controversial new nuclear power plants could not continue until it was decided what would be done with the radioactive wastes.

1982 (42:14-24)

PART VI

U.S. Federalism and IGR Bibliography: *PAR* Volumes 1-43

U.S. Federalism and IGR Bibliography: *PAR* Volumes 1-43

Vieg, John Albert, "Working Relationships in Governmental Agricultural Programs," 1: 141-148.

Hovde, B. J., "The Local Housing Authority," 1:167-175.

Ellis, William J., "The Case for State-Local Administration," 1:233-239.

Hodson, William, "The Case for Retaining the Federal W.P.A.," 1:239-241.

Stewart, Frank M. and Ronald M. Ketcham, "Intergovernmental Contracts in California,' 1:242-248.

Durisch, Lawrence L., "Local Government and the T.V.A. Program," 1:326-334.

Anderson, William, "Local Government Units and Areas," 1:408-409.

Uhl, Raymond, "Administrative Regions in Virginia," 2:50-53.

Bane, Frank, "Cooperatiave Government in Wartime," 2:95-103.

May, Samuel C. and Robert E. Ward, "Coordinating Defense Activities in a Metropolitan Region," 2:104-112.

Englebert, Ernest and Kenneth Wernimont, "Administrative Aspects of the Federal-State Legislative Relationship," 2:126-140.

Reed, Thomas H., "Home Rule for Whom?" 2:171-175.

Stassen, Harold E., "E Pluribus Unum," 2:187-194.

Parkman, Henry, Jr., "The Local Rationing Board in Massachusetts," 2:195-198.

Field, Oliver P. and John E. Stoner, "The Charlestown Coordinator," 3:42-50.

Finer, Herman, "The Case for Local Self Government," 3:51-58.

Staples, Abram P., "Federal-State Regulation of Utilities," 3:168-171.

Watson, George H., "State Participation in Gasoline Rationing," 3:213-222.

Morrow, Glenn D., "Supervision of County Debts in Kentucky," 3:335-352.

Rohrlich, George F., "Consolidation of Unemployment Insurance and the Problem of Centralization," 4:43-50.

Dobbins, W. and R. F. Leonard, "Community Planning in North Alabama," 4:220-225.

Weidner, Edward W., "State Supervision of Local Government in Minnesota," 4:226-233.

Chatters, Carl H., "Intergovernmental Fiscal Relations," 4:364-367.

Gill, Corrington, "Federal-State-City Cooperation in Congested Production Areas," 5:28-33.

Friedrich, Carl J., *et al.*, "Planning for the Greater Boston Metropolitan Area," 5:113-116.

Bauer, John, "Metropolitan Utility Supply and Organization," 5:127-134.

Luginbuhl, Martha, "Local Responsibility for Health Service," 6:30-41.

Caldwell, Lynton K., "Perfecting State Administration: 1940-1954," 7:25-36.

Kurtz, Maxine, "The Tri-County Regional Planning Commission," 7:113-122.

Lancaster, Lane W., "Stimulating Local Government," 7:277-281.
Reed, Thomas H., "Progress in Metropolitan Integration," 9:1-10.
Lutz, Edward A., "Intergovernmental Relations at the Grass Roots," 9:119-125.
Gallagher, Hubert R., "State Reorganization Surveys," 9:252-256.
Stevenson, Adlai E., "Reorganization from the State Point of View," 10:1-6.
Ader, Emile B., "State Budgetary Controls of Federal Grants-in-Aid," 10:87-92.
Egger, Rowland, "In One Consent," 10:262-269.
Moore, Lyman S., "How Well Are States and Cities Prepared for the Emergency?" 11:81-87.
Crook, Stanley K., "The Pacific Coast Board of Inter-Governmental Relations," 11:103-108.
Public Administration Clearing House, "Intergovernmental Relationships and Highways," 12:67.
Gant, George F., "The Southern Regional Education Program," 12:106-111.
Redfield, Charles E. and Edward A. Lutz, "Get the Folks out of the Mud!" 12:126-131.
Jones, Victor, "Metropolitan Studies," 13:57-63.
Davidson, C. Girard, "Integration of Conflicting Regional Programs," 13:129-133.
Conference Report (Rosalind G. Baldwin, rapporteur), "Intergovernmental Relations," 14:149-151.
Cope, O. K. and M. D. Tarshes, "Consolidation of City-County Health Functions in San Diego," 14:170-179.
Grant, Daniel R., "Federal-Municipal Relationships and Metropolitan Integration," 14: 259-267.
Durisch, Lawrence L. and Robert E. Lowry, "State Watershed Policy and Administration in Tennessee," 15:17-20.
Schaeffer, Wendell G., "Miami Looks at the Problems of Metropolitan Governments," 15:35-38.
Havard, William C. and Bruce B. Mason, "Local Participation in Solving a Water Problem," 15:210-217.
Bain, Chester W., "Annexation: Virginia's Not-so-Judicial System," 15:251-262.
Farmer, Hallie, "The Governments of All Our States," 15:283-286.
Jones, Victor, "Six Functions in Search of a Government," 16:52-59.
Gaus, John M., "Federalism and Intergovernmental Relations," 16:102-109.
Craine, Lyle E., "Natural Resources and Government," 16:212-223.
Casella, William N., Jr., "County Government in Transition," 16:223-231.
Zimmer, Basil G. and Amos H. Hawley, "Approaches to the Solutions of Fringe Problems: Preferences of Residents in the Flint Metropolitan Area," 16:258-268.
Jamison, Judith Norvell and Richard Bigger, "Metropolitan Coordination in Los Angeles," 17:164-169.
Williams, G. Mennen, "Federal-State Relations," 17:225-230.
Moseley, John D., "The States: A Citizen Concern," 17:272-278.
Chute, Charlton F., "The Honolulu Metropolitan Area: A Challenge to Traditional Thinking," 18:7-13.
Morlan, Robert L., "Toward City-School District Rapprochment," 18:113-117.
Woodbury, Coleman, "Great Cities, Great Problems, Great Possibilities," 18:332-340.
Martin, James W., "Administrative Dangers in the Enlarged Highway Program," 19: 164-172.
Birkhead, Guthrie S., "Extending States Boundaries—but not Horizons," 19:265-268.
Shore, William B., "Cooperation Grows Among Government Units," 19:279-282.
Martin, James W., "Federal-State Highway Relations," 20:121.
Bosworth, Karl A. "Light in the Shadows of the Domes," 20:161-165.
Jacob, Herbert, "By Land or By C," 20:169-171.
Long, Norton E., "Sayre and Kaufman's New York: Competition Without Chaos," 21: 23-40.

Shore, William B., "New Ripples in Federalism's Marble Cake: States, U.S. Eye Metropolitan Problems," 21:45-52.

Cornog, Geoffrey Y., "Facilitating Intergovernmental Communication," 21:119.

Adrian, Charles R., "Metropology: Folklore and Field Research," 21:148-157.

Press, Charles, "Research on the Metropolis: Foundation for Conservation," 22:88-95.

Wegner, Robert L., "The Metropolitan Data Center Projects," 22:145-146.

Watson, George H., "More and More Local Finance," 22:153-157.

Gittell, Marilyn, "Metropolitan Mayor: Dead End," 23:20-24.

Grossman, Howard J. and Robert A. Cox, "Coordination: Teamwork in a Small Community," 23:35-39.

Keenan, Boyd R., "The Midwest's CIC: Experiment in Regional Cooperation," 23:40-44.

Coke, James G., "Stability and Change: Local Government in the Philadelphia Metropolitan Area," 23:186-191.

Kammerer, Gladys M., "The Politics of Metropolis: Still a Frontier," 23:240-246.

Musicus, Milton, "Reappraising Reorganization," 24:107-112.

Ostrom, Vincent, "The American Public Enterprise System," 24:136-137.

Campbell, Alan K., and Seymour Sacks, "Administering the Spread City," 24:141-152.

Warren, Robert, "Political Form and Metropolitan Reform," 24:180-187.

Fox, Irving K., "New Horizons in Water Resources Administration," 25:61-69.

Wright, Deil S., "The Advisory Commission on Intergovernmental Relations: Unique Features and Policy Orientation," 25:193-202.

Goldbach, John, "Local Formation Commissions: California's Struggle Over Municipal Incorporations," 25:213-220.

Haefele, Edwin T., "Urban Transport: Who Decides?" 25:234-239.

Price, Reginald C., "Some Decisions in the State's Development of California's Waters During the 1960s," 25:290-296.

Banovetz, James M., "Metropolitan Studies: An Appraisal," 25:297-301.

Elazar, Daniel J., "The Continuing Study of the Partnership," 26:56-58.

Aleshire, Robert A., "The Metropolitan Desk: A New Technique in Program, Teamwork," 26:87-95.

Beckman, Norman, "How Metropolitan Are Federal and State Policies?" 26:96-106.

Woodworth, James R., "Newer Grant-in-Aid Concepts: The Case of Food and Drug Programs," 26:107-109.

Seidman, Harold, "Coordination of Federal Grant-in-Aid Programs," 26:330-333.

Scott, Stanley, "The Metropolitan Scene: Some Recent Views," 26:334-343.

Ransone, Coleman B., Jr., "Scholarly Revolt in Dullsville: New Approaches to the Study of State Government," 26:343-352.

Cho, Yong H., "The Effect of Local Governmental Systems on Local Policy Outcomes in the United States," 27:31-38.

Kee, Woo Sik, "State and Local Fiscal Systems and Municipal Expenditures," 27:39-41.

Gross, Bertram M., "The Administration of Economic Development Planning: Principles and Fallacies," 27:51-56.

Walker, David B., "State and Local Manpower: A Challenge to Creative Federalism," 27:56-59.

Stover, Carl F., "Industry, Technology, and Metropolitan Problems," 27:112-117.

Jones, Roger W., "Developments in Goverment Manpower: A Federal Perspective," 27:134-141.

Muskie, Edmund S., "Manpower: The Achilles Heel of Creative Federalism," 27:193-194.

Ink, Dwight A., "Establishing the New Department of Housing and Urban Development," 27:224-228.

Gittell, Marilyn, "Professionalism and Public Participation in Educational Policy-Making: New York City, A Case Study," 27:237-251.

Rosenthal, Albert H., "The Current Scene: Approaches and Reproaches," 28:3-9.
Anderson, William, "The Myths of Tax Sharing," 28:10-14.
Hearle, Edward F. R., "Regional Commissions: Approach to Economic Development," 28: 15-18.
Hamilton, Randy, "The Regional Commissions: A Restrained View," 28:19-22.
Carey, William D., "Intergovernmental Relations: Guide to Development," 28:22-25.
Campbell, Jack M., "Are the States Here to Stay?" 28:26-29.
Duggar, George S., "Urban Concepts and Metropolitan Restructuring," 28:78-84.
Stahl, O. Glenn, "Intergovernmental Personnel Act-A Progress Report," 28:182-183.
Reeves, H. Clyde, "Role of State Governments in Our Intergovernmental System," 28: 267-270.
Fagin, Henry, "Perspectives on the City," 28:287-292.
Caulfield, Henry P., Jr., "Environmental Management: Water and Related Land," 28: 306-311.
Wood, Robert C., "Federal Role in the Urban Environment," 28:345-347.
Campbell, Alan K., "Fiscal Outputs: Determinants and Policy Consequences," 28:571-577.
Kaufman, Herbert, "Administrative Decentralization and Political Power," 29:3-15.
Miller, S. M. and Martin Rein, "Participation, Poverty, and Administration," 29:15-25.
Gilbert, Charles E., "Of Marble Cakes and Stately Mansions," 29:87-94.
Brogden, John Carl, "Los Angeles County Assessment Appeals Board: Retrospect and Prospect," 29:298-302.
Grant, Daniel R., "Intergovernmental Megalopolity: A Comparison of Perspectives," 29: 318-323.
Beckman, Norman, "Revenue Sharing for What," 29:540-546.
Scott, Stanley, "The Study of Urban Government: First Steps Toward an International Discipline," 29:546-552.
"Governors' View on Federal-State and State-Local Relations—Comments of Nine Governors," 30:27-41.
Ink, Dwight and Alan L. Dean, "A Concept of Decentralization," 30:60-63.
Harman, B. Douglas, "The Block Grant: Readings from a First Experiment," 30:141-153.
Reeves, H. Clyde, "Have State Policies Produced the Current Urban Problem?" 30:155-160.
Schmandt, Henry J., "Metropolitan America: A Mixed Bag of Problems," 30:188-193.
Dillon, Conley H., "The Setting," 30:264-265.
Wood, Robert C., "Needs and Prospects," 30:265-268.
Walker, David B., "Response: Relevant Research Required," 30:269-270.
Hulcher, W. E., "Another Viewpoint," 30:270-272.
Seidman, Harold, "Response: New Aspects for Attention," 30:272-274.
Delguidice, Dominic, "The City as Full Partner," 30:287-293.
Campbell, Roald F., "Federal Influences on Educational Policy," 30:346-352.
Haskew, Laurence D., "The State and Educational Policy," 30:359-365.
Scott, Mel, "The Federal-State Partnership in the Arts," 30:376-386.
Fitch, Lyle C., "Governing Megacentropolis: The People," 30:481-488.
Cohen, Henry, "Governing Megacentropolis: The Constraints," 30:488-497.
Matthewson, Kent, "Governing Megacentropolis: The Leader," 30:506-512.
Bloomberg, Warner, Jr., "Governing Megacentropolis: The Goals," 30:513-520.
Zimmerman, Joseph F., "Metropolitan Reform in the U.S.: An Overview," 30:531-543.
Friesema, H. Paul, "Community Political Analysis: Out of the Circle," 30:571-578.
Warren, Robert, "Federal-Local Development Planning: Scale Effects in Representation and Policy Making," 30:584-595.
Sundquist, James L. and David W. Davis, "Organizing U.S. Social and Economic Development," 30:625-630.
Gove, Samuel K., "State of the States," 30:655-660.

Johnson, Bert W., "Governance of the Municipality: Fracture and Divorce," 31:187-191.
Leach: Richard H., "Federalism: Continuing Predicament," 31:217-223.
Stewart, Richard E., "The Future of Federalism in Insurance Regulation," 31:441-443.
Kraemer, Kenneth L., "USAC: An Evolving Intergovernmental Mechanism for Urban Information Systems Development," 31:543-551.
Long, Norton E., "The City as an Underdeveloped Country," 32:57-63.
Sternberg, Carl W., "Collective Bargaining in the Public Service: Labor Management Relations in State and Local Government," 32:102-107.
Vanagunas, Stanley, "Sharing Crime Control Funds," 32:127-134.
Kennedy, David J., "The Law of Appropriateness: An Approach to a General Theory of Intergovernmental Relations," 32:135-143.
Stenberg, Carl W., "Citizens and the Administrative State: From Participation to Power," 32:190-198.
Mogulof, Melvin B., "Federal Agency Action and Inaction: The Federal Regional Council Experience," 32:232-240.
Hallman, Howard W., "Federally Funded Citizen Participation," 32:421-427.
Elazar, Daniel J., "Fiscal Questions and Political Answers in Intergovernmental Finance," 32:471-478.
Schick, Allen, "Five Theories in Search of an Urban Crisis," 32:546-552.
Howard, Lawrence C., "Executive Development: An Intergovernmental Perspective," 33:101-110.
Haefele, Edwin T., "General Purpose Representatives at the Local Level," 33:177-179.
Murphy, Robert T., "The Regional Commission System," 33:179-184.
Benjamin, Gerald, "The Process of Change in Federal-Local Relations," 33:188-193.
Stokes, B. R., "Bay Area Rapid Transit: A Transportation Planning Breakthrough," 33:206-214.
Olcott, S. A., "Innovative Approaches to Urban Transportation Planning," 33:215-224.
Wildner, Ralph R., "Transport Investment and Appalachian Development," 33:225-235.
Mertins, Herman, Jr., "The 'New Federalism' and Federal Transportation Policy," 33:243-252.
Ostrom, Elinor, Roger B. Parks, and Gordon P. Whitaker, "Do We Really Want to Consolidate Urban Police Forces?: A Reappraisal of Some Old Assertions," 33:423-432.
Martin, Philip L., "The Hatch Act in Court: Some Recent Developments," 33:443-447.
Hebert, F. Ted, "The Politics of Revenue Raising," 33:473-478.
Long, Norton E., "Have Cities A Future?" 33:543-552.
Lugar, Richard, "Public Administration: Target for the 70s," 33:557-560.
Belmonte, Robert M., "State and County Relationships: An Imperfection in the Fabric of American Federalism," 33:561-563.
Porter, David O., and Teddie Wood Porter, "Social Equity and Fiscal Federalism," 34:36-43.
Kloman, Erasmus H., "Public Participation in Technology Assessment," 34:52-61.
Aron, Joan B., "Regional Governance for the New York Metropolitan Region: A Reappraisal," 34:260-264.
Stanley, David T., "How Safe the Streets, How Good the Grant?" 34:380-389.
Bresnick, David, "Should Public Administrators Care About Educational Policy?" 34:404-407.
Capoccia, Victor A., "Chief Executive Review and Comment: A Preview of New Federalism in Rochester, New York," 34:462-470.
Gilbert, Neil and Harry Specht, "Picking Winners: Federal Discretion and Local Experience as Bases for Planning Grant Allocation," 34:565-574.
Mikesell, John L., "Administration and the Public Revenue System: A View of Tax Administration," 34:615-624.

Murphy, John C., "General Revenue Sharing's Impact on County Government," 35:131-135.

Caputo, David A. and Richard L. Cole, "General Revenue Sharing Expenditure Decisions in Cities Over 50,000," 35:136-142.

Carroll, Michael A., "The Impact of General Revenue Sharing on the Urban Planning Process—An Initial Assessment," 35:143-150.

Browne, Edmond, Jr., and John Rehfuss, "Policy Evaluation, Citizen Participation, and Revenue Sharing in Aurora, Illinois," 35:150-157.

Levitan, Sar A. and Joyce K. Zickler, "Block Grants for Manpower Programs," 35:191-197.

Stephenson, Charles M. and William N. Wiley, "A New Approach to New Town Development and Governance," 35:205-208.

Lovell, Catherine H., "The Future of the Intergovernmental Process: Will Revenue Sharing Be Continued?" 35:211-216.

Stowe, Eric and John Rehfuss, "Federal New Towns Policy: Muddling Through at the Local Level," 35:222-228.

Burby, Raymond J., Shirley F. Weiss and Robert B. Zehner, "A National Evaluation of Community Services and the Quality of Life in American New Towns," 35:229-239.

Kirk, Frank A., "State Policy Issues in New Towns and Large-Scale Developments," 35: 246-249.

Fucik, William C., "The Challenge of Implementing Federally Assisted New Communities," 35:249-256.

DeNicholas, Robert P., "A Model Personnel System for New Jersey Counties and Municipalities," 35:287-289.

Aron, Joan B., "Decision Making in Energy Supply at the Metropolitan Level: A Study of the New York Area," 35:340-345.

Newton, Robert D., "Towards an Understanding of Federal Assistance," 35:372-377.

Conaway, O. B., Jr., "The Intergovernmental Personnel Programs: Record, Problems, Potential," 35:396-399.

Shannon, John and Frank Tippett, "Slumpflation and the Recent Local Tax Trends," 35: 527-533.

Macaluso, Ann C., "Background and History of the Study Committee on Policy Management Assistance," 35:695-700.

Study Committee on Policy Management Assistance, "Strengthening Public Management in the Intergovernmental System," 35:700-705.

Burgess, Philip M., "Capacity Building and the Elements of Public Management," 35: 705-716.

Schick, Allen, "The Intergovernmental Thicket: The Questions Still Are Better than the Answers," 35:717-722.

Sherwood, Frank P., "Dealing with Dominance: The Center's Role in an Increasingly Unbalanced System," 35:723-728.

Stone, Donald C., "Achieving a Capable and Manageable Federal System," 35:728-737.

Jones, Harry H., "Evaluation Bases and Management," 35:737-742.

Higgs, Louis D., "Mapping the Federal Assistance Effort: The Pieces of a Puzzle, But Where's the Picture?" 35—743-748.

Wright, J. Ward, "Building the Capacities of Municipal Governments," 35:748-754.

Shapek, Raymond A., "Problems and Deficiencies in the Needs Assessment Process," 35: 754-758.

Paulhus, Norman G., Jr., "Policy Management Assistance in Mission Agencies," 35:758-763.

Olson, Kenneth C., "The States, Governors, and Policy Management: Changing the Equilibrium of the Federal System," 35:764-770.

RuBino, Richard G., "State Policy Management: A Question of the Will to Act," 35:771-774.

Gilmer, Jay, James W. Guest, and Charles Kirchner, "The Impact of Federal Programs and Policies on State-Local Relations," 35:774-779.

Feller, Irwin, "Issues in Design of Federal Programs to Improve the Policy Management Capabilities of State Legislatures," 35:780-786.

Scott, Paul and Robert J. Macdonald, "Local Policy Management Needs: The Federal Response," 35:786-794.

Lindley, Christopher, "Changing Policy Management Responsiblities of Local Legislative Bodies," 35:794-797.

Colman, William G., "Recipient Unit Eligibility Criteria Under a Federal Assistance Program to Strengthen State and Local Policy Management Capability," 35:798-801.

Van Meter, Elena C., "Citizen Participation in the Policy Management Process," 35:804-812.

Bryce, Herrington J., "Problems of Policy Management and Implementation by Local Government: A Minority Perspective," 35:812-818.

Porter, David O. and Eugene A. Olsen, "Some Critical Issues in Government Centralization and Decentralization," 36:72-84.

Lieske, Joel A., "In Quest of the Manpower Grail: Politics, Planning, and Pluralism," 36: 327-333.

Michel, Robert H., "The Future Direction of Income Transfer Programs," 36:603-607.

Ross, John P. and Richard D. Gustely, "Changing the Intrastate General Revenue Sharing Formula: A Discussion of the Issues," 36:655-660.

Bahl, Roy, "The Outlook for State and Local Government Finances," 36:683-687.

Florestano, Patricia S., "State and Local Government Revisited: The State of the Art Since Coleman Ransone," 36:695-699.

Almy, Timothy A., "City Managers, Public Avoidance, and Revenue Sharing," 37:19-27.

Pachon, Harry P. and Nicholas P. Lovrich, "The Consolidation of Urban Public Services: A Focus on the Police," 37:38-47.

Murin, William J., "Urban Transportation Planning, Politics, and Policy Making," 37:89-97.

Rehfuss, John, "Suburban Development and Governance," 37:111-120.

McIntyre, Douglas I., "Merit Principles and Collective Bargaining: A Marriage or Divorce," 37:186-190.

Wanamaker, Daniel K. and Paul Stansbury, "Riding the Circuit with the Kentucky Public Administration Specialist," 37:290-293.

Pikarsky, Milton, "The Challenge of Public Administration," 37:396-399.

Doerksen, Harvey, "Water, Politics, and Ideology: An Overview of Water Resources Management," 37:444-448.

Conway, Nicholas T. and Gregory L. Simay, "The Energy Research and Development: A Partnership Between Federal and Local Government," 37:711-713.

Magazine, Alan H. and Beatrice G. Shields, "The Paperwork Forest: Can State and Local Governments Find a Way Out?" 37:725-729.

Jones, William A. and C. Bradley Doss, "Local Officials Reaction to Federal 'Capacity-Building,' " 38:64-69.

Adams, Bruce and Betsy Sherman, "Sunset Implementation: A Positive Partnership to Make Government Work," 38:78-81.

Hagerty, James Emmett, "Criminal Justice: Toward a New Federal Role," 38:173-176.

Newton, Robert D., "Administrative Federalism," 38:252-255.

Hayford, Stephen L., "Local Government Residency Requirements and Labor Relations: Implications and Choices for Public Administrators," 38:482-486.

McCaffery, Jerry and John H. Bowman, "Participatory Democracy and Budgeting: The Effects of Proposition 13," 38:530-538.

Schneider, Mark and David Swinton, "Policy Analysis in State and Local Government: Introductory Comments," 39:12-16.

Van Horn, Carl E., "Evaluating the New Federalism: National Goals and Local Implementors," 39:17-22.

Mead, Lawrence M., "Institutional Analysis for State and Local Government," 39:26-30.

Boruch, Robert F., *et al.,* "Randomized Experiments for Evaluating and Planning Local Programs: A Summary on Appropriateness and Feasibility," 39:36-40.
Gregg, James M. H. and Robert F. Diegelman, "Red Tape on Trial: Elements of a Successful Effort to Cut Burdensome Federal Reporting Requirements," 39:171-179.
Kraemer, Kenneth L. and James L. Perry, "The Federal Push to Bring Computer Applications to Local Governments," 39:260-270.
Newman, Monroe and Brinley J. Lewis, "Regional Resource Allocation," 39:355-362.
Gary, T. Jack, Jr., "A Single Audit of Federally Assisted Programs?" 39:389-394.
Lovell, Catherine H., "Coordinating Federal Grants From Below," 39:432-439.
Rosenfeld, Raymond A., "Local Implementation Decisions for Community Development Block Grants," 39:448-457.
Mock, Ron, "Intergovernmental Power and Dependence," 39:556-561.
Finkle, Arthur L., "Local Personnel Standards in the Federal Grant-in-Aid System," 39: 572-574.
Stavisky, Leonard P., "Federal Funding and Educational Policy Making: A State Perspective," 39:588-594.
Terrell, Paul, "Beyond the Categories: Human Services Managers View the New Federal Aid," 40:47-54.
Mikulecky, Thomas J., "Intergovernmental Relations Strategies for the Local Manager," 40:379-381.
Mosher, Frederick C., "The Changing Responsibilities and Tactics of the Federal Government," 40:541-552.
Goering, John M., "Towards a National Policy for Neighborhoods: A Conversation Between a Policy Maker and a Social Scientist," 40:553-560.
Skok, James E., "Federal Funds and State Legislatures: Executive-Legislative Conflict in State Government," 40:561-567.
Sternberg, Carl W., "Beyond the Days of Wine and Roses: Intergovernmental Management in a Cutback Environment," 41:10-20.
Clavel, Pierre and Harvey M. Jacobs, "Planning and National Urban Policy," 41:87-92.
Eribes, Richard A. and John S. Hall, "Revolt of the Affluent: Fiscal Controls in Three States," 41:107-121.
Florestano, Patricia S., "Revenue-Raising Limitations on Local Government: A Focus on Alternative Responses," 41:122-131.
Bowman, John H., "Urban Revenue Strutures: An Overview of Patterns, Trends, and Issues," 41:131-143.
McKinney, Jerome B., "Process Accountability and the Creative Use of Intergovernmental Resources," 41:144-150.
Straussman, Jeffrey D., "More Bang for Fewer Bucks? Or How Local Governments Can Rediscover the Potentials (and Pitfalls) of the Market," 41:150-158.
Lovell, Catherine H., "Evolving Local Government Dependency," 41:189-202.
Menzel, Donald C., "Implementation of the Federal Surface Mining Control and Reclamation Act of 1977," 41:212-219.
Groszyk, Walter S. and Thomas J. Madden, "Managing Without Immunity: The Challenge for State and Local Government Officials in the 1980s," 41:268-278.
Lovell, Catherine and Charles Tobin, "The Mandate Issue," 41:318-331.
Kettl, Donald F., "The Fourth Face of Federalism," 41:366-371.
Warren, Charles R., "Sharing Management Capacity: Is There a Federal Responsibility?" 41:381-387.
Vaughan, Claude M., Jr., and James K. Sharpe, "The Public Utility Regulatory Policies Act: Implications for Regulatory Commission Reform," 41:387-391.
Doolittle, Fred, "Auditing Disputes in Federal Grant Programs: The Case of AFDC," 41:430-436.

Hickman, Dale, Robert Berne, and Leanna Stiefel, "Taxing over Tax Limits: Evidence from the Past and Policy Lessons for the Future," 41:445-453.

Gormley, William T., Jr., "Statewide Remedies for Public Underrepresentation in Regulatory Proceedings," 41:454-462.

Lamare, Judith L., "Intergovernmental Finance, Productivity, and the Local Match Question: The Case of California's Transit Subsidy Policy," 41:463-470.

Flowers, George A., Jr., Jerome S. Legge, Jr., Paul E. Radford, and David H. Wiltsee, "Targeting Funds for Economic Development in Rural Georgia: The Experience of the Georgia Department of Community Affairs," 41:485-488.

Honadle, Beth Walter, "A Capacity-Building Framework: A Search for Concept and Purpose," 41:575-580.

Stevens, John M. and Robert D. Lee, Jr., "Patterns of Policy Analysis Use for State Governments: A Contingency and Demand Perspective," 41:636-644.

Gargan, John J., "Consideration of Local Government Capacity," 41:649-658.

Beckman, Norman, "Intergovernmental Relations: The Future Is Now," 41:693-701.

Stavisky, Leonard P., "State Legislatures and the New Federalism," 41:701-710.

Poister, Theodore H., "Federal Transportation Policy for the Elderly and Handicapped: Responsive to Real Needs?" 42:6-14.

Kearney, Richard C. and Robert B. Garey, "American Federalism and the Management of Radioactive Wastes," 42:14-24.

King, John Leslie, "Local Government Use of Information Technology: The Next Decade," 42:25-36.

Danzinger, James N. and Peter Smith Ring, "Fiscal Limitations: A Selective Review of Recent Research," 42:47-55.

Edner, Sheldon M. and Edward Weiner, "Urban Transportation: A Time for Change," 42: 84-89.

Cigler, Beverly A. and Michael L. Vasu, "Housing and Public Policy in America," 42:90-96.

Lorenz, Patsy Hashey, "The Politics of Fund Raising Through Grantsmanship in the Human Services," 42:244-251.

Barkenbus, Jack N., "Federal Energy Policy Paradigms and State Energy Roles," 42:410-418.

Sunshine, Eugene S., "Minimizing the Disappointment of Unsuccessful Applicants in Grant Programs," 42:479-480.

Wilms, Wellford W., "Soft Policies for Hard Problems: Implementing Energy Conserving Building Regulations in California," 42:553-561.

McCurdy, Howard E., "Public Administration in the Wilderness: The New Environmental Management," 42:584-590.

Wenner, Lettie M., "Energy Policy," 42:591-596.

Hamilton, Randy, "The World Turned Upside Down: The Contemporary Revolution in State and Local Government Capital Financing," 43:22-31.

Kidwell, David S. and Robert J. Rogowski, "Bond Banks: A State Assistance Program That Helps Reduce New Issue Borrowing Costs," 43:108-113.

McGowan, Robert P. and John M. Stevens, "Local Government Initiatives in a Climate of Uncertainty," 43:127-136.

Spurrier, Robert L., Jr., "Paying the Piper in Federal Civil Rights Litigation," 43:199-208.

Agranoff, Robert and Valerie A. Lindsay, "Intergovernmental Management: Perspectives from Human Services Problem Solving at the Local Level," 43:227-237.

McGowan, Robert and John M. Stevens, "Local Government Management: Reactive or Adaptive?" 43:260-267.

Buntz, C. Gregory and Beryl A. Radin, "Managing Intergovernmental Conflict: The Case of Human Services," 43:403-410.

Johnson, Arthur T., "Municipal Administration and the Sports Franchise Relocation Issue," 43:519-528.

Comparative Federalism and IGR Bibliography: *PAR* Volumes 1-43

Lepawsky, Albert, "Canadian Federalism in Transition," 1:76-81.

Crane, Jacob and William L. C. Wheaton, "The British White Paper on Local Government," 5:135-140.

Ebenstein, William, "Federalism in Germany," 6:285-290.

Crouch, Winston W., "Trends in British Local Government," 7:254-262.

Cohen, Enmeline W., "Aspects of Local Government in England and Wales," 11:253-259.

Crouch, Winston W., "Metropolitan Government in Toronto," 14:85-95.

Harris, John S., "Central Government Inspection of Local Services in Britain," 15:26-34,

Ferris, John P., "Organization for Regional Economic Development Projects: A Middle East Experience," 25:128-134.

Hansen, Niles M., "Central-Local Cooperative Financing for Local Public Investment: Can the Belgian Experience Be Borrowed?" 26:169-173.

Henderson, Keith M., "Charting a New Terrain: Comparative Local Administration," 27: 142-147.

Scott, Stanley, "The Study of Urban Government: First Steps Towards an International Discipline," 29:546-552.

Smallwood, Frank, "Reshaping Local Government Abroad: Anglo-Canadian Experiments," 30:521-530. Comment by: Lionel D. Feldman, 31:323-333.

Burns, Ronald M., "Intergovernmental Relations in Canada," 33:14-22.

Plunkett, Thomas J., "Structural Reform of Local Government in Canada," 33:40-51.

Romero, Miguel Acosta, "Mexican Federalism: Conception and Reality," 42:399-404.